PERSONAL GROWTH AND BEHAVIOR 91/92

Eleventh Edition

Annual Editions

A Library of Information from the Public Press

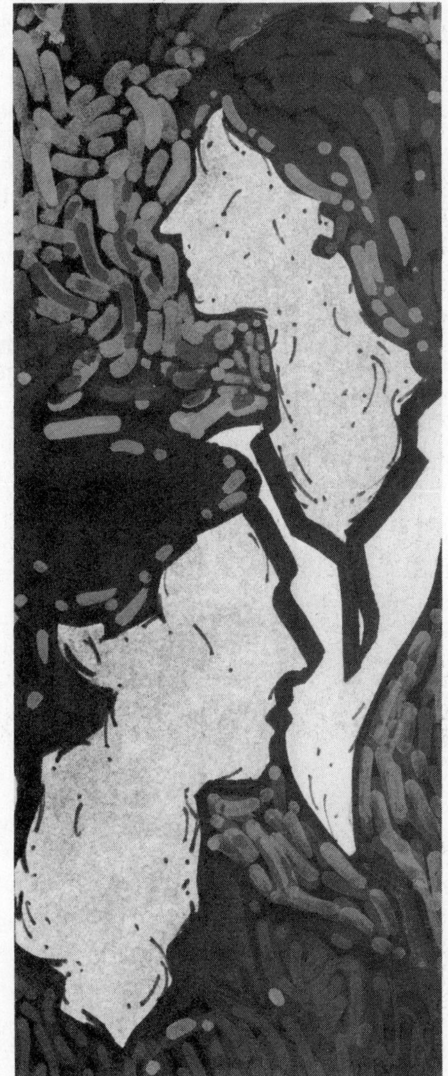

Editor

Karen G. Duffy
SUNY College, Geneseo

Karen G. Duffy is a full professor in the Department of Psychology and an adjunct professor of the School of Business at SUNY Geneseo. She received her B.S. in psychology from St. Lawrence University in 1968 and a Ph.D. in personality and social psychology from Michigan State University in 1973. Active as a certified mediator in community and family disputes, she is also a member of the New York State Executive Board for Employee Assistance Programs and is affiliated with the Eastern Psychological Association.

Cover illustration by Mike Eagle

The Dushkin Publishing Group, Inc.
Sluice Dock, Guilford, Connecticut 06437

The Annual Editions Series

Annual Editions is a series of over fifty volumes designed to provide the reader with convenient, low-cost access to a wide range of current, carefully selected articles from some of the most important magazines, newspapers, and journals published today. Annual Editions are updated on an annual basis through a continuous monitoring of over 200 periodical sources. All Annual Editions have a number of features designed to make them particularly useful, including topic guides, annotated tables of contents, unit overviews, and indexes. For the teacher using Annual Editions in the classroom, an Instructor's Resource Guide with test questions is available for each volume.

VOLUMES AVAILABLE

Africa
Aging
American Government
American History, Pre-Civil War
American History, Post-Civil War
Anthropology
Biology
Business and Management
Business Ethics
Canadian Politics
China
Comparative Politics
Computers in Education
Computers in Business
Computers in Society
Criminal Justice
Drugs, Society, and Behavior
Early Childhood Education
Economics
Educating Exceptional Children
Education
Educational Psychology
Environment
Geography
Global Issues
Health
Human Development
Human Resources
Human Sexuality
Latin America
Macroeconomics
Management
Marketing
Marriage and Family
Microeconomics
Middle East and the Islamic World
Money and Banking
Nutrition
Personal Growth and Behavior
Psychology
Public Administration
Race and Ethnic Relations
Social Problems
Sociology
Soviet Union and Eastern Europe
State and Local Government
Third World
Urban Society
Violence and Terrorism
Western Civilization, Pre-Reformation
Western Civilization, Post-Reformation
Western Europe
World History, Pre-Modern
World History, Modern
World Politics

Library of Congress Cataloging in Publication Data
Main entry under title: Annual editions: Personal growth and behavior. 1991–92.
1. Personality—Periodicals. 2. Adjustment (Psychology)—Periodicals. I. Duffy, Karen, *comp.*
II. Title: Personal growth and behavior.
155'.2'05 75–20757 ISBN 1-56134-005-7

Eleventh Edition

Manufactured by The Banta Company, Harrisonburg, Virginia 22801

Editors/ Advisory Board

Members of the Advisory Board are instrumental in the final selection of articles for each edition of Annual Editions. Their review of articles for content, level, currentness, and appropriateness provides critical direction to the editor and staff. We think you'll find their careful consideration well reflected in this volume.

To the Reader

In publishing ANNUAL EDITIONS we recognize the enormous role played by the magazines, newspapers, and journals of the *public press* in providing current, first-rate educational information in a broad spectrum of interest areas. Within the articles, the best scientists, practitioners, researchers, and commentators draw issues into new perspective as accepted theories and viewpoints are called into account by new events, recent discoveries change old facts, and fresh debate breaks out over important controversies.

Many of the articles resulting from this enormous editorial effort are appropriate for students, researchers, and professionals seeking accurate, current material to help bridge the gap between principles and theories and the real world. These articles, however, become more useful for study when those of lasting value are carefully *collected, organized, indexed,* and *reproduced* in a *low-cost format*, which provides easy and permanent access when the material is needed. That is the role played by *Annual Editions*.

Under the direction of each volume's *Editor*, who is an expert in the subject area, and with the guidance of an *Advisory Board*, we seek each year to provide in each *ANNUAL EDITION* a current, well-balanced, carefully selected collection of the best of the public press for your study and enjoyment. We think you'll find this volume useful, and we hope you'll take a moment to let us know what you think.

Do you know any identical twins? Scientists tell us that identical twins should be quite similar. The twins may very well look alike, each with red hair, freckles, and a small nose. If you know the twins well, you have probably developed a strategy for telling them apart. In fact, to you the twins might indeed look quite different but to a stranger appear identical. You might also have come to appreciate the twins' unique personalities, interests, and abilities. One prefers classical piano; the other blasts her rock and roll. One likes to read romance novels; the other is a tomboy and spends her fall afternoons playing touch football.

If identical twins who share the same genes are different, imagine how unique the rest of us are compared to one another. Some of us are adventurous and fantasize about the safaris we cannot afford. Others of us are timid; the closest we would get to Africa is seeing the continent on television. A few people tell bawdy jokes while others shrink in horror at the punch lines.

What makes us all so unique and interesting? This and other questions are not new. We have been curious about human nature for thousands of years. The answers to this question, however, are incomplete at present because attempts to address it are new or just developing. Psychology, the science that can and should answer such questions and the primary focus of this book, is only about 100 years old. This may seem old to you, but it is comparatively young. Other disciplines such as mathematics, medicine, and philosophy are thousands of years old. Through psychology and related social sciences, this anthology will help you explore the answers to the question of uniqueness, as well as other questions you ponder about human nature. The purpose of this anthology is to compile the newest, most complete, and most readable articles that examine individual behavior and adjustment, as well as the dynamics of personal growth and relationships.

This anthology is revised each year, and reflects both traditional viewpoints and emerging perspectives on people's behavior. Thanks to the editorial board's valuable advice, this edition has been completely revised. Those of you familiar with past editions will notice that all articles in the current edition are dated 1983 or newer, with many articles from 1989 and 1990.

Annual Editions: Personal Growth and Behavior 91/92 is comprised of six units, each of which serves a distinct purpose. The first unit is concerned with issues related to self-identity. For example, one theory addressed in this anthology, humanism, hypothesizes that self-concept is in a perpetual state of change, while a contrasting perspective, behaviorism, maintains that there exists no such entity as self-concept. This section includes other articles that are critical of humanism or the self theories and offer alternative perspectives such as behaviorism. The second unit provides information on not *how* but *why* a person develops in a particular way. In other words, the factors that determine individual growth: physiology, heredity, experience, or some combination of all. The third unit deals with common problems of the different stages of development: infancy, childhood, adolescence, adulthood, and old age. The fourth and fifth units are similar in that they address problems of adjustment—problems that occur in interpersonal relationships and problems created for the individual by society, respectively. For example, unit four contains articles on topics such as intimacy and interpersonal persuasion, while unit five includes articles on prejudice, bystander apathy, and sex roles. The final unit focuses on coping, or in the face of some of these problems, how most people adjust or cope.

This anthology will stimulate and challenge you. It will provide you with many answers, but will also provoke many questions. Perhaps it will inspire you to continue your study of the burgeoning fields that are exploring personal growth and behavior.

Your feedback on this edition would be particularly valuable for future revisions. Please take a moment to fill out and return the article rating form on the last page. Thank you.

Karen Grover Duffy

Karen Grover Duffy
Editor

Contents

Unit 1

Becoming a Person: Seeking Self-Identity

Seven selections discuss the psychosocial development of an individual's personality. Attention is given to values, life-styles, and the self-concept.

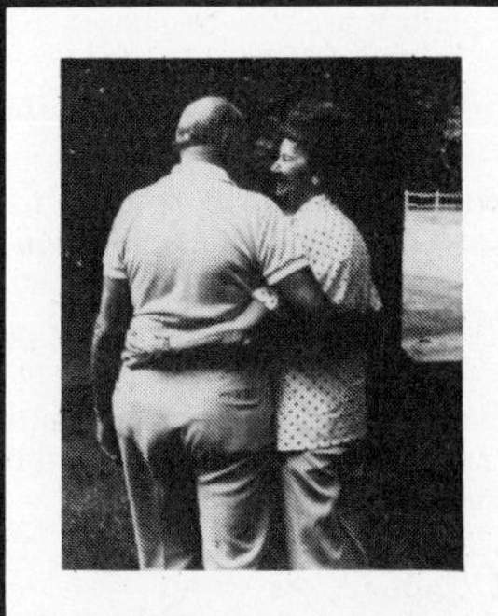

Unit 2

Determinants of Behavior: Motivation, Environment, and Physiology

Ten articles examine the effects of nutrition, culture, genes, and chemically sponsored emotions on an individual's behavior.

Unit 3

Problems Influencing Personal Growth

Fourteen articles consider aging, development, self-image, depression, and social interaction and their influences on personal growth.

Unit 4

Relating to Others

Seven articles examine some of the dynamics involved in relating to others. Topics discussed include friendship, jealousy, the importance of family ties, and self-esteem.

Unit 5

Dynamics of Personal Adjustment: The Individual and Society

Eight selections discuss some of the problems experienced by individuals as they attempt to adjust to society.

Unit 6

Enhancing Human Adjustment: Learning to Cope Effectively

Eight selections examine some of the ways an individual learns to cope successfully within today's society. Topics discussed include therapy, depression, stress, and interpersonal relations.

The concepts in bold italics are developed in the article. For further expansion please refer to the Topic Guide, the Index, and the Glossary.

Topic Guide

This topic guide suggests how the selections in this book relate to topics of traditional concern to students and professionals involved with the study of personal growth and behavior. It is useful for locating articles which relate to each other for reading and research. The guide is arranged alphabetically according to topic. Articles may, of course, treat topics that do not appear in the topic guide. In turn, entries in the topic guide do not necessarily constitute a comprehensive listing of all the contents of each selection.

TOPIC AREA	TREATED IN:
Mental Illness	46. Psychotherapy's Value 48. Wounded Healers 49. Beating Depression 51. When Stress Becomes Distress
Menopause	28. Not Past Their Prime
Middle Age	28. Not Past Their Prime 30. Reaching the Child Within Us
Mood	12. Winter Blues 13. Food, Mood, and Behavior
Motivation	1. Abraham Maslow and the New Self 7. The Risks of Rewards
Neurology	9. New Connections 11. Making of a Mind 13. Food, Mood, and Behavior
Nutrition	13. Food, Mood, and Behavior
Optimism/ Pessimism	54. Healthy Pleasures
Parenting	20. Dr. Spock Had It Right 21. Sad Legacy of Abuse 24. Scared Serious 27. Understanding and Preventing Teen Suicide
Personal Style	35. The Language of Persuasion 50. The Trusting Heart
Personality/ Personality Theories	1. Abraham Maslow and the New Self 2. Erikson, in His Own Old Age 4. Personality: Major Traits Found Stable 8. Major Personality Study 29. Meet the People 53. Health's Character
Prejudice	32. A Theory of Success and Failure 46. Psychologists Find Ways to Break Racism's Hold
Psychobiology	9. New Connections 10. A Pleasurable Chemistry 13. Food, Mood, and Behavior 14. Guns and Dolls 17. Second Thoughts About a Gene for Alcoholism 28. Not Past Their Prime
Psychosocial Development	2. Erikson, in His Own Old Age 18. The Changing Meanings of Age 20. Dr. Spock Had It Right 21. Sad Legacy of Abuse 22. Children After Divorce 23. The Taming of the Tube 40. The American Man in Transition 46. Psychologists Find Ways to Break Racism's Hold

TOPIC AREA	TREATED IN:
Psychotherapy	47. Psychotherapy's Value 48. Wounded Healers 49. Beating Depression 51. When Stress Becomes Distress 53. Health's Character
Relating to Others	21. Sad Legacy of Abuse 34. Art of Anger Difficult for Women 35. The Language of Persuasion 36. "They Have Ears, But Hear Not" 38. The Dance of Intimacy 41. Success at Failure 44. No Life to Live 45. When Bystanders Just Stand By 50. The Trusting Heart
Seasonal Affective Disorder	12. Winter Blues
Self-Defeating Behavior	41. Success at Failure
Self/Identity	1. Abraham Maslow and the New Self 41. Success at Failure 52. Ridden With Guilt
Sex/Gender Roles	14. Guns and Dolls 23. The Taming of the Tube 34. Art of Anger Difficult for Women 39. The Indispenable Woman 40. The American Man in Transition
Shame/Guilt	52. Ridden With Guilt
Support (Groups/ Social)	41. Success at Failure 44. No Life to Live
Stress	6. Managing Stress and Living Longer 51. When Stress Becomes Distress
Success/Failure	32. A Theory of Success and Failure
Suicide	27. Understanding and Preventing Teen Suicide
Television	23. The Taming of the Tube
Twenties Generation	16. Proceeding With Caution
Type A	50. The Trusting Heart
Violence	23. The Taming of the Tube

Becoming a Person: Seeking Self-Identity

A baby sits in front of a mirror and looks at herself. A chimpanzee sorts through photographs while its trainer watches carefully for the chimp's reaction. What do each of these events have in common? "Nothing," you say. Wrong! Both are examples of techniques used to investigate self-concept.

The baby has a red dot on her nose. The researchers watch to see if the child reaches for the dot in the mirror or touches her own nose. In recognition of the fact that the image she sees in the mirror is her own, the baby touches her real nose, not the nose in the mirror.

The chimpanzee has been trained to sort photographs into a human and an animal pile. If the chimp was raised with humans, the researcher wants to know into which pile, animal or human, the chimp will place its own picture. Is the chimp's concept of itself animal or human?

Research such as this is designed to investigate how self-concept develops. Most psychologists believe that people develop a personal identity or sense of self—the knowledge of who you are, what you like and dislike, what feelings are characteristic of you, and why you behave as you do. It is knowledge of your gender, race, age, self-worth, and much more. Strong positive or negative feelings are usually attached to this identity. Psychologists are just beginning to understand how and when this sense of self develops. Most psychologists do not believe that infants are born with a sense of self, but rather that children slowly develop self-concept as a consequence of their experiences.

This section of the book delineates some of the popular viewpoints regarding how the sense of self develops, and how that identity guides behavior. Therefore, it lays the important foundation for the rest of the units in this book. The first article explores how self develops and how it directs our behavior. In "Abraham Maslow and the New Self," Abraham Maslow reveals his popular concept of human motivation. He and other humanists feel that people actively seek growth experiences and continue to change and develop over a lifetime. Erik Erikson's classic theory is explained in the next article. Unlike Sigmund Freud and other psychoanalysts, Erikson felt that there are many stages of personal growth, and the challenges at each stage are psychosocial rather than psychosexual in nature. Erikson, as did Maslow, concludes that people are continually changing or growing, but Erikson's theory is more psychoanalytic in conception. Both Maslow's and Erikson's theories, however, emphasize that a sense of self is not consistent over a lifetime; as experience changes, so does the person. In the next article the new theories on analyzing dreams by psychiatrist and neuroscientist Allan Hobson are presented.

Humanistic and psychoanalytic ideas have not gone unchallenged by other psychologists. For instance, some theorists, known in psychology as trait theorists, believe that personality traits or characteristics are established in childhood. Such traits are typical of an individual from situation to situation (at home, school, or church) and throughout a lifetime. Only major events, perhaps surviving a terrible natural disaster, can change personality traits; traits do not yield easily to everyday experiences.

On the other hand, behaviorists, another group of psychologists, are convinced that people do not have a sense of self at all. Individuals do not ever really come to "know" themselves. Instead, they simply behave from moment to moment, based on either past learning experiences or on immediate stimuli in their environments. There is no self-concept upon which people regularly rely or reflect.

The next two articles offer these alternative viewpoints, known respectively as the trait or dispositional approach and behaviorism. In "Personality: Major Traits Found Stable Through Life," the author claims that most personality traits remain constant over time in contrast with the growth theory of Maslow. The work of an influential contemporary psychologist, B. F. Skinner, is presented in the next article. Skinner claims there is no self-concept that directs behavior.

"Managing Stress and Living Longer" points out the ineffective methods most people use to handle stress. Jerome Murray presents effective methods for stress management.

In the final article, "The Risks of Rewards," Skinner is taken to task for his notion of positive reinforcement. We are recognizing today that reinforcement of behavior might undermine another very positive side of human

Unit 1

nature, intrinsic motivation or the motivation to simply do something because it is satisfying or stimulating in and of itself.

Looking Ahead: Challenge Questions

Does the sense of self develop the same way in each individual? Are there various aspects of self such as gender that develop faster than other aspects? Can one type of experience influence identity more than another type?

Are there more similarities or differences between people from the same culture? Does age or sex play a role in uniqueness—are men more alike as a group than women, for example?

Is self-concept stable, or does it change regularly? What events create change? How could an individual change his or her self-concept? Is psychotherapy the best way to achieve change?

Besides career choice, how might your sense of self direct your behavior? Does self-concept direct behavior in interpersonal relations? Do individuals have a number of selves, and do they show different ones to different people? If so, is this normal, or does it signal maladjustment?

Suppose someone developed on a desert island with no human contact. What might this individual be like? How might the person appear to others who have been raised in civilization?

Is self a uniquely human concept? Could animals develop a sense of self? How would you test animals for self-concept?

How and when do you think children develop a sense of self? How do people show others that they have a sense of self? Do children understand their own behavior or others' behavior first? Which word, "yes" or "no," is usually added first to a child's vocabulary? What impact does this have on the child's development?

What do you think is responsible for guiding our behavior, our past reinforcement history or intrinsic motivation? Do you feel that different behaviors are guided by different forces?

With the coming of this relatively little-known scientist, a uniquely American school of psychology blossomed. Before Maslow—who, like his colleagues, had been trained in the precepts of Freud and Jung—the emphasis in psychiatry was on neurotic behavior, psychosis, the disorders of the mind. Maslow, in contrast, accentuated the positive, stressing self-help and human potential. In its basic optimism, Maslow's thinking was as American as cherry pie—and a lot more healthy.

Abraham Maslow and the New Self

To him, man was not a mass of neuroses but a wealth of potential

by George Leonard

Humanistic Psychology

He wrote with none of the dark grandeur of a Freud or the learned grace of an Erik Erikson or the elegant precision of a B.F. Skinner. He was not a brilliant speaker; in his early years he was so shy he could hardly bring himself to mount the podium. He traveled little; Brooklyn was his home for nearly half his life. The branch of psychology he founded has not achieved a dominant position in the colleges and universities. He died in 1970, but a full-scale biography remains to be written.

And yet, Abraham Maslow has done more to change our view of human nature and human possibilities than has any other American psychologist of the past fifty years. His influence, both direct and indirect, continues to grow, especially in the fields of health, education, and management theory, and in the personal and social lives of millions of Americans.

Maslow confronts us with paradoxes. He started out as a behaviorist, a skilled experimenter, and then went on to demonstrate the crippling limitations of just that kind of psychology in the study of human affairs. He coauthored a textbook on abnormal psychology, a classic in its field, and then went on to investigate, not the pathological, but the exceptionally healthy person. Considering himself a Freudian, he went on to take Freudian psychology out of the basement of warring drives and inevitable frustration, up into the spacious, previously unexplored upper stories of the human personality, where entirely different, non-Freudian rules seemed to prevail.

Working ten to twelve hours a day in the shadow of a heart condition that was to kill him at sixty-two, Maslow produced a rich and varied body of work, one that has altered our way of thinking about human needs and motivations, neurosis and health, experience and values. Some of his theories are still controversial, especially in their particulars, but no one can deny that this dogged and daring explorer has radically revised our picture of the human species and has created a vastly expanded map of human possibilities.

Abraham H. Maslow was born on April 1, 1908, in

a Jewish slum in Brooklyn, the first of seven children. His father, a cooper by trade, had come to America from Kiev, then had sent for a hometown cousin to join him as his wife. Young Maslow's childhood was generally miserable. He was alienated from his mother ("a pretty woman, but not a nice one," he later told English writer Colin Wilson) and afraid of his father ("a very vigorous man, who loved whiskey and women and fighting"). His father's business succeeded, and when Abe was nine the family moved out of the slums and into the first of a series of lower-middle-class houses, each slightly more comfortable than the one preceding it. But these moves took the family into Italian and Irish neighborhoods and made Abe the victim of terrifying anti-Semitism. He was not only Jewish but also, by his own account, a peculiar-looking child, so underweight that the family doctor feared he might get tuberculosis. "Have you ever seen anyone uglier than Abe?" his father mused aloud at a family gathering.

Reading was his escape, the library his magic kingdom. And when he chose to go to Brooklyn Borough High School, an hour-and-a-half's journey from his home, Abe got his first taste of success. He became a member of the chess team and of the honor society Arista. He edited the Latin magazine and the physics magazine, for which, in 1923, at the age of fifteen, he wrote an article predicting atom-powered ships and submarines. In terms of sheer, raw intelligence, Maslow was a true prodigy. Tested years later by the psychologist Edward L. Thorndike, he registered an IQ of 195, the second highest Thorndike ever encountered.

At eighteen, Maslow enrolled in New York's City College. It was free and his father wanted Abe to study law. But Maslow found the school impersonal and the required courses dull. He skipped classes, made poor grades, and was put on probation for the second semester.

PHOTOGRAPH: HENRY GROSSMAN

HE LOVED THE LIFE OF THE MIND.

No matter. Maslow was intoxicated with the rich artistic and intellectual life of New York City in the vintage year of 1927. He discovered the music of Beethoven and the plays of Eugene O'Neill. He went to two concerts a week at Carnegie Hall and sold peanuts to get into the theater. He attended lectures by Will Durant and Bertrand Russell and Reinhold Niebuhr. Like most young American intellectuals of that period, he became a socialist and an atheist.

But if Maslow was in love with the life of the mind, he was even more in love—blissfully, hopefully—with his cousin Bertha. And it was during the year he was nineteen that he experienced two of the great moments of his life, the kinds of moments he was later to call "peak experiences." The first came when he read William Graham Sumner's *Folkways*, a book that introduced him to the idea of cultural evolution, forever disabused him of the assumption that his own society was the "fixed truth from which everything else was a foolish falling away," and triggered a lifelong interest in anthropology. By his own account, he was never again the same.

IT WAS DURING THE YEAR HE WAS NINETEEN THAT HE EXPERIENCED TWO OF THE GREAT MOMENTS OF HIS LIFE, THE KINDS HE WOULD LATER CALL "PEAK EXPERIENCES."

The second peak experience of that year came when he kissed Bertha. Previously, he had never dared to touch her. His frustration was indeed so painful that it drove him to leave New York City for a semester at Cornell. When he returned, Bertha's sister Anna took matters into her own hands by literally pushing him into Bertha's arms. "I kissed her," Maslow later told Colin Wilson, "and nothing terrible happened—the heavens didn't fall, and Bertha accepted it, and that was the beginning of a new life.... I was accepted by a female. I was just deliriously happy with her. It was a tremendous and profound and total love affair."

By now it was clear that Maslow would not become a lawyer, and he went away to the University of Wisconsin to study psychology in earnest. A few lonely, frustrated months later, Abe wired Bertha that they were going to get married. The wedding took place in New York during the December holidays of 1928. Bertha returned to Wisconsin with him and enrolled as a student.

Thus began Abraham Maslow's life as a psychologist. It was a life that would be graced with an extraordinary succession of mentors, distinguished scholars who were somehow drawn to this shy, brilliant young man and wanted him to work with them; they invited him to meals, drove him to meetings, helped get him jobs. One might say that these mentors served an emotional function as surrogate mothers and fathers, but if the Fates had conspired to choose ideal professional influences, they could not have done a better job.

As an undergraduate, Maslow became a lab assistant to William H. Sheldon, who later was to achieve fame with his theory of constitutional types (endomorph, mesomorph, ectomorph). Sheldon and other professors provided a solid grounding in classical laboratory research. Professor Harry Harlow, the noted primate researcher, eventually became Maslow's chief mentor at Wisconsin. In 1932 Harlow shared authorship of a paper on the intelligence of primates with Maslow, and the twenty-four-year-old undergraduate was so inspired by seeing his name in print in the *Journal of Comparative Psychology* that he spent all of his next summer vacation, helped by Bertha, repeating the experiment with every primate in the Bronx Park Zoo.

As a graduate student at Wisconsin, Maslow came up with a truly original line of research. He discovered that the incessant mounting behavior of primates, which involved males mounting males, females mounting females, and females mounting males, as well as the "conventional" mounting of females by males, had more to do with dominance than with sexuality. This activity was, in fact, a means of sorting out the hierarchy of the primate horde. What's more, he learned that the ferocity involved in dominance behavior tends to fade away as one goes up the primate intelligence scale: the monkey uses its dominance position to tyrannize; the chimpanzee, to protect.

Maslow moved from Wisconsin to Columbia University as the eminent behaviorist Edward Thorndike's research associate. And he continued his work on dominance and sexuality, going from simple dominance in animals to dominance-feeling in humans to the relationship between self-esteem and sexuality. In 1936, while still at Columbia, he began doing Kinsey-type interviews with female college students, possibly inspiring Kinsey's own work, which began some two years later. Maslow's interviews showed that highly dominant women, regardless of their sex drives, are more likely to be sexually active and experimental than are less dominant women. But he also found—and this is important in terms of his later work—that "any discussion of dominance must be a discussion of insecure people, that is, of slightly sick people.... Study of carefully selected psychologically secure individuals indicates clearly that their sexual lives are little determined by dominance-feeling." Here was a hint, a seed: there seems to exist a state of psychological health that transcends at least one lower drive.

HE FOUND HIMSELF INCREASINGLY ALONE OUT ON THE FRONTIERS OF HUMAN KNOWLEDGE..."A DANIEL BOONE," ONE WHO ENJOYS BEING THE "FIRST IN THE WILDERNESS."

During this period of inspired excitement and feverish work, Maslow continued to collect mentors. One of them was Alfred Adler, an early disciple of Freud who eventually broke with his master.

Maslow also sat at the feet of such eminent psychologists and anthropologists as Erich Fromm, Kurt Goldstein, Karen Horney, and Margaret Mead—some of them refugees from the Nazi terror. It was the late Thirties and New York was both an exciting and a sobering place for a Jewish intellectual.

Of all his mentors, Ruth Benedict, the anthropologist, and Max Wertheimer, the founder of the European Gestalt school of psychology, had the greatest influence on Maslow's life. Both became good friends and often came to dinner with him and Bertha at their modest Brooklyn home. Maslow admired Benedict and Wertheimer inordinately. Not only were they giants in their fields, but they were also, to put it simply, wonderful human beings. He began making notes on these exceptional people. Nothing he had learned in psychology equipped him to understand them. How could they be what they so clearly were in a world of savage, repressed Freudian drives and Nazi horrors? Who was the real human species-type, Hitler or Benedict and Wertheimer?

These questions helped set the stage for the major turning point in Maslow's life, one that was to change psychology and our view of the human personality for all time. The year, as best as it can be reconstructed, was 1942; the place, New York City. By now, though not a great lecturer, Maslow was a beloved teacher, so popular that the college newspaper characterized him as the Frank Sinatra of Brooklyn College. He was working very hard, sometimes teaching nights as well as days for the extra income. He adored his daughters, who were now two and four; their innocence and potential in a darkening world sometimes moved him to tears. And the war was always in the back of his mind. He was too old to be drafted for military service but he wanted to make his contribution in the fight against Hitler. He wanted somehow to enlist himself in the larger enterprise of helping create a world in which there would be no Hitlers, in which "good people" would prevail.

It was in that emotional climate that he happened upon a parade of young American servicemen on their way to combat duty. And he was overcome by the evils of war, the needless suffering and death, the tragic waste of human potential. He began weeping openly. Against the backdrop of those times, the conventional, step-by-step psychology he had been doing was entirely inadequate. He knew he would have to change his life and career. It would have been easy enough to stay on his present course. His research credentials were firmly established. His recently published *Principles of Abnormal Psychology*, coauthored with Bela Mittelmann, was being well received. Maslow was undoubtedly on his way to a successful career in mainstream psychology. But now, tears streaming down his cheeks, he determined to take a more difficult, more uncertain course.

The direction of his exploration was set by a flash of insight that came to him while he was musing over his notes on Ruth Benedict and Max Wertheimer, trying to puzzle out the pattern that made these two people so very different from the neurotic, driven people who are usually the subject of psychological study. As he wrote years later, "I realized in one wonderful moment that their two patterns could be gener-

SELF-ACTUALIZING PEOPLE, MASLOW DISCOVERED, ARE MORE LIKELY TO HAVE PEAK EXPERIENCES—THAT IS, EPISODES OF DELIGHT, HEIGHTENED CLARITY, EVEN REVELATION.

alized. I was talking about a kind of person, not about two noncomparable individuals. There was a wonderful excitement in that. I tried to see whether this pattern could be found elsewhere, and I did find it elsewhere, in one person after another."

Like many historic breakthroughs, this one, in retrospect, seems obvious, so simple a child might have hit upon it: Up until that time, the field of psychology had by and large concentrated on mental illness, neglecting or entirely ignoring psychological *health*. Symptoms had been relentlessly pursued, abnormalities endlessly analyzed. But the normal personality continued to be viewed primarily as a vague, gray area of little interest or concern. And *positive* psychological health was terra incognita.

From the moment of the turning point at the parade in New York City, Maslow would devote his life and his thought to the exploration of this unknown land, of what he called in his last book "the farther reaches of human nature." In this exploration, he would find it necessary to leave his mentors behind. Though he would go on to form his own network of colleagues and supporters, he would find himself increasingly alone out on the frontiers of human knowledge. He was to become, in his words, "a reconnaissance man, a Daniel Boone," one who enjoys being "first in the wilderness."

Maslow stayed at Brooklyn College until 1951, then went to Brandeis University, in Waltham, Massachusetts, where he became chairman of the psychology department. In 1969 he moved to Menlo Park, California. A special fellowship set up by an industrialist would give him unlimited time for writing. But time was short; he died a year later. Still, in the twenty-seven years after the turning point in his career, he published close to a hundred articles and books that add up to a great synthesis, a bold and original psychological theory.

Maslow's theory is built upon his finding that human needs can be arranged in a hierarchy, beginning with the physiological needs for oxygen, water, food, and the like, then moving up through the needs for safety, belongingness, love, and esteem. Each lower need is, in Maslow's term, "prepotent" to the one above it. A very hungry person, for example, will quickly forget hunger if deprived of oxygen. Generally, each of the lower needs must be met before the one above it emerges. Taken this far, his "hierarchy of needs" is a useful but not particularly shattering formulation. For one thing, it avoids the twists and turns in the Freudian notion that all so-called higher feelings and actions are merely disguised versions of the primary drives of sex and ego-need; tenderness, for example, is seen by Freud as nothing more than "aim-inhibited sexuality." But Maslow goes even further: After all of the "deficiency-needs" listed above are fairly well satisfied, then a need for "self-actualization" emerges. This "being-need" is just as real, just as much a part of human nature as are the deficiency-needs.

The concept of self-actualization crystallized during Maslow's moment of insight about Ruth Benedict and Max Wertheimer, but it evolved and developed through years of studying exceptionally healthy and successful individuals. Self-actualization is, in short, the tendency of every human being—once the basic deficiency-needs are adequately fulfilled—to *make real* his or her full potential, to become everything he or she can be. The self-actualizing person is the true human species-type; a Max Wertheimer is a more accurate representation of the human species than is a Hitler. For Maslow, the self-actualizing person is not a normal person with something added, but a normal person with nothing taken away. In a "synergic" society—the term is Benedict's—what is good for the development and well-being of the individual is also good for the development and well-being of the society. Our type of society is obviously not synergic, which accounts for the rarity of self-actualizing people. Though the physiological needs of most of our citizens are fulfilled, the safety needs are hardly to be taken for granted, what with the prevalence of dog-eat-dog competition and crime. And many lives are lacking in an adequate supply of belongingness, love, and esteem. Maslow sees these lacks, these "holes" in the development of a person, as a prime cause of mental illness. Indeed, for Maslow, neurosis can be viewed largely as a deficiency disease. Thus, the Maslovian thesis cries out against the injustice that deprives so many people of their most basic needs and suggests major reforms in our ways of relating, especially in the family.

For those people who somehow transcend the deficiency-needs, self-actualization becomes a growth process, an unfolding of human nature as it potentially could be. Maslow defines this "true" human nature in terms of the characteristics of self-actualizing people, using not just personal interviews but also the study of such historical figures as Thomas Jefferson, Albert Einstein, Eleanor Roosevelt, Albert Schweitzer, and Jane Addams.

One of the most striking characteristics of these people is that they are strongly focused on problems *outside* of themselves. They generally have a mission in life; they delight in bringing about justice, stopping cruelty and exploitation, fighting lies and untruth. They have a clear perception of reality, along with a keen sense of the false, the phony. They are spontaneous and creative, sometimes displaying what might be called a mature childlikeness, a "second naiveté." They are autonomous, not bound tightly to the customs and assumptions of their particular culture. Their character structure is highly democratic, so that their friendships tend to cut across the dividing lines of class, education, politics, and ethnic background. At the same time, they are marked by a certain detachment and a need for privacy; they generally limit themselves to a relatively small circle of close friends. Significantly, they do not lump people or ideas in the usual categories but rather tend to see straight through "the man-made mass of concepts, abstractions, expectations, beliefs and stereotypes that most people confuse with the world."

Self-actualizing people, Maslow discovered, are far more likely than others to have peak experiences—that is, episodes of delight and heightened clarity and even revelation, during which all things seem to flow in perfect harmony. Through numerous interviews and questionnaires, he found that even ordinary people take on self-actualizing qualities during peak experiences. He also comes very close to saying that such experiences provide a glimpse into the realm of Being, into ultimate reality itself.

Here is another paradox: Maslow the self-proclaimed atheist insisting upon the importance of a class of human experience that includes the experiences of the greatest religious figures back through the ages. But he himself was always filled to the brim with a religious wonder, with a profound sense of what Rudolf Otto calls *das Heilige*, "the holy"; and he never shrank from presenting the transcendent realm of Being forcefully, even if he did so in a secular, psychological context. At the turn of the century William James had written eloquently about the mystic experience, but most psychologists ignored this entire aspect of human life or dismissed it as some kind of compensation mechanism. For Freud, who confessed he had never had such an experience, the "oceanic feeling" is mere infantile regression. Maslow's courage in bringing the peak experience out of the closet has since been validated by several studies and polls showing its universality and value.

When people reach the stage of self-actualization, according to Maslow, many of the assumptions of conventional psychology are overturned. For example, human motivation prior to Maslow was generally treated in terms of tension reduction, and impulses were considered to be dangerous. But Maslow points out that this is true only in the realm of the lower needs. The "growth-needs" of the self-actualizing person ware not mere itches to be relieved by scratching. The higher tensions (problems to be solved, human relations to be deepened) can be pleasurable. Creative impulses, then, are to be welcomed and trusted.

By opening up the previously hidden area of psychological health, Maslow provides a new kind of guidance for the human journey. Self-actualizing people, he argues, are good choosers. When given an opportunity, they gravitate toward what is good for them and, in his view, good for the human race. "So far as human value theory is concerned," Maslow writes in his 1962 book, *Toward a Psychology of Being*, "no theory will be adequate that rests simply on the statistical description of the choices of unselected human beings. To average the choices of good and bad choosers, of healthy and sick people, is useless. Only the choices and tastes and judgment of healthy human beings will tell us much about what is good for the human species in the long run."

In the 1950s Maslow began to see his work as part of a Third Force in psychology, representing a decisive, positive move beyond standard Freudian psychology, with its sickness-oriented view of humankind, and beyond behaviorism, which tends to treat the individual as a mere point between stimulus and response. With his generous, inclusive spirit, Maslow viewed Third Force psychology as large enough to hold Adlerians, Rankians, Jungians, Rogerians, neo-Freudians, Talmudic psychologists, Gestaltists, and many others. In 1961 his mailing list, which had long been used to circulate papers and ideas, became the basis for the *Journal of Humanistic Psychology*. A year later Maslow was a guiding force in starting the Association for Humanistic Psychology, whose founding members included Charlotte Bühler, Kurt Goldstein, David Riesman, Henry Murray, and Lewis Mumford, Two of the most influential founders were Rollow May, who was instrumental in introducing European existential psychology to the U.S., and Carl Rogers, whose humanistic, client-centered approach to psychotherapy and counseling has since spread throughout the world.

MASLOW'S THEORY, EVEN IF IT IS INCOMPLETE, NEVER FAILS TO CHALLENGE US WITH A SPINE-TINGLING VISION OF INDIVIDUAL POTENTIAL, HEALTH, AND A SYNERGIC SOCIETY.

The summer of 1962 was to see two events that would play a major role in Maslow's influence on the culture. The first involved his appointment as a visiting fellow to Non-Linear Systems, a high-tech plant in Del Mar, California. Here, Maslow first realized that his theories could be applied to management. He discovered that there were just as many self-actualizing people in industry—perhaps more—than in the universities, and he got the idea that a humane, enlightened management policy devoted to the development of human potential could also be the most effective. He called this concept "eupsychian management," which became the title of his 1965 book on the subject. As it turned out, Maslow's ideas foreshadowed those that are now associated with the best of Japanese management, and it is hard to find a book on management theory today that does not give a prominent place to Abraham Maslow.

The second event of that summer was synchronistic—to use a word coined by Jung to describe coincidences that are more than just that. Abe and Bertha were driving down California's Highway 1 for a holiday, and their progress was slower than anticipated on that spectacular and tortuous coast road. Looking for a place to spend the night, they saw a light and drove off the road down a steep driveway toward what they took to be a motel. They were astonished to find that almost everybody there was reading the recently published *Toward a Psychology of Being* and enthusiastically discussing Maslovian ideas.

The Maslows had stumbled upon what was to become Esalen Institute on the eve of its opening to the public. The institute's cofounder, Michael Murphy, had just bought a dozen copies of the book and given them to the members of his staff. Later, Maslow and Murphy became close friends and Maslow became a major influence on Esalen and on the entire counterculture of the 1960s.

This association was to raise some eyebrows among Maslow's conservative colleagues. The first press reports on the newly minted human-potential movement were, to be as charitable as possible, sensationalized and uninformed, and a less courageous man might have pulled back. But Maslow was not one to flinch under fire. "Esalen's an experiment," he told Bertha. "I'm glad they're trying it." And later, in public symposia, Maslow called Esalen "potentially the most important educational institution in the world."

Maslow's influence on America, transmitted through this lineage, can hardly be overstated. What has happened is that the counterculture of the 1960s has become a major and influential segment of the mainstream culture of the 1980s. This development has been largely ignored by the established journals of opinion but is clearly seen in the surveys of Louis Harris and Daniel Yankelovich, in the sophisticated Trend Reports of John Naisbitt, and in Naisbitt's recent best seller, *Megatrends*.

It is also becoming clear that while the quest for self-actualization might lead some people to a narrow preoccupation with the self, the number who go to this extreme is small, and the "me first" stage is generally temporary, a way station on the journey to social consciousness. This is seen in the Values and Lifestyles (VALS) Program of SRI International, a California-based research and consulting organization, which has adapted Maslow's hierarchy of needs to an analysis of the U.S. population and which numbers some of the nation's most successful corporations among its subscribers. The VALS study shows that the "Inner-Directeds," those who might be said to be on the path toward self-actualization, now make up 21 percent of all Americans and represent the fastest-growing segment of the population. Of this 21 percent, only 3 percent are in the self-centered, narcissistic "I-am-me" category. The Inner-Directeds, for the most part, tend to move inexorably toward social consciousness, service to

BORN APRIL 1, 1908

At Brooklyn College in 1943, Maslow was a much-loved teacher, so popular that the school newspaper characterized him as the Frank Sinatra of Brooklyn College.

PHOTOGRAPH • COURTESY OF MRS. BERTHA MASLOW

Dossier

Abraham Maslow

was born on April 1, 1908, in Brooklyn. The eldest of seven children, he remembered "clinging" to his father. "I have no memory," he wrote, "of expecting anything from my mother." He later called his mother a "schizophrenogenic... one who makes crazy people.... I was awfully curious to find out why I didn't go insane."

In elementary school he met anti-Semitism and a teacher he later described as a "horrible bitch." Challenging his reputation as the class's best speller, the teacher made Maslow stand up and spell one word after another. When he finally missed one—*parallel*—the teacher publicly concluded, "I knew you were a fake."

Throughout his adolescence he was intensely shy and, he recalled, "terribly unhappy, lonely, isolated, self-rejecting." A loving uncle, his mother's brother, looked after him. "He may have saved my life, psychically," Maslow said.

He left New York for Cornell University partly because of his strong passion for his cousin Bertha: "I had not yet touched Bertha.... And this was getting kind of rough on me—sexually, because I was very powerfully sexed...."

At the University of Wisconsin his professors accepted him as a colleague. Still, he was amazed when, one day in a men's room, a professor stepped up to the urinal next to his. "How did I think that professors urinated?" he later marveled. "Didn't I know they had kidneys?"

At Columbia University he found the initial research he conducted for psychologist E. L. Thorndike boring. He wrote Thorndike a note saying so—even though he stood to lose his job during the Depression. Far from firing Maslow, Thorndike respected his opinion.

For all his popularity with students, Maslow was terrified of public speaking until he was over fifty. In 1925 a paper he wrote never got published because he fled a conference rather than read it. In 1959 he delivered a talk, then for days afterward stayed in bed recovering from it.

He suffered his first heart attack in 1945 and never again was completely healthy. He had an arthritic hip, and though he was always tired, he had trouble sleeping. Only in the year before his death did a doctor discover that Maslow's chronic fatigue was a form of hypoglycemia. For years the ailment had made him crabby, inhibited his work, and stifled his sex life.

Until the age of thirty he considered himself a socialist—"Fabian rather than Marxist." He said he dropped socialism after Franklin Roosevelt put "our whole socialist programme... into law" and he didn't see "any great miracles occur."

After his bar mitzvah, at thirteen, he became "a fighting atheist." Yet later in life, when offers came to teach at other universities, he would not leave his teaching job at Brandeis. "Why?" he asked himself. "Partly it's the Jewish business. I have been so proud of the great Jewish university—I didn't realize how much—and I feel like a rat deserting the sinking ship... just the way I did when I left Brooklyn and abandoned the poor Jewish students whom nobody loved but me. The guilt of upward mobility."

In 1954 he wrote, "Human nature is not nearly as bad as it has been thought to be.... In fact it can be said that the possibilities of human nature have customarily been sold short...."

He enjoyed art museums, shopping, and reading science fiction. He admired J. D. Salinger. ("... read *Fanny and Zooey*.... He says in his way what I've been trying to say. The novelist can be *so* much more effective.") He also liked Betty Friedan's *The Feminine Mystique,* which discusses his views on sex and dominance. ("A passionate book—I was swept along unintentionally.")

In 1969 the White House invited him to join a committee to define national goals, but he was too sick to attend. He was miffed by the popular press's indifference to his work: "A new image of man... a new image of nature, a new philosophy of science, a new economics, a new everything, and they just don't notice it."

Still, at fifty-six he wrote: "With my troubles about insomnia and bad back and conflict over my role in psychology and... in a certain sense, *needing* psychoanalysis, if anyone were to ask me 'Are you a happy man?' I'd say 'yes, yes!' Am I lucky?... The darling of fortune? Sitting as high up as a human being ever has? Yes!"

Five years later, on June 8, 1970, he died of a heart attack. *The New York Times* published no obituary.

"[Maslow's is] a voice that has not been heard before ... it is hard to do justice to ... the challenge of Maslow's amazingly fertile mind; his combining of teacher, seer, ... physician, visionary, social planner, critic; his ambition in tying together all varieties of apparently unrelated phenomena; his unstoppable optimism."

—JOYCE CAROL OATES

DIED JUNE 8, 1970

others, and personal integration—which should come as no surprise to anyone who has given Maslow more than a cursory reading.

Critics argue that Maslow did not adequately deal with the problem of evil, with humanity's darker side, and there is something to this criticism. But Maslow himself was aware that he had much more work to do, "at least two hundred years' worth," he told Bertha shortly before his death. True, Maslow's theory might not be complete, but it never fails to challenge us with a spine-tingling vision of individual potential and health and of a synergic society.

Despair is often comfortable, in some circles even fashionable, and it is easy enough to dismiss or even ridicule Maslow's challenge. After all, nothing is more difficult or painful than to look clearly at your own wasted potential, then start doing something about it. But ever-increasing numbers of Americans are taking the challenge. For example, the fastest-growing movement in health management today involves the field of holistic, health-oriented approaches to the physical that Maslow applied to the psychological. If anything can solve the crisis of medical depersonalization and rising costs, it is this classically Maslovian shift: more and more people working against a pathogenic environment and society while taking personal responsibility for their own positive good health.

In spite of his unorthodox views, Maslow was elected to the presidency of the American Psychological Association in 1967, and now, more than twelve years after his death, his voice is still being heard, even if indirectly, even if by people who barely know his name. Warren Bennis, professor of management at USC, recalls it as "that incredibly soft, shy, tentative, and gentle voice making the most outrageous remarks." Bennis also remembers Maslow for "a childlike spirit of innocence and wonder—always wearing his eyebrows (as Thomas Mann said about Freud) continually raised in a constant expression of awe."

Still, it takes another characteristic to join the shyness, the outrageousness, and the awe into a complete human being, and that is courage, which is the essence of Abraham Maslow's story. Psychologist James F.T. Bugental, who served as the first president of the Association for Humanistic Psychology, lived near Maslow during the last year of his life. "Abe used to go for his walks," Bugental recalls, "and he'd come by our house. We had this myth that one of the cans of beer in the refrigerator was his, and he'd always say, 'Is my beer cold?'

"And he'd drink his beer and get a little sentimental and sometimes show us pictures of his granddaughter and weep because she was so beautiful and innocent and would have to lose her innocence. And sometimes he would talk about the time in his childhood when he'd have to go through a tough Irish neighborhood to get to the library, and about how he would plan his route and sometimes get chased and sometimes get beat up. But he never let that stop him. He went to the library even though he might have to get beat up.

"That's the way I see his life. He never stopped doing what he thought he had to do, even though he might get beat up. He had courage, just plain courage."

Erikson, In His Own Old Age, Expands His View of Life

In partnership with his wife, the psychoanalyst describes how wisdom of the elderly is born.

Daniel Goleman

In his ninth decade of life, Erik H. Erikson has expanded the psychological model of the life cycle that he put forward with his wife, Joan, almost 40 years ago.

Their original work profoundly changed psychology's view of human development. Now, breaking new ground, they have spelled out the way the lessons of each major stage of life can ripen into wisdom in old age. They depict an old age in which one has enough conviction in one's own completeness to ward off the despair that gradual physical disintegration can too easily bring.

"You've got to learn to accept the law of life, and face the fact that we disintegrate slowly," Mr. Erikson said.

On a recent afternoon, in a rare interview, they sat in their favorite nook in a bay window of Mrs. Erikson's study on the second floor of their Victorian house near Harvard Square in Cambridge, Mass. "The light is good here and it's cozy at night," Mrs. Erikson told a visitor.

Although Mr. Erikson has a comfortable study downstairs, and Mrs. Erikson, an artist and author in her own right, has a separate workroom, they prefer to spend their time together in this quiet corner, in the spirit of their lifelong collaboration.

Mr. Erikson, who never earned an academic degree (he is usually called Professor Erikson), deeply affected the study of psychology. Many believe that his widely read books made Freud pertinent to the struggles of adult life and shaped the way people today think about their own emotional growth. He gave psychology the term "identity crisis."

When Mr. Erikson came to this country in 1933 from Vienna, he spoke little English. Mrs. Erikson, a Canadian, has always lent her editorial hand to those writings of her husband on which she did not act as co-author.

As Mr. Erikson approaches 87 years of age and Mrs. Erikson 86, old age is one topic very much on their minds.

Their original chart of the life cycle was prepared in 1950 for a White House conference on childhood and youth. In it, each stage of life, from infancy and early childhood on, is associated with a specific psychological struggle that contributes to a major aspect of personality.

In infancy, for instance, the tension is between trust and mistrust; if an infant feels trusting, the result is a sense of hope.

In old age, according to the new addition to the stages, the struggle is between a sense of one's own integrity and a feeling of defeat, of despair about one's life in the phase of normal physical disintegration. The fruit of that struggle is wisdom.

"When we looked at the life cycle in our 40's, we looked to old people for wisdom," Mrs. Erikson said. "At 80, though, we look at other 80-year-olds to see who got wise and who not. Lots of old people don't get wise, but you don't get wise unless you age."

Originally, the Eriksons defined wisdom in the elderly as a more objective concern with life itself in the face of death. Now that they are at that stage of life, they have been developing a more detailed description of just what the lessons of each part of life lend to wisdom in old age. For each earlier stage of development they see a parallel development toward the end of life's journey.

For instance, the sense of trust that begins to develop from the infant's experience of a loving and supportive environment becomes, in old age, an appreciation of human interdependence, according to the Eriksons.

"Life doesn't make any sense without interdependence," Mrs. Erikson said. "We need each other and the sooner we learn that the better for us all."

The second stage of life, which begins in early childhood with learning control over one's own body, builds the sense of will on the one hand, or shame and doubt on the other. In old age, one's experience is almost a mirror image of what it was earlier as the body deteriorates and one needs to learn to accept it.

In "play age" or preschool children, what is being learned is a sense of initiative and purpose in life, as well as a sense of playfulness and creativity, the theory holds.

Two lessons for old age from that stage of life are empathy and resilience, as the Eriksons see it.

"The more you know yourself, the more patience you have for what you see in others," Mrs. Erikson said. "You don't have to accept what people do, but understand what leads them to do it. The stance this leads to is to forgive even though you still oppose."

The child's playfulness becomes, too, a sense of humor about life. "I can't imagine a wise old person who can't laugh," said Mr. Erikson. "The world is full of ridiculous dichotomies."

At school age, the Erikson's next stage, the child strives to become effective and industrious, and so develops a sense of competence; if he or she does not, the outcome is feelings of inferiority.

The Completed Life Cycle

In the Eriksons' view, each stage of life is associated with a specific psychological conflict and a specific resolution. In a new amplification, lessons from each of the earlier stages mature into the many facets of wisdom in old age, shown in column at right.

Conflict and resolution	Culmination in old age
Old Age Integrity vs. despair: wisdom	Existential identity; a sense of integrity strong enough to withstand physical disintegration.
Adulthood Generativity vs. stagnation: care	Caritas, caring for others, and agape, empathy and concern.
Early Adulthood Intimacy vs. isolation: love	Sense of complexity of relationships; value of tenderness and loving freely.
Adolescence Identity vs. confusion: fidelity	Sense of complexity of life; merger of sensory, logical and aesthetic perception.
School Age Industry vs. inferiority: competence	Humility; acceptance of the course of one's life and unfulfilled hopes.
Play Age Initiative vs. guilt: purpose	Humor; empathy; resilience.
Early Childhood Autonomy vs. shame: will	Acceptance of the cycle of life, from integration to disintegration.
Infancy Basic trust vs. mistrust: hope	Appreciation of interdependence and relatedness.

HUMILITY IN OLD AGE

In old age, as one's physical and sensory abilities wane, a lifelong sense of effectiveness is a critical resource. Reflections in old age on the course one's life has taken—especially comparing one's early hopes and dreams with the life one actually lived—foster humility. Thus, humility in old age is a realistic appreciation of one's limits and competencies.

The adolescent's struggle to overcome confusion and find a lifelong identity results in the capacity for commitment and fidelity, the Eriksons hold. Reflections in old age on the complexity of living go hand in hand with a new way of perceiving, one that merges sensory, logical and esthetic perception, they say. Too often, they say, people overemphasize logic and ignore other modes of knowing.

"If you leave out what your senses tell you, your thinking is not so good," Mrs. Erikson said.

In young adulthood, the conflict is between finding a balance between lasting intimacy and the need for isolation. At the last stage of life, this takes the form of coming to terms with love expressed and unexpressed during one's entire life; the understanding of the complexity of relationships is a facet of wisdom.

"You have to live intimacy out over many years, with all the complications of a long-range relationship, really to understand it," Mrs. Erikson said. "Anyone can flirt around with many relationships, but commitment is crucial to intimacy. Loving better is what comes from understanding the complications of a long-term intimate bond."

She added: "You put such a stress on passion when you're young. You learn about the value of tenderness when you grow old. You also learn in late life not to hold, to give without hanging on; to love freely, in the sense of wanting nothing in return."

In the adult years, the psychological tension is between what the Eriksons call generativity and caring on the one hand and self-absorption and stagnation on the other. Generativity expresses itself, as Mrs. Erikson put it, in "taking care to pass on to the next generation what you've contributed to life."

Mr. Erikson sees a widespread failing in modern life.

"The only thing that can save us as a species is seeing how we're not thinking about future generations in the way we live," he said. "What's lacking is generativity, a generativity that will promote positive values in the lives of the next generation. Unfortunately, we set the example of greed, wanting a bigger and better everything, with no thought of what will make it a better world for our great-grandchildren. That's why we go on depleting the earth: we're not thinking of the next generations."

UNDERSTANDING GENERATIVITY

As an attribute of wisdom in old age, generativity has two faces. One is "caritas," a Latin word for charity, which the Eriksons take in the broad sense of caring for others. The other is "agape," a Greek word for love, which they define as a kind of empathy.

The final phase of life, in which integrity battles despair, culminates in a full wisdom to the degree each earlier phase of life has had a positive resolution, the Eriksons believe. If everything has gone well, one achieves a sense of integrity, a sense of completeness, of personal wholeness that is strong enough to offset the downward psychological pull of the inevitable physical disintegration.

Despair seems quite far from the Eriksons in their own lives. Both continue to exemplify what they described in the title of a 1986 book, "Vital Involvement in Old Age." Mr. Erikson is writing about, among other things, the sayings of Jesus. Mrs. Erikson's most recent book, "Wisdom and the Senses," sets out evidence that the liveliness of the senses throughout life, and the creativity and playfulness that this brings, is the keystone of wisdom in old age.

"The importance of the senses came to us in old age," said Mr. Erikson, who now wears a hearing aid and walks with a slow, measured dignity.

In her book, Mrs. Erikson argues that modern life allows too little time for the pleasures of the senses. She says: "We start to lose touch with the senses in school: we call play, which stimulates the senses and makes them acute, a waste of time or laziness. The schools relegate play to sports. We call that play, but it isn't; it's competitive, not in the spirit of a game."

The Eriksons contend that wisdom has little to do with formal learning. "What is real wisdom?" Mrs. Erikson asked. "It comes from life experience, well digested. It's not what comes from reading great books. When it comes to understanding life, experiential learning is the only worthwhile kind; everything else is hearsay."

Mr. Erikson has been continuing a line of thought he set out in a Yale Review article in 1981 on the sayings of Jesus and their implications for the sense of "I," an argument that takes on the concept of the "ego" in Freudian thought.

"The trouble with the word 'ego' is its technical connotations," Mr. Erikson said. "It has bothered me that 'ego' was used as the translation of the German word 'Ich.' That's wrong. Freud was referring to the simple sense of "I."

The Eriksons contend that wisdom has little to do with formal learning.

Another continuing concern for the Eriksons has been the ethics of survival, and what they see as the urgent need to overcome the human tendency to define other groups as an enemy, an outgrowth of the line of thinking Mr. Erikson began in his biography of Gandhi.

Mr. Erikson was trained in psychoanalysis in Vienna while Freud was still there, and worked closely with Freud's daughter Anna in exploring ways to apply psychoanalytic methods to children. That expertise made him welcome at Harvard, where he had his first academic post.

There he began the expansion of Freud's thinking that was to make him world famous. By describing in his books "Childhood and Society" and "Identity and the Life Cycle" how psychological growth is shaped throughout life, not just during the formative early years that Freud focused on, Mr. Erikson made a quantium leap in Freudian thought.

Over the years since first coming to Harvard, Mr. Erikson has spent time at other universities and hospitals, including Yale in the late 1930's, the University of California at Berkeley in the 40's, the Austen Riggs Center in Stockbridge, Mass., in the 50's, and again at Harvard through the 60's. Until last year, the Eriksons lived in Marin County near San Francisco, but it is to Cambridge that they returned.

One lure was grandchildren nearby. Their son Kai, with two children, is a professor of sociology at Yale, and their daughter Sue, with one child, also lives nearby.

Informally, Mr. Erikson still continues to supervise therapists. "The students tell me it's the most powerful clinical supervision they've ever had," said Margaret Brenman-Gibson, a professor of psychology in the psychiatry department at Cambridge City Hospital, a part of Harvard Medical School.

In Cambridge, the Eriksons share a rambling three-story Victorian with three other people: a graduate student, a professor of comparative religion and a psychologist. The housemates often take meals together.

"Living communally," said Mrs. Erikson, "is an adventure at our age."

What DREAMS Are (Really) Made Of

The psychiatrist and neuroscientist Allan Hobson suggests replacing the traditional Freudian view—that dreams stem from unacceptable, hidden wishes and fears—with a more commonsense theory. Dreams, he says, are caused by spontaneous electrochemical signals in the brain, and their meaning is transparent, not obscure

EDWARD DOLNICK

Edward Dolnick is a contributing editor of In Health, *formerly called* Hippocrates.

IN THE SPRING OF 1900, SHORTLY AFTER THE PUBLICATION of *The Interpretation of Dreams*, Sigmund Freud wrote a letter to a friend. "Do you suppose," he asked, "that someday one will read on a marble tablet on this house: 'Here, on July 24, 1895, the secret of the dream revealed itself to Dr. Sigm. Freud'?"

Freud's faith in his theory never wavered. Nine years later he told an American lecture audience that "the interpretation of dreams is in fact the royal road to a knowledge of the unconscious. It is the securest foundation of psychoanalysis and the field in which every worker must acquire his convictions and seek his training."

Two decades after that, looking back on *The Interpretation of Dreams* in his old age, Freud still felt pride of authorship. "It contains," he wrote, "even according to my present-day judgement, the most valuable of all the discoveries it has been my good fortune to make. Insight such as this falls to one's lot but once in a lifetime."

The world has echoed that verdict. Virtually all scholars of psychoanalysis agree with Freud that his dream book was his most important work. Perhaps more significant, Freud's dream theory has become an inescapable part of modern culture. Even people who reject much of Freudian theory as dubious or bizarre, who would never give credence to talk of Electra complexes or penis envy, make an exception for dreams.

We all accept, as a commonplace, that dreams bubble up from a troubled subconscious, that they represent hidden and mysterious wishes, and that they require deciphering. In both popular culture and high culture these notions are generally accepted without argument. As Walt Disney's Cinderella put it, "A dream is a wish your heart makes when you're fast asleep." Move from Hollywood to Harvard and the view doesn't change much. In a discussion of a book called *Dream Time,* Sven Birkerts, a Cambridge-based literary critic, notes in passing, "Ah, but we are all now children of Freud. We know that nothing in dreams is really accidental."

In 1977 Freud's dream theory was finally commemorated with the plaque he had hoped for. In that same year, by coincidence, a campaign began that would enlist all the tools of modern neuroscience in an effort to dethrone Freud and to vanquish the cult of the dream.

Chief among the would-be debunkers is a Harvard psychiatrist and neuroscientist named Allan Hobson. In a steady series of books and lectures and research papers and debates he has argued that the psychoanalytic theory of dreams is a museum piece, as outdated as theories of possession by demons. Not surprisingly, he has an alternative theory.

Hobson is fifty-seven, trim, and a bit above medium height, with wispy white hair and a long, thin nose, which was rearranged by muggers a couple of decades ago. He is an animated man, a good talker, whose voice rises and whose delivery speeds up as he works his way to a punch line. He made his reputation as a scientist, but his fascination with dreams has led him into diverse realms.

On one wall of his lab hangs a fan letter from Federico Fellini. Hobson is a film buff who has spent time on the set with Fellini and written an essay on Bergman's dream imagery. Now, on a winter morning in his office at the Massachusetts Mental Health Center, a facility affiliated with Harvard Medical School, he is recounting a dream from the previous night.

Hobson was talking with a woman at what seemed to be a reunion of his medical school class. What was strange, what made the dream "dreamy," was that he couldn't quite place her. "Only eight women were in my class, and I know them all," he says. "Some of the data suggested classmate A, but the woman's actual appearance was closer to that of classmate B, though not precisely."

What is the psychological significance of that confusion? Hobson's voice grows loud and indignant. "That was the best I could do. It's the best that my mind could do under the circumstances." He pauses for breath and adds a soupçon of incredulity to the mix, his voice now almost a squeak. "It's not my *mother*, or somebody else that's stuck in there dressed like my medical school classmates. My mind, or brain-mind, was making the best of a bad job. It was trying to fit the thing together into some whole meaning, and it didn't work."

That picture of the dreamer as a kind of sorcerer's apprentice, racing madly to keep up with a flood of imagery, is central to Hobson's theory. Every night, he says, the dreaming brain automatically generates a barrage of signals that we do our best to assemble into a coherent story. The imagery itself has no "message," but the mind, waking or dreaming, cannot help investing its world with meaning. "I walk out this door," Hobson says, swinging his chair around his tiny office, "and I see the coatrack standing there. It's got *my* coat on it, *my* hat, but when I look at it, I see a person."

He snorts in derision at his own gullibility. "It's happened fifty times. I fill in, I project. I know that it happens, but I look around startled. That's clear evidence that in the waking state I'm taking bits of form and filling in the holes. And that's what happens in dreams."

This view stands conventional thinking about dreaming on its head. Dreams are caused by electrochemical signals darting helter-skelter around the brain, like untied balloons released in a room. The familiar expression "I had a dream" should probably be reversed: "A dream had me."

Why Dreams Are Bizarre

LIKE THE ANONYMOUS NOVELIST WHOM NOEL Coward described as "every other inch a gentleman," Allan Hobson is intermittently a modest fellow. His theory is bold—it aims to supplant Freud, after all—but many of his claims for it are surprisingly limited.

To begin with, Hobson has restricted his attention to the formal properties of dreams, the features that all dreams share. He wants to know why dreams are bizarre, why they are vivid, and why they are hard to remember. The specifics of a given dream—why I dreamed of my grandfather last night—lie outside his reach.

The theory is not a ploy to dismiss dreams. Hobson is inordinately fond of them and has kept a dream journal off and on since 1973. One night recently I heard a family friend who had come to Hobson's house for dinner proffer a dream the way a guest of another household might present a bottle of wine or a dessert.

Hobson does not deny that dreams have meaning. They are revealing, he says, much as interpretations of Rorschach inkblots can be. The particular narrative that a dreamer fashions from randomly generated signals does reflect his preoccupations and hopes and fears.

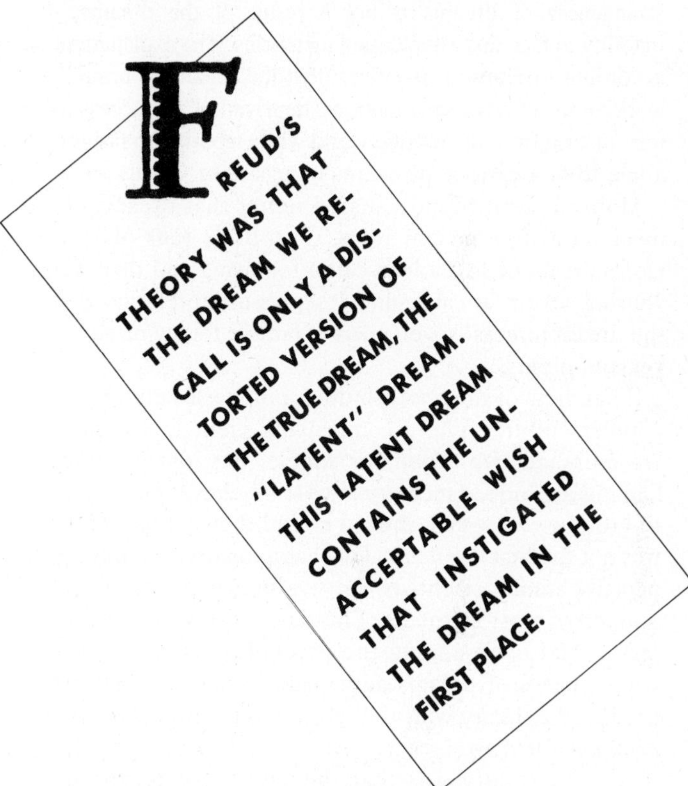

The dispute isn't over whether dreams have a meaning but over where their meaning lies. Hobson's dreamer reveals himself by what he *adds* to a jumble of apparently unrelated elements. Freud's view was just the opposite. The unconscious, he said, teems with secret, forbidden wishes that we cannot bear to acknowledge. To guard our sleep, a censor disguises and *subtracts* information from our dreams so that we can endure them. Dreams seem strange and full of gaps and scene shifts because the censor has gotten to the newsstand ahead of us, tearing out incriminating pages, blacking out key sentences, disguising photographs.

Hobson concedes that we all walk around with painful memories that we do our best to banish. But he emphatically rejects Freud's view that those repressed memories are the cause of dreams. Instead, he says, dreams are caused by the brain's spontaneous self-activation while we sleep.

On the most general level, Hobson and Freud are in accord. Like Freud, Hobson believes that dreams are psychologically significant. Like Freud, Hobson rejects the dismissive view of one of Freud's scientifically minded predecessors that the dreaming brain is analogous to "the ten fingers of a man who knows nothing of music wandering over the keys of the piano."

But on the specific nature of dreams Hobson has little use for Freud. Dreams are not obscure but transparent; they are not censored but unedited; dreaming is not triggered by daily events that resurrect buried memories but is a process as automatic as breathing. Most important, the characteristic strangeness of dreams is not a result of the dreamer's inability to face up to unpleasant memories. The explanation, according to Hobson, is simply that the dreaming brain is working under adverse conditions, deprived of any access to information from the outside world while laboring to fashion a tale from a cascade of internally generated signals.

Hobson's and Freud's shared belief that dreams are meaningful has ancient roots. The Bible tells of Pharaoh's dream of seven lean cattle following and then devouring seven fat cattle and Joseph's interpretation that the dream forecast seven years of famine following seven years of plenty.

That view of dreams as hidden prophesies endures in popular culture. The accompanying view, that dreams are messages from gods or angels, has lost its hold. Dreams are indeed messages, we still believe, but thanks to Freud we now look inward to find their source. Freud was not the first intellectual to champion dreams, but, especially among scientists, he was in a minority. In the opinion of most scientists of his day, dreams were mental froth. And even among the psychologists and writers whose views of dreams anticipated Freud, no one had produced a theory with the scope and detail of *The Interpretation of Dreams*.

Freud's theory was that the dream we recall, the "manifest" dream, is only a distorted version of the true dream, the "latent" dream. This latent dream contains the unacceptable wish that instigated the dream in the first place. The point of the nearly 500 pages of *The Interpretation of Dreams* is to explain how the two forms of the dream are related, and how the latent dream can be uncovered.

Hobson's theory is far less ornate. Where a physiological explanation is at hand, he says, a psychological explanation is unnecessary. "The nonsensical features of dreams are not a psychological defense," Hobson insists, "any more than the disoriented ramblings of a patient with Alzheimer's disease are."

Such barbs are aimed at Freud, but Hobson isn't a doctrinaire follower of any therapeutic school. "The scientific evidence is very strong in favor of the idea that it is therapists, and not therapies, that help people," he says. "There's very little evidence that one school or one technique is better than another. The only exception is behavior therapy, which is probably the treatment of choice for phobias."

In some ways, though, Hobson's view of dreaming is similar to Jung's. Hobson doesn't have much use for Jung's archetypical symbols, but he does follow Jung in seeing dreaming as creative rather than neurotic. And he agrees with Jung that dreams are undisguised.

The meaning, he says, is right out on the surface, shouting to the rooftops. "When I'm up for promotion or tenure and there's a really unbelievable administrative botch of the whole thing," he says, "I have *five years* of dreams where I'm missing trains, missing boats, I don't have my papers, my dossier's not in order."

He has rattled off that list of calamities at tobacco-auctioneer speed and now can hardly sit still. "*This is a transparent reflection of my concern about my credentials*," he roars. "*No problem!* It's not a disguise of my fear of failure or my anxiety that I'm going to succeed. My anxiety is, I'm afraid either those bureaucrats won't get my records straight or they'll say no promotion."

To venture more-elaborate explanations, Hobson says, is a kind of showing off, an entertaining but empty display of intellectual ingenuity. This is a point Hobson circles back to repeatedly, sometimes sounding as enamored of "plain talk and common sense" as a Fourth of July orator praising the homespun wisdom of the American people.

That is an odd stance for a scientist to take (common sense surely tells us that, say, the earth is flat), and in his more considered moments Hobson instead invokes one of the patron saints of science, William of Occam. That fourteenth-century philosopher spelled out the doctrine now known as Occam's razor, which says that a simple explanation that fits the facts is preferable to a complex one. Never introduce more than is required for an explanation, Occam declared, or, in Hobson's free translation, "Given two alternative theories, one of which is straightforward and the other convoluted, you pays your money and you takes your choice."

Hobson wields Occam's razor with the flair and self-righteousness of a knight of old brandishing his sword. Does Freud say that we dream because at night, when our defenses are down, lurid thoughts escape from the dungeon of the unconscious? *Whhsssst!* cuts the razor. We dream because the sleeping brain automatically sparks itself into life every ninety minutes or so. Does Freud say that dreams are bizarre because we censor and disguise their true message? *Whhsssst!* Dreams are bizarre because they're constructed from random bits and pieces. Does Freud say that we forget dreams largely because even in censored form they're too painful to acknowledge? *Whhsssst!* We forget them because the dreaming brain happens to be deprived of certain chemicals that are essential for storing memories.

The Origins of Hobson's Theory

THE SCIENCE UNDERLYING HOBSON'S THEORY of dreaming stems from a discovery by a most unlikely Archimedes, a ne'er-do-well graduate student named Eugene Aserinsky. In 1952 Aserinsky was studying physiology at the University of Chicago. In the dozen years before that he had tried college but left without a degree, begun dental school but dropped out, served in the Army, and been a social worker. He had never earned even a bachelor's degree. Now he was, in his words, a "stray cat" whom a kindly professor had taken in, and he was working on a "nonsensical idea" that no one else was interested in.

For no very clear reason Aserinsky wanted to know how a person's eyes move while he is asleep. The best way to tackle the problem, he decided, was to observe a sleeper for a full night. The most convenient research subject available was his eight-year-old son, Armond.

Aserinsky found an ancient, broken-down electroencephalograph machine, abandoned in a university basement. His plan was to tape electrodes near Armond's eyes and use the electroencephalograph, a machine akin to a lie detector, to record any eye movements.

For week after frustrating week the machine malfunctioned. "It would break down with one ailment and I would fix that, and it would break down with something else," Aserinsky recalls. Throughout this period the pens attached to the EEG would occasionally interrupt their slow, wavy tracing of Armond's eye movements and begin marking spiky peaks and valleys.

The interruptions seemed to show that the brain was occasionally as active in sleeping as in waking. That didn't make sense, and Aserinsky figured he still hadn't fixed his machine. Scientists thought of the sleeping brain as like a house late at night, the day's hubbub of activity replaced by the quiet hum of rest. We wake refreshed, conventional wisdom had it, because the brain has had a break from work. Aserinsky's research adviser was one of the leading proponents of this view. Either Aserinsky had made a startling discovery or his machine was still broken, and he didn't know which.

He phoned the manufacturers. They couldn't help. He managed to reach the scientist who was the reigning authority on the EEG, and this man advised Aserinsky to abandon the project. "If I had a suicidal nature, this would have been the time," Aserinsky says. Even today, safe in retirement, his tone as he tells the story recalls the panicky young man he was. "I was married, I had a child, I'd been in universities for twelve years with no degree to show for it. I'd already spent a couple of years horsing around on this. I was absolutely finished."

Finally he saw the solution. He could record the movements of each eye independently. Eyes move in tandem, and if the pens did too, that would suggest that the spiky patterns probably weren't caused by mechanical problems. This strategy of double-checking the machine turned out to be an old idea, but, Aserinsky says, "it saved my life."

Episodes of rapid eye movement, Aserinsky was soon convinced, came periodically throughout the night. "Well, it was a pretty quick jump to think of dreaming," Aserinsky says. "But that wasn't an idea I readily accepted. As a physiologist, I was more interested in blood and guts than in behavior."

Aserinsky now recruited a number of volunteers; he woke them up when their eyes began twitching and they reported that they had indeed been dreaming. His adviser asked for a demonstration but, wary of cheating, turned down Aserinsky's offer to recruit a volunteer and insisted that his own daughter be the test subject. She fell asleep. Soon after, her father's theory that the sleeping brain is resting was "totally demolished," Aserinsky says. "It doesn't exist anymore, except in the Annals of Peculiar Notions."

In the following years discoveries about rapid-eye-movement sleep tumbled out of laboratories around the world. Wake someone up during REM sleep and about 80 percent of the time he or she will report vivid, elaborate, hallucinatory dreams; wake the person during one of the bursts of particularly intense eye movement that punctuate REM sleep and the odds rise to 95 percent. But if the sleeper isn't wakened, the dream will almost certainly be lost. Dreams melt quickly: 95 percent of what we dream, perhaps 99 percent, is never remembered.

REM sleep begins some ninety minutes after we fall asleep. The brain begins running at full speed, blood pressure rises, breathing quickens, and the heart beats faster. Muscles become totally relaxed and unresponsive, though eyes and extremities may twitch. The dreamer is floating free in a self-created universe, his churning brain trying to keep its bearings without any cues from the outside world.

Episodes of REM-sleep are separated by calmer, deeper periods of sleep. We may dream during these hiatuses, but such dreams are rarer than REM-sleep ones and tend to be briefer and less bizarre. And every ninety minutes we automatically shift back into REM sleep.

We pass through four or five such dream episodes a night. They grow longer as the night goes on, and total about two hours. Because bed partners tend to fall asleep at roughly the same time and to wake each other by jostling or snoring, their pathways to REM sleep are roughly synchronized. "It may be biologically trivial but it is nonetheless charming," Hobson says, that "by sleeping together, couples increase the chances of dreaming together."

REM sleep has been found in all mammals studied to date except the spiny anteater, and, to a limited extent, in birds and some reptiles. (Any cat or dog owner watching his pet's twitching eyes and paws could have anticipated Aserinsky's discovery.) A newborn baby spends about eight hours a day in REM sleep. And before birth, at about thirty weeks after conception, the developing infant appears to spend almost all its time in REM sleep.

Just what infants (let alone animals) could be dreaming about is unclear. David Foulkes, a psychologist at Emory University, in Atlanta, has done the best work on the dreams of children. By monitoring children in a sleep lab and waking them at intervals, he found that children aged three to seven rarely reported that they'd been dreaming. After the age of seven children seem to dream about as often as adults.

The nature of dreams, as well as their frequency, changes with age. The earliest dreams are brief and almost devoid of action—a child might dream of herself asleep in a bathtub. At age five, six, or seven dreams become much longer but the dreamer still figures only rarely as an active participant in the dreams. By age eight or nine children's dreams begin to become as complex and lengthy as adult ones.

Any of the REM-sleep discoveries could have called Freud's dream theory into question. If dreams are caused by wishes, as Freud proposed, why should those wishes come every ninety minutes? If dreams are caused by repressed sexual desires, what unmentionable fantasies is a newborn baby entertaining? What of Fido asleep in front of the fireplace?

The challenge to Freud is not so much that the sleeping brain turns out to be active (his hardworking censor fits nicely with that finding) as that it is active at recurrent, predictable intervals. We dream with clockwork regularity. That poses no problem for physiology, which has long focused on explaining the body's rhythms. For psychology, however, and especially for a theory that dreams reflect individual and idiosyncratic hopes and fears, that regularity is a major mystery.

But the scientific assault on Freud waited another generation. The fortress, apparently, was strong, and didn't have to be abandoned just because of some sniper fire from the physiologists' camp. What was needed, in addition to criticism of Freud, was a scientifically based theory that could serve as an alternative to Freudian ideas.

Developing one was the mission that Allan Hobson saw for himself. The confrontational style that was required came naturally. He says, "One of the most important things that has happened to me is that I went to school in England when I was nineteen and was exposed to formal debate."

He absorbed the lessons well. To this day he can address a single listener in tones more appropriate to a prosecutor making a closing argument to a jury. After summarizing a critic's charges, he will say, "I submit to you that that is absurd." "What is most objectionable," he will cry, as he conjures up a flock of dream-interpreting psychoanalysts, "is that they do it under the mantle of science when it's not science at all. That is a lie."

Hobson seems genuinely fond of confrontation. "Some people count their blessings with the number of enemies they have," one of his colleagues observes, "and I think Allan is like that." But, surprisingly, he is on good terms with most of these "enemies." The sparring is serious, but Hobson seems not to take it personally. "He's the best psychologist working on dreams," he says of one researcher, and adds in the next breath, "He thinks my theory is bunk, just totally useless."

To the debater's combativeness Hobson adds a showman's flair. In 1977 he helped design an art exhibit *cum* science experiment that drew 10,500 visitors. The main attraction of the Dreamstage show was a volunteer sleeping behind a one-way mirror while hooked up to gadgets that continuously monitored his brain waves, eye position, and muscle tone. An audience sat in a darkened adjacent room watching colored lights paint those waves of information along the walls. At the same time, a synthesizer converted the waves into music, in effect a kind of improvised jazz composed by the sleeper. When he rolled over or began dreaming, the music grew louder and faster, and crowds of visitors scurried to the one-way mirror to see what was happening.

The Assault Begins

This attack on Freud began in 1977, when Hobson and his longtime collaborator, Robert McCarley, a psychiatrist who teaches at Harvard, published two papers on dreaming in the *American Journal of Psychiatry*. The articles, written in dry and rigorous prose, were explicitly intended as assaults on psychoanalysis. "I would admit to having created some heat where light might have been more useful," Hobson says, "but I can tell you, they weren't paying any attention until I turned the heat up a bit." Hobson and McCarley caught the eye of the psychiatric community. The articles generated more letters to the editor than any papers the journal had ever before published. Most were from outraged analysts, who perceived correctly that Hobson and McCarley were deeply skeptical of the theories that guided their profession.

The two articles amounted to a one-two punch. First came a critique of Freud's "antique neurobiology." Freud's dream theory, Hobson and McCarley argued, was based on the brain science of the 1890s, which is now universally agreed to be obsolete. Since those biological ideas had proved false, a psychology built on them must also be mistaken.

The first decade of Freud's career was devoted to neurobiology and neurology. Freud produced a spate of technical papers on such topics as the nerve cells of crayfish. In 1895, at the age of thirty-eight, he began an ambitious essay now known as the "Project for a Scientific Psychology." Memory, cognition, dreaming, and more were all to be explained biologically, in terms of the activity of brain cells. "The intention," Freud announced, "is to furnish a psychology that shall be a natural science."

That goal was never achieved. After a few months of frenzied work in 1895, Freud left the "Project" unfinished. Abandoning neuroscience, he turned his efforts to psychology. His theory of dreams, Freud later said, was based on a lengthy, painful self-analysis in the mid-1890s rather than on any theory of how the brain works. By probing his own emotions and earliest memories with ruthless honesty, psychoanalytic history has it, Freud unearthed such prizes as the Oedipus complex, the stages of sexual development, and the source of "accidental" slips of the tongue. His most important tool was free association, mainly with respect to the material from dreams. Hobson and McCarley didn't buy it. The self-analysis story, they insisted, was a myth. Freud's dream theory was simply a translation of the "Project" into a form that concealed its origins in neurobiology.

The second paper described Hobson and McCarley's own theory. In the years since it was written, Hobson has continued to refine his model. (McCarley, still a friend and ally, has gone his own way.) The fullest account appears in Hobson's 1988 book *The Dreaming Brain*.

Dreaming is so familiar that we tend to overlook its strangeness. In Hobson's summary,

> We see things, but the lights are out; we imagine running, flying, or dancing the tango, but are paralyzed; we explain the bizarre proceedings to our full satisfaction, but the logic by which we do so is as bizarre as the proceedings; we have intense emotional involvement in the action, but we forget the whole business as soon as it is over. What is going on?

That question, like What is time?, is easy to ask but maddeningly hard to answer. The brain, estimated to contain between 20 billion and 100 billion nerve cells, is one of the most complicated regions in the universe. The brain's nerve cells communicate in chemical messages called neurotransmitters, and each nerve cell, or neuron, is in simultaneous communication with upwards of 10,000 others. Each cell sends between two and a hundred messages every second, ceaselessly, day and night.

By a process that no one claims to understand, this electrified mound of gray-white Jell-O–like matter somehow becomes conscious. Brain becomes mind. But a daunting chasm separates the two. Physiologists assess one side of the territory, psychologists and therapists the other.

Hobson has a more ambitious (some would say ludicrously ambitious) goal. He want to travel back and forth across the body-mind chasm, using dreams as the bridge. Formidable as that task would seem to be, the strategy is straightforward, because the discovery of REM sleep provides a physiological handle on a psychological state. But the human brain is difficult to study experimentally. So research into the workings of the brain must detour by way of animal subjects.

Most of what sleep physiologists know about the living brain they've learned from cats. That may sound like a peculiar choice for research intended to explain the mystery of thought, but it is a practical one. Cat and human brains are roughly similar in design, and for a student of sleep a better subject would be hard to find.

A generation or so ago new tools were developed that provide more-detailed pictures of the brain at work than EEGs could offer. These are microelectrodes that record not electrical activity in general but the activity of single cells in particular. The tiny probes revealed that many neurons in the visual areas of the brain fire at least as often in REM sleep as they do in waking.

That was a surprise. When a wide-awake cat eyes the world, its visual cortex lights up with activity. Let that cat fall asleep, eyes shut tight in a black room, and the same cells will light up just as intensely. The brain interprets its own internally generated signals as if they had come from outside.

Similarly, brain cells that have to do with physical activity fire as intensely in REM sleep as in waking. "As far as the neurons are concerned," Hobson says, "the brain is both seeing and moving in REM sleep."

None of this was known in Freud's day. For Freud, for example, the question of why dreams are so intensely visual was a tricky one. Dreams represent a regression to infancy, he argued, and therefore a return to a mental life dominated by imagery rather than thought. For Hobson, matters are simpler. Dreams are visual because the dreaming brain is bombarded by internally generated signals that make it think it is seeing. (And sensations of taste and smell and pain are rare in dreams because the appropriate regions of the brain aren't as effectively activated.)

Why do dreamers find themselves trying to run but unable to move? Freud suggested that we are stalemated because our conscious wishes and our unconscious desires are in conflict. Hobson refers instead to physiological studies showing that in REM sleep we are effectively paralyzed. Though our dreams are full of effortless movement, things often go wrong when we try to exert our will and move voluntarily. Then a stalemate does occur, in the best Freudian tradition, but it is between the mind giving the command "Run!" and muscles that are blocked from acting. The dreamer *can't* move, so he can't flee the dragon chasing him.

Much of Hobson's research has sought answers to a different layer of questions. He, and many others, wanted to find the brain cells that trigger REM sleep. The search focused on the brainstem, a structure atop the spinal column that regulates such "primitive" functions as body temperature and appetite. A French researcher named Michel Jouvet had already homed in on a region of the brainstem called the pons, in 1962. But which cells in the pons were the crucial ones?

Like most questions in neurophysiology, this one was difficult to answer. When you probe with microelectrodes, a tiny miss can land you in a region of cells with a role entirely different from that of the target cells. Moreover, the components of the brain are interconnected in a bewilderingly complex fashion. To test a theory that certain brain cells are essential to REM sleep, for instance, you might try destroying them. But, in the glum words of one neuroscientist, "when you make a hole, you're going to cut down all the telephone wire that goes through that area as well as the telephone pole."

In 1973 Hobson made an accidental discovery, a "thrilling" find that he calls "the highlight of my scientific career." While looking for cells that fired only in REM sleep, he found a cell that *stopped* firing in REM sleep. Though this was the opposite of what he had sought, Hobson kept watching. When REM sleep ended, the cell began firing. When REM sleep resumed, the cell stopped again.

Hobson's microelectrode had missed its target by a millimeter. His mistake had taken him to a region of the brainstem called the locus ceruleus. Other laboratories made similar findings, locating additional populations of so-called REM-off cells elsewhere in the brainstem, and a new picture of the dreaming brain emerged.

The idea is that the brainstem contains clusters of cells that trigger REM sleep and other clusters of cells that turn REM sleep off. Whether we are dreaming or not depends on which group of cells has the upper hand. Hobson has described this cellular interplay as "a sort of continuous war whose effects spread from the brain stem throughout the brain, taking the mind hostage. This battle for the mind occurs regularly—and silently—every night in our sleep. And the only outward sign may be the fleeting recollection of a dream as we read the morning newspaper!"

The war is regulated by a curious clock that operates in ninety-minute cycles. Hobson's colleague McCarley developed a theory about its workings after studying the problems of Canadian fur trappers in the 1800s.

Trappers sold fur pelts from lynx and snowshoe hares, but because the lynx preyed on the hares, the populations of the two species fluctuated in balance. When the hare population was large, the lynx population grew large. Eventually, more and more predators meant fewer and fewer hares. Less food for the predators meant, eventually, fewer predators, which meant more hares and thus, eventually, more predators. And so on and on, the two populations rising and falling in cycles, the timing of which depended chiefly on the reproduction rates of the lynx and hares.

All that had been worked out in detail by nineteenth-century mathematicians. The pleasant surprise for McCarley was that he could use essentially the same model to explain the periodic onset of dreaming. Instead of lynx and hares, he had cells that turn on in REM sleep and cells that turn off in REM sleep. Moreover, the two populations of brain cells functionally silence each other. Just as prey and predators compete for territory, the two populations of cells compete for control of the mind. In slow oscillations repeated through the night, first one group holds sway and we sleep deeply, and then the other takes over and we move into REM sleep, and dream.

The model is appealingly tidy, not least because it has several testable consequences. The cells that turn on REM sleep seem to do so by releasing a neurotransmitter called acetylcholine, which is broken down by an enzyme in the brain. If you inject a substance that mimics acetylcholine into the brainstem, you should increase REM sleep. If you block the enzyme that breaks down acetylcholine, you should also increase REM sleep.

And so you do. The model has a flip side, too, that can equally well be tested. The brain cells that turn off REM sleep release their own neurotransmitters. Like playground monitors whose job is to keep rowdy children quiet, these substances tamp down the activity of the cells they come in contact with. Enhance the effect of *these* neurotransmitters and you should see less REM sleep. Break them down—blindfold the playground monitor—and you should see more REM sleep.

That is what Hobson predicts, but the results of tests of this half of his model aren't in yet. In any event, REM sleep in cats, which is what is being studied in these experiments, is not dreaming in human beings. And experiments with people have to be oblique, for reasons relating to ethics. In 1978, however, researchers at the National Institute of Mental Health devised a way to test Hobson's model on human beings. A substance that imitates acetylcholine was given to volunteers intravenously, while they slept. As expected, they quickly entered a long, intense phase of REM sleep. More tellingly, when they were awakened, they reported that they had been dreaming. For the first time, dreams had been triggered artificially.

Hobson's Critics Have Their Say

Hobson's theory of dreaming has something to offend everyone. His many scientific critics say that it is premature. The great majority of them concede that the research itself is careful and solid, but they insist that not enough is known about the brain to justify theories of how and why we dream.

Hobson is happy to concede that his theory of dreaming is far from proved. "I agree it's incomplete," he says. "It's very important to admit that. But I'd also say that you have to make a distinction between the specific burdens of a dream theory and a general theory of consciousness. If you're interested in why dreams are bizarre, my theory has to interest you. If you want it to solve the whole mind-body question at a single stroke and create a completely detailed theory of human consciousness, you're going to be disappointed."

"In one generation we've got a rough blueprint of a theory," Hobson continues. "What do you want? Let's go on and build a house. That's going to take a while, probably on the order of hundreds of years. But the door is open to establishing a physical theory of consciousness."

That's daring and vision if you like Hobson, grandstanding if you don't. He concedes that his manner has provoked some of his peers. In one notorious instance, involving a dispute over the properties of a particular group of brain cells, Hobson took years to acknowledge that his critics had been right and he had been wrong.

The skepticism has lingered. "He's extraordinarily clever, one of the most creative people in the field," one critic who wishes to remain anonymous acknowledges, "but if you really look into the details of what he says, you say, 'This isn't true, and that's not true,' and the whole thing just falls apart."

Hobson is unruffled by such charges. "If you're bold and ambitious," he says, "you can expect a lot of people not to like that." He points out that he has proposed a conceptual model for thinking about dreaming, and he notes (correctly) that even most of his detractors, while criticizing him on details, accept the framework he has suggested. "Allan's an unusual scientist, in that he does propose fairly general theories," says Robert Moore, the chairman of the neurology department at the State University of New York at Stony Brook. "I think people who say he's a flimflam artist are the ones who aren't smart enough to do that kind of thing themselves."

But Hobson's scientific critics can also muster substantive objections. Over the years, Hobson has modified his model of the dreaming brain significantly. He argued originally, for example, that one particular localized group of cells triggered REM sleep, but he now maintains that the trigger is distributed in multiple locations. Even McCarley, Hobson's collaborator of sixteen years, has reservations about this approach.

And some predictions implicit in the model haven't panned out. Several distinct groups of cells that turn off in REM sleep have been identified, for example. According to Hobson, those cells secrete neurotransmitters that block REM sleep. Destroy the cells, therefore, and you would expect to disrupt the REM-sleep cycle. But when such cell groups were destroyed in laboratory animals, the REM-sleep cycle continued.

Is that because the system is redundant? This is Hobson's explanation, and he points out that no one has destroyed all the cells at once. Or is Hobson simply wrong?

"I think that to be useful a scientific theory has to be fairly specific, to go out on a limb and make predictions

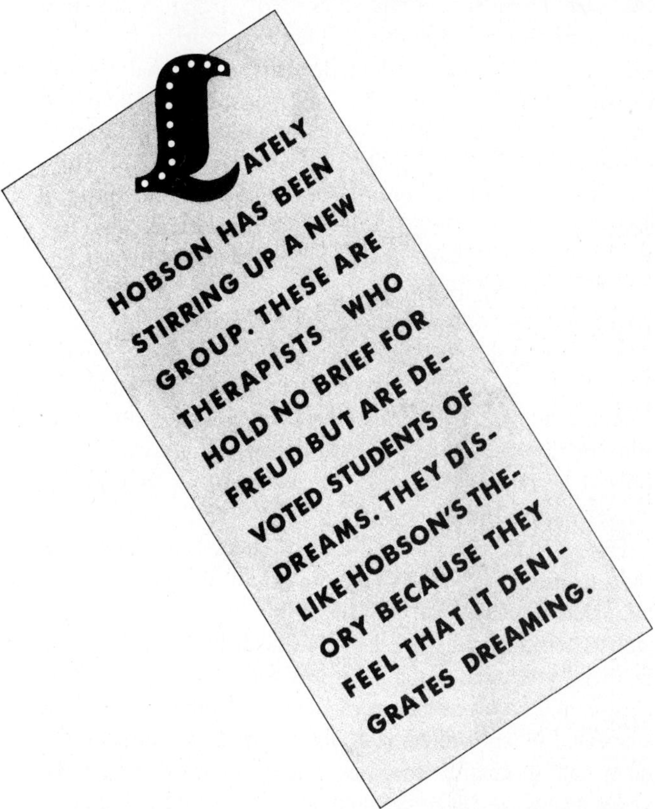

that could be refuted," says Jerome Siegel, a physiologist at the University of California-Los Angeles and a longtime rival of Hobson's. "His initial version of the theory did make predictions, and they were refuted. Now his theory seems to have evolved to the point where it makes fewer predictions and the predictions are too vague to refute."

Such charges may sound as if they could be resolved simply, by weighing facts impartially. But in the end, the quarrel over Hobson's model of the dreaming brain comes down to the kind of judgment call we are all familiar with. Hobson looks at his theory and sees a trusty old car that might need an oil change or a new set of spark plugs. His scientific rivals look at the same car and see a patched-together jalopy that has outlived its usefulness.

Much as he perturbs some of his fellow physiologists, the harshest attacks on Hobson come from outside science. For traditional psychoanalysts, Hobson's approach was doomed from the start, because of his refusal to use their methods. "I can't convince anybody that there are microbes in this world unless I apply a light microscope," says Theodore Shapiro, the editor of the *Journal of the American Psychoanalytic Association.* "I can't tell you anything about the ultrastructure of cells unless I apply an electron microscope. How can Hobson say anything about the insights to be derived from dreams if he doesn't apply the psychoanalytic method?"

The New Dream Interpreters

LATELY HOBSON HAS BEEN STIRRING UP A NEW group. These are therapists who hold no brief for Freud but are devoted students of dreams. They dislike Hobson's theory because they feel that it denigrates dreaming. Their opposition is significant, for while these are lean days for psychoanalysis, the dream business is booming. Anyone interested in the meaning of dreams may choose among fifty or more psychology and self-help books. Dozens of colleges and universities around the country, including such unlikely schools as Notre Dame and the Stanford School of Business, offer courses on working with dreams.

The new dream interpreters don't follow an explicit party line, but they tend to share several beliefs. Dreams can be triggered by any emotional concern, they maintain, and are not the result of repressed wishes alone. Dreams needn't have to do with sex. Dreams don't employ or reflect a universal symbolism. Dreams use symbols as metaphors to convey meaning rather than as disguises to obscure it.

Hobson has no quarrel with those ideas. Nonetheless, he rails against what he calls "the dream-cult people." Doffing his scientist's lab coat in favor of his psychiatrist's tweed jacket, he mounts his attack. "I've never had an experience in therapy of feeling that a dream was a turning point of treatment," he says, "or a revelation of a truth not otherwise suspected or known, or anything else of that nature. And I have had successful therapies where dreams were almost never discussed. I'd *rather* talk about dreams. I think they're fun. I think that a full view of human experience includes them. And sometimes I'd have to grant that I learned something important from them. But is the dream *uniquely* valuable, *uniquely* informative? I would have to say a qualified no. I am just not sure it's all that useful."

That is heresy to the dream groups, who have pruned and trimmed the Freudian garden but who continue to huddle under the familiar old tree at its center. Freud's approach to dream interpretation was off-target, they say, but his basic insight was valid: dreams *are* a royal road to the unconscious, messages to ourselves that convey truths we might otherwise miss. Perhaps the best-known dream psychologist, Gayle Delaney, has built her entire career around that belief. Delaney knows and likes Hobson, and she shares his anti-Freudianism, but she insists that dreams are invaluable in therapy. "Doing psychology without using dreams, she says, is like doing orthopedics without using x-rays."

Skeptics look at Delaney and never get past her celebrity: she has written a best seller on dreams, and she was the host of a radio show on which people phoned in their dreams. And she lives and works in San Francisco. But she resents those who would dismiss her as "a California touchy-feely." Not many minutes had passed in our conversation before she pointed out that she "graduated with highest honors from Princeton."

Delaney has heard people tell her tens of thousands of dreams over the years. Dreamers have characteristic styles, she says. She believes that dreams use symbols and metaphors unique to each dreamer to convey important messages with an uncanny compactness. She repeats the dream of a woman named Barbara as an example: "I was in a pool swimming with my eight-year-old son on my back. I would swim under the water while my son's head would stay above it. I did this in several short bursts, while my husband was supposed to take a picture of us in this position. But somehow he wasn't getting the picture taken. I was beginning to feel as if I was going to drown if he didn't get it soon. Each time I surfaced, I asked him, 'Did you get the picture?' Each time his answer was 'Not yet.'"

To Delaney, the message was blatant. The dreamer felt she was drowning under her child-care responsibilities, and her husband didn't get the picture. Did the dream reveal anything that Barbara didn't already know? "Dreams take you to a point where you can feel things that you don't allow yourself to feel or think while you're awake," Delaney says. "I would agree that at some level you know it—dreams don't come out of the ether and tell you what God wants for you. Our dreams tell us what we should know but don't let ourselves know."

Hobson bristles at such talk. He thinks this business of "approaching the dream in hushed tones" is cultishness. If the function of dreaming is to convey information, how do we explain that ninety-nine messages in every hundred are lost before they are delivered?

A therapist can learn about a client in any number of ways that have nothing to do with dreaming, Hobson says. Inkblots or free association or simply asking someone what he did the day before would serve equally well. "I do most of my therapy without any special recourse to dreams," Hobson says. "I don't feel I need to do that to find out what's going on. And I rarely find out from discussing dreams what I didn't already know."

Here therapists and psychoanalysts of all persuasions join forces to tackle Hobson. By focusing so much of his attention on the bizarreness of dreams, they say, Hobson dismisses them too glibly. Listen to foreigners telling stories, one analyst says, and if you don't bother to learn their language, their tales will sound like gibberish. "Dreaming is involuntary poetry," another analyst says—and sometimes understanding poetry is hard work.

Undoubtedly, these therapists continue, we have some conscious knowledge of our hopes and fears. But Hobson is missing the point if he thinks that dreams simply restate in symbolic or ornate language truths that we already grasp.

"The point of Freud's work on dreams," says Mardi

Horowitz, a professor of psychiatry at the University of California–San Francisco, "was that we tend to be consciously aware of our more proximal wishes, which are to solve our workaday problems, but we tend to be only dimly aware of why it's so imperative that we solve those problems. Perhaps we have to solve our problems or we'll be unloved, or some thought like that. Freud was presenting the idea that the deepest and most unrecognized wishes—unconscious wishes—might sometimes be found in dreams."

Faced with such challenges from psychotherapists, Hobson retreats just long enough to slip back into his lab coat. There's nothing wrong with therapists' interpreting dreams, he says. Their interpretations may even be right. "But the burden of proof is on them to show either that their knowledge is richer or that their results are better," he says.

Above all, they should make clear that their interpretations lack a foundation in science. "I'd have no quarrel if they'd tell patients, 'This isn't based on science; it's more like interpreting literary texts.' I say to them, 'Stand up and be counted. Don't say you're a doctor if you're an artist.'"

Dreams as Neurotic Symptoms

DESPITE THE INTENSITY OF HIS ANTI-FREUDIAN critique, Hobson's approach to dreaming is in a sense an homage to Freud. Freud made dreams a subject worthy of serious study, after centuries in which they had been brushed aside as the stuff of fortune-tellers. And both Hobson and Freud, in their efforts to explain the bizarre discontinuities and images of dreams, have taken for granted that these are the central and obvious issue to explore.

In addition, the scientific approach to psychology, which Hobson follows, is the one with which Freud himself began. Freud's early attempt to establish psychology on a solid scientific foundation, his "Project for a Scientific Psychology," was a major effort. "[It] does not precisely read like an early draft of psychoanalytic theory," notes the historian and Freud partisan Peter Gay, "but Freud's ideas on the drives, on repression and defense, on the mental economy with its contending forces of energies, and on the human animal as the wishing animal, are all adumbrated here."

James Strachey, a translator of Freud and the editor of the standard English-language edition of his works, wrote, "The Project's invisible ghost haunts the whole series of Freud's theoretical writings to the very end." Throughout his life Freud clung to the hope that someday science would vindicate his early attempts to ground psychology in physiology.

Now Allan Hobson has stepped forward, proclaimed himself the voice of modern science, and announced that Freud had it all wrong. The role is an odd one for Hobson. As a college student, he was a "Freud idolater" who read and reread everything Freud wrote. His college honors thesis was on Freud and Dostoevsky. Even today Hobson happily acknowledges, "Freud is brilliant. And the dream theory is wonderful, it's compelling and beautifully written and developed, and it's rich."

Freud's ambition extended far beyond interpreting the dreams of individual patients. His real goal was a theory of the mind. The key to such a synthesis was a crucial analogy: dreams are caused by the festering of unacceptable wishes, just as neuroses are caused by the repressing of unacceptable emotions or memories.

"Freud regarded dreams as if they were neurotic symptoms," writes Anthony Storr, a British psychiatrist sympathetic to Freud. "Since normal people dream, Freud's theory of dreams supported the idea that neurotic and normal cannot be sharply distinguished, and paved the way for establishing psycho-analysis as a general theory of the mind which applied to everyone."

Hobson's charge that this revolutionary theory of the mind is in fact based on Freud's abandoned "Project for a Scientific Psychology" is a serious one, since, as noted, everyone today agrees that the 1890s neurobiology of the "Project" is worthless. Freud and his contemporaries thought of the brain as a "passive reflex" machine that could act only in response to messages from outside. A dream was triggered by an event from daily life—say, a run-in with the boss—that somehow unearthed and activated a hidden wish from long ago. That is in sharp contrast with today's picture of a self-activating brain that can both create and cancel its own energy.

Brain cells are now known to be of two types, excitatory and inhibitory. Excitatory cells transmit electrochemical impulses that increase the activity of the cells they contact; inhibitory cells decrease that activity. In Freud's day only excitatory cells were known. "This meant," one scientist explains, "that once you got a notion in your head, it was doomed to run around in there forever until you finally decided to do something about it. Or, alternatively, until *it* found a way to trick you into unconsciously expressing it in some unintended action—like the famous 'Freudian slip.'"

Similarly, it was thought that repressed wishes would boil and bubble endlessly in the cauldron of the unconscious, until they managed to emerge, suitably disguised, as dreams. In essence, Hobson argues that Freud's dream theory came into being in a somewhat comparable way: the brain-based picture of the mind that he labored over in the "Project" never panned out, but eventually it emerged, suitably translated into psychological terms, as *The Interpretation of Dreams*.

But, oddly, this feature of Hobson's argument seems not to faze the analytic community. "It never dawns on psychoanalysts," says Frank Sulloway, a historian of science and a revisionist Freud scholar, "that if Freud was wrong about the general properties of dreams, he might also have been wrong about the interpretation of specific dreams. If you say that the whole dream theory is based on outmoded biology, they say, 'We'll give you that and keep everything else.' It's as if they lived in a building and someone said, 'The first floor's about to collapse,' and they said, 'We don't care; we live on the tenth floor.'"

Even on the tenth floor signs of trouble are visible. Significant numbers of strict Freudian analysts are still treating patients, but psychoanalysis has been in decline since the 1960s. Hundreds of alternate forms of psychotherapy have sprung up, the psychoanalytic-training institutes are hard pressed for students, and the leading psychiatric journals have cut down on their psychoanalytically based articles. "It's almost dead," says Robert Moore, the Stony Brook neurologist. "I know of no institution looking for a chief of psychiatry that's looking for a psychoanalyst."

The decline of psychoanalysis is due largely to the rise of biology. Depression, manic depression, schizophrenia, and other mental illnesses seem to be yielding some of their secrets to neurobiology. With support from the National Institute of Mental Health, Congress has declared the 1990s the "decade of the brain."

Freud's dream-analysis technique, in particular, has fallen out of favor with some psychoanalysts. Despite Freud's insistence that dream interpretation is "the securest foundation of psychoanalysis," contemporary analysts seem to believe that following the weaving course of a patient's free associations to each dream element takes too long and is too much trouble. Freud's approach to dreams in therapy may eventually suffer the cruelest of all fates—to be deemed not wrong but irrelevant.

Nevertheless, the decline of Freud within the therapeutic community seems not to have significantly affected his reputation in the rest of the academic world, where his standing is as high as it ever was. Many debunking books and articles have appeared, most of them the work of historians or philosophers, but they have not had lasting impact. They are published, they win prizes and respectful audiences, and then their message is forgotten.

Great numbers of literary critics, social scientists, and historians continue to march to a Freudian drummer. Every day sees the publication of a new psychobiography of someone or other, or a new psychoanalytically based work of literary scholarship. On campus, at least, Auden's words remain apt: Freud is "no more a person now but a whole climate of opinion."

Dreams as Creative Opportunities

As INTELLECTUAL FASHIONS CHANGE, DREAMING falls in and out of favor. It remains as mysterious as ever. For two hours in every twenty-four, for six years in an average lifetime, we are mad as hatters. Why? What is dreaming for?

Dreaming seems to be important. We can't decide to dream or not to dream, and if some sleep researcher prevents us from dreaming one night, we make up for it the next.

Hobson, in many ways an optimistic man, has devised a much sunnier answer than Freud did to the question Why dream? "Instead of seeing the dream process as some sort of laundry for kinky thoughts," he says, "I see it as a resourceful artist producing all kinds of wonderful new solutions."

In this view, dreaming is a virtual parody of scientific thinking, in which every idea can be considered, even outlandish notions can be pursued, and anything is possible. And, indeed, numerous problems have been solved in dreams. Robert Louis Stevenson dreamed the plot of *The Strange Case of Dr. Jekyll and Mr. Hyde.* Elias Howe claimed that the crucial idea for his sewing machine came to him in a dream, after years of struggle. In all his failed models the needle's eye was in the middle of the shaft. One night Howe dreamed he had been captured by a tribe of savages who carried spears with eye-shaped holes near the tip.

At least one dreamer earned a Nobel Prize. Otto Loewi, a German-born physiologist and pharmacologist, wanted to know how nerves send signals. Do they simply transmit electricity, like tiny wires, or do they also send chemical signals? Loewi was studying frogs, trying to learn why stimulating the vagus nerve causes the heart to slow. Unlike his peers, he believed that chemicals were somehow involved, but he couldn't think how to prove he was right.

On Easter Sunday of 1920 the answer came to him in a dream. Loewi woke up, scrawled it down, and fell back asleep. In the morning he couldn't read his writing and he couldn't remember his dream.

"The next night, at three o'clock, the idea returned," he wrote later. "I got up immediately, went to the laboratory, and performed the experiment." Loewi's inspiration was to stimulate the vagus nerve of one frog, thus slowing its heart, and then to transfer blood from that frog's heart to a second frog. When the second heart slowed too, Loewi had proved that the vagus nerve acted by releasing a chemical. The chemical turned out to be acetylcholine, the very substance that is now known to be the neurotransmitter that triggered Loewi's dream in the first place.

Hobson likes such stories, but he is wary of them too. "Nobody ever tells you about all the cockamamie ideas that didn't work," he says. "You don't hear about the guy who went off for ten years and worked on this crazy idea that occurred to him in a dream. In fact, you don't even know whether two days later it would have occurred to him at breakfast." He laughs, but then turns crabby. "You never hear anybody raise those questions!" he shouts. "Because, again, that's the dream mystique. You want to believe this thing's wonderful."

In fact, the notion of problem-solving in dreams is one that therapists of all sorts rush to embrace. The idea rests on the commonsensical premise that we work to make sense of our lives while we're awake and the process continues while we're asleep.

Perhaps the best-known advocate of this view is Rosalind Cartwright, the chairman of the psychology department at Rush University, in Chicago. The function of dreaming, she says, is to give the mind a chance to sort uninterrupted through emotional issues that we are too preoccupied to untangle during our waking lives. The process goes on automatically, whether or not we can recall our dreams later.

"In dreaming, you update the program of who you are every night," Cartwright says. "If nothing much has changed in your life, you get a night off to play or be creative or tell jokes to yourself, or you just have a dull night of nothing much going on. But when you're going through crises, you need to revise who you are, and you have to update that program in a dramatically new way."

To test her theory, Cartwright has spent several years studying men and women who are going through divorces and are depressed. She has found that their dreams differ in key ways from those of people who are happily married. For people whose lives are going along smoothly, the first dream of the night is typically brief and dull: "I went shopping." In Cartwright's reading, the dream hasn't much work to do. For most of the depressed subjects in her studies, however, the first dream comes much sooner than it does for others, lasts much longer, and is far more complicated.

And the dreams are terrible, endless and masochistic rehashes of mistakes made and opportunities lost. One of the supposed benefits of anti-depressant medications, in fact, is that they suppress dreaming. But with a nudge from therapy sessions during the day, dreams change during the course of the night. Dreamers become more angry and less depressed. "When they do that," Cartwright says, "they recover. It's a predictor that dreaming has gone into high gear, has stirred up the feelings to be worked through. When I see those people at follow-up, they're no longer depressed."

Hobson is almost visibly ambivalent about such stories. On the one hand, he is perfectly happy to concede that dreaming has a constructive, creative side. It fits with his theory that the dreamer fashions a plot from whatever materials happen to be at hand, and it furnishes ammunition against "the peculiar modern, psychoanalytic tendency to view even the normal as somehow neurotic."

On the other hand, as a good scientist, Hobson is fearful of venturing too far into speculative talk of "purpose." And to talk about the purpose of dreaming is to pile intangible on intangible. He is more comfortable speculating about the purpose of REM sleep.

For example, we spend more time in REM sleep as infants in the womb than we ever will again. Why? Hobson suggests that infants prior to birth are literally "making up their minds," working on tasks that are somehow essential to cognitive development.

Some experiments with adults also seem to link REM sleep and intellectual work. Volunteers deprived of REM sleep by experimenters have more trouble solving complicated puzzles than do people deprived of non-REM sleep. And people trying to assimilate new information—students of a foreign language, for example—show an increase in REM sleep.

But because REM sleep is distributed so widely throughout the animal kingdom, no such explanation is adequate. Both opossums and moles spend substantial amounts of time in REM sleep, for instance, and neither species is noted for perspicacity.

The hardheaded scientific attitude is to dismiss dreams altogether. All mammals undergo REM sleep, the argument runs, human beings in particular have powerful minds, and the combination yields the strange experiences we call dreams. Dreaming isn't *for* anything; it just happens. Occasionally Hobson talks in this vein, speculating that "dreaming is just the noise the brain makes while it automatically sorts and files," but more often he takes a softer line.

He prefers to think of REM sleep as a time when the brain refreshes and readjusts itself, a notion that explains why we have so much trouble remembering our dreams. The explanation is based on a striking observation: the brain cells that turn off in REM sleep release neurotransmitters that are crucial to attention, learning, and memory.

"You have these systems firing all day long like a metronome," Hobson says, "with zillions and zillions of packets of neurotransmitter being bled out over the day, and your attention sort of runs down. At a certain point the sleep system kicks in, you go to bed, and before you know it these neuronal systems are shut down. Your metabolic rate doesn't go to zero—you continue to manufacture enzymes and neurotransmitters, and all the packets just get filled up again. You wake up in the morning and you say, 'God, I feel good. I feel sharp.' "

The brain is ready for another day's work, but the night's dreams are lost, because the dreamer was deprived of the very substances necessary to lay down memories. Hobson's explanation of REM sleep has still another facet. The dreaming brain also carries out what he calls an "active maintenance" program to test its own circuitry. While the dreamer is barely connected with the outside world, dreaming provides a chance "to run through your repertoire of instinctive behaviors with the clutch pressed in, to make sure they're still working in the proper way."

For Hobson, such armchair speculation is an intellectual version of sport. Ask him a question or give him an analogy to consider and he engages his whole body in the attempt to find an answer. He twists in his chair, throws his arms out, and casts his eyes around to address invisible listeners in every corner of the room. He starts an explanation headed one way, sees a grinning tackler lying in wait, and cuts back in the opposite direction. Sometimes he arrives far downfield, visibly proud of himself. Occasionally he doubles back and forth so often that when he finally runs out of steam he has made hardly any progress.

The picture is far from that of the stereotype of the scientist as a bloodless logic machine. Indeed, the romantic accusation that science banishes beauty by dissecting it might better be directed at Freud than at Hobson.

In a curious way, the two men have exchanged roles. Hobson, the neurophysiologist, who might be expected to play the level-headed spokesman for the hard sciences, has devised a theory of dreams that leaves a great deal of room for chance. Dreams are unpredictable and improvised, he argues. The dreamer's own interpretation can be as valid as a therapist's. Freud, the psychologist, who might have emphasized the variety of human experience, proposed a rigidly determinist, reductionist theory of dreams. Every feature of a dream, no matter how trivial, is deeply significant. Every dream, "invariably and indisputably," has the same cause. Dreams can be interpreted only by following the psychoanalytic method.

The years between the two theories saw the most extensive scientific progress the world has ever known. One might have expected steady progress in revealing the dream in its true guise. But the science of dreaming has brought a different, more humbling message: the dream was undisguised all along. Like Poe's purloined letter, it lay hidden in plain sight.

Freud's dream interpretations were brilliant, so brilliant that in the end he outsmarted himself. It now appears that his rival Carl Jung came nearer the mark. "I was never able to agree with Freud that the dream is a 'façade' behind which its meaning lies hidden—a meaning already known but maliciously, so to speak, withheld from consciousness," Jung wrote. "To me dreams are a part of nature, which harbors no intention to deceive, but expresses something as best it can, just as a plant grows or an animal seeks its food as best it can."

Personality: Major Traits Found Stable Through Life

Daniel Goleman

Studies challenge theories that see transitions.

The largest and longest studies to carefully analyze personality throughout life reveal a core of traits that remain remarkably stable over the years and a number of other traits that can change drastically from age to age.

The new studies have shown that three basic aspects of personality change little throughout life: a person's anxiety level, friendliness and eagerness for novel experiences. But other traits, such as alienation, morale and feelings of satisfaction, can vary greatly as a person goes through life. These more changeable traits largely reflect such things as how a person sees himself and his life at a given point, rather than a basic underlying temperament.

One of the recently completed studies followed 10,000 people 25 to 74 years old for nine years. Another involved 300 couples first tested in 1935. The studies are joined by a new analysis of more than two dozen earlier studies of lifetime personality and a study of twins that looks at the genetic contribution.

The recent work poses a powerful challenge to theories of personality that have emphasized stages or passages—predictable points in adult life—in which people change significantly.

The new research is "a death knell" for the passage theories of adult personality, in the view of a researcher who conducted one of the new studies. "I see no evidence for specific changes in personality due to age," said the researcher, Paul T. Costa Jr. "What changes as you go through life are your roles and the issues that matter most to you. People may think their personality has changed as they age, but it is their habits that change, their vigor and health, their responsibilities and circumstances—not their basic personality."

But the new work has not made converts of the theorists who see adult life through the framework of passages. Rather they assert that simple pencil and paper tests cannot discern the richness inherent in the maturing personality. A theory proposed by Daniel Levinson, a psychologist at Yale University, suggests a series of sometimes troubled transitions between psychological stages; Erik Erikson coined the term "identity crisis" for the difficulties some young people have in settling on a life course.

Proponents of the most recent studies say, however, that the notion of passages, built on clinical interviews, was never objectively tested.

Some of the strongest evidence for the stability of the core personality throughout adulthood comes from a study by Dr. Costa and Robert McCrae, psychologists at the National Institute on Aging in Baltimore. They interviewed thousands of people in 100 places throughout the United States in 1975, and again in 1984.

The researchers found virtually no change in the three key personality traits. Their report in a recent issue of the Journal of Gerontology asserts that a person who was calm and well-adjusted at 25 years of age would remain so at 65, while a person who was emotionally volatile at 25 would be about the same at 65. Their findings represented averages, however, and could not reflect the changes in some individuals that might have been brought on by, for instance, psychotherapy or a personal catastrophe.

ONLY THE FORM CHANGES

"There is no evidence of any universal age-related crises; those people who have crises at one point or another in life tend to be those who are more emotional," said Dr. Costa. "Such people experience some degree of distress through most of life; only the form of the trouble seems to change."

A mellowing in midlife, found by other studies, has now been shown to relate more to a muting of some of a person's more extreme feelings than to any change in the overall pattern of personality.

The new studies find no increase in irritability with aging. "The stereotype that people become cranky and rigid as they age does not hold up," said Dr. Costa. "The calm, outgoing, adventurous young person is going to stay that way into old age, given good health. Those who are dogmatic and closed to experience early in life remain that way."

The greatest changes in core personality occur in childhood and from adolescence to early adulthood, according to Dr. Costa. "After 25, as William James said, character is set in plaster," he said. "What does change is one's role in life, and the situations that influence your temporary behavior one way or another."

Support for Dr. Costa's large study comes from a recent study of twins that found an important genetic influence on the three main traits. Early childhood experiences, the investigators concluded, are not the main influence in shaping the most persistent of personality traits, though they may shape them to some degree, as they do all personality.

In this study of 203 pairs of twins at Indiana University, the researchers, Michael Pogue-Geile and Richard Rose, administered a personality test when the subjects were 20, and again when they were 25. The researchers were looking to see whether fraternal twins changed in the same ways as identical twins in that time, which is one of the stages of turbulent transition proposed by some theorists. If a particular trait is genetically determined it will tend to change more similarly in identical twins than it will in fraternal twins.

There was evidence of significant genetic influence on the three main personality traits of anxiety or emotionality, friendliness and openness to new things.

Life experience also shaped these basic traits. But it had a far greater influence on other personality traits, including alienation, morale and feelings of satisfaction. These traits change so much over the course of adult life that there is virtually no relationship between their levels when a person is in his 20's and when he is in his 60's, according to James Conley, who studied 300 couples who were tested in 1935, 1955 and 1980, when the researchers were able to interview 388 of the original 600 men and women.

"If you try to predict how alienated or satisfied with life people will be in their later years from how they seem in college, you will fail abysmally," he said.

Dr. Conley is among those finding that the three basic traits change little over a lifetime. In addition to the study of couples, he has reviewed data from more than two dozen other long-term personality studies.

Some personality traits may make certain crises in life more probable. For instance, the study of couples suggests that specific combinations of personality in a marriage are explosive. Over the course of 45 years, the highest probability of divorce occurred in those marriages where both the husband and wife were emotionally volatile and the husband had little impulse control.

"The evaluations in 1935, by five friends, of the personalities of an engaged couple was highly predictive of which marriages would break up," Dr. Conley said, "If you have a couple with emotional hair triggers, and where the husband philanders, gambles, drinks, or loses jobs, a break-up is almost certain. Some marriages broke up right away: some took 45 years to end. Data from younger couples suggests that today the dangerous combination of personalities is the same, except now it can be either the wife or the husband whose impulsiveness triggers the trouble."

Critics say the new studies lack necessary subtlety.

Walter Mischel, a psychologist at Columbia University, wrote an influential article in 1968 arguing that the variation in expression of a given trait from situation to situation is so great that the notion of personality traits itself was of little use in accounting for how people behave.

VARIATIONS WITH SITUATION

"There is lots of evidence for the stability of some traits, such as extroversion, over time," Dr. Mischel said in a recent interview. "But the same person may be quite outgoing in some circumstances, and not at all in others."

Kenneth Craik, a psychologist at the University of California at Berkeley, said, "The belief for 10 to 15 years after Mischel's critique was that the situation determined far more than personality about how people behave." Now, within the last few years, he said, "personality and situation are seen by most researchers as having about equal influence."

Researchers are concluding that the influence of one situation or another on how a person acts may also create the impression that personality itself changes more than is the case; apparent changes in personality may actually reflect temporary circumstances.

"Any trait can vary with the moment," said Seymour Epstein, a personality psychologist at the University of Massachusetts at Amherst. "You need to look at the person in many situations to get a stable rating of that trait."

And people seem to differ in how much situations affect their actions, according to research by Mark Snyder, a psychologist at the University of Minnesota. In "Public Appearances, Private Reality," published recently by W.H. Freeman & Company, Dr. Snyder reviews evidence showing that some people are virtual chameleons, shaping themselves to blend into whatever social situation they find themselves, while others are almost oblivious to the special demands and expectations of differing situations, being more or less the same person regardless of where they are.

The situation-oriented, Dr. Snyder has found, are skilled at social roles: At a church service, they display just the right combination of seriousness and reserve; at a cocktail party they become the friendly and sociable extrovert.

Those less affected by situations are more consistent in their behavior, putting less effort into role-playing: They have a smaller wardrobe, wearing the same clothes in more situations, than do the situation-oriented.

It is as though each type were playing to a different audience, one inner, the other outer, says Dr. Snyder.

Those adept at situations flourish in jobs where they deal with a range of different groups, Dr. Sndyer reports.

Embattled Giant of Psychology Speaks His Mind

Daniel Goleman
Special to The New York Times

CAMBRIDGE, Mass.—B.F. Skinner is a creature of carefully shaped habit. At the age of 83, he has fashioned a schedule and environment for himself that is in perfect keeping with his theories of behavioral reinforcement.

Dr. Skinner's personal Skinner box—his own self-contained environment of positive reinforcements—is his basement office in his home here, a 1950's flat-top set among charming New England-style saltboxes.

"I spent a lot of time creating the environment where I work," Dr. Skinner said as he recently led a visitor through the home where he and his wife, Yvonne, live. "I believe people should design a world where they will be as happy as possible in old age."

Burrhus Frederic Skinner, the chief architect of behaviorism, uses the office to marshal a crusade against what he sees as grave mistakes in psychology that have left his own once pre-eminent theories in decline.

Behaviorism holds that people act as they do because of the rewards and punishments—positive and negative reinforcements—they have received. The mind and such things as memory and perception cannot be directly observed, and so, in Dr. Skinner's view, are unworthy of scientific study.

B.F. Skinner, the architect of behaviorism, battles 'grave mistakes' in rival approaches.

Much of Dr. Skinner's efforts now aim at meeting two major challenges to behaviorism: brain science, the study of links between brain and behavior, and cognitive psychology, the study of how the mind perceives, thinks and remembers and how goals and plans influence behavior.

During the recent visit, Dr. Skinner, known to colleagues as Fred, was in the midst of preparing a talk week at psychology's major annual convention.

It is to maximize his productivity in such writing, and to conserve energy in his later years, that Dr. Skinner has designed this environment. He sleeps in the office, in a bright yellow plastic tank just large enough for the mattress it contains, a small television and some narrow shelves and controls. The bed unit, which bears some resemblance to a sleeper on a train, is one of those used by the Japanese in stacks in tiny hotel rooms, Dr. Skinner explained.

The office-bedroom suits Dr. Skinner's habits well: he goes to bed each night at 10 P.M. sleeps three hours, then rolls out of bed to his nearby desk, where he works for one hour. Then he goes back to bed for another three hours, getting up to begin his day at 5 A.M.

POSITIVE REINFORCEMENT: MUSIC

In these early morning hours Dr. Skinner puts in about three hours of writing, which he considers to be his main work. After his writing, he walks a mile or so to his office at Harvard University, where he answers mail and attends to other business. And then, for reinforcement, he spends the afternoon listening to music—which he loves—on the quadrophonic tape deck in his office.

This schedule, with its work output and rewards, allows Dr. Skinner to continue to act as the undisputed leader of modern behaviorism. As such, he fights a continuing battle for his ideas on many fronts, many of which he touched on in the wide-ranging interview.

"I think cognitive psychology is a great hoax and a fraud, and that goes for brain science, too," Dr. Skinner said. "They are nowhere near answering the important questions about behavior."

Dr. Skinner is still vigorous in arguing his cause. In addition to the speech opposing cognitive psychology he is giving at the annual meeting of the American Psychological Association, next month he will publish in the American Psychologist an article attacking not only cognitive psychology, but also other enemies of his brand of behaviorism: humanistic psychology and other nonbehaviorist psychotherapies.

Humanists, Dr. Skinner writes in his article, have attacked behaviorism as undermining people's sense of freedom and have denounced its claims that the environment determines what people achieve. And, he writes, psychotherapists—apart from those who practice a behaviorist approach—rely too much on inferences they make about what is supposedly going on inside their patients, and too little on direct observation of what they do.

The use of punishment is another issue Dr. Skinner still feels impassioned about. He is an ardent opponent of the use of punishment, such as spanking, or using "aversives"—such as pinches and shocks—with autistic children.

"What's wrong with punishments is that they work immediately, but give no long-term results," Dr. Skinner said. "The responses to punishment are either the urge to escape, to counterattack or a stubborn apathy. These are the bad effects you get in prisons or schools, or wherever punishments are used."

One of the ways Dr. Skinner feels behaviorist techniques have been under-appreciated is in the failure of teaching machines to find wide acceptance in the schools. The machines, which can be computerized, break a topic like division or Russian history into small, manageable concepts, and methodically teach each so a student gets the reinforcement of knowing he has mastered it before moving on to the next.

The learning devices had a great advantage over the classroom teacher, according to Dr. Skinner. "Schools were invented to extend a tutor to more than one student at once," Dr. Skinner said. "That's O.K. with three or four, but when you have 30 or more in a classroom, the teacher is no longer able to give the student the reinforcement of a 'right' before moving on to the next task."

Such machines are widely used now in industrial education, but are not widely used in schools.

REWARDS OF WORK

Dr. Skinner continues to act as a social philosopher, a role he played most prominently with his 1948 book "Walden Two," which described a behaviorist utopia. In an article last year in the American Psychologist in which he examined "What is Wrong With Daily Life in the Western World," Dr. Skinner charged that common practices had eroded the natural relationship between what people do and the pleasing effects that would reinforce their activities.

For instance, in Dr. Skinner's view, fixed salaries do not reinforce workers because they are paid whether or not they do more than the minimum job. If workers were paid on a commission or by the piece their pay would be a direct reinforcer for their labors, and they would work with more effort and pleasure, according to behaviorist principles.

Another aspect of modern life Dr. Skinner criticizes, in all seriousness, is labor-saving devices, such as dishwashers or frozen dinners, which he sees as depriving people of the small satisfactions that accomplishing something brings. "We've destroyed all the reinforcers in daily life," said Dr. Skinner. "For example, if you wash a dish, you've accomplished something, done something that gives you a pleasing result. That is far more reinforcing than putting the dishes in with some powder and then taking them about again."

The device for which Dr. Skinner may be most famous, the original "Skinner box," was a large glass-enclosed, climate-controlled baby crib with equipment to keep infants amused and well-exercised. Dr. Skinner is still pained by the rumors that his daughters, who used the box, became psychotic or suicidal as a result. Today one daughter is an artist and writer living in London, and the other is a professor of educational psychology at Indiana University; both are married.

When Dr. Skinner first began in the 1930's and 1940's to develop the principles of what he calls "radical behaviorism"—to distinguish it from the earlier theories of Pavlov and Watson—he argued that a scientific psychology could only study behavior that can be directly observed. For that reason, Skinnerian behaviorists have studied the laws of learning through observing responses such as the pecking of a pigeon, and avoided the "black box" of the inner workings of the mind.

In recent decades, though, advances in devices for monitoring faculties such as attention have spurred studies linking the brain and mental activity. If he were starting his research today, Dr. Skinner was asked, would he avail himself of these techniques?

"If I had it all to do again, I would still call the mind a black box," Dr. Skinner said. "I would not use any of the new techniques for measuring information processing and the like. My point has always been that psychology should not look at the nervous system or so-called mind—just at behavior."

For Dr. Skinner, the mind is irrelevant to understanding why people behave as they do. In his view, most assumptions about mental life made by laymen and psychologists alike are based on fallacies. In his address next week before the American Psychological Association, he will argue that all the words that describe mental activities actually refer to some behavior.

"No one invented a word for mental experience that comes from the mind," Dr. Skinner said. "They all have their roots in a reference to action.

"To contemplate, for instance, means to look at a template, or picture. 'Consider' comes from roots meaning to look at the stars until you see a pattern. 'Compare' means to put things side by side to see if they match."

"All the words for mental experience go back to what people do," Dr. Skinner continued. "Over thousands of years, people have used these terms to express something that goes on in their bodies. But these are action terms; they do not mean that these things are going on inside the mind."

"The cognitive revolution is a search inside the mind for something that is not there," Dr. Skinner said. "You can't see yourself process information; information-processing is an inference from behavior—and a bad one, at that. If you look carefully at what people mean when they talk about the mind, you find it just refers to how they behave."

One of the major disputes between the cognitive and behaviorist viewpoints is whether a person's actions are guided by goals and plans, or whether they are a result of that person's history of rewards and punishments. For Dr. Skinner, there is no question. "Behavior is always reinforced behavior," he said.

Despite their differences with other points of view, behaviorists are influential in many psychology departments, and the school of thought remains prominent, particularly among those who are trying to apply its principles in areas like psychotherapy, industrial motivation and remedial education. From the 1930's through the 1960's, behaviorism dominated academic psychology; in the 1960's the so-called cognitive revolution began and would go on to sweep psychology.

There is no precise estimate of the numbers of behaviorists, although there are 1,228 members of the division of the psychological association that is devoted to behaviorist research and applications. The strongholds of behaviorism tend to be in colleges in the South and Midwest, according to Kurt Salzinger, a psychologist at Polytechnic University in Brooklyn who is the new president of the behaviorist division.

Dr. Skinner concedes that behaviorism is on the decline while the cognitive school of thought is increasingly popular among psychologists. There is now a move afoot to reconcile the two approaches.

"Behaviorism was right in saying the task of psychology is to account for what people do, but wrong in ruling out talking about what's going on in the head that generates what people do," said Stephan Harnad, one of the editors of a collection of Dr. Skinner's major papers, along with more than 150 comments by leading scholars. The book is scheduled to be published this winter by the Cambridge University Press.

He considers much of recent psychology to be 'a great hoax and a fraud.'

"That left behaviorists only able to talk about a person's history of rewards and punishments," Dr. Harnad said. "But that accounts for almost nothing of what we can do—our perception, our being able to remember something and our speech. This calls for a cognitive theory."

As the field evolves, an increasing number of behaviorists are violating Dr. Skinner's tenets by studying mental activity. "My major research now is a collaborative project with a cognitive scientist," said Richard Herrnstein, a psychologist who is a former colleague of Dr. Skinner at Harvard University. "We're studying how organisms perceive shapes; we're doing studies of pigeons, humans and computers. I'm pretty comfortable with much of the cognitive school, and I consider myself a behaviorist."

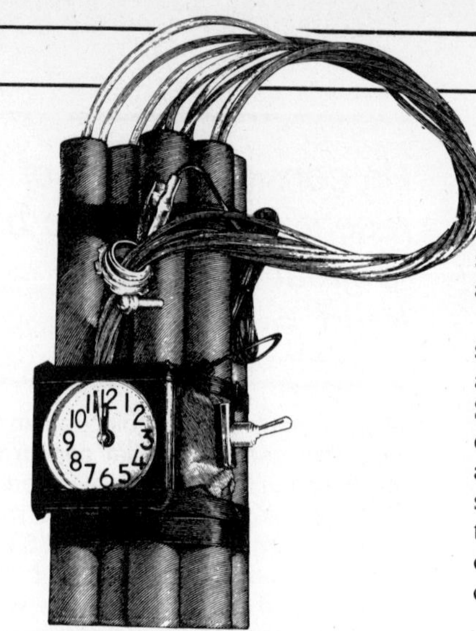

MANAGING STRESS AND LIVING LONGER

"Every person is born with a genetically predetermined amount of stress-coping energy. . . . When it is depleted, death occurs."

Jerome Murray

Dr. Murray, a clinical psychologist, lecturer, and consultant from Santa Rosa, Calif., is author of From Uptight to All Right.

WARNING! Even though you rigorously follow a stress management program, stress still could be ravaging you and shortening your life. This is true because most people's definition of stress management is erroneous.

To the average person, it means learning to relax and enjoy life, taking time to mellow out in comfortable, stress-free environments, exercising regularly, and a healthy diet. Many, believing themselves to be engaged in pursuing greater health and self-fulfillment, energetically practice relaxation techniques, yoga, meditation, and biofeedback. They play tennis every weekend, jog faithfully, watch their cholesterol intake, and take pride in their enlightened lifestyle.

Millions of dollars are spent annually on gym memberships, exercycles, and other means of improving cardiovascular efficiency. Multimillion-dollar industries have been created to service these enthusiasts' need for clothing and shoes.

The problem is one of timing. Much of the damage attributable to stress has occurred before these stress management efforts even have begun. Permitting yourself to be bombarded by stressors during the day and trying to undo the damage evenings and weekends is the classic "too little, too late." Living a hectic and frenzied life compounded by pressure and frustration and punctuated by periodic attempts to relax and exercise is a parody of stress management. More accurately, it is an endeavor to manage *dis*tress, not stress.

While managing distress effectively is not to be decried, it is analogous to fighting a fire. Even with sophisticated apparatus, the best strategy is to avoid the conflagration in the first place. This means learning to prevent stress from becoming distress, expanding the range of one's coping skills, and not allowing stressors to continue unabated.

Even though distress management techniques have their place, they frequently are nothing more than expensive padlocks to put on a barn already empty of horses. The elimination of stress isn't the answer either. True stress management is distress *prevention*.

In an experiment to find out what would happen in a stress-free environment, subjects were placed in a deprivation tank, where they floated in water warmed to body temperature. The drug curare was used to paralyze muscle movement. Eyes were blindfolded, ears were plugged, and there was nothing to smell or taste, or sensations to which the subjects had to adjust. After a period of relaxation, they began to hallucinate and have delusional thoughts—they became psychotic. Lacking stimulation, the brain produced its own. The marvelous mechanisms of brain and body require stimulation to function. The issue is, how much, how frequent, and how long?

Stress is the body's non-specific response to stressors such as frustrations, conflicts, and pressures. In more general terms, they are known as adjustment demands. Every adjustment we make in life takes its toll in stress.

Yet, stressors, as the deprivation tank illustrates, can not and should not be avoided. They are essential to mental and physical health. Without the stress of learning, there would be no education. Without the stress of exercise, bodies would be flabby and unable to perform.

Stressors are inevitable and even necessary. They serve to condition our minds and bodies, enabling greater performance. Stressors can stimulate growth and confidence and actually assist in keeping us alive. The problem occurs when the stressors exceed our coping ability or continue too long. When that happens, stress becomes distress, and that is the issue of concern.

There are two human conditions having the greatest potential for producing distress—impotence and isolation. When they are experienced, the human organism is at its most vulnerable to stress.

Resist the impulse to jump to conclusions—this type of impotence refers to a psychological state in which we feel a demand to act, but lack the authority or ability.

If you took psychology in college, you may remember studying the "executive monkey" experiment, conducted at the Walter Reed Army Institute of Research. Two monkeys were strapped upright in a plastic box permitting limited movement, a console in front of each of them with a light and a button. The light was turned on 10 seconds before the monkeys received a jarring shock to their feet. The button would prevent the shock if it was pushed within the 10-second grace period. The monkeys learned this fact faster than most graduate students.

The researchers then added an inventive twist. They disconnected a wire to one of the buttons, reconnecting it to the other. Now, one monkey controlled the shock for both. Being responsible for another and having decision-making power, he was dubbed the executive monkey. After 23 days of this pressure, the executive monkey expired. A post-mortem revealed the beginning of atherosclerosis, incipient renal failure, and a perforated duodenal ulcer. The surviving non-executive monkey was sacrificed to the cause of science and found to be without physiological abnormality.

The moral was supposed to be that executives were prone to stress-related diseases because they have responsibility for others. At first examination, that interpretation had face validity, and overstressed executives sympathized with the deduction. It duly was printed in most general psychology textbooks and taught to undergraduates.

However, that conclusion was not supported by attempted replications. Every other attempt to duplicate the original results failed. Each time, it was the monkey whose button didn't work that developed ulcers. He knew he was going to get shocked, but was helpless to prevent it. This state is identified as responsibility without authority, better known in corporations as mid-level management.

The most devastating type of stress is not heavy responsibility—it is having a sense of responsibility without the power to do anything about it. Responsibility won't kill you as long as your buttons work, but feeling responsible for something over which you have no authority will send you to an early grave.

To avoid the distressful consequences of feeling impotent, limit your sense of responsibility to those areas over which you have authority. Parents who agonize over the behavior of children whose age precludes parental authority suffer from impotence. Employees who feel stymied in their careers because of the perceived inadequacies of their supervisors are making themselves impotent. Anyone who laments the quality of his or her life because of inability to control the actions of another suffers from distress. In effect, they are saying to others, "I am powerless to improve the quality of my life unless you change." That produces a feeling of impotence and heightened vulnerability to stress.

This does not suggest that attempts to influence the lives of others are inconsequential. Sometimes, efforts to influence others succeed, causing them to change in ways that enhance the complexion of your life. However, don't be misled—influence is not authority. If others do not respond positively to your efforts to modify their behavior, don't make yourself impotent by persisting in your efforts. Keep the responsibility where the authority is. Ask yourself: "What can I do to live a more successful life even though this other person is not cooperating with my pursuit of happiness?"

That is the only effective question to ask. It focuses the issue on what *you* do—not what others do or don't do. By concentrating on the authority you have to enrich your own life, you will minimize feelings of impotence. This reduces susceptibility to distress and has another important benefit—you'll be happier and more productive.

Isolation

There is ample evidence that vulnerability to stress is intensified by the lack of close, bonded relationships. Social research confirms that we derive something from attachments that, in effect, serve to immunize us from stress. This "need for nearness" is manifested in strivings to feel wanted, needed, and valued. It is met by establishing intimate social bonds and involves the feeling of belonging and being loved. Even the need for self-esteem is an expression of the necessity for nearness. When we feel good about ourselves, it strengthens our confidence that we are worthy of belonging.

Historically, marriage and family have been the prime source for meeting nearness needs. In this age of anxiety, when tranquilizers are the most frequently prescribed medicine, it is not surprising that these institutions are less secure than ever before. Broken families seem to be the rule, not the exception. Sadly, family and marriage do not offer the stability and support they once did.

Actuarial statistics reveal that married people live longer than single people. We simply don't do as well alone as we do when we have intimacy. As the divorce rate escalates, so does vulnerability to stress.

Increasingly, health specialists are adopting the attitude that disrupted social bonds affect the body's immune system, increasing susceptibility to disease. The California Department of Mental Health found the following correlation between social ties and health:

- People who isolate themselves from others face two to four times the risk of premature death.
- Terminal cancer strikes isolated people more often than those with bonded relationships.
- The rates of mental hospitalization are five to 10 times greater for separated, divorced, and widowed persons than for married people.
- Pregnant women under stress and without supportive relationships have three times the number of complications than expectant mothers with intimate ties who are equally stressed.
- Women who can confide in a close friend are much less likely to become depressed.

Moreover, studies indicate the mortality rate of widowers is 40-60% higher during the first six months of bereavement. If remarriage occurs, mortality rates return to normal.

The health risk vulnerability of people lacking committed social bonds is dramatized further by a study examining death rates for smokers and non-smokers. Not surprisingly, those who smoke have higher death rates than people who don't. The most revealing statistic is that, in both smoking and non-smoking populations, single, widowed, and divorced men had the highest rates. Divorced men who smoked had the highest rates of all. Being alone is bad enough; feeling unwanted is worse. If the loss of established relationships increases stress vulnerability, creating loving, committed relationships is the best safeguard against it.

Several microcosmic population groups have been found with high percentages of centenarians. Efforts to discover the secret of their long lives have been inconclusive. The first, in the U.S.S.R. area of Georgia, led physically active lives, which led to the acceptance of cardiovascular fitness as the explanation. This conjecture was weakened by the discovery of a similar group in India that had a high percentage of its populace living past 100 years of age despite being extremely sedentary in lifestyle. Eventually, the revelation of their high-fiber diet led to its attribution as the genesis of their longevity. In still another community in the Peruvian Andes, the aged not only weren't active, their diet was primarily home-made beer.

Further reflection on these populations reveals only one common tie—in every instance, the communities valued and respected their elders. There were no mandatory retirement age or convalescent homes. There was no segregation by age at all. The older members of each group were involved in community activities, including meaningful work, and were valued for their experience and knowledge. They felt needed, wanted, and loved.

Every person is born with a genetically predetermined amount of stress-coping energy. Using this energy exacts a physiological toll known as aging. When it is depleted, death occurs. The most rapid depletion occurs in conditions of distress.

Think of yourself as a vehicle and the stress-coping energy as gas in your car. The size of your gas tank, set at birth, and how well your engine is tuned determine how much mileage your vehicle will get. Many people treat their lives just like cars. They "run out of gas" long before they should because they don't take care of their "engine" or "drive" sensibly. While you can't change the size of your gas tank, you can do two things to maximize your mileage—keep your engine tuned and don't take any unnecessary trips.

The next time you impotently rage at the "idiot" going 40 in the fast lane, ask yourself: Is it worth it? It could cost you seconds of your life. Do you really want to waste your finite stress-coping energy on someone you don't even know?

Permitting the feeling of responsibility without a corresponding authority to act is like revving the car's engine with the brakes on. It may sound impressive, but it's a waste of gas.

The next time you decide to "write off" any of the people in your life because they have offended you, ask yourself: Can I afford it? Do you really want to lose the potential support and nourishment represented by that relationship? Doesn't it make more sense to salvage it?

As important as diet and exercise are to "tuning up your engine," they are not as crucial as avoiding the feeling of isolation. Making and maintaining loving relationships is the single most important way to stress-proof your personality. Minimizing feelings of impotence and isolation are the philosophical heart of stress management.

THE RISKS OF REWARDS

Alfie Kohn

ALFIE KOHN *is the author of* The Brighter Side of Human Nature: Altruism and Empathy in Everyday Life *(Basic Books, 1990) and* No Contest: The Case Against Competition *(published in paperback by Houghton Mifflin, Co., 1987).*

Prizes and praise may send kids the wrong message

If there's one thing that will excite a fifth- or sixth-grader, it's a free movie ticket. That's what psychologist James Garbarino figured, so when he asked 12 girls individually to try to teach a new game to a younger child, he promised each one a ticket if she did a good job. He also asked another group of students to try their hand at tutoring, but he said nothing to these girls about a reward.

What Garbarino wanted to know was which group would teach more effectively. What he found was that those who were after the tickets took longer to communicate ideas, got frustrated more easily and ended up with pupils who didn't understand the game as well as the children who learned from girls who were not promised a reward.

Before you dismiss these results as a fluke, consider the findings from a few other experiments:

- Children who expected to receive a prize for making collages or telling stories proved to be less imaginative at both tasks than those who weren't promised anything.
- Two or three weeks after being told they would get an award for drawing with felt-tip markers, preschoolers were less interested in using the markers than their peers who didn't expect to be rewarded.
- Teenagers who were offered a reward for remembering details of a newspaper story they had recently read had poorer recall than those who received nothing for their efforts.

What's going on here? Don't rewards motivate people? The answer is: Sure—they motivate people to get rewarded. Unfortunately, this is often at the expense of interest in, or excellence at, whatever it is they're doing. Contrary to B.F. Skinner's famous theory of positive reinforcement, which suggested that we perform better when we expect to get something out of it, some psychologists now report that it often doesn't make sense to use rewards as a way to encourage children to learn, create or be caring and responsible. In fact, a growing number of studies indicate that emphasizing grades and special privileges or even lavishing praise can actually be counterproductive.

The Wrong Motivation

Despite this research, most of us cling to the belief that children will do what we want them to do if we make it worth their while. In a well-meaning attempt to promote reading among schoolchildren, for example, the Pizza Hut restaurant chain sponsors a five-month reading-for-reward program called BOOK IT! that dangles free pizza before children to induce them to read more. Only half in jest, John Nicholls, professor of education at the University of Illinois in Chicago, says that the likely long-term consequence of this strategy is "a lot of fat kids who don't like to read."

Why Nicholls says this is related to what he and other specialists call "intrinsic motivation"—doing something just because you find it worthwhile, because it seems valuable in its own right. As almost every parent knows, children naturally seek out situations that arouse their curiosity and allow them to prove their competence. They don't have to be bribed in order to learn new words or ideas. In fact, children who are intrinsically motivated are more likely to do high-quality, creative work—or to be well-behaved—than those who are driven by the prospect of a reward.

But here's the kicker: Rewards are not only relatively ineffective as motivators, they can kill intrinsic motivation. Children may make up stories just because it's fun. But once they are rewarded for it, they come to see themselves as acting mostly to get the prize. As Brandeis University social psychologist Teresa Amabile puts it, "We look to those extrinsic pressures and say, 'That must be why I'm doing this.' " The fascination with the task mysteriously vanishes along the way and eventually the child can't be bothered to do it unless there's some reward at stake.

An old joke illustrates this principle. An elderly man, harassed for weeks by the taunts of neighborhood children, finally devises a scheme. He offers to pay the children a dollar each if they'll return the next day and yell their insults again. They do so eagerly and he pays them as promised. "If you come back tomorrow, I'll give you 25 cents," he tells them. They do and collect their quarters. "From now on I'll pay you a penny," the old man announces. The children are contemptuous. "A penny? Forget it!" they reply. And they never return.

Using rewards, the old man "bought off" the children's intrinsic motivation to taunt him, which, of course, was exactly his plan. Unhappily, it is also what countless parents and teachers unwittingly do every single day: undermine interest in reading, thinking and creating just by rewarding these behaviors.

The same is true for getting children to behave responsibly and help others. It's tempting to promise another hour of television or an extra dessert if a child does what you want. But "our long-range goal is for children to develop internal principles, to be good because they understand it's right rather than because they've been paid," explains Marilyn Watson, program director of the Child Development Project, a San Ramon, California, program that works through the schools to encourage children to become caring and socially skilled. "Our job as parents and teachers is to help them see what's right, not to manipulate them with rewards."

A generation ago, disciplining children through positive reinforcement was presented as a progressive alternative to punishment, both in the classroom and at home. Instead of being spanked, humiliated or sent to his room, a child might receive extra privileges for behaving well. But studies show that positive reinforcement doesn't help a child internalize good behavior any more than does punishment. Specialists say the key to helping children develop a sense of responsibility is to explain the reason for a request—or allow them to help create their own solutions to problems.

Likewise, one study after another has found that the worst plan for encouraging children to be generous is to reward or praise them for acting that way. Two Canadian researchers found that seven- and eight-year-olds who were praised for donating marbles to poor children were not as helpful a week or two later as those who were led to think of themselves as donating because they were basically caring people. Another study, published just last year, showed that the children of mothers who believed in using rewards as motivators were less altruistic than their peers.

What Makes Rewards Toxic?

The evidence that rewards often undermine intrinsic motivation and performance is becoming so difficult to deny that psychologists have moved on to trying to figure out why this happens.

One key reason is that people who think of themselves as working for a reward feel controlled by it—as if the rewarder were in charge of their behavior, according to Richard Ryan, associate professor of psychology at the University of Rochester. "To the extent that one's experience of being self-determined is limited, one's creativity will be reduced as well," he says.

Nicholls, meanwhile, prefers to distinguish between thinking about what you're doing, which he calls "task involvement," and thinking about whether you're succeeding at it better than others, which he calls "ego involvement." The more emphasis that is placed on the task itself, the more children keep wanting to do it. It gives them a chance to feel proficient, and it also taps their natural curiosity. Praise and grades can have the opposite effect because they often make children more ego-involved and less interested in the task itself.

Other researchers are concerned about the message given by the promise of a reward. The British educator A.S. Neill said it is "tantamount to declaring that the activity is not worth doing for its own sake." All a child has to hear is that he or she will get a cookie or a gold star for completing a task, and the child tends to conclude that it is probably unpleasant or the bribe wouldn't be necessary.

In fact, anything that's presented as a means rather than an end will come to be viewed as less enjoyable. In one experiment, Mark R. Lepper of Stanford University told some preschoolers that they couldn't draw with pastel crayons until they had first spent some time drawing with felt-tip markers, or vice versa. When he checked back several weeks later, he discovered that the children no longer expressed much interest in whichever kind of drawing he had made a prerequisite for the other.

Some experts on creativity point out that rewards can be bad news for still another reason: They encourage children (and adults) to focus narrowly and superficially on a task, to do it as quickly as possible and to take few risks. "If they feel, 'This is something I have to get through to get the prize,' they're going to be less creative," says Amabile.

Maybe that's why studies find that the more children think about a reward, the more likely they are to choose the easiest possible task: They want the goody, not the challenge. Thus, says Nicholls, the child who is encouraged to think of reading as a way to get free pizza is likely to pick books that are short and simple. He or she is thinking about plowing through them quickly rather than appreciating the joys of reading. Indeed, even high achievers concentrate on quantity rather than quality when grades are at stake—a finding that led John Condry of Cornell University to dub rewards "the enemies of exploration."

It's important, though, that we don't regard reduced intrinsic interest as bad only because of its effects on how well children learn. As Ryan and his colleagues have noted, "Intrinsic motivation...is positively related not only to achievement per se, but also to children's self-esteem, perceived cognitive competence [how able they feel] and sense of control." If grades and other rewards reduce students' love of learning, then the consequences include how they come to think of themselves, not just how well they do in school.

Safer Rewards

What does all this mean in the real world? How should a parent or teacher react to these findings? Obviously, children like to receive praise and, at least until significant changes are made in our schools, will be confronted with grades. The solution is not to eliminate all rewards but to "detoxify" them. Here are some strategies:

- Don't make feedback seem controlling. Children ought to feel as if they play a role in deciding how to learn and behave. While praise that seems to reduce their sense of autonomy probably will make them less interested in a task, basic information about how well they're doing can actually increase motivation. Relate praise to the task, saying: "This is an interesting piece of work," rather than "You're so smart."
- Avoid comparing a child with siblings (or with yourself as a child) either in the way praise is phrased or rewards are set up. Even though most of us have been taught that competition is a useful motivator, many studies have shown just the reverse. "Understanding excellence as superiority over others can bring second-best results," says Nicholls.
- If you must give a reward, make it a surprise. An unexpected goody after a child has done something well is less damaging than a reward promised at the outset.
- Make rewards similar to the activities themselves. If you feel obliged to give children something in order to encourage them to read, give them books.
- Emphasize intrinsic motivation, not rewards. Do everything you can to help your child forget about grades. Rather than asking who did the best on a quiz or what the teacher thought of the child's assignment, Nicholls suggests asking: "Do you understand the subject better now than when you took the test? What's fun about this assignment? What's your opinion on the topic you've been discussing in class?"

Overall, the rule of thumb is: If we want children eventually to *want* to do something, it doesn't make sense to bribe them to do it.

Determinants of Behavior: Motivation, Environment, and Physiology

On the front pages of every newspaper, in practically every televised newscast, and on many magazine covers the problems of substance abuse haunt us. Innocent children are killed when caught in the crossfire of guns of drug lords. Prostitutes selling their bodies for drug money spread the deadly AIDS virus. The white-collar middle manager loses his job because he embezzled company money to support his cocaine habit.

Why do people turn to drugs? Why isn't the adverse publicity about the ruination of human lives diminishing the drug problem? Why can some people consume two cocktails and stop, while others feel helpless against the inebriating seduction of alcohol? Why do some people choose heroin as their drug of choice when others crave marijuana?

The cause of individual behavior, such as drug abuse or drinking, is the focus of this section. If physiology, either body chemistry or genes, is the determinant of our behavior, then solutions to such puzzles as alcoholism lie in the field of psychobiology (the study of behavior in relation to biological processes). However, if experience as a function of our environment and learning creates personality and subsequent behavior, normal or not, then researchers must take a different tack and explore features of the environment responsible for certain behaviors. A third explanation involves some complex interaction between experience and biology. If this interaction accounts for individual characteristics, scientists then have a complicated task ahead of them.

Conducting research designed to unravel the determinants of behavior is difficult. Scientists must call upon their best design skills to develop studies that will yield useful and replicable findings. A researcher hoping to examine the role of experience in personal growth and behavior needs to be able to isolate one or two stimuli or environmental factors that seem to control a particular behavior. Imagine trying to sufficiently delimit the complexity of the world so that only one or two events would stand out as the causes of an individual's alcoholism. Likewise, researchers interested in psychobiology need refined, technical knowledge. Suppose a scientist hopes to show that a particular form of mental illness is inherited. One cannot merely examine family histories, since family members can learn maladaptive patterns from one another. The researcher's ingenuity will be challenged; he or she must use intricate techniques such as comparing children to their adoptive parents, as well as to their biological parents. Such volunteer subjects will be difficult to find, and even then, the data may be hard to interpret.

The articles in this section are meant to familiarize you with a variety of hypothesized determinants of behavior. The first set of articles side with the view that our personality is a consequence of our *physiology*. "Major Personality Study Finds That Traits Are Mostly Inherited," divulges research that has found major personality traits appear to be mostly inherited. In "New Connections," Sandra Blakeslee shares the result of recent research on the brain suggesting that there are three stages of brain development that might help explain age-related differences in learning ability. The third article about physiology, "A Pleasurable Chemistry," pertains to endorphins—chemicals in our bloodstreams that dictate the pleasantness with which we perceive experiences.

The next set of articles supports the viewpoint that our self-concepts are a consequence of our *experiences*. In "Making of a Mind" by Kathleen McAuliffe, evidence is presented that early learning forms the foundation for later personality and behavior. In "Winter Blues," Richard Laliberte highlights recent research that demonstrates how seasonal changes often affect our moods, sometimes dramatically. Luckily, there is a solution for individuals who find such fluctuations problematic: increasing the number of hours spent under artificial lights. In "Food, Mood, and Behavior," the reader will learn how various foods are converted into neurotransmitters that alter performance and moods.

The *interactionist explanation* is also represented in this section. This viewpoint holds that we are a function of some complex interplay of physiology and experience. Two diverse articles offering this viewpoint are presented for your reading. "Guns and Dolls" features the interactionist explanation for sex differences, while "Second Thoughts About a Gene for Alcoholism" offers the same explanation for addiction.

"Proceeding With Caution" covers the generation of young adults ages 18 through 29. This article finds them skeptical of the baby boomer generation's values, and they are balking at work and marriage. What will this generation offer society?

Looking Ahead: Challenge Questions

Based on your experience observing children, what would you say most contributes to their personal growth:

Unit 2

physiological factors or environmental factors? Parents surely play a significant role in any child's development; who else has an impact, and how significant are they compared to the parents?

What is most responsible for sex differences: biology or learning? Is it important for people to behave differently from each other? What would society be like if everyone behaved the same way?

Are there individual foods or food groups that seem to affect people's health? Are there substances other than food, drugs, and alcohol that alter our moods, and if so, how so? Are parents and schools morally responsible for what children consume? How and where might knowledge of how food affects behavior and mood be useful?

Do you think foods influence performance and sense of well-being? Why or why not? Why is the study of neurotransmitters important; where can this information be utilized?

Do you have any personality traits that you feel you also possessed as a child? If some traits changed, why do you think they changed? Do you think early experience is more important than later experience? With regard to addictions, what do you think accounts for them—early or later experiences, or something physiological?

Major Personality Study Finds That Traits Are Mostly Inherited

Data on twins will fuel nature vs. nurture debate.

Daniel Goleman

The genetic makeup of a child is a stronger influence on personality than child rearing, according to the first study to examine identical twins reared in different families. The findings shatter a widespread belief among experts and laymen alike in the primacy of family influence and are sure to engender fierce debate.

The findings are the first major results to emerge from a long-term project at the University of Minnesota. Since 1979, more than 350 pairs of twins in the project have gone through six days of extensive testing that has included analysis of blood, brain waves, intelligence and allergies.

The results on personality are being reviewed for publication by the Journal of Personality and Social Psychology. Although there has been wide press coverage of pairs of twins reared apart who met for the first time in the course of the study, the personality results are the first significant scientific data to be announced.

For most of the traits measured, more than half the variation was found to be due to heredity, leaving less than half determined by the influence of parents, home environment and other experiences in life.

The Minnesota findings stand in sharp contradiction to standard wisdom on nature versus nurture in forming adult personality. Virtually all major theories since Freud have given far more importance to environment, or nurture, than to genes, or nature.

Even though the findings point to the strong influence of heredity, the family still shapes the broad suggestion of personality offered by heredity; for example, a family might tend to make an innately timid child either more timid or less so. But the inference from this study is that the family would be unlikely to make the child brave.

The 350 pairs of twins studied included some who were raised apart. Among these separately reared twins were 44 pairs of identical twins and 21 pairs of fraternal twins. Comparing twins raised separately with those raised in the same home allows researchers to determine the relative importance of heredity and of environment in their development. Although some twins go out of their way to emphasize differences between them, in general identical twins are very much alike in personality.

But what accounts for that similarity? If environment were the major influence in personality, then identical twins raised in the same home would be expected to show more similarity than would the twins reared apart. But the study of 11 personality traits found differences between the kinds of twins were far smaller than had been assumed.

"If in fact twins reared apart are that similar, this study is extremely important for understanding how personality is shaped," commented Jerome Kagan, a developmental psychologist at Harvard University. "It implies that some aspects of personality are under a great degree of genetic control."

The traits were measured using a personality questionnaire developed by Auke Tellegen, a psychologist at the University of Minnesota who was one of the principal researchers. The questionnaire assesses many major aspects of personality, including aggressiveness, striving for achievement, and the need for personal intimacy.

For example, agreement with the statement "When I work with others, I like to take charge" is an indication of the trait called social potency, or leadership, while agreement with the sentence "I often keep working on a problem, even if I am very tired" indicates the need for achievement.

Among traits found most strongly determined by heredity were leadership and, surprisingly, traditionalism or obedience to authority. "One would not expect the tendency to believe in traditional values and the strict enforcement of rules to be more an inherited than learned trait," said David Lykken, a psychologist in the Minnesota project. "But we found that, in some mysterious way, it is one of the traits with the strongest genetic influence."

Other traits that the study concludes were more than 50 percent determined by heredity included a sense of well-being and zest for life; alienation; vulnerability or resistance to stress; and fearfulness or risk seeking.

Another highly inherited trait, though one not commonly thought of as part of personality, was the capacity for becoming rapt in an aesthetic experience, such as a concert.

Vulnerability to stress, as measured on the Tellegen test, reflects what is commonly thought of as "neuroticism," according to Dr. Lykken. "People high in this trait are nervous and jumpy, easily irritated, highly sensitive to stimuli, and generally dissatisfied with themselves, while those low on the trait are resilient and see themselves in a positive light," he said. "Therapy may help vulnerable people to some extent, but they seem to have a built-in susceptibility that may mean, in general, they would be more content with a life low in stress."

The need to achieve, including ambition and an inclination to work hard toward goals, also was found to be genetically influenced, but more than half of this trait seemed determined by life experience. The same lower degree of hereditary influence was found for impulsiveness and its opposite, caution.

The need for personal intimacy appeared the least determined by heredity among the traits tested; about two-thirds of that tendency was found to depend on experience. People high in this trait have a strong desire for emotionally intense relationships; those low in the trait tend to be loners who keep their troubles to themselves.

"This is one trait that can be greatly strengthened by the quality of interactions in a family," Dr. Lykken said. "The more physical and emotional intimacy, the more likely this trait will be developed in children, and those children with the strongest inherited tendency will have the greatest need for social closeness as adults."

No single gene is believed responsible for any one of these traits. Instead, each trait, the Minnesota researchers propose, is determined by a great number of genes in combination, so that the pattern of inheritance is complex and indirect.

No one believes, for instance, that there is a single gene for timidity but rather a host of genetic influences. That may explain, they say, why previous studies have found little connection between the personality traits of parents and their children. Whereas identical twins would share with each other the whole constellation of genes that might be responsible for a particular trait, children might share only some part of that constellation with each parent.

That is why, just as a short parent may have a tall child, an achievement-oriented parent might have a child with little ambition.

The Minnesota findings are sure to stir debate. Though most social scientists accept the careful study of twins, particularly when it includes identical twins reared apart, as the best method of assessing the degree to which a trait is inherited, some object to using these methods for assessing the genetic component of complex behavior patterns or question the conclusions that are drawn from it.

Further, some researchers consider paper-and-pencil tests of personality less reliable than observations of how people act, since people's own reports of their behavior can be biased. "The level of heritability they found is surprisingly high, considering that questionnaires are not the most sensitive index of personality," said Dr. Kagan. "There is often a poor relationship between how people respond on a questionnaire and what they actually do."

"Years ago, when the field was dominated by a psychodynamic view, you could not publish a study like this," Dr. Kagan added. "Now the field is shifting to a greater acceptance of genetic determinants, and there is the danger of being too uncritical of such results."

Seymour Epstein, a personality psychologist at the Univer-

The Roots of Personality

The degree to which eleven key traits of personality are estimated to be inherited, as gauged by tests with twins. Traits were measured by the Multidimensional Personality Questionnaire, developed by Auke Tellegen at the University of Minnesota.

SOCIAL POTENCY **61%**

A person high in this trait is masterful, a forceful leader who likes to be the center of attention.

TRADITIONALISM **60%**

Follows rules and authority, endorses high moral standards and strict discipline.

STRESS REACTION **55%**

Feels vulnerable and sensitive and is given to worries and easily upset.

ABSORPTION **55%**

Has a vivid imagination readily captured by rich experience, relinquishes sense of reality.

ALIENATION **55%**

Feels mistreated and used, that "the world is out to get me."

WELL-BEING **54%**

Has a cheerful disposition, feels confident and optimistic.

HARM AVOIDANCE **51%**

Shuns the excitement of risk and danger, prefers the safe route even if it is tedious.

AGGRESSION **48%**

Is physically aggressive and vindictive, has taste for violence and is "out to get the world."

ACHIEVEMENT **46%**

Works hard, strives for mastery and puts work and accomplishment ahead of other things.

CONTROL **43%**

Is cautious and plodding, rational and sensible, likes carefully planned events.

SOCIAL CLOSENESS **33%**

Prefers emotional intimacy and close ties, turns to others for comfort and help.

The New York Times/Dec. 1, 1986

sity of Massachusetts, said he was skeptical of precise estimates of heritability. "The study compared people from a relatively narrow range of cultures and environments," he said. "If the range had been much greater—say Pygmies and Eskimos as well as middle-class Americans—then environment would certainly contribute more to personality. The results might have shown environment to be a far more powerful influence than heredity," he said.

Dr. Tellegen himself said: "Even though the differences between families do not account for much of the unique attributes of their children, a family still exercises important influence. In cases of extreme deprivation or abuse, for instance, the family would have a much larger impact—though a negative one—than any found in the study. Although the twins studied came from widely different environments, there were no extremely deprived families."

Gardner Lindzey, director of the Center for Advanced Studies in the Behavioral Sciences in Palo Alto, Calif., said the Minnesota findings would "no doubt produce empassioned rejoinders."

"They do not in and of themselves say what makes a given character trait emerge," he said, "and they can be disputed and argued about, as have similar studies of intelligence."

For parents, the study points to the importance of treating each child in accord with his innate temperament.

"The message for parents is not that it does not matter how they treat their children, but that it is a big mistake to treat all kids the same," said Dr. Lykken. "To guide and shape a child you have to respect his individuality, adapt to it and cultivate those qualities that will help him in life."

"If there are two brothers in the same family, one fearless and the other timid, a good parent will help the timid one become less so by giving him experiences of doing well at risk-taking, and let the other develop his fearlessness tempered with some intelligent caution. But if the parent shelters the one who is naturally timid, he will likely become more so."

The Minnesota results lend weight and precision to earlier work that pointed to the importance of a child's temperament in development. For instance, the New York Longitudinal Study, conducted by Alexander Thomas and Stella Chess, psychiatrists at New York University Medical Center, identified three basic temperaments in children, each of which could lead to behavioral problems if not handled well.

"Good parenting now must be seen in terms of meeting the special needs of a child's temperament, including dealing with whatever conflicts it creates," said Stanley Grossman, a staff member of the medical center's Psychoanalytic Institute.

NEW CONNECTIONS

When it's time to make changes in your life, what role does your brain play?

SANDRA BLAKESLEE

Sandra Blakeslee *of Los Angeles writes on science and health for* The New York Times *and is coauthor of* Second Chances.

Suppose you are contemplating a major change in your life. You want to redefine a relationship, stop smoking, lose weight, go back to school or switch careers. You go to the bookstore, read up on the appropriate changes, and now you know which strategies are supposed to work.

But there's one aspect of personal change you probably won't find in the self-help books. It has to do with your brain and the vast network of interconnecting cells that account for everything you do, think, feel, remember and believe. When you set out to alter course, what are you up against? How did your brain get to be the way it is in the first place? What is the biological basis for the behavior or thought patterns you want to change?

Recent brain research has begun to explain why it's so much easier to buy those how-to books than make enduring changes in our lives. To some degree, the adult brain is designed to be set in its ways. If the brain changed with every whim, we'd be mental chameleons, unable to make commitments, hold onto values or stick with difficult tasks.

Fortunately, however, the adult brain is also designed to accommodate change. The possibility for change—both original growth and the reworking of established pathways—is built into the physical and chemical structure of the human nervous system. We learn and adapt.

Researchers have found that the human brain undergoes three distinctly different stages of development. Before you are born, the processes are largely biological and preprogrammed. Then from birth to your early 20s, your brain is fundamentally shaped by experience and the emotions that surround those events. Finally, in adulthood your brain is more or less set—but not in concrete. Change is still possible; it's just more subtle and may require extra effort.

You can't think away a habit.

To appreciate what your brain must go through to learn something new or steer a fresh course, it helps to understand how it evolved into an orchestrated array of billions of cells with trillions of connections. In an intricate dance of nature and nurture, genes and environment interact to shape each of us into a unique human being. As we mature, biological choices are made: We hone the skills that will mark our adult lives—but lose the potential for others.

BIRTH: MASSIVE CELL DEATH

Your brain begins as a small group of cells that proliferate explosively. Midway through gestation, this proliferation ends, and the neurons—the nerve cells that send and receive the messages that compose all your thoughts and actions—begin a second great expansion. The cell axons—long, thin projections with which neurons communicate—travel all over the brain, seeking out the receiving stations of other neurons.

Once an axon finds a compatible target, it releases a chemical neurotransmitter across the synapse (the tiny gap between cells), thus establishing a communication link. Eventually, neurons make countless such connections, building up complex circuits. Late in gestation, the brain is wired and ready for the next major phase—massive cell death.

That the brain loses billions of cells right before birth may seem startling. But nature doesn't want to risk coming up short; it overproduces and then prunes the excess. This pruning continues until the emerging brain builds up its essential functional networks. It's now ready to face the world.

GROWING UP: NETWORKING

Soon after birth, another growth phase begins. Surviving neurons sprout additional axons and set about making enormous numbers of new synaptic connections. The brain's wiring gets increasingly complicated, building vast neural networks that may or may not be useful later in childhood. The neocortex—the outer part of the brain devoted to higher mental processes—actually thickens in the first three years of life as this explosive growth continues. At the same time, the growing brain begins interacting with its environment to solidify important circuits.

By age three, the healthy brain achieves three-quarters of its adult weight, and the number of synaptic connections reaches its maximum. And once again, it's time for another massive pruning—this time directed by experience.

University of Chicago studies show that right after the toddler years, the number of connections begins to decline and keeps dropping until it finally stabilizes in the early adult years. Positron emission tomography (PET) scans of infants and children also show the metabolic activity of the brain's cortex reaches a maximum—about double the adult level—around age three, says Dr. Harry Chugani, an associate professor of pediatrics and neurology at UCLA. It stays high until around age nine and then slows until it stabilizes in young adulthood.

These observations strongly suggest that between the toddler years and young adulthood, experience literally sculpts the brain. Although growth is an essential element in brain maturation, the dominant theme is loss. Many researchers believe that synaptic connections not recruited early in life—say, by age nine or 10—are slowly eliminated as you mature.

Language capacity is thought to represent this kind of process. Little children are equipped with a brain that allows them to learn to speak any language flawlessly—be it the complex tones of Mandarin Chinese or the odd clicks of the !Kung bushmen. If English is your native tongue, you learned to pronounce the incredibly difficult (for most of the world) American "r." As you learned English, your brain recruited synaptic circuits dedicated to replicating the sound system of your mother tongue. Had you been consistently exposed to two or three languages in early childhood, you could have spoken each with native fluency, because your brain would have recruited special circuits for each.

But after age nine, this ability starts to decline. Unused synaptic circuits, scientists theorize, begin to die off. Although many children acquire second languages in later childhood—and speak them fluently—linguists can almost invariably tell that the second language isn't the native tongue. Similarly, if you had musical talent and your parents had waited until you were 10 or 11 before bringing you to a master teacher to be trained for a concert career, the teacher probably would have told them it was too late—no matter how talented you were.

On the other hand, the loss of unused synapses has benefits. As child psychologists have noted, children acquire new cognitive powers as they grow older. In some ways, the more children lose, the more they seem to gain. The stages of development described by psychologist Jean Piaget may, in fact, mirror stages of brain maturation driven by synaptic pruning.

According to Piaget, from 12 to young adulthood—a time of massive pruning—children lose some versatility but gain the ability to focus. They master logical thought and manipulate abstract ideas; they begin to think about astronomy and infinity, when just a few years before they couldn't fathom how far it was to Grandma's house. They also begin to solidify basic beliefs about the world. Researchers at the University of Michigan have found that the political beliefs people adopt in their late teens and early 20s tend to endure for life. Many of our basic attitudes are similarly ingrained.

When it comes to laying down learning and memory circuits, researchers are finding that emotions play a critical role—and may make learned patterns difficult to change in later life. When a memory is formed, neurons undergo structural changes that affect the strength of synaptic connections. Much of what you remember depends on your emotional state—fear, excitement, surprise—at the time, your alertness and the nature of the event itself, says Dr. Larry R. Squire, professor of psychiatry at the University of California in San Diego.

Trivial events are best forgotten. But if the event is important, your brain modulates its storage through neurotransmitters and hormones associated with specific emotional states. Adrenaline, for example, can indirectly strengthen the connection between neurons in a memory trace. This would explain why emotional responses are so difficult to change as we get older. Emotional patterns established in the early years—habits, phobias or simply ways of relating to people—have left strong memory traces in our brains that are hard to alter.

ADULTHOOD: CHANGING COURSE

For about 20 years, nature and nurture conspire to create a brain uniquely yours—a brain shaped by a singular set of experiences, memories and emotions. When you become an adult, it's time to settle down, neurologically speaking. But even though your brain is mature, a lifetime of experience still to come will continue to modify your nervous system and make further change possible. Animal evidence supports this idea, Squire says. For example, rats housed in enriched environments up to old age develop brains with especially dense synaptic connections and thick cortical regions, compared with animals confined in empty cages.

The details of how the human brain maintains its plasticity are still unknown. But the repertoire of our neural connections is probably never complete, says Dr. Dale Purves, professor of neurobiology at Washington University in St. Louis. New connections are apparently constructed, and old ones removed, throughout the adult years.

What exactly happens to the adult nervous system when we want to make a change or break a habit? "Our understanding of the process is very sketchy," Squire says. New learning must entail structural change in the neurons and synapses. But instead of a whole new pathway being formed, he says, the existing pathways may be reshaped. To form a new habit, you might alter an old pathway, instead of laying down an entirely new one. Rather than disappearing, the old pathway would simply weaken.

This idea makes sense, Squire continues, because memory formation is such a dynamic process. As time passes, depending on their relevance to your life, certain memories fade. When you forget or "unlearn," a memory circuit is progressively weakened. At the same time, other memories are strengthened as their traces become more highly organized and strongly connected.

Old memory traces can also be reactivated to your advantage. Though unused circuits can fade away, they probably never disappear. Say you studied calculus in high school but have not used it since. If your son or daughter should need help 20 years later, you can reread the calculus text and rapidly regain your knowledge by reactivating the pathways.

Clearly, with a little effort adults are capable of change. It's still possible to learn a language, take up the guitar, or adopt new roles in life. But change is less facile than it was in childhood. As we acquire new skills and abilities and lay down fresh synaptic pathways, we must practice, practice, practice. We can learn just about anything. It just takes a little longer.

The change must come through experience. You can't think away a habit. It has to be *actively eliminated* through new behavior that modifies old circuits or establishes alternative pathways.

This is one reason it's so difficult to make changes in adulthood. When, for example, you decide to lose weight, it's not simply a matter of putting less food on your plate. All the visual and olfactory cues that give rise to strong emotions about food must be rewired. Genes also play a role, Squire adds.

If you have invested powerful emotions in a relationship you now want to change, you can't simply wish for change to happen. You must work at establishing a new set of emotional responses to that person, which will override the earlier feelings. As everyone knows, this is one of life's most difficult tasks.

Whether you take advantage of the fact or not, the adult brain remains extremely flexible into old age. Although some of our abilities decline, we compensate. We make lists to shore up a shaky memory. But neurobiologists have shown that we can continue to lay down new synaptic networks well into our 80s or 90s. Being human means we are endowed with superior ability to learn, grow and even alter course. In other words, we change.

A Pleasurable Chemistry

Endorphins, the body's natural narcotics, aren't something we have to run after. They're everywhere.

Janet L. Hopson

Janet L. Hopson, who lives in Oakland, California, gets endorphin highs by contributing to Psychology Today.

Welcome aboard the biochemical bandwagon of the 1980s. The magical, morphine-like brain chemicals called endorphins are getting a lot of play. First we heard they were responsible for runner's high and several other cheap thrills. Now we're hearing that they play a role in almost every human experience from birth to death, including much that is pleasurable, painful and lusty along the way.

Consider the following: crying, laughing, thrills from music, acupuncture, placebos, stress, depression, chili peppers, compulsive gambling, aerobics, trauma, masochism, massage, labor and delivery, appetite, immunity, near-death experiences, playing with pets. Each, it is claimed, is somehow involved with endorphins. Serious endorphin researchers pooh-pooh many or most of these claims but, skeptics notwithstanding, the field has clearly sprinted a long way past runner's high.

Endorphin research had its start in the early 1970s with the unexpected discovery of opiate receptors in the brain. If we have these receptors, researchers reasoned, then it is likely that the body produces some sort of opiate- or morphine-like chemicals. And that's exactly what was found, a set of relatively small biochemicals dubbed "opioid peptides" or "endorphins" (short for "endogenous morphines") that plug into the receptors. In other words, these palliative peptides are sloshing around in our brains, spines and bloodstreams, apparently acting just like morphine. In fact, morphine's long list of narcotic effects was used as a treasure map for where scientists might hunt out natural opiates in the body. Morphine slows the pulse and depresses breathing, so they searched in the heart and lungs. Morphine deadens pain, so they looked in the central and peripheral nervous systems. It disturbs digestion and elimination, so they explored the gut. It savages the sex drive, so they probed the reproductive and endocrine systems. It triggers euphoria, so they scrutinized mood.

Nearly everywhere researchers looked, endorphins or their receptors were present. But what were they doing: transmitting nerve impulses, alleviating pain, triggering hormone release, doing several of these things simultaneously or disintegrating at high speed and doing nothing at all? In the past decade, a trickle of scientific papers has become a tidal wave, but still no one seems entirely certain of what, collectively, the endorphins are doing to us or for us at any given time.

Researchers do have modern-day sextants for their search, including drugs such as naloxone and naltrexone. These drugs, known as opiate blockers, pop into the endorphin receptors and block the peptides' normal activity, giving researchers some idea of what their natural roles might be. Whatever endorphins are doing, however, it must be fairly subtle. As one researcher points out, people injected with opiate blockers may feel a little more pain or a little less "high," but no one gasps for breath, suffers a seizure or collapses in a coma.

Subtle or not, endorphins are there, and researchers are beginning to get answers to questions about how they touch our daily lives—pain, exercise, appetite, reproduction and emotions.

•ANSWERS ON ANALGESIA: A man falls off a ladder, takes one look at his right hand—now cantilevered at a sickening angle—and knows he has a broken bone. Surprisingly, he feels little pain or anxiety until hours later, when he's home from the emergency room. This physiological grace period, which closely resembles a sojourn on morphine, is a common survival mechanism in the animal world, and researchers are confident that brain opiates are responsible for such cases of natural pain relief. The question is how do they work and, more to the point, how can we make them work for us?

The answers aren't in, but researchers have located a pain control system in the periaquaductal gray (PAG), a tiny region in the center of the brain, and interestingly, it produces opioid peptides. While no one fully understands how this center operates, physicians can now jolt it with electric current to lessen chronic pain.

One day in 1976, as Navy veteran Dennis Hough was working at a hospital's psychiatric unit, a disturbed patient snapped Hough's back and ruptured three of his vertebral discs. Five years later, after two failed back operations, Hough was bedridden with constant shooting pains in his legs, back and shoulders and was depressed to the point of suicide. Doctors were just then pioneering a technique of implanting platinum electrodes in the PAG, and Hough soon underwent the skull drilling and emplacement. He remembers it as "the most barbaric thing I've ever experienced, including my tour of duty in Vietnam," but the results were worth the ordeal; For the past seven years, Hough has been able to stimulate his brain's own endorphins four times a day by producing a radio signal from a transmitter on his belt. The procedure is delicate—too much current and his eyes flutter, too little and the pain returns in less than six hours. But it works dependably, and Hough not only holds down an office job now but is engaged to be married.

Researchers would obviously like to find an easier way to stimulate the brain's own painkillers, and while they have yet to find it, workers in many labs are actively developing new drugs and treatments. Some physicians have tried direct spinal injections of endorphins to alleviate postoperative pain. And even the most cynical now seem to agree that acupuncture works its magic by somehow triggering the release of endorphins. There may, however, be an even easier path to pain relief: the power of the mind.

Several years ago, neurobiologist Jon Levine, at the University of California, San Francisco, discovered that the placebo effect (relief) based on no known action other than the patient's belief in a treatment) can itself be blocked by naloxone and must therefore be based on endorphins. Just last year Levine was able to quantify the effects: One shot of placebo can equal the relief of 6 to 8 milligrams of morphine, a low but fairly typical dose.

Another line of research suggests that endorphins may be involved in self-inflicted injury—a surprisingly common veterinary and medical complaint and one that, in many cases, can also be prevented with naloxone. Paul Millard Hardy, a behavioral neurologist at Boston's New England Medical Center, believes that animals may boost endorphin levels through self-inflicted pain and then "get caught in a self-reinforcing positive feedback loop." He thinks something similar may occur in compulsive daredevils and in some cases of deliberate self-injury. One young woman he studied had injected pesticide into her own veins by spraying Raid into an intravenous needle. This appalling act, she told Hardy, "made her feel better, calmer and almost high."

Hardy also thinks endorphin release might explain why some autistic children constantly injure themselves by banging their heads. Because exercise is believed to be an alternate route to endorphin release, Hardy and physician Kiyo Kitahara set up a twice-a-day exercise program for a group of autistic children. He qualifies the evidence as "very anecdotal at this point" but calls the results "phenomenal."

•RUNNER'S HIGH, RUNNER'S CALM: For most people, "endorphins" are synonymous with "runner's high," a feeling of well-being that comes after an aerobic workout. Many people claim to have experienced this "high," and remarkable incidents are legion. Take, for example, San Francisco runner Don Paul, who placed 10th in the 1979 San Francisco Marathon and wound up with his ankle in a cast the next day. Paul had run the 26 miles only vaguely aware of what turned out to be a serious stress fracture. Observers on the sidelines had to tell him he was "listing badly to one side for the last six miles." He now runs 90 miles per week in preparation for the U.S. men's Olympic marathon trial and says that when he trains at the level, he feels "constantly great. Wonderful."

Is runner's high a real phenomenon based on endorphins? And can those brain opiates result in "exercise addiction"? Or, as many skeptics hold, are the effects on mood largely psychological? Most studies with humans have found rising levels of endorphins in the blood during exercise.

However, says exercise physiologist Peter Farrell of Pennsylvania State University, "when we look at animal studies, we don't see a concurrent increase in the brain." Most circulating peptides fail to cross into the brain, he explains, so explaining moods like runner's high based on endorphin levels in the blood is questionable. Adds placebo expert Jon Levine, "Looking for mood changes based on the circulating blood is like putting a voltmeter to the outside of a computer and saying 'Now I know how it works.' " Nevertheless, Farrell exercises religiously: "I'm not going to waste my lifetime sitting around getting sclerotic just because something's not proven yet."

Murray Allen, a physician and kinesiologist at Canada's Simon Fraser University, is far more convinced about the endorphin connection. He recently conducted his own study correlating positive moods and exercise—moods that could be blocked by infusing the runner with naloxone. Allen thinks these moods are "Mother Nature's way of rewarding us for staying fit" but insists that aerobic exercisers don't get "high." Opioid peptides "slow down and inhibit excess activity in the brain," he says. "Many researchers have been chasing after psychedelic, excitable responses." The actual effect, he says, is "runner's calm" and extremes leading to exhaustion usually negate it.

In a very similar experiment last year, a research team at Georgia State University found the mood-endorphin link more elusive. Team member and psychologist Wade Silverman of Atlanta explains that only those people who experience "runner's high" on the track also noticed it in the lab. Older people and those who ran fewer, not more, miles per week were also more likely to show a "high" on the test. "People who run a lot—50 miles per week or more—are often drudges, masochists, running junkies," says Silverman. "They don't really enjoy it. It hurts." For optimum benefits. Silverman recommends running no more than three miles per day four times a week.

Silverman and Lewis Maharam, a sports medicine internist at Manhattan's New York Infirmary/Beekman Downtown Hospital, both agree that powerful psychological factors—including heightened sense of self-esteem and self-discipline—contribute to the "high" in those who exercise moderately. Maharam would still like to isolate and quantify the role of endorphins, however, so he could help patients "harness the high." He would like to give people "proper exercise prescriptions," he says, "to stimulate the greatest enjoyment and benefit from exercise. If we could encourage the 'high' early on, maybe we could get people to want to keep exercising from the start."

The questions surrounding exercise, mood and circulating endorphins remain. But even if opioids released into the bloodstream from, say, the adrenal glands don't enter the brain and give a "high" or a "calm," several studies show that endorphins in the blood do bolster the immune system's activity. One way or the other, regular moderate exercise seems destined to make us happy.

•APPETITE CLOCKS AND BLOCKS: Few things in life are more basic to survival and yet more pleasurable than eating good food—and where survival and pleasure intersect, can the endorphins be far behind? To keep from starving, an animal needs to know when, what and how much to eat, and researchers immediately suspected that opioid peptides might help control appetite and satiety. People, after all, have long claimed that specific foods such as chili peppers or sweets give them a "high." And those unmistakably "high" on morphine or heroin experience constipation, cravings and other gastrointestinal glitches.

Indeed, investigators quickly located opiate receptors in the alimentary tract and found a region of the rat's hypothalamus that—when injected with tiny amounts of beta endorphin—will trigger noshing of particular nutrients. Even a satiated rat will dig heartily into fats, proteins or sweets when injected with the peptide. Neurobiologist Sarah Leibowitz and her colleagues at Rockefeller University produced this result and also found that opiate blockers would prevent the snack attack—strong evidence that endorphins help regulate appetite. The opiates "probably enhance the hedonic, pleasurable, rewarding properties" of fats, proteins and sweets—foods that can help satiate an animal far longer than carbohydrates so it can survive extended periods without eating.

Intriguingly, rats crave carbohydrates at the beginning of their 12-hour activity cycles, but they like fats, proteins or sweets before retiring—a hint that endorphins control not just the nature but the timing of appetites. Leibowitz suspects that endorphins also help control cravings in response to stress and starvation, and that disturbed endorphin systems may, in part, underlie obesity and eating disorders. Obese people given opiate blockers, for example, tend to eat less; bulimics often gorge on fat-rich foods; both bulimics and anorexics often have abnormal levels of endorphins; and in anorexics, food deprivation enhances the release of opiates in the brain. This brain opiate reward, some speculate, may reinforce the anorexic's self-starvation much as self-injury seems to be rewarding to an autistic child.

Researchers such as Leibowitz are hoping to learn enough about the chemistry of appetite to fashion a binge-blocking drug as well as more effective behavioral approaches to over- or undereating. In the meantime, people who try boosting their own endorphins through exercise, mirth or music may notice a vexing increase in their taste for fattening treats.

•PUBERTY, PREGNANCY AND PEPTIDES: Evolution has equipped animals with two great appetites—the hunger for food to prevent short-term disintegration and the hunger for sex and reproduction to prevent longer-term genetic oblivion. While some endorphin researchers were studying opioids and food hunger, others began searching for a sex role—and they found it.

Once again, drug addiction pointed the way: Users of morphine and heroin often complain of impotence and frigidity that fade when they kick their habits. Could natural opioids have some biochemical dampening effect on reproduction? Yes, says Theodore Cicero of Washington University Medical School. Endorphins, he says, "play an integral role—probably the dominant role—in regulating reproductive hormone cycles."

This formerly small corner of endorphin research has "exploded into a huge area of neurobiology," Cicero says, and researchers now think the opioid peptides help fine-tune many—perhaps all—of the nervous and hormonal pathways that together keep the body operating normally.

Cicero and his colleagues have tracked the byzantine biochemical loops through which endorphins, the brain, the body's master gland (the pituitary), the master's master (the hypothalamus) and the gonads exchange signals to ensure that an adult animal can reproduce when times are good but not when the environment is hostile. Cicero's work helped show that beta endorphin rules the hypothalamus and thus, indirectly, the pituitary and gonads.

The Washington University group also sees "a perfect parallel" between the brain's ability to produce endorphins and the onset of puberty: As the opioid system matures, so does the body sexually. A juvenile rat with endorphins blocked by naloxone undergoes puberty earlier; a young rat given opiates matures far later than normal and its offspring can have disturbed hormonal systems. Cicero calls the results "frightening" and adds, "there couldn't possibly be a worse time for a person to take drugs than during late childhood or adolescence."

Endorphins play a critical role in a later reproductive phase, as well: pregnancy and labor. Women in their third trimester sometimes notice that the pain and pressure of, say, a blood pressure cuff, is far less pronounced than before or after pregnancy. Alan Gintzler and his colleagues at the State University of New York Health Science Center in Brooklyn found that opioid peptides produced inside the spinal cord probably muffle pain and perhaps elevate mood to help a woman deal with the increasing physical stress of pregnancy. Endorphin activity builds throughout pregnancy and reaches a peak just before and during labor. Some have speculated that the tenfold drop from peak endorphin levels within 24 hours of delivery may greatly contribute to postpartum depression.

•CHILLS, THRILLS, LAUGHTER AND TEARS: Just as the effects of morphine go beyond the physical, claims for the opioid peptides extend to purely esthetic and emotional, with speculation falling on everything from the pleasure of playing with pets and the transcendence of near-death experiences to shivers over sonatas and the feeling of well-being that comes with a rousing laugh or a good cry.

Avram Goldstein of Stanford University, a pioneer in peptide research, recently collected a group of volunteers who get a spine-tingling thrill from their favorite music and gave them either a placebo or an opiate blocker during a listening session. Their shivers declined with the blocker—tantalizing evidence that endorphins mediate rapture, even though the mechanics are anyone's guess.

Former *Saturday Review* editor Norman Cousins may have spawned a different supposition about endorphins and emotion when he literally laughed himself out of the sometimes fatal disease ankylosing spondylitis. He found that 10 minutes of belly laughing before bed gave him two hours of painfree sleep. Before long, someone credited endorphins with the effect, and by now the claim is commonplace. For example, Matt Weinstein, a humor consultant from Berkeley, California, frequently mentions a possible link between endorphins, laughter and health in his lectures on humor in the workplace. His company's motto: If you take yourself too seriously, there's an excellent chance you may end up seriously ill.

Weinstein agrees with laughter researcher William Fry, a psychiatrist at Stanford's medical school, that evidence is currently circumstantial. Fry tried to confirm the laughter-endorphin link experimentally, but the most accurate way to assess it would be to tap the cerebrospinal fluid. That, Fry says, "is not only a difficult procedure but it's not conducive to laughter" and could result in a fountain of spinal fluid gushing out with the first good guffaw. Confirmation clearly awaits a less ghoulish methodology. But in the meantime, Fry is convinced that mirth and playfulness can diminish fear, anger and depression. At the very least, he says, laughter is a good aerobic exercise that ventilates the lungs and leaves the muscles relaxed. Fry advises patients to take their own humor inventory, then amass a library of books, tapes and gags that dependably trigger hilarity.

Another William Frey, this one at the University of Minnesota, studies the role of tears in emotion, stress and health. "The physiology of the brain when we experience a change in emotional state from sad to angry to happy or vice versa is an absolutely unexplored frontier," Frey says. And emotional tears are a fascinating guidepost because "they are unique to human beings and are our natural excretory response to strong emotion." Since all other bodily fluids are involved in removing something, he reasons, logic dictates that tears wash something away, too. Frey correctly predicted that tears would contain the three biochemicals that build up during stress: leucine-enkephalin, an endorphin, and the hormones prolactin and ACTH. These biochemicals are found in both emotional tears and tears from chopping onions, a different sort of stress.

Frey is uncertain whether tears simply carry off excess endorphins that collect in the stressed brain or whether those peptides have some activity in the tear ducts, eyes, nose or throat. Regardless, he cites evidence that people with ulcers and colitis tend to cry less than the average, and he concludes that a person who feels like crying "should go ahead and do it! I can't think of any other physical excretory process that humans alone can do, so why suppress it and its possibly healthful effects?"

All in all, the accumulated evidence suggests that if you want to use your endorphins, you should live the unfettered natural life. Laugh! Cry! Thrill to music! Reach puberty. Get pregnant. Get aerobic. Get hungry, Eat! Lest this sound like a song from *Fiddler on the Roof*, however, remember that stress or injury may be even quicker ways to pump out home-brew opioids. The bottom line is this: Endorphins are so fundamental to normal physiological functioning that we don't have to seek them out at all. We probably surf life's pleasures and pains on a wave of endorphins already.

Test yourself by imagining the following: the sound of chalk squeaking across a blackboard; a pink rose sparkling with dew; embracing your favorite movie star; chocolate-mocha mousse cake; smashing your thumb with a hammer. If any of these thoughts sent the tiniest tingle down your spine, then you have have just proved the point.

The newborn's brain: registering every flash of color, caress, scent, and other stimuli vital to the

MAKING OF A MIND

KATHLEEN McAULIFFE

"Give me a child for the first six years of life and he'll be a servant of God till his last breath."

—Jesuit maxim

A servant of God or an agent of the devil; a law-abiding citizen or a juvenile delinquent. What the Jesuits knew, scientists are now rapidly confirming—that the mind of the child, in the very first years, even months, of life, is the crucible in which many of his deepest values are formed. It is then that much of what he may become—his talents, his interests, his abilities—are developed and directed. The experiences of his infancy and childhood will profoundly shape everything from his visual acuity to his comprehension of language and social behavior.

What underlies the child's receptivity to new information? And why do adults seem to lose this capacity as they gain more knowledge of the world around them? Why is it that the more we know, the less we *can* know?

Like a Zen koan, this paradox has led scientists down many paths of discovery. Some researchers are studying development processes in infants and children; others search the convoluted passages of the cortex for clues to how memory records learning experiences. Still others are studying the degree to which learning is hardwired—soldered along strict pathways in the brains of animals and humans.

Another phenomenon recently discovered: Long after patterns of personality have solidified, adults may tap fresh learning centers in the brain, new nerve connections that allow intellectual growth far after fourscore years.

Although much research remains to be done, two decades of investigation have yielded some dramatic—and in some instances unexpected—insights into the developing brain.

An infant's brain is not just a miniature replica of an adult's brain. Spanish neuroscientist José Delgado goes so far as to call the newborn "mindless." Although all the nerve cells a human may have are present at birth, the cerebral cortex, the gray matter that is the seat of higher intellect, barely functions. Surprisingly, the lower brain stem, the section that we have in common with reptiles and other primitive animals, dictates most of the newborn's actions.

This changes drastically in the days, weeks, and months after birth, when the cerebral cortex literally blossoms. During this burst of growth, individual brain cells send out shoots in all directions to produce a jungle of interconnecting nerve fibers. By the time a child is one year old, his brain is 50 percent of its adult weight; by the time he's six, it's 90 percent of its adult weight. And by puberty, when growth trails off, the brain will have quadrupled in size to the average adult weight of about three pounds.

How trillions of nerve cells manage to organize themselves into something as complex as the human brain remains a mystery. But this much is certain: As this integration and development proceeds, experiences can alter the brain's connections in a lasting, even irreversible way.

To demonstrate this, Colin Blakemore, professor of physiology at Oxford University, raised kittens in an environment that had no horizontal lines. Subsequently, they were able to "see" only vertical lines. Yet Blakemore had tested their vision just before the experiment began and found that the kittens had an equal number of cells that responded to each type of line.

Why had the cats become blind to horizontal lines? By the end of the experiment, Blakemore discovered that many more cells in the animals' brains responded to vertical lines than horizontal lines.

As the human brain develops, similar neurological processes probably occur. For example, during a test in which city-dwelling Eurocanadians were exposed to sets of all types of lines, they had the most difficulty seeing oblique lines. By comparison, the Cree Indians, from the east coast of James Bay, Quebec, perceived all orientations of lines equally well. The researchers Robert Annis and Barrie Frost, of Queens University, in Kingston, Ontario, attributed this difference in visual acuity to the subjects' environments. The Eurocanadians grow up in a world dominated by vertical and horizontal lines, whereas the Indians, who live in tepees in coniferous forests, are constantly exposed to surroundings with many different types of angles.

The sounds—as well as the sights—that an infant is exposed to can also influence his future abilities. The phonemes *rah* and *lah*, for instance, are absent from the Japanese language, and as might be expected, adults from that culture confuse English words containing *r* and *l*. (Hence the offering of steamed "lice" in sushi bars.) Tests reveal that Japanese adults are quite literally deaf to these sounds.

Infants, on the other hand, seem to readily distinguish between speech sounds. To test sensitivity to phonemes, researchers measure changes in the infants' heartbeats as different speech sounds are presented. If an infant grows familiar with one sound and then encounters a new sound, his heart rate increases. Although the evidence is still incomplete, tests of babies from linguistic backgrounds as varied as Guatemala's

Spanish culture, Kenya's Kikuyu-speaking area, and the United States all point to the same conclusion: Infants can clearly perceive phonemes present in any language.

The discovery that babies can make linguistic distinctions that adults cannot caused researchers to wonder at what age we lose this natural facility for language. To find out, Janet Werker, of Dalhousie University, in Nova Scotia, and Richard Tees, of Canada's University of British Columbia, began examining the language capabilities of English-speaking adolescents. Werker and Tees tested the subjects to see whether they could discriminate between two phonemes peculiar to the Hindi language.

"We anticipated that linguistic sensitivity declines at puberty, as psychologists have commonly assumed," Werker explains.

The results were surprising. Young adolescents could not make the distinction, nor could eight-year-olds, four-year-olds, or two-year-olds. Finally, Werker and Tees decided to test infants. They discovered that the ability to perceive foreign phonemes declines sharply by one year of age. "All the six-month-olds from English-speaking backgrounds could distinguish between the Hindi phonemes," Werker says. "But by ten to twelve months of age, the babies were unable to make this distinction."

The cutoff point, according to Werker, falls between eight and twelve months of age. If not exposed to Hindi by then people require a lot of learning to catch up. Werker found that English-speaking adults studying Hindi for the first time needed up to five years of training to learn the same phoneme distinctions any six-month-old baby can make. With further testing, Werker succeeded in tracking down one of the learning impairments that thwarted her older subjects. Although there is an audible difference, the adult mind cannot retain it long enough to remember it. "The auditory capabilities are there," Werker says. "It's the language-processing capabilities that have changed."

Even a brief introduction to language during the sensitive period can permanently alter our perception of speech. Werker and Tees tested English-speaking adults who could not speak or understand a word of Hindi, although they had been exposed to the language for the first year or two of life. They found that these adults had a major advantage in learning Hindi, compared with English-speaking adults who lacked such early exposure.

Werker and Tees's studies show that there is an advantage in learning language within the first year of life. But when it comes to learning a second tongue another study has revealed some startling findings: Adults actually master a second language more easily than school-age children do.

For four years Catherine Snow, of the Harvard Graduate School of Education, studied Americans who were learning Dutch for the first time while living in Holland. "When you control for such factors as access to native speakers and the daily exposure level to the language," Snow says, "adults acquire a large vocabulary and rules of grammar more quickly than children do. In my study, adults were found to be as good as children even in pronunciation, although many researchers contend that children have an advantage in speaking like natives."

Obviously not all learning stops when the sensitive period comes to a close. This observation has led some researchers to question the importance of early experiences. What would happen, for example, if a child did not hear a single word of any language until after one year of age? Would the propensity to speak be forfeited forever? Or could later exposure to language make up the deficit?

Because of the unethical nature of performing such an experiment on a child, we may never know the answer to that question. But some indications can be gleaned from animal studies of how early deprivation affects the development of social behavior.

"It's probably fair to say that if you want bright kids, you should cuddle them a lot when they're babies because that increases the number of neural connections."

In *An Outline of Psychoanalysis*, Sigmund Freud refers to "the common assertion that the child is psychologically the father of the man and that the events of his first years are of paramount importance for his whole subsequent development." At the University of Wisconsin Primate Laboratory, the pioneering studies of Harry and Margaret Harlow put this belief to the test on our closest living relative—the rhesus monkey.

"Our experiments indicate that there is a critical period somewhere between the third and sixth month of life," write the Harlows, "during which social deprivation, particularly deprivation of the company of [the monkey's] peers, irreversibly blights the animal's capacity for social adjustment."

When later returned to a colony in which there was ample opportunity for interacting with other animals, the experimental monkeys remained withdrawn, self-punishing, and compulsive. Most significantly, they grew up to be inept both as sexual partners and parents. The females never became impregnated unless artificially inseminated. We don't know whether humans, like Harlow's monkeys, must establish close bonds by a certain age or be forever doomed to social failure. But an ongoing longitudinal study, the Minnesota Preschool Project, offers the encouraging finding that emotionally neglected four-year-olds can still be helped to lead normal, happy lives. To rehabilitate the children, the teachers in the project provide them with the kind of intimate attention that is lacking at home.

Perhaps one of the Harlows' observations sheds light on why the project was successful: During the critical period for social development, the Harlows found that even a little bit of attention goes a long way. During the first year of life, for example, only 20 minutes of playtime a day with other monkeys was apparently sufficient for the animals to grow into well-adjusted adults. L. Alan Sroufe, codirector of the Minnesota Project, tells the story of one four-year-old boy who was constantly defiant—the kind of child who would hit the other children with a toy fire truck. Instead of sending him to a corner, the teacher was instructed to remove him from the group and place him with another teacher. The message they hoped to impart: We are rejecting your behavior, but we're not rejecting you. Within a few months, the antisocial little boy learned to change his behavior.

If children aren't exposed to positive social situations until adolescence, however, the prognosis is poor. Like any complex behavior, human socialization requires an elaborate series of learning steps. So by adolescence, the teenager who missed out on many key social experiences as a child has a tremendous handicap to overcome.

Researchers are finding that each stage of life demands different kinds of competencies. This may be why sensitive learning periods exist. "When a baby is born it has to do two things at the same time," says biochemist Steven Rose, of England's Open University. "One is that it has to survive as a baby. The second is that it has to grow into that very different organism, which is a child and then finally an adult. And it is not simply the case that everything the baby does is a miniature version of what we see in the adult."

For example, the rooting reflex, which enables the baby to suckle, is not a preliminary form of chewing: There's a transitional period in which the child must begin eating solid foods. And then other sorts of skills become necessary—the child must learn to walk, talk, form friendships, and when adulthood is reached, find a sexual partner. "But the child does not have to know all that at the beginning," Rose says. "So sensitive periods are necessary because we have to know how to do certain things at certain times during development."

During the course of a sensory system's development, several sensitive periods occur. In the case of human vision, for example, depth perception usually emerges by two months of age and after that remains relatively stable. But it takes the first five years of life to acquire the adult level of visual acuity that allows us to see fine details. And during that prolonged period, we are vulnerable to many developmental problems that can cause this process to go awry. For example, a drooping lid or an eye covered by a cataract—virtually anything that obstructs vision in one of the child's eyes for as few as seven days—can lead to a permanent blurring of sight. This condition, known as amblyopia is one of the most common ophthalmological disorders. Treatment works only if carried out within the sensitive period, before the final organization of certain cells in the visual cortex becomes fixed. After five years of age, no amount of visual stimulation is likely to reorganize the connections laid down when the young nervous system was developing.

Like molten plastic, the nervous system is, at its inception, highly pliable. But it quickly settles into a rigid cast—one that has been shaped by experience. Just what neurological events set the mold is not known. Some suggestive findings, however, come from the research of John Cronly-Dillon, a professor of ophthalmic optics at the University of Manchester Institute of Science and Technology, in England.

Working with colleague Gary Perry, Cronly-Dillon studied growth activity in the visual cortex of rat pups reared under normal light conditions. To measure growth, researchers monitored the rate at which certain cells synthesized tubulin, a protein vital for forming and maintaining nerve connections. The researchers found that tubulin production in the visual cortex remained at a low level until day 13, which marks the onset of the sensitive period for visual learning. It coincides with the moment when the animal first opens its eyes. At that time, tubulin production soars, indicating a rise in growth activity.

Cronly-Dillon and Perry found that the rat's visual cortex continues to grow for the next week and then declines. By the end of the critical period, when the pup is roughly five weeks old, tubulin production drops to the level attained before the eyes open.

To Cronly-Dillon the surplus of tubulin at the beginning of the critical period and its subsequent cutback have profound implications. "It means that an uncommonly large number of nerve connections can exist at the peak of the critical period, but only a small fraction of them will be maintained at the end," he says. "So the question, of course, is which nerve connections will be kept?"

If Cronly-Dillon is correct, experience probably stabilizes those connections most often used during the sensitive period. "So by definition," he says, "what remains is most critical for survival."

Cronly-Dillon's work elaborates on a theory Spanish neurophysiologist Ramon Y Cajal advanced at the turn of the century. According to this view, which has been gaining broader acceptance in recent times, brain development resembles natural selection. Just as the forces of natural selection ensure the survival of the fittest, so do similar forces preserve the most useful brain circuits.

The beauty of this model is that it could explain why the brain is as exquisitely adapted to its immediate surroundings, just as the mouthparts of insects are so perfectly matched to the sexual organs of the flowers they pollinate. The textures, shapes, sounds, and odors we perceive best may have left their imprint years ago in the neural circuitry of the developing mind.

There is also a certain economic appeal to this outlook: Why, for example, should Japanese adults keep active a neural circuit that permits the distinction between *r* and *l* sounds when neither of these linguistic components is present in their native tongue?

Yet another economic advantage of the theory is that it would explain how nature can forge something as intricate as the brain out of a relatively limited amount of genetic material. "It looks as though what genetics does is *sort of* make a brain," Blakemore says. "We only have about one hundred thousand genes—and that's to make an entire body. Yet the brain alone has trillions of nerve cells, each one forming as many as ten thousand connections with its neighbors. So imagine the difficulty of trying to encode every step of the wiring process in our DNA."

This vast discrepancy between genes and connections, according to Blakemore, can be overcome by encoding in the DNA the specifications for a "rough brain." "Everything gets roughly laid down in place," Blakemore says. "But the wiring of the young nervous system is far too rich and diffuse. So the brain overconnects and then uses a selection process to fine-tune the system."

The brain of an eight-month-old human fetus is actually estimated to have two to three times more nerve cells than an adult brain does. Just before birth, there is a massive death of unnecessary brain cells, a process that continues through early childhood and then levels off. Presumably many nerve connections that fall into disuse vanish. But that is only part of the selection process—and possibly a small part at that.

According to Blakemore, many neural circuits remain in place but cease to function after a certain age. "I would venture a guess," he says, "that as many as ninety percent of the connections you see in the adult brain are nonfunctional. The time when circuits can be switched on or off probably varies for different parts of the cerebral cortex—depending on what functions they control—and would coincide with the sensitive period of learning. Once the on–off switch becomes frozen, the sensitive period is over."

This doesn't mean, however, that new circuits can't grow. There appears to be a fine-tuning of perception coinciding with these developmental events. And as the brain becomes a finer sieve, filtering out all but a limited amount of sensory input, its strategy for storing information appears to change.

"Studies indicate that as many as fifty percent of very young children recall things in pictures," says biochemist Rose. "And by the time we're about four or five, we tend to lose our eidetic [photographic] memory and develop sequential methods of recall."

To Rose, who is studying the neurological mechanisms that underlie learning, this shift in memory process may have an intriguing logic. "To be a highly adaptable organism like man, capable of living in a lot of different environments, one must start out with a brain that takes in everything," Rose explains. "And as you develop, you select what is important and what is not important to remember. If you went on remembering absolutely everything, it would be disastrous."

The Russian neurologist A. R. Luria had a patient cursed with such a memory—the man could describe rooms he'd been in years before, pieces of conversations he'd overheard. His memory became such an impediment that he could not hold even a clerk's job; while listening to instructions, so many associations for each word would arise that he couldn't focus on what was being said. The only position he could manage was as a memory man in a theatrical company.

"The crucial thing then," Rose says, "is that you must learn what to *forget*."

Some components of the brain, however, must retain their plasticity into adulthood—otherwise, no further learning would be possible, says neuroscientist Bill Greenough, of the University of Illinois, at Urbana-Champaign. While the adult brain cannot generate new brain cells, Greenough has uncovered evidence that it does continue to generate new *nerve connections*. But as the brain ages, the rate at which it produces these connections slows.

If the young brain can be likened to a sapling sprouting shoots in all directions, then the adult brain is more akin to a tree, whose growth is confined primarily to budding regions. "In the mature brain," Greenough says, "neural connections appear to pop up systematically, precisely where they're needed."

Early experience, then, provides the foundation on which all subsequent knowledge and skills build. "That's why it's extraordinarily difficult to change certain aspects of personality as an adult," says neuroscientist Jonathan Winson, of Rockefeller University. "Psychiatrists have an expression: 'Insight is wonderful, but the psyche fights back.' Unfortunately, one of the drawbacks of critical-period learning is that a lot of misconceptions and unreasonable fears can become frozen in our minds during this very vulnerable period in our development."

Greenough acknowledges that the system isn't perfect; nevertheless, it works to our advantage because you can't build on a wobbly nervous system. "You've got to know who your mother is, and you've got to have perceptual skills," he explains. "These and other types of learning have to jell quickly, or all further development would halt."

Can these insights into the developing brain help educators to devise new strategies for teaching?

"We're a very long way from being able to apply the work of neurobiologists to what chalk-faced teachers are trying to do," says Open University's Rose.

But he can see the rough outline of a new relationship between neurobiology and education, which excites him. "We can now say with considerable certainty that there are important advantages to growing up in an enriched environment," he says. "That does not mean that you should be teaching three-year-olds Einstein's theory of relativity on the grounds that you will be turning them into geniuses later on. But it's probably fair to say that if you want bright kids, you should cuddle them a lot as babies because that increases the number of neural connections produced in the brain."

Although early learning tends to overshadow the importance of later experience, mental development never ceases. Recent studies indicate that our intellectual abilities continue to expand well into our eighties, provided the brain has not been injured or diseased. Most crucial for maintaining mental vigor, according to Greenough, is staying active and taking on new challenges. In his rat studies, he found that lack of stimulation—much more than age—was the factor that limited the formation of new neural connections in the adult brain.

As long as we don't isolate ourselves as we grow older, one very important type of mental faculty may even improve. Called crystallized intelligence, this ability allows us to draw on the store of accumulated knowledge to provide alternate solutions to complicated problems. Analyzing complex political or military strategies, for example, would exploit crystallized intelligence.

There is a danger in believing that because the brain's anatomical boundaries are roughly established early in life, all mental capabilities are restricted, too. "Intelligence is not something static that can be pinned down with an I.Q. test like butterflies on a sheet of cardboard," says Rose. "It is a constant interplay between internal processes and external forces."

To be sure, many types of learning do favor youth. As violinist Isaac Stern says, "If you haven't begun playing violin by age eight, you'll never be great." But in the opinion of Cronly-Dillon, the best time for learning other types of skills may be much later in life. Although he will not elaborate on this until further studies are done, he believes we may even have sensitive periods with very late onsets. "There's a real need," Cronly-Dillon says, "to define all the different types of sensitive periods so that education can take advantage of biological optimums."

It is said that the ability to learn in later life depends on the retention of childlike innocence. "This old saw," insists Cronly-Dillon, "could have a neurological basis."

WINTER BLUES

Richard Laliberte

RICHARD LALIBERTE *is a writer based in New York City.*

During my last winter in North Dakota, I nearly snapped. Because I grew up there, the cold, darkness and isolation brought on by this nether season were entirely familiar; but that year, 1983, was distinctive. During one 10-day stretch, temperatures never got above zero with wind chills as low as 100 degrees below. My car died. My friends' cars died. I spent a lot of time alone in my dark, virtually windowless studio apartment.

Finally, one Saturday in February there was a heat wave—temperatures in the 20s. People joyously got out and about. That afternoon a huge cloud of snow hit suddenly and the mercury plunged. Twenty-three people died throughout the area, including a man, his son and two other boys whose car stalled on a drift-prone road near the airport.

By March, I hated most of the other forces at work in my world: my love life, my financial situation, my professional status. But mostly, I was sick of winter.

Physical rigors aggravated by general dissatisfactions: That was how I'd always interpreted the toll on my psyche that year. I didn't know it then, but during this winter of discontent researchers at the National Institute of Mental Health (NIMH) in Bethesda, Maryland, were in the midst of studies establishing a relationship between seasons and moods. They went on to define a condition they called seasonal affective disorder, or SAD. When I heard about it, I wondered: Could that have been my problem?

Mood-Changing Hormone

The influence of the seasons on health has been observed for ages. Hippocrates noted that "Some are well or ill adapted to summer, others are well or ill adapted to winter." Such notions were generally pooh-poohed by modern medicine until the mid-1980s. Now research indicates that most of us experience at least some degree of seasonal change. In a 1987 telephone survey of 416 adults in Montgomery County, Maryland, 92 percent of the respondents reported varying degrees of seasonal change in mood and behavior. Dr. Norman Rosenthal, NIMH director of seasonal studies and author of *Seasons of the Mind: Why You Get the Winter Blues & What You Can Do About It* (Bantam, 1989), says that up to a quarter of the population may suffer from SAD or a mild variation of it.

"To me, that's a lot," he says—more than he and his colleagues had expected. "If you had told me when we started our research that a quarter of the population was affected, I would have told you it was nonsense."

The discovery—or rediscovery—of seasonal influences on people began with animal research. The seasons have long been known to affect animals profoundly: Many are fertile only during certain times of the year. Light, it seems, triggers seasonal reproductive changes through the hormone melatonin. Every night, melatonin is secreted into the bloodstream by the pea-size pineal gland at the base of the brain. This secretion tapers off at dawn, marking the duration of darkness and providing animals with a seasonal time cue.

How light suppresses secretion and whether melatonin causes similar cues in people are unclear, but in 1982 Dr. Alfred Lewy of NIMH made a crucial discovery: Melatonin secretion in humans also can be suppressed by light. This, and the fact that information from the eye travels along nerve pathways to the hypothalamus—part of the limbic system that regulates emotions and basic body functions—led NIMH researchers to try using bright lights to treat a man named Herb Kern.

Kern came to NIMH bearing a number of notebooks in which he'd kept scrupulous track of regular seasonal fluctuations in his mood and behavior going back some 15 years. He figured light had something to do with his emotional swings and asked NIMH researchers for help. They suggested he artificially lengthen his winter day by six hours using a two-by-four-foot box that emitted high-intensity fluorescent light softened by a diffusing screen.

The results were dramatic. Kern's mood improved noticeably within three days. Similarly dramatic results were also being achieved by Dr. Peter S. Mueller, a psychologist in private practice in Princeton, New Jersey, who pioneered research into the relationship between seasons and energy levels. These successes led to controlled experiments, both in the United States and abroad, with larger groups of people who reported seasonal disturbances in mood, eating habits, sleeping patterns or energy levels—and there was no shortage of volunteers. In fact, researchers were surprised not only by the number of people who came to them for experimental light treatment, but by the similarity of their conditions.

Because of the consistency of both symptoms and light-treatment results, a version of SAD was accepted with remarkable speed into the bible of psychology, the *Diagnostic and Statistical Manual of Mental Disorders* (American Psychiatric Press). SAD is now known well enough to prompt a New England liquor store to offer sufferers relief with a "SAD sale." SAD is one of the fastest-growing areas of biomedical research, with a lot of questions still open, such as what type of light therapy works best, whether alternative treatments exist and how many people could benefit from treatment. Back in my hometown, the disorder is now treated at Fargo Clinic.

The Urge to Hibernate

The classic symptoms often begin in the fall with a feeling of anxiety over the approaching winter. During winter months, sufferers typically feel like hibernating. They become lethargic, spend more time sleeping, crave sweet and starchy foods, gain weight, withdraw from other people and lose interest in sex. A less common summer syndrome brings opposite symptoms in many cases: insomnia and loss of appetite and weight. (Sex drive falls in summer too.) SAD is four times as likely to show up in women. The reason for this isn't clear, but the association of depression with premenstrual syndrome and the existence of postpartum depression suggest that endocrine changes may influence mood.

NIMH researchers estimate that in the United States, 6 percent of us—about 10 million people—suffer from full-blown SAD. These are the people affected most severely and explicitly, the hibernators who find seasonal change so debilitating that it can affect jobs and relationships. They suffer from the disorder defined in the *Diagnostic and Statistical Manual*, which specifies the conditions necessary for a seasonal depression to be clinically identified. Among them:

- Depression occurs within a particular 60-day period—say, from the beginning of October to the end of November.
- Full remissions also occur within a particular 60-day period—say, mid-February to mid-April.
- These changes have happened at least three times in three separate years, two of which were consecutive.
- Seasonal episodes outnumber nonseasonal episodes by more than three to one.
- There haven't been any extenuating seasonal stresses, such as being unemployed every winter.

The scientists who conducted the Maryland survey, led by Dr. Siegfried Kasper of the University of Bonn, West Germany, say that clinical SAD represents the extreme end of a spectrum of seasonality affecting a large percentage of the population. Within that spectrum are people who don't meet the clinical criteria for SAD but notice the same symptoms to a lesser degree. Their seasonal doldrums may make them feel less energetic, less efficient and less sociable, but they are able to work around their difficulties, consider themselves normal and don't seek treatment.

In the Kasper study, 27 percent of the respondents said seasonal changes were a problem for them—a figure close to that of a similar study by Dr. Michael Terman, director of the light-therapy unit at New York State Psychiatric Institute, Columbia-Presbyterian Medical Center, in New York City. Both Kasper and Terman say the evidence suggests that the spectrum of seasonality also includes a larger segment of people who find seasonal change less troublesome, but experience it nonetheless.

"What this means," Terman says, "is that seasonality is the norm, not the exception."

One way to separate the different levels of severity is with a survey called the Seasonal Pattern Assessment Questionnaire, or SPAQ. It asks how your sleep, social activity, mood, weight, appetite and energy level change throughout the year. A low score could mean your depression is caused by something else—a very real possibility.

"There are only so many different behavioral manifestations of depression, but there can be many different underlying mechanisms," says psychiatrist Robert N. Moreines, coauthor of *Light Up Your Blues: Understanding and Overcoming Seasonal Affective Disorders* (Berkley, 1989), who treats SAD patients at Fair Oaks Hospital in Summit, New Jersey.

Adds Terman: "If you had one bad year in 10, there could be a hundred different reasons for it."

There is no laboratory test for SAD; diagnosis is based solely on case history. The SPAQ survey helps determine whether you experience seasonal changes in mood and behavior that are consistent and sustained from year to year. If you do, you might be helped by light therapy.

Under the Lights

Generally, treatment consists of sitting, often in one's own home, at a specified distance from the front of a metal box containing bright fluorescent lights. The illumination from a typical light box, which costs around $450, is about five times brighter than that found in a well-lit room. How much time is spent in front of the box depends on the person, the time of year and the geographic location. Since northern latitudes receive less light in winter, more supplementary light may be needed. A typical person with SAD in the northern United States may need as little as half an hour of light therapy a day in mid-September, six hours a day or more in January and February. There's some debate about the effectiveness of shorter treatments with brighter light and about what time of day is best.

"The procedure is innocuous," says Terman, "and you know quickly if it's working. Within seven to 10 days, you know unambiguously if the symptoms have gone away." Most patients improve significantly within two to four days.

There are other ways to treat depression, and often patients undergoing light therapy have tried other methods, or may find them beneficial. Light therapy can be applied in conjunction with psychotherapy or it can complement the use of antidepressant medication, often allowing the patient to take lower drug dosages.

Knowing all this about SAD, I still wondered if I had a problem. My history gave me red herrings instead of real clues. After that memorably depressing winter, I accepted a job in New York, where there's a bit more light in winter and the incidence of SAD is slightly lower. But I was living again in a dark apartment, working in a dark office—and my job depressed me more than winter ever did. About the time I got a job where I was happy, I also moved into a much brighter apartment. I didn't know if the seasons or other forces were at work.

I took the SPAQ survey. My score fell at the low end of the range, well below the numbers associated with even a subsyndromal disorder. Clearly, I don't have SAD, or even a diagnosable case of the winter blues, because my experiences with the seasons provide few consistent or sustained patterns. That seemed somehow unsatisfactory, because I've always felt my mood take an introspective turn in fall and winter.

Both Rosenthal and Moreines say that this seasonal introspection, even my interest in the subject, suggests a mild syndrome. Part of me wants to be affected by the seasons, to feel a cosmic kinship with nature—a relationship patients in light therapy often find moving, Terman says. "Many people experience a deep sense of surprise that such a simple environmental manipulation can affect them to the core," he explains. "We're not used to being so deeply tied to our environment."

Food, Mood, and Behavior

Lesley Barton

Lesley Barton is a free-lance writer specializing in the sciences. She has more than 12 years of experience in medical and biological research laboratories.

You missed breakfast, you've been surviving on coffee all morning, and now it's time to meet someone for lunch. This is an important new client and you want her business. You've arranged to have lunch at a nearby restaurant specializing in Italian food. When you arrive, the tantalizing odors make you realize you are incredibly hungry. You start munching on homemade bread and order a tempting pasta dish topped with garlic sausage and served with a glass of excellent Italian wine. Your hunger pangs are now under control and the small talk is over. You and your client are getting down to business. But even though you know you prepared well for this meeting, you don't really feel in control. You're too relaxed, almost groggy. You don't feel alert and you're missing details. Your client has not been hooked, and now you're afraid the deal might not go through.

Or perhaps you are to give an after-dinner talk but a short nap sounds like a better idea. Or you're responsible for a late-afternoon presentation but you've just run out of energy. Do any of these situations sound familiar? If they do, they could easily be avoided. Your relaxed manner and inattentiveness could very well be related to what you just ate or when you had your last meal.

Foods can influence the production and function of chemicals in the brain. Certain chemicals are directly involved in determining mood, mental energy, performance, and behavior. Some foods will increase your mental alertness, motivation, and energy levels. The same foods under certain conditions will increase tension and irritability. Others act as natural tranquilizers, making you sluggish and sleepy.

Psychologists and nutritionists alike have begun using diet to improve their patients' performance and sense of well-being. Data from her own research prompted Judith Wurtman, a nutrition counselor and biochemist at the Massachusetts Institute of Technology, to write the book *Managing Your Mind and Mood Through Food.* In it she claims you can "learn how to use food to shift at will from a state of mind that works against you into one that works for you." This can be done without days or weeks of preconditioning. "Your brain chemistry reacts quickly the first and every time you eat foods," Wurtman says. From her own experience Wurtman claims she often feels distracted and irritable by 4:30 p.m. But if she eats a small box of Cheerios (without milk), then within 15 minutes she is back on track and able to continue working until 7 or 7:30 p.m.

This may sound just a little too simple to be true. However, an understanding of how chemicals in the brain work will help to explain. Many of the foods we eat supply us with various proteins. Within the body, protein is broken down into its components known as amino acids, and some of these amino acids are used to make brain chemicals known as neurotransmitters. "Too many of the neurotransmitters in certain brain areas can result in an elated mood," says Fathy Messiha, a professor of pharmacology at the University of North Dakota. "A deficiency or too few of them can cause mood swings toward depression."

Three brain chemicals are dopamine, norepinephrine, and serotonin. One amino acid, tyrosine, is important in making dopamine and norepinephrine, and another—tryptophan—is important in making serotonin. "Dopamine and norepinephrine are associated with increased muscle activity, more aggressive behavior, and your emotional states," Messiha says. "Serotonin is associated with sleep and calmness."

However, tyrosine and tryptophan are not available to the brain in equal amounts at all times. "What you eat is not necessarily going to go to the brain," says Messiha. "Mother Nature provides us with a barrier to protect us from circulating chemicals." Although both these amino acids are supplied by eating protein, tyrosine is available in much larger amounts. The various pathways that these amino acids must use to get to the brain are also used by other amino acids. Because tryptophan is less plentiful, less of it is able to get to the brain. As a result, less serotonin, the calming chemical, is produced.

So how do we increase the serotonin levels in our brains? It's simple. Just eat carbohydrates without protein. Candies, jams, breads, and pastas trigger the release of insulin, which not only regulates blood-sugar levels but also keeps the amino acids moving through the bloodstream so they can hook up with various cells throughout the body. Tryptophan levels are not affected by insulin, and soon there is more tryptophan relative to other amino acids in the bloodstream. Now it is able to enter the brain, where it can be converted to serotonin—which can provide a calming effect. Therefore, according to Wurtman, by eating foods high in

Reprinted with permission from *USAir Magazine*, July 1990, pp. 82, 84-85. *USAir Magazine*, published by Pace Communications, Inc., Greenboro, North Carolina.

20th, as the period of formal education lengthened and the transition to adulthood was increasingly delayed. A stage called youth took on its modern meaning only a few decades ago, as growing numbers of young people, after leaving high school and before marrying or making occupational choices, opted for a period of time to explore various life roles.

It was only a few decades ago, too, that middle age became identified, largely a reflection of the historically changing rhythm of events in the family cycle. With fewer children per family, and with births spaced closer together, middle age became defined as the time when children grow up and leave the parents' home. In turn, as the concept of retirement took hold, old age came to be regarded as the time following retirement from the labor force. It was usually perceived as a distinct period marked by the right to lead a life of leisure, declining physical and intellectual vigor, social disengagement and, often, isolation and desolation.

Life periods were closely associated with chronological age, even though age lines were seldom sharply drawn.

But the distinctions between life periods are blurring in today's society. The most dramatic evidence, perhaps, is the appearance of the so-called "young-old." It is a recent historical phenomenon that a very large group of retirees and their spouses are healthy and vigorous, relatively well-off financially, well-integrated into the lives of their families and communities and politically active. The term "young-old" is becoming part of everyday parlance, and it refers not to a particular age but to health and social characteristics. A young-old person may be 55 or 85. The term represents the social reality that the line between middle age and old age is no longer clear. What was once considered old age now characterizes only that minority of older persons who have been called the "old-old," that particularly vulnerable group who often are in need of special support and special care.

When, then, does old age now begin? The usual view has been that it starts at 65, when most people retire. But in the United States today the majority begin to take their Social Security retirement benefits at 62 or 63; and at ages 55 to 64 fewer than three of every four men are in the labor force. At the same time, with continued good health, some people are staying at work, full-time or part-time, into their 80s. So age 65 and retirement are no longer clear dividers between middle age and old age.

Alternatively, old age is often said to begin when poor health creates a major limitation on the activities of everyday life. Yet in a 1981 survey, half of all people 75 to 84 reported no such health limitations. Even in the very oldest group, those older than 85, more than a third reported no limitations due to health, and another one-third reported minor limitations; only one in three said they were unable to carry out any of their everyday activities. So health status is also becoming a poor age marker.

It is not only in the second half of life that the blurring of life periods can be seen. Adults of all ages are experiencing changes in the traditional rhythm and timing of events of the life cycle. More men and women marry, divorce, remarry and divorce again up through their 70s. More stay single. More women have their first child before they are 15, and more do so after 35. The result is that people are becoming grandparents for the first time at ages ranging from 35 to 75. More women, but also increasing numbers of men, raise children in two-parent, then one-parent, then two-parent households. More women, but also increasing numbers of men, exit and reenter school, enter and reenter the work force and undertake second and third careers up through their 70s. It therefore becomes difficult to distinguish the young, the middle-aged and the young-old—either in terms of major life events or the ages at which those events occur.

MORE MEN AND WOMEN MARRY, DIVORCE, REMARRY AND DIVORCE AGAIN UP THROUGH THEIR 70S.

The line between adolescence and adulthood is also being obscured. The traditional transitions into adulthood and the social competencies they implied—full-time jobs, marriage and parenthood—are disappearing as markers of social age. For some men and women, the entry into a job or profession is being delayed to age 30 as education is prolonged. For others, entry into the work force occurs at 16 or 17. Not only are there more teenage pregnancies but also more teenage women who are mothering their children. All this adds up to what has been aptly called "the fluid life cycle."

This is not to deny that our society still recognizes differences between adolescents, young people and old people, and that people still relate to each other accordingly. Yet we are less sure today where to place the punctuation marks in the life line and just what those punctuation marks should be. All across adulthood, age has become a poor predictor of the timing of life events, just as it is a poor predictor of health, work status, family status, interests, preoccupations and needs. We have conflicting images rather than stereotypes of age: the 70-

year-old in a wheelchair, but also the 70-year-old on the tennis court; the 18-year-old who is married and supporting a family, but also the 18-year-old college student who brings his laundry home to his mother each week.

Difference among individuals, multiple images of age groups and inconsistencies in age norms were surely present in earlier periods of our history, but as our society has become more complex, the irregularities have become increasingly a part of the social reality.

These trends are reflected in public perceptions, too. Although systematic research is sparse, there are a few studies that show a diminishing public consensus about the periods of life and their markers. In the early 1960s, for instance, a group of middle-class, middle-aged people were asked about the "best" ages for life transitions (such as completing school, marrying, retiring) and the ages they associated with such phrases as "a young man," "an old woman" and "when a man (or woman) has the most responsibilities." When the same questions were asked of a similar group of people two decades later, the earlier consensus on every item of the questionnaire had disappeared. In the first study, nearly 90 percent had replied that the best age for a woman to marry was between 19 and 24; in the repeat study, only 40 percent gave this answer. In the first study, "a young man" was said to be a man between 18 and 22; in the repeat study, "a young man" was anywhere from 18 to 40. These findings are based on a very small study, but they illustrate how public views are changing.

In some respects, the line between childhood and adulthood is also fading. It is a frequent comment that childhood as we once knew it is disappearing. Increasingly children and adults have the same preferences in styles of dress, forms of language, games and television shows. Children know more about once-taboo topics such as sex, drugs, alcoholism, suicide and nuclear war. There is more adult-like sexual behavior among children, and more adult-like crime. At the same time, with the pressures for achievement rising, we have witnessed the advent of "the hurried child" and "the harried child."

We have also become accustomed to the descriptions of today's adults as narcissistic, self-interested and self-indulgent. Yuppies are described in the mass media as the pace-setters. While they work hard to get ahead, they are portrayed as more materialistic even than the "me" generation that preceded them, interested primarily in making money and in buying the "right" cars, the "best" housing and the most expensive gourmet foods. Overall, today's adults have fewer lasting marriages, fewer lasting commitments to work or community roles, more uncontrolled expressions of emotion, a greater sense of powerlessness—in short, more childlike behavior.

This picture may be somewhat overdrawn. Both children and adults are continually exhorted to "act your age," and they seldom misunderstand what that means. Yet the expectations of appropriate behavior for children and adults are certainly less differentiated than they once were. We are less sure of what intellectual and social competencies to expect of children—not only because some children are teaching their teachers how to use computers, but also because so many children are streetwise by age 8 and so many others, in the wake of divorce, are the confidantes of their parents by age 12.

Some observers attribute the blurring of childhood and adulthood primarily to the effects of television, which illuminates the total culture and reveals the secrets that adults have traditionally withheld from children. But it is not only television. A report in *The New York Times* underlines the fact that children are being socialized in new ways today by parents, schools, churches and peer groups as well. The Girl Scouts of the U.S.A., according to the *Times* article, had decided finally to admit 5-year-olds. The national executive director was quoted as saying, "The decision to admit five-year-olds reflects the change in the American labor market. Women are working for part or all of their adult lives now. The possibilities are limitless but you need to prepare. So we think six is not too early to learn about career opportunities, and we also think that girls need to learn about making decisions. When you're five, you're not too young."

The blurring of traditional life periods does not mean that age norms are disappearing altogether. We still have our regulations about the ages at which children enter and exit from school, when people can marry without the consent of parents, when they are eligible for Social Security benefits. And less formal norms are still operating. Someone who moves to the Sun Belt to lead a life of leisure is socially approved if he is 70, but not if he is 30. An unmarried mother meets with greater disapproval if she is 15 than if she is 35. A couple in their 40s who decide to have another child are criticized

SOMEONE WHO MOVES TO THE SUN BELT TO LEAD A LIFE OF LEISURE IS SOCIALLY APPROVED IF HE'S 70, BUT NOT IF HE IS 30.

for embarrassing their adolescent children. At the door of a discotheque a young person who cannot give proof of being "old enough" may be refused admission, while inside a gray-haired man who dances like those he calls youngsters meets the raised eyebrows and mocking remarks of the other dancers. As in these examples, expectations regarding age-appropriate behavior still form an elaborate and pervasive system of norms, expectations that are woven into the cultural fabric.

Both legal and cultural age norms are mirrored in the ways people behave and the ways they think about their own lives. Today, as in the past, most people by the time they are adolescents develop a set of anticipations of the normal, expectable life cycle: expectations of what the major life events and turning points will be and when they should occur. People internalize a social clock that tells them if they are on time or not.

Although the actual timing of life events for both women and men has always been influenced by various life contingencies, the norms and the actual occurrences have been closely connected. It may be less true today, but most people still try to marry or have a child or make a job change when they think they have reached the "right" age. They can still easily report whether they were early, late or on time with regard to one life event after another. "I married early," we hear, or "I had a late start because I served in Vietnam."

The life events that occur on time do not usually precipitate life crises, for they have been anticipated and rehearsed. The so-called "empty nest," for instance, is not itself stressful for most middle-aged parents. Instead, it is when children do not leave home at the appropriate time that stress occurs in both the parent and the child. For most older men, if it does not occur earlier than planned, retirement is taken in stride as a normal, expectable event. Widowhood is less often a crisis if it occurs at 65 rather than at 40.

It is the events that upset the expected sequence and rhythm of the life cycle that cause problems—as when the death of a parent comes during one's adolescence rather than in middle age; when marriage is delayed too long; when the birth of a child comes too early; when occupational achievement is slowed; when the empty nest, grandparenthood, retirement, major illness or widowhood occurs "out of sync." Traditional timetables still operate.

For the many reasons suggested earlier, the traditional time schedules do not in today's society produce the regularities anticipated by adolescents or young adults. For many men and women, to be out of sync may have lost some of its importance, but for others, the social clocks have not stopped ticking. The incongruities between the traditional norms and the fluid life cycle represent new freedoms for many people; for other people, new uncertainties and strains.

There is still another reality to be reckoned with. Some timetables are losing their significance, but others are more compelling than ever. A young man may feel he is a failure if he has not "made it" in his corporation by the time he is 35. A young woman may delay marriage because of her career, but then hurry to catch up with parenthood. The same young woman may feel under pressure to marry, bear a child and establish herself in a career all within a five-year period—even though she knows she is likely to live to 85.

Sometimes both traditional and nontraditional views are in conflict in the mind of the same person. The young woman who deliberately delays marriage may be the same woman who worries that she has lost status because she is not married by 25. A middle-aged man starts a second family, but feels compelled to justify himself by explaining that he expects to live to see his new children reach adulthood. Or an old person reports that because he did not expect to live so long, he is now unprepared to take on the "new ways" of some of his peers. Some people live in new ways, but continue to think in old ways.

IT IS WHEN CHILDREN DO NOT LEAVE HOME AT THE APPROPRIATE TIME THAT STRESS OCCURS IN BOTH PARENT AND CHILD.

Given such complications, shall we say that individuals are paying less or more attention to age as a prod or a brake upon their behavior? That age consciousness is decreasing or increasing? Whether or not historical change is occurring, it is fair to say that one's own age remains crucial to every individual, all the way from early childhood through advanced old age. A person uses age as a guide in accommodating to others, in giving meaning to the life course, and in contemplating the time that is past and the time that remains.

In sum, there are multiple levels of social and psychological reality based on social age, and in modern societies, on calendar age as the marker of social age. The complexities are no fewer for the individual than for society at large.

DON'T ACT YOUR AGE!

Life stages no longer roll forward in a cruel numbers game

Carol Tavris, Ph.D.

Carol Tavris *is a social psychologist and writer, and author of* Anger: The Misunderstood Emotion.

A friend of mine has just had her first baby. Not news, exactly. It's not even news that she's 45 years old. The news is it's not news that a 45-year-old woman has just had her first baby.

Another friend, age 32, has decided to abandon the pursuit of matrimony and remodel her kitchen instead. The news is that her parents and friends don't think she's weird. They're giving her a Not-Wedding party.

It used to be that all of us knew what we were supposed to be doing at certain ages. The "feminine clock" dictated that women married in their early 20s, had a couple of kids by 30 (formerly the baby deadline), maybe went back to work in their 40s, came down with the empty nest blues in their 50s, and faded into grandmotherhood in their 60s. The "masculine clock" ticked along as men marched up the career ladder, registering their promotions and salaries with notches at each decade.

Nowadays, many women are following the masculine clock; many men are resetting their schedules; and huge numbers of both sexes have stopped telling time altogether. This development is both good news and bad.

The good news is that people are no longer expected to march in lock step through the decades of life, making changes on schedule. "No one is doing things on time anymore," says Dr. Nancy Schlossberg, an adult development expert at the University of Maryland, and the author of the forthcoming *Overwhelmed: Coping with Life's Ups and Downs* (Lexington Books). "Our lives are much too irregular and unpredictable. In my classes I've seen women who were first-time mothers at 43 and those who had their first baby at 17. I just met a woman who is newly married—at age 65. She quit her job, and with her husband is traveling around on their yacht writing articles. You can bet she won't be having an age-65 retirement crisis. She's having too much fun."

The bad news is that without timetables, many people are confused about what they're "supposed" to be doing in their 20s, 30s, 40s and beyond. They have confused *age* (a biological matter) with *stage* (a social matter). Women ask: "When is the best time to have children—before or after I've started working?" Men want to know: "Since I can't make up my mind about marriage, work, children and buying a dog, is it possible I'm having a midlife crisis even though I'm only 32?"

Although confusion can be unsettling, I prefer it to the imposed phoniness of the "life stage" theories of personal development. Actually, I date my dislike of stage theories to my childhood. My parents used to keep Gesell's *The First Five Years of Life* and *The Child From Five to Ten* on the highest shelf of their library (right next to Rabelais), and I *knew* they were consulting these volumes at regular intervals to check on my progress. I was

NO ONE IS DOING THINGS ON TIME ANYMORE.

indignant. For one thing, a 9¾-year-old person finds it humiliating to be lumped with six-year-olds. For another, I was sure I wasn't measuring up, though what I was supposed to be measuring up to I never knew.

I survived Gesell's stages only to find myself, as a college student in the '60s, assigned to read Erik Erikson's theory of the eight stages of man. Every few years in childhood, and then every 10 years or so after, Erikson said, people have a special psychological crisis to resolve and overcome.

The infant must learn to trust, or will forever mistrust the world. The toddler must develop a sense of autonomy and independence, without succumbing to shame and doubt. The school-aged child must acquire competence at schoolwork, or will risk lifelong feelings of inferiority. Teenagers, naturally, must overcome the famous "identity crisis," or they will wallow in "role confusion" and aimlessness. Once you have your identity, you must learn to share it; if you don't master this "intimacy crisis," you might become lonely and isolated. To Erikson, you're never home free. Older adults face the crises of stagnation versus generativity, and, in old age, "ego integrity" versus despair.

It turned out, of course, that Erikson meant the ages of "man" literally, but none of us knew that in those days. We female students all protested that our stages were out of order—but that was just further evidence, our instructor said, of how deviant, peculiar and irritating women are. Erikson's theory, he said, was a brilliant expansion of Freud's stage theory (which stopped at puberty). If women didn't fit, it was their own damned fault.

In the 1970s, stage theory struck again with an eruption of popular books. (Stage theories recur in predictable stages.) Journalist Gail Sheehy published *Passages: Predictable Crises of Adult Life* (no one asked how a crisis, by definition a "turning point" or "a condition of instability," could be predictable). Harvard psychiatrist George Vaillant, now at Dartmouth, studied privileged Harvard (male) students, and concluded that men go through orderly stages even if their lives differ. Yale psychiatrist Daniel J. Levinson, in *The Seasons of a Man's Life*, argued that the phases of life unfold in a natural sequence, like the four seasons. This book had nothing to say about women's seasons, possibly because women were continuing to irritate academics by doing things unseasonably.

By this time I was really annoyed. I wasn't having any of my crises in the right order. I hadn't married when I was supposed to, which put my intimacy and generativity crises on hold; leaving my job created an identity crisis at 32, far too late. My work-linked sense of competence, having reached a high of +9, now plunged to -2, and I was supposed to have resolved *that* one at around age seven.

I had only to look around to realize I was not alone. All sorts of social changes were detonating around me. Women who had been homebodies for 35 years were running off to start businesses, much to the annoyance of their husbands, who were quitting their businesses to take lute lessons. People who expected to marry didn't. People who expected to stay married didn't. Women who expected never to work were working. Men who expected never to care about babies were cooing over their own. Expectations were out the window altogether.

LIFE AS A FAN

Eventually, stages no longer mattered, either. Psychological theories—which follow what people actually do—have had to change to keep up with the diversity of modern life. In recent years, researchers have discovered a few things that, once and for all, should drive a stake through the idea of fixed, universal life stages:

The psychology and biology of aging are not the same thing. Many of the problems of "old age" stem from psychological, not physical, losses. They would afflict most people at any age who were deprived of family, close friends, meaningful activity, intellectual stimulation and control over what happens to them. Today we've learned to distinguish the biology of normal aging from the decline caused by illness: Conditions once thought inevitable—osteoporosis, senility, excessive wrinkling, depression—can result from poor nutrition, overmedication, lack of exercise, cell damage or disease. **For example, only 15% of people over 65 suffer serious mental impairment, and half of those cases are due to Alzheimer's disease.**

EXPERTS CAN'T AGREE ON WHERE TO LOCATE "MIDLIFE."

These findings have played havoc with the basic definition of "old." It used to be 50. Then it was 60, then 70. Today there are so many vibrant octogenarians that "old" is getting even older. Researchers can't even agree on where to locate "midlife" (30 to 50? 40 to 60? 35 to 65?), let alone what problems constitute a midlife crisis.

Although children progress through biologically determined "stages," adults don't. Children go through a stage of babbling before they talk; they crawl before they walk; they wail before they can say, "Can we discuss this calmly, Mom?" These developments are governed by maturational and biological changes dictated by genes. But as children mature, genes become less of a driving force on their development, and the environment has greater impact.

Bernice Neugarten, a professor of behavioral science at the University of Chicago, observes that the better metaphor for life is a fan, rather than stages. When you open a fan, you can see all its diverse pieces linked at a common point of origin. As people age, their qualities and experiences likewise "fan out," which is why, she says, you find greater diversity in a group of 70-year-olds than in a passel of seven-year-olds.

The variety and richness of adult life can't be crammed into tidy "stages" anymore. Stage theorists such as Erikson assumed that growth is fixed (by some biological program or internal clock), progressive (you grow from a lower stage to a higher one), one-way (you grow up, not down; become more competent, not less), cumulative (reflecting your resolution of previous stages), and irreversible (once you gain a skill, there's no losing it).

Yet it has proven impossible to squash the great variety of adult experience into a fixed pattern, and there is no evidence to support the idea of neat stages that occur in five- or 10-year intervals. Why must you master an "identity crisis" before you learn to love? Don't issues of competence and inferiority recur throughout life? Why is the need for "generativity" relevant only to 30-year-olds?

EVENTS AND NONEVENTS

For all these reasons, new approaches to adult development emphasize not how old people are, but what they are doing. Likewise, new studies find that *having* a child has stronger psychological effects on mothers than the age at which they have the baby. (New mothers of any age feel more nurturing and less competent.) Entering the work force has a strong positive effect on your self-esteem and ambition, regardless of when you start working. Men facing retirement confront similar issues at 40, 50 or 60. Divorced people have certain

THE NEW APPROACH: NOT HOW OLD YOU ARE, BUT WHAT YOU ARE DOING.

common problems, whether they split at 30 or 50.

In their book *Lifeprints* (McGraw-Hill), Wellesley College psychologists Grace Baruch and Rosalind Barnett and writer Caryl Rivers surveyed 300 women, ages 35 to 55. They found that the differences among the women depended on what they were doing, not on their age. A career woman of 40, for example, has more in common with a career woman of 30 than with an unemployed woman her age.

At the heart of *Lifeprints* is the heretical notion that "there is no one lifeprint that insures all women a perpetual sense of well-being—nor one that guarantees misery, for that matter. American women today are finding satisfying lives in any number of role patterns. Most involve trade-offs at different points in the life cycle."

Instead of looking for the decade landmarks or the "crises" in life, the *transitions* approach emphasizes the importance of shifting from one role or situation to another. What matters are the events that happen (or fail to happen) and cause us to change in some way. Maryland's Schlossberg describes four kinds of transitions:

■ **Anticipated** transitions are the events you plan for, expect and rehearse: going to school, getting married, starting a job, getting promoted, having a child, retiring at 65. These are the (previously) common milestones of adult life, and because they're predictable, they cause the least difficulty.

■ **Unanticipated** transitions are the things that happen when you aren't prepared: flunking out of school, being fired, having a baby after being told you can't, being forced to retire early. Because these events are bolts from the blue, they can leave you reeling.

■ **Nonevent** transitions are the changes you expect to happen that don't: You don't get married; you can't have children; you aren't promoted; you planned to retire but need to keep working for the income. The challenge here is knowing when to accept these ongoing events as specific transitions and learning to live with them.

■ **Chronic Hassle** transitions are the situations that may eventually require you to change or take action, but rumble along uncomfortably for a long stretch: You aren't getting along with your spouse; your mother gets a chronic illness and needs constant care; you have to deal with discrimination at work; your child keeps getting into trouble.

There are no rules: An anticipated change for one person (having a baby) might be unanticipated for another. An upsetting "nonevent" transition for one person (not getting married) can be a planned decision for another and thus not a transition at all. And even unexpected good news—you recover despite a hopeless diagnosis—can require adjustment. This approach acknowledges that nonevents and chronic situations cause us to change just as surely as dramatic events do, though perhaps less consciously.

Seeing our lives in terms of these transitions, says Schlossberg, frees us from the old stereotypes that say we "should" be doing one thing or another at a certain time in our lives. But it also helps us understand why we can sail through changes we thought would be traumatic—only to be torpedoed by transitions expected to be a breeze. Our reactions have little to do with an internal clock, and everything to do with expectations, goals and, most of all, what else is happening to us.

For example, says Schlossberg, people have very different reactions to "significant" birthdays. For some, 30 is the killer; for others it's 50. For an aunt of mine, who breezed through decade markers without a snivel, 70 was traumatic. "To determine why a birthday marker creates a crisis," says Schlossberg, "I'd ask what was going on in the person's life, not their age. How old were they when their last parent died? How is their work going? Have they lost a loved one?" If they see a birthday as closing down options, then the event can feel negative, she adds.

"All of us carry along a set of psychological needs that are important throughout our lives, not just at one particular age or stage," says Schlossberg. "We need to feel we *belong* to a family, group or community, for example. Changing jobs, marriages or cities often leaves people feeling temporarily left out.

"We also need to feel we matter to others, that we count. At some phases of life, people are burdened by mattering too much to too many people. Many women in their 30s must care for children, husbands and parents, to say nothing of working at their paid jobs. At other phases, people suffer from a sense of mattering too little."

In addition to belonging and "mattering," says Schlossberg, people need to feel they have a reasonable amount of control over their lives; they need to feel competent at what they do; they need identity—a strong sense of who they are; and they need close attachments and commitments that give their lives meaning.

These themes, says Schlossberg, reflect our common humanity, uniting men and women, old and young. A freshman in college and a newly retired man may both temporarily feel marginal, "out of things." A teenager and her grandmother may both feel they don't "matter" to enough other people, and be lonely as a result. A man may feel he has control over his life until he's injured in a car accident. A woman's identity changes when she goes back to school in midlife. A newly divorced woman of 30 and a recently laid-off auto worker of 40 may both feel inadequate and incompetent. When people lose the commitments that give their lives meaning, they feel adrift.

"By understanding that these emotional feelings are a normal response to what is going on in your life, and not an inevitable crisis that occurs at 23 or 34, or whatever," says Schlossberg, "people can diagnose their problems more accurately—and more important, take steps to fix them." If you say, "No wonder I'm miserable; I'm having my Age 30 Decade Panic," there's nothing to do but live through it—getting more panicked when you're still miserable at age 36½.

But if you can say, "No wonder I'm miserable—I don't feel competent at work, I don't feel I matter to enough people, I feel like a stranger in this neighborhood," then more constructive possibilities present themselves. You can learn new skills, join new groups, start a neighborhood cleanup committee, and quit whining about being 30.

None of this means that age doesn't matter, as my 83-year-old mother would be the first to tell you. She mutters a lot about irritating pains, wrinkles, forgetfulness and getting shorter. But mostly my mother is too busy to complain, what with her paralegal counseling, fund-raising, organizing programs for shut-in older women, traveling around the world, and socializing. She knows she belongs; she matters to many; she has countless commitments; she knows who she is.

A WOMAN'S IDENTITY CHANGES WHEN SHE GOES BACK TO SCHOOL.

And yet the transitions approach reminds us that adult concerns aren't settled, once and for all, at some critical stage or age. It would be nice if we could acquire a sense of competence in grammar school and keep it forever, if we had only one identity crisis per lifetime, if we always belonged. But adult development is more complicated than that, and also more interesting. As developmental psychologist Leonard Pearlin once said, "There is not one process of aging, but many; there is not one life course, but many courses; there is no one sequence of stages, but many." The variety is as rich as the diversity of human experience.

Let's celebrate the variety—and leave stages to children, geologists, rocket launches and actors.

Dr. Spock had it right

Studies suggest that kids thrive when parents set firm limits

Using the serious tone once reserved for childhood ailments such as diphtheria and measles, a recent article in a journal published by the American Academy of Pediatrics described a new illness sweeping the nation: The "spoiled-child syndrome." Children exhibiting symptoms of the disease are excessively "self-centered and immature," as a result of parental failure to enforce "consistent, age-appropriate limits." Often, the article goes on to suggest, spoiled children grow into spoiled adolescents and adults, never learning how to delay gratification or tolerate not getting their own way.

Whether or not the epidemic of spoiled brats is genuine, the wave of parental anxiety on the subject of discipline is undeniable. Today's parents are torn by conflicting instincts and conflicting theories on permissiveness vs. discipline. On the one hand are feelings of guilt, particularly on the part of two-income parents who feel they don't spend enough time with their children and want to make every available minute a pleasant one; on the other are growing fears over drugs and violence in society. A recent national survey by Louis Harris & Associates reveals that most people—64 percent of those polled—say parents just don't do a good job disciplining their children.

Burdens of the past. Behind the parental concerns over doing the "right" thing is a long-running scientific debate. Several recently completed studies that tracked more than 100 children for nearly 20 years have provided the first objective test of which disciplinary styles work best, and all point in the same direction. Parents who are not harshly punitive, but who set firm boundaries and stick to them, are significantly more likely to produce children who are high achievers and who get along well with others.

Over the ages, child-rearing theories have changed as faddishly as fashions, reflecting a continual shift between viewing children as innocents who need little adult intervention and as inherently evil, and in dire need of straightening out. "The normal child is healthy in every way. His manners need no correcting. . . . So, when they cry or scream or are upset, we should understand that it means something is disturbing them, and we must try to discover what they need and give it to them," wrote Greek physician Galen in A.D. 175, perhaps the first doctor on record to advise demand feedings. In the 18th century, French philosopher Jean Jacques Rousseau envisioned the child as an unspoiled creature of nature, a noble savage best left unfettered by society's constraints, as did 17th-century English philosopher John Locke.

By the turn of the century in America, with the coming of the Industrial Age and the increasing faith placed in scientific experts, the idea of giving the young unbridled freedom fell severely out of favor. The prevailing view of eminent child experts, such as pediatrician L. Emmett Holt, author of *The Care and Feeding of Children,* called for strict, regimented conditioning to create good eating, sleeping and social habits in children. "Infants who are naturally nervous should be left much alone . . . and should never be quieted with soothing sirups or the pacifier," Holt wrote. In 1928, John Watson, a leader of the behaviorist school of psychology, applied Holt's principles to the child's mind. The result, the immensely popular *Psychological Care of Infant and Child,* is horrifying by modern parenting standards. Watson advocated molding babies by scientific control, with strict 4-hour feeding and sleeping schedules (just tune out the wailing), toilet training at 6 months—before the infant can sit up—and no thumb sucking, hugging or kissing. "Mother love is a dangerous instrument" that could wreck a child's chance for future happiness, Watson warned. The only physical contact he sanctioned between parent and child was a brisk handshake each morning.

The theorizing, and the receptions various theories received, often seems to have had more to do with cultural attitudes than with science. Dr. Benjamin Spock, who popularized Freudian theory and research on child psychology in his famous 1945 work, *The Common Sense Book of Baby and Child Care,* was seized upon by war-weary Americans who were looking for ways to free themselves of old conventions and who interpreted his emphasis on nurturing, gentleness and following common-sense instincts as a sanction of permissiveness. Later, in the 1960s and '70s, Spock became a political target when critics such as minister Norman Vincent Peale and Spiro Agnew blamed his so-called permissiveness for drugs, student riots, promiscuity and other excesses of the counterculture. Both, in fact, garbled Spock's message; he consistently urged parents to assert their authority at home. Through four editions, he never wavers from his 1945 message that the child "needs to feel that his mother and father, however agreeable, still have their own rights, know how to be firm, won't let him be unreasonable or rude. . . . It trains him from the beginning to get along reasonably with other people. The spoiled child is not a happy creature even in his own home."

Although Spock didn't condone permissiveness, other influential theorists did, as recently as a generation ago. A case in point is Scottish educator A. S. Neill in *Summerhill: A Radical Approach to Child Rearing,* which became popular in the United States after its publication in 1960. Neill, who established the progressive Summerhill School in Suffolk, England, during the 1920s, practiced and preached a philosophy of noninterference. Summerhill students chose whether or not they wanted to attend class, do homework, wear clothes, smoke cigarettes and experiment with sex. During the 1960s, Neill's child-rearing theories played a part in the creation of alternative schools and communes across America.

Friendly persuasion. The recent studies tend to support Spock's view that the most effective disciplinary style emphasizes warmth, verbal give-and-take and exertion of control without a parent acting like the child's jailer. The best evidence comes from a set of longitudinal studies conducted by psychologist Diana Baumrind of the University of California at Berkeley's Institute of Human Development. In her studies of approximately 150 middle-class, well-educated parents and children over a 20-year period, Baumrind identified three disciplinary styles that produced markedly different behavior traits in pre-school-age children. "Authoritarian" parents ("do it because I'm the parent") were more likely to have discontented, withdrawn and distrustful children. "Permissive" parents ("do whatever you want") had children who were the least self-reliant and curious about the world, and who took the fewest risks. "Authoritative" parents ("do it for this reason") were more likely to have self-reliant, self-controlled, contented children.

Baumrind's research teams collected and analyzed data at three intervals, when the subjects of her study reached ages 5, 10 and 15. One of her most interesting findings is that during adolescence "authoritative" parents are as effective in preventing their children's experimentations with drugs as the more restrictive "authoritarian" parents.

Baumrind's research dovetails with the clinical experiences of pediatrician Dr. Glenn Austin, who has applied her theories to his young patients and their parents in Los Altos, Calif. Austin has found that parents whose actions fit into Baumrind's category of "authoritative" make the most effective disciplinarians. For example, Austin cites how certain parents effectively break their children of the habit of throwing tantrums. They tune out the child until the tantrum ceases, or if that becomes intolerable, carry the child to his room, without "scolding or fussing or attempting to control the child's actions."

In Austin's summary of one of Baumrind's studies, he found that 85 percent of children raised by authoritative parents were "fully competent," which meant they possessed a long list of positive attributes including a sense of identity, a willingness to pursue tasks alone and a healthy questioning of adult authority, compared with 30 percent of children raised by authoritarian parents and 10 percent of children raised by permissive parents. While both boys and girls raised by authoritative parents turned out to be fully or partially "competent," major differences were found between boys and girls raised by other types of parents. For instance, authoritarian parents appeared to dominate their boys more than their girls: Only 18 percent of the boys were fully competent, compared with 42 percent of the girls.

Other research supports the insight that the key to a successful disciplinary strategy is helping the child develop inner controls, a process Freud called "internalization." University of Minnesota Prof. L. Alan Sroufe, who has studied 500 children in the past 18 years, found that the limits and boundaries parents imposed, before the child could regulate himself, served as a safety net that helped the child operate and develop his own internal controls. Authoritative parents usually establish an early pattern of trust through responding to a child's needs, meaning what they say and then following through. "If parents stick to a few rules that they're clear about, then their kids will be more compliant within those limits," Sroufe says. When parental expectations are not met, the principle of "minimum sufficiency," or less is more, should guide the punishment, because if the punishment is too harsh, that's what the child will focus on, not the behavior the punishment is intended to change.

Adjusting to conditions. Another study supports the view that inner controls are more apt to kick in when parents adjust their disciplinary style to external conditions. Psychologists Arnold Sameroff of Brown University's Bradley Hospital and Al Baldwin and Clara Baldwin at the University of Rochester studied 150 families over 13 years and confirmed that the most effective parental discipline matches the actual dangers facing the child. For example, in high-crime, inner-city neighborhoods, children whose parents imposed restrictive curfews and household rules, but displayed warmth as well as strictness, performed better than average in school. Conversely, in low-risk, suburban neighborhoods, the children of restrictive parents performed worse than average in school.

Although these studies are as objective as anyone can get, they can't bestow upon parents any magic formulas for preventing brattiness or rearing angels. Perhaps the most striking theme to emerge from all the scientific data is that establishing a pattern of love and trust and acceptable limits within each family is what really counts, and not lots of technical details. The true aim of discipline, a word that has the same Latin root as *disciple,* is not to punish unruly children but to teach and guide them and help instill inner controls. For in the end, as every mother and father know, parenting is far more of an art than a science.

by Beth Brophy

Sad Legacy Of Abuse: The Search For Remedies

Studies aim to learn why some abused children grow up to be abusers, and why most do not.

Daniel Goleman

Children and adults who were victims of child abuse are coming under intensified study by researchers who hope to learn what distinguishes those who go on to become abusers themselves from those who grow up to be good parents.

In the hope of finding ways to break the tragic cycle, the new research is identifying particular experiences in childhood and later in life that allow a great many abused children to overcome their sad legacy.

Studies also now indicate that about one-third of people who are abused in childhood will become abusers themselves. This is a lower percentage than many experts had expected, but obviously poses a major social challenge. The research also confirms that abuse in childhood increases the likelihood in adulthood of problems ranging from depression and alcoholism to sexual maladjustment and multiple personality.

The studies are also uncovering specific factors that help many victims grow into a well-adjusted adulthood, and factors that push others toward perpetuating the pattern of violence. The findings should help therapists improve treatment of abused children or formerly abused adults, helping them recover from their trauma.

"Studies showing that a high proportion of troubled adults were abused in childhood tell only part of the story," said Dr. Richard Krugman, a professor of pediatrics at the University of Colorado Medical School and director of the C. Henry Kempe Center for Prevention and Treatment of Child Abuse and Neglect. "There are substantial numbers of men and women who were abused as children, but who are not themselves child abusers, drug abusers, criminals or mentally disturbed."

Key factors found to worsen the long-term impact of abuse are: abuse that started early, abuse that lasted for a long time, abuse in which the perpetrator had a close relationship to the victim, abuse that the child perceived as particularly harmful, and abuse that occurred within a cold emotional atmosphere in the family. These factors, researchers say, help identify which children need treatment most urgently.

Victims of abuse frequently respond to the trauma by denying that any abuse occurred or by blaming themselves for the abuse, which they often view as justified discipline from adults, the studies show. But many victims can overcome the trauma with the emotional support of a friend or relative or through therapy that makes them aware that they were not to blame for abuse inflicted by their parents. Victims of abuse can almost always benefit from therapy to deal with the psychological effects of being so terribly treated, such as a damaged sense of self-worth and conflicts between wanting to love their parents while recognizing the abuse that happened.

"Child abuse" refers to a range of maltreatment. In addition to physical harm and sexual abuse, researchers also include serious neglect of a child's emotional and physical needs and forms of emotional abuse such as incessant berating of a child. They are finding that the long-lasting effects of all these kinds of abuse share much in common.

In any given year, from 1 percent to 1.5 percent of American children are subject to abuse of some kind, according to Dr. Krugman. By the time they reach adulthood, about one in four men and women have experienced at least one episode of abuse at some point during childhood.

Numerous studies have found those who were victims of child abuse to be more troubled as adults than those who were not. There are disproportionate numbers of victims of abuse among prostitutes, violent criminals, alcoholics and drug abusers, and patients in psychiatric hospitals.

The more severe the abuse, the more extreme the later psychiatric symptoms. For instance, a study by Judith Herman, a psychiatrist in Somerville, Mass., found that among women who had been victims of incest, although half seemed to have recovered well by adulthood, those who suffered forceful, prolonged, intrusive abuse, or who were abused by fathers or step-fathers, had the most serious problems later in life.

Virtually all those who suffer from multiple personality, a rare but severe psychiatric disorder, have a history of being severely abused; the disorder is thought to stem from ways some children try to mentally isolate themselves against the horror of unremitting abuse.

The emotional support of a nurturing adult can help victims overcome the trauma.

A 1985 study of all 15 adolescents in the United States who were condemned murderers found that 13 had been victims of extreme physical or sexual abuse. In nine cases the abuse was so severe—characterized as "murderous" by the researchers—that it led to neurological damage. Similarly, a study of nine women imprisoned for fatal child abuse found that all of them had experienced severe maltreatment themselves.

While all these studies depict an alarming pattern, researchers point out that the statistics do not reflect the large numbers of abused children who do not suffer from these problems.

That abused children need not go on to abuse their own children was shown in a study of more than 1,000 pregnant women, 95 of whom had been abused as children. The report, by William Altemeier, a pediatrician at Vanderbilt University Medical School, and his colleagues, was published in 1986 in the journal *Child Abuse and Neglect*.

Strongest Predictive Factor

The study found that the strongest predicter from childhood of becoming an abusive parent was not having been abused, but rather having felt as a child that one was unloved and unwanted by one's parents—an attitude common, of course, among abused children, but also found in families in which there is no overt abuse.

However, studies in which there have been more careful observations of mothers and their children have found a stronger link between having been abused in childhood and being an abusive parent. In a survey of such studies, Joan Kaufman and Edward Zigler, psychologists at Yale, concluded that 30 percent is the best estimate of the rate at which abuse of one generation is repeated in the next.

Denial that one has been abused is emerging as a source of trouble later in life. Researchers find that many adults who were abused as children do not think of themselves as having been victimized. For instance, three-quarters of men in one study who described punishments that, by objective standards, constitute abuse—such as being burned for an infraction of a minor household rule—denied that they had been abused.

About 30 percent of victims become abusive parents.

That phenomenon is common among those who go on to become child abusers, according to Dr. Krugman, and is part of the cycle by which abused children become abusive parents.

"When you ask them if they were ever abused, they tell you, 'No,' " Dr. Krugman said. "But if you ask them to describe what would happen if they broke a rule, they'll say something like, 'I was locked in a closet for a day, then beaten with a belt until I was black and blue.' Then you ask them, was that abuse? and their answer is, '!No, I was a bad kid and my parents had to beat me to make me turn out okay.' "

While there has been much attention by psychotherapists in recent years on women who were sexually abused in childhood, a more recent focus is on men who suffered sexual abuse. Such men are much more reticent than women about admitting what happened to them and dealing with the trauma, according to Mike Lew, co-director of The Next Step Counseling Centre in Newton, Mass., and author of "Victims No Longer," (Nevraumont) about the problem.

Children fare better after abuse, researchers have found, when they have someone in their life—a relative, teacher, minister, friend—who is emotionally nurturing.

In helping a child recover from abuse, "you need to counteract the child's expectations that adults will be deeply uncaring," explained Martha Erickson, a psychologist at the University of Minnesota.

Among adult victims of childhood abuse who are in therapy, a common refrain from patients is that "it just wasn't that bad," said Terry Hunt, a psychologist in Cambridge, Mass., who specializes in their problem. "The key to their treatment is facing the fact that their parents were so cruel to them; they've bought the parent's word that they were bad and deserved it. The damage shows up in their intimate relationships: they're waiting to get hit or used again."

Many adults refuse to acknowledge that they were abused as children.

One of the crucial differences between those abused children who go on to become abusers and those who do not, he said, is whether they have the insight that their parents were wrong to abuse them.

Often, Dr. Hunt finds, the most troubled among his patients are those who were told as children, by adults other than their abusing parent, that the abuse was justified.

"If an abused child thinks, 'that was wrong, they shouldn't have done that to me—I'm not that bad,' then he can still love his parents, but decide not to repeat the abuse when he becomes a parent," said Dr. Krugman. "The child somehow gets the message that what happened is not his fault, that he is not to blame."

When parents are not the abusers, how they react to its discovery is crucial. In a study of children who had been involved in sex rings, those who had fewest lasting problems in later years were the children whose parents had been understanding of the child, according to Ann Burgess, a professor of nursing at the University of Pennsylvania medical school.

"These kids recovered with no symptoms, while those whose parents blamed them had the worst outcome," Dr. Burgess said.

The factors that lead some children to become abusers while others become excellent parents is being revealed in research at the University of Minnesota. Psychologists there are currently studying a group of children born to parents with a high probability of becoming abusers. Not all those in the study were abused as children; they were selected instead because they were poor, single, got pregnant at an early age, and had chaotic households—all factors that correlate highly with child abuse.

In addition to physical and sexual abuse—the two varieties most often studied—the researchers are also studying children whose physical care is neglected, those whose parents constantly berate and criticize them and those whose parents are completely unresponsive to their emotional needs.

Followed From Birth

The study, one of the few that has followed children from birth, is finding that there are different emotional effects from each of the different kinds of abuse, and that these effects change from age to age. For instance, children whose mothers were emotionally cold during infancy had emotional and learning problems at the age of six that were as severe as—and sometimes more severe—than those found in children whose mothers had been physically abusive but emotionally responsive during their infancy.

When the same children were studied between the ages of four and six, the most serious problems were found in those whose mothers neglected their physical care.

The study is also finding general effects that come from maltreatment of any kind.

"The earlier the maltreatment occurs, the more severe the consequences," said Martha F. Erickson, a psychologist at the University of Minnesota, who is one of those conducting the study. Dr. Erickson, with Byron Egeland and Robert Pianta, two colleagues, will publish early findings from the study in a chapter to appear in "Child Maltreatment," a book to be published by Cambridge University Press in May.

Many of the lifelong psychological effects of abuse stem from a lack of nurturance, they conclude, a lack that lies behind all the kinds of maltreatment.

The Minnesota researchers report that among those abused children who go on to become abusing parents, there is little repetition of a specific type of abuse.

For instance, of 13 women who had been sexually abused, six were physically abusing their children; of 47 who had been physic abused, 8 were physical abusers by the time their children reached six years, while 8 neglected their children, and 6 had homes where children were being sexually abused, often by a boyfriend of the mother.

CHILDREN AFTER DIVORCE

WOUNDS THAT DON'T HEAL

Judith S. Wallerstein

Judith S. Wallerstein is a psychologist and author of "Second Chances: Men, Women & Children a Decade After Divorce," published by Ticknor & Fields. This article, adapted from the book, was written with the book's co-author, Sandra Blakeslee, who is a regular contributor to The New York Times.

As recently as the 1970's, when the American divorce rate began to soar, divorce was thought to be a brief crisis that soon resolved itself. Young children might have difficulty falling asleep and older children might have trouble at school. Men and women might become depressed or frenetic, throwing themselves into sexual affairs or immersing themselves in work.

But after a year or two, it was expected, most would get their lives back on track, at least outwardly. Parents and children would get on with new routines, new friends and new schools, taking full opportunity of the second chances that divorce brings in its wake.

These views, I have come to realize, were wishful thinking. In 1971, working with a small group of colleagues and with funding from San Francisco's Zellerback Family Fund, I began a study of the effects of divorce on middle-class people who continue to function despite the stress of a marriage breakup.

That is, we chose families in which, despite the failing marriage, the children were doing well at school and the parents were not in clinical treatment for psychiatric disorders. Half of the families attended church or synagogue. Most of the parents were college educated. This was, in other words, divorce under the best circumstances.

Our study, which would become the first ever made over an extended period of time, eventually tracked 60 families, most of them white, with a total of 131 children, for 10, and in some cases 15, years after divorce. We found that although some divorces work well—some adults are happier in the long run, and some children do better than they would have been expected to in an unhappy intact family—more often than not divorce is a wrenching, long-lasting experience for at least one of the former partners. Perhaps most important, we found that for virtually all the children, it exerts powerful and wholly unanticipated effects.

Our study began with modest aspirations. With a colleague, Joan Berlin Kelly—who headed a community mental-health program in the San Francisco area—I planned to examine the short-term effects of divorce on these middle-class families.

We spent many hours with each member of each of our 60 families—hearing their first-hand reports from the battleground of divorce. At the core of our research was the case study, which has been the main source of the fundamental insights of clinical psychology and of psychoanalysis. Many important changes, especially in the long run, would be neither directly observable nor easily measured. They would become accessible only through case studies: by examining the way each of these people processed, responded to and integrated the events and relationships that divorce brings in its wake.

We planned to interview families at the time of decisive separation and filing for divorce, and again 12 to 18 months later, expecting to chart recoveries among men and women and to look at how the children were mastering troubling family events.

We were stunned when, at the second series of visits, we found family after family still in crisis, their wounds wide open. Turmoil and distress had not noticeably subsided. Many adults were angry, and felt humiliated and rejected, and most had not gotten their lives back together. An unexpectedly large number of children were on a downward course. Their symptoms were worse than they had been immediately after the divorce. Our findings were absolutely contradictory to our expectations.

Dismayed, we asked the Zellerbach Fund to support a follow-up study in the fifth year after divorce. To our surprise, interviewing 56 of the 60 families in our original study, we found that although half the men

From *The New York Times* Magazine, January 22, 1989, pp. 19–21, 41–44. Adapted from *Second Chances: Men, Women & Children a Decade After Divorce*, by Judith S. Wallerstein and Sandra Blakeslee.

and two-thirds of the women (even many of those suffering economically) said they were more content with their lives, only 34 percent of the children were clearly doing well.

Another 37 percent were depressed, could not concentrate in school, had trouble making friends and suffered a wide range of other behavior problems. While able to function on a daily basis, these children were not recovering, as everyone thought they would. Indeed most of them were on a downward course. This is a powerful statistic, considering that these were children who were functioning well five years before. It would be hard to find any other group of children—except, perhaps, the victims of a natural disaster—who suffered such a rate of sudden serious psychological problems.

The remaining children showed a mixed picture of good achievement in some areas and faltering achievement in others; it was hard to know which way they would eventually tilt.

The psychological condition of these children and adolescents, we found, was related in large part to the overall quality of life in the post-divorce family, to what the adults had been able to build in place of the failed marriage. Children tended to do well if their mothers and fathers, whether or not they remarried, resumed their parenting roles, managed to put their differences aside, and allowed the children a continuing relationship with both parents. Only a handful of kids had all these advantages.

We went back to these families again in 1980 and 1981 to conduct a 10-year follow-up. Many of those we had first interviewed as children were now adults. Overall, 45 percent were doing well; they had emerged as competent, compassionate and courageous people. But 41 percent were doing poorly; they were entering adulthood as worried, underachieving, self-deprecating and sometimes angry young men and women. The rest were strikingly uneven in how they adjusted to the world; it is too soon to say how they will turn out.

At around this time, I founded the Center for the Family in Transition, in Marin County, near San Francisco, which provides counseling to people who are separating, divorcing or remarrying. Over the years, my colleagues and I have seen more than 2,000 families—an experience that has amplified my concern about divorce. Through our work at the center and in the study, we have come to see divorce not as a single circumscribed event but as a continuum of changing family relationships—as a process that begins during the failing marriage and extends over many years. Things are not getting better, and divorce is not getting easier. It's too soon to call our conclusions definitive, but they point to an urgent need to learn more.

It was only at the 10-year point that two of our most unexpected findings became apparent. The first of these is something we call the sleeper effect.

A divorce-prone society is producing its first generation of young adults, men and women so anxious about attachment and love that their ability to create enduring families is imperiled.

The first youngster in our study to be interviewed at the 10-year mark was one who had always been a favorite of mine. As I waited for her to arrive for this interview, I remembered her innocence at age 16, when we had last met. It was she who alerted us to the fact that many young women experience a delayed effect of divorce.

As she entered my office, she greeted me warmly. With a flourishing sweep of one arm, she said, "You called me at just the right time. I just turned 21!" Then she startled me by turning immediately serious. She was in pain, she said.

She was the one child in our study who we all thought was a prime candidate for full recovery. She had denied some of her feelings at the time of divorce, I felt, but she had much going for her, including high intelligence, many friends, supportive parents, plenty of money.

As she told her story, I found myself drawn into unexpected intricacies of her life. Her trouble began, typically, in her late teens. After graduating from high school with honors, she was admitted to a respected university and did very well her freshman year. Then she fell apart. As she told it, "I met my first true love."

The young man, her age, so captivated her that she decided it was time to have a fully committed love affair. But on her way to spend summer vacation with him, her courage failed. "I went to New York instead. I hitchhiked across the country. I didn't know what I was looking for. I thought I was just passing time. I didn't stop and ponder. I just kept going, recklessly, all the time waiting for some word from my parents. I guess I was testing them. But no one—not my dad, not my mom—ever asked me what I was doing there on the road alone."

She also revealed that her weight dropped to 94 pounds from 128 and that she had not menstruated for a year and a half.

"I began to get angry," she said. "I'm angry at my parents for not facing up to the emotions, to the feelings in their lives, and for not helping me face up to the feelings in mine. I have a hard time forgiving them."

I asked if I should have pushed her to express her anger earlier.

She smiled patiently and said, "I don't think so. That was exactly the point. All those years I denied feelings. I thought I could live without love, without sorrow, without anger, without pain. That's how I coped with the unhappiness in my parents' marriage. Only when

I met my boyfriend did I become aware of how much feeling I was sitting on all those years. I'm afraid I'll lose him."

It was no coincidence that her acute depression and anorexia occurred just as she was on her way to consummate her first love affair, as she was entering the kind of relationship in which her parents failed. For the first time, she confronted the fears, anxieties, guilt and concerns that she had suppressed over the years.

Sometimes with the sleeper effect the fear is of betrayal rather than commitment. I was shocked when another young woman—at the age of 24, sophisticated, warm and friendly—told me she worried if her boyfriend was even 30 minutes late, wondering who he was with and if he was having an affair with another woman. This fear of betrayal occurs at a frequency that far exceeds what one might expect from a group of people randomly selected from the population. They suffer minute to minute, even though their partners may be faithful.

In these two girls we saw a pattern that we documented in 66 percent of the young women in our study between the ages of 19 and 23; half of them were seriously derailed by it. The sleeper effect occurs at a time when these young women are making decisions with long-term implications for their lives. Faced with issues of commitment, love and sex in an adult context, they are aware that the game is serious. If they tie in with the wrong man, have children too soon, or choose harmful life-styles, the effects can be tragic. Overcome by fears and anxieties, they begin to make connections between these feelings and their parents' divorce:

"I'm so afraid I'll marry someone like my dad."

"How can you believe in commitment when anyone can change his mind anytime?"

"I am in awe of people who stay together."

We can no longer say—as most experts have held in recent years—that girls are generally less troubled by the divorce experience than boys. Our study strongly indicates, for the first time, that girls experience serious effects of divorce at the time they are entering young adulthood. Perhaps the risk for girls and boys is equalized over the long term.

When a marriage breaks down, men and women alike often experience a diminished capacity to parent. They may give less time, provide less discipline and be less sensitive to their children, since they are themselves caught up in the maelstrom of divorce and its aftermath. Many researchers and clinicians find that parents are temporarily unable to separate their children's needs from their own.

In a second major unexpected finding of our 10-year study, we found that fully a quarter of the mothers and a fifth of the fathers had not gotten their lives back on track a decade after divorce. The diminished parenting continued, permanently disrupting the child-rearing functions of the family. These parents were chronically disorganized and, unable to meet the challenges of being a parent, often leaned heavily on their children. The child's role became one of warding off the serious depression that threatened the parents' psychological functioning. The divorce itself may not be solely to blame but, rather, may aggravate emotional difficulties that had been masked in the marriage. Some studies have found that emotionally disturbed parents within a marriage produce similar kinds of problems in children.

These new roles played by the children of divorce are complex and unfamiliar. They are not simple role reversals, as some have claimed, because the child's role becomes one of holding the parent together psychologically. It is more than a caretaking role. This phenomenon merits our careful attention, for it affected 15 percent of the children in our study, which means many youngsters in our society. I propose that we identify as a distinct psychological syndrome the "overburdened child," in the hope that people will begin to recognize the problems and take steps to help these children, just as they help battered and abused children.

One of our subjects, in whom we saw this syndrome, was a sweet 5-year-old girl who clearly felt that she was her father's favorite. Indeed, she was the only person in the family he never hit. Preoccupied with being good and helping to calm both parents, she opposed the divorce because she knew it would take her father away from her. As it turned out, she also lost her mother who, soon after the divorce, turned to liquor and sex, a combination that left little time for mothering.

A year after the divorce, at the age of 6, she was getting herself dressed, making her own meals and putting herself to bed. A teacher noticed the dark circles under her eyes, and asked why she looked so tired. "We have a new baby at home," the girl explained. The teacher, worried, visited the house and discovered there was no baby. The girl's story was designed to explain her fatigue but also enabled her to fantasize endlessly about a caring loving mother.

Shortly after this episode, her father moved to another state. He wrote to her once or twice a year, and when we saw her at the five-year follow-up she pulled out a packet of letters from him. She explained how worried she was that he might get into trouble, as if she were the parent and he the child who had left home.

"I always knew he was O.K. if he drew pictures on the letters," she said. "The last two really worried me because he stopped drawing."

Now 15, she has taken care of her mother for the past 10 years. "I felt it was my responsibility to make sure that Mom was O.K.," she says. "I stayed home with her instead of playing or going to school. When she got mad, I'd let her take it out on me."

I asked what her mother would do when she was angry.

"She'd hit me or scream. It scared me more when she screamed. I'd rather be hit. She always seemed so much bigger when she screamed. Once Mom got drunk and passed out on the street. I called my brothers, but they hung up. So I did it. I've done a lot of things I've never told anyone. There were many times she was so upset I was sure she would take her own life. Sometimes I held both her hands and talked to her for hours I was so afraid."

In truth, few children can rescue a troubled parent. Many become angry at being trapped by the parents' demands, at being robbed of their separate identity and denied their childhood. And they are saddened, sometimes beyond repair, at seeing so few of their own needs gratified.

Since this is a newly identified condition that is just being described, we cannot know its true incidence. I suspect that the number of overburdened children runs much higher than the 15 percent we saw in our study, and that we will begin to see rising reports in the next few years—just as the reported incidence of child abuse has risen since it was first identified as a syndrome in 1962.

The sleeper effect and the overburdened-child syndrome were but two of many findings in our study. Perhaps most important, overall, was our finding that divorce has a lasting psychological effect on many children, one that, in fact, may turn out to be permanent.

Children of divorce have vivid memories about their parents' separation. The details are etched firmly in their minds, more so than those of any other experiences in their lives. They refer to themselves as children of divorce, as if they share an experience that sets them apart from all others. Although many have come to agree that their parents were wise to part company, they nevertheless feel that they suffered from their parents' mistakes. In many instances, conditions in the post-divorce family were more stressful and less supportive to the child than conditions in the failing marriage.

If the finding that 66 percent of the 19- to 23-year-old young women experienced the sleeper effect was most unexpected, others were no less dramatic. Boys, too, were found to suffer unforeseen long-lasting effects. Forty percent of the 19- to 23-year-old young men in our study, 10 years after divorce, still had no set goals, a limited education and a sense of having little control over their lives.

In comparing the post-divorce lives of former husbands and wives, we saw that 50 percent of the women and 30 percent of the men were still intensely angry at their former spouses a decade after divorce. For women over 40 at divorce, life was lonely throughout the decade; not one in our study remarried or sustained a loving relationship. Half the men over 40 had the same problem.

In the decade after divorce, three in five children felt rejected by one of their parents, usually the father—whether or not it was true. The frequency and duration of visiting made no difference. Children longed for their fathers, and the need increased during adolescence. Thirty-four percent of the youngsters went to live with their fathers during adolescence for at least a year. Half returned to the mother's home disappointed with what they had found. Only one in seven saw both mother and father happily remarried after 10 years. One in two saw their mother or their father undergo a second divorce. One in four suffered a severe and enduring drop in the family's standard of living and went on to observe a lasting discrepancy between their parents' standards of living.

We found that the children who were best adjusted 10 years later were those who showed the most distress at the time of the divorce—the youngest. In general, pre-schoolers are the most frightened and show the most dramatic symptoms when marriages break up. Many are afraid that they will be abandoned by both parents and they have trouble sleeping or staying by themselves. It is therefore surprising to find that the same children 10 years later seem better adjusted than their older siblings. Now in early and mid-adolescence, they were rated better on a wide range of psychological dimensions than the older children. Sixty-eight percent were doing well, compared with less than 40 percent of older children. But whether having been young at the time of divorce will continue to protect them as they enter young adulthood is an open question.

Our study shows that adolescence is a period of particularly grave risk for children in divorced families. Through rigorous analysis, statistical and otherwise, we were able to see clearly that we weren't dealing simply with the routine angst of young people going through transition but rather that, for most of them, divorce was the single most important cause of enduring pain and anomie in their lives. The young people told us time and again how much they needed a family structure, how much they wanted to be protected, and how much they yearned for clear guidelines for moral behavior. An alarming number of teenagers felt abandoned, physically and emotionally.

For children, divorce occurs during the formative years. What they see and experience becomes a part of their inner world, influencing their own relationships 10 and 15 years later, especially when they have witnessed violence between the parents. It is then, as these young men and women face the developmental task of establishing love and intimacy, that they most feel the lack of a template for a loving relationship between a man and a woman. It is here that their anxiety threatens their ability to create new, enduring families of their own.

As these anxieties peak in the children of divorce throughout our society, the full legacy of the rising divorce rate is beginning to hit home. The new families being formed today by these children as they reach adulthood appear particularly vulnerable.

Because our study was such an early inquiry, we did not set out to compare children of divorce with children from intact families. Lacking fundamental knowledge about life after the breakup of a marriage, we could not know on what basis to build a comparison or control group. Was the central issue one of economics, age, sex, a happy intact marriage—or would any intact marriage do? We began, therefore, with a question—What is the nature of the divorce experience?—and in answering it we would generate hypotheses that could be tested in subsequent studies.

This has indeed been the case. Numerous studies have been conducted in different regions of the country, using control groups, that have further explored and validated our findings as they have emerged over the years. For example, one national study of 699 elementary school children carefully compared children six years after their parents' divorce with children from intact families. It found—as we did—that elementary-age boys from divorced families show marked discrepancies in peer relationships, school achievement and social adjustment. Girls in this group, as expected, were hardly distinguishable based on the experience of divorce, but, as we later found out, this would not always hold up. Moreover, our findings are supported by a litany of modern-day statistics. Although one in three children are from divorced families, they account for an inordinately high proportion of children in mental-health treatment, in special-education classes, or referred by teachers to school psychologists. Children of divorce make up an estimated 60 percent of child patients in clinical treatment and 80 percent—in some cases, 100 percent—of adolescents in inpatient mental hospital settings. While no one would claim that a cause and effect relationship has been established in all of these cases, no one would deny that the role of divorce is so persuasively suggested that it is time to sound the alarm.

All studies have limitations in what they can accomplish. Longitudinal studies, designed to establish the impact of a major event or series of events on the course of a subsequent life, must always allow for the influence of many interrelated factors. They must deal with chance and the uncontrolled factors that so often modify the sequences being followed. This is particularly true of children, whose lives are influenced by developmental changes, only some of which are predictable, and by the problem of individual differences, about which we know so little.

Our sample, besides being quite small, was also drawn from a particular population slice—predominately white, middle class and relatively privileged suburbanites.

Despite these limitations, our data have generated working hypotheses about the effects of divorce that can now be tested with more precise methods, including appropriate control groups. Future research should be aimed at testing, correcting or modifying our initial findings, with larger and more diverse segments of the population. For example, we found that children—especially boys and young men—continued to need their fathers after divorce and suffered feelings of rejection even when they were visited regularly. I would like to see a study comparing boys and girls in sole and joint custody, spanning different developmental stages, to see if greater access to both parents counteracts these feelings of rejection. Or, does joint custody lead to a different sense of rejection—of feeling peripheral in both homes?

It is time to take a long, hard look at divorce in America. Divorce is not an event that stands alone in childrens' or adults' experience. It is a continuum that begins in the unhappy marriage and extends through the separation, divorce and any remarriages and second divorces. Divorce is not necessarily the sole culprit. It may be no more than one of the many experiences that occur in this broad continuum.

Profound changes in the family can only mean profound changes in society as a whole. All children in today's world feel less protected. They sense that the institution of the family is weaker than it has ever been before. Even those children raised in happy, intact families worry that their families may come undone. The task for society in its true and proper perspective is to strengthen the family—all families.

A biblical phrase I have not thought of for many years has recently kept running through my head: "Watchman, what of the night?" We are not I'm afraid, doing very well on our watch—at least for our children. We are allowing them to bear the psychological, economic and moral brunt of divorce.

And they recognize the burdens. When one 6-year-old boy came to our center shortly after his parents' divorce, he would not answer questions; he played games instead. First he hunted all over the playroom for the sturdy Swedish-designed dolls that we use in therapy. When he found a good number of them, he stood the baby dolls firmly on their feet and placed the miniature tables, chairs, beds and, eventually, all the playhouse furniture on top of them. He looked at me, satisfied. The babies were supporting a great deal. Then, wordlessly, he placed all the mother and father dolls in precarious positions on the steep roof of the doll house. As a father doll slid off the roof, the boy caught him and, looking up at me, said, "He might die." Soon, all the mother and father dolls began sliding off the roof. He caught them gently, one by one. "The babies are holding up the world," he said.

Although our overall findings are troubling and serious, we should not point the finger of blame at divorce per se. Indeed, divorce is often the only rational solution to a bad marriage. When people ask whether they should stay married for the sake of the children, I have to say, "Of course not." All our evidence shows that children exposed to open conflict, where parents terrorize or strike one another, turn out less well-adjusted than do children from divorced families. And although we lack systematic studies comparing children in divorced families with those in unhappy intact families, I am convinced that it is not useful to provide children with a model of adult behavior that avoids problem-solving and that stresses martyrdom, violence or apathy. A divorce undertaken thoughtfully and realistically can teach children how to confront serious life problems with compassion, wisdom and appropriate action.

Our findings do not support those who would turn back the clock. As family issues are flung to the center of our political arena, nostalgic voices from the right argue for a return to a time when divorce was more difficult to obtain. But they do not offer solutions to the wretchedness and humiliation within many marriages.

Still we need to understand that divorce has consequences—we need to go into the experience with our eyes open. We need to know that many children will suffer for many years. As a society, we need to take steps to preserve for the children as much as possible of the social, economic and emotional security that existed while their parents' marriage was intact.

Like it or not, we are witnessing family changes which are an integral part of the wider changes in our society. We are on a wholly new course, one that gives us unprecedented opportunities for creating better relationships and stronger families—but one that also brings unprecedented dangers for society, especially for our children.

THE TAMING OF THE TUBE

Judy O'Brien Goldman

JUDY O'BRIEN GOLDMAN *is a free-lance writer in Brooklyn who is trying to make peace with her television set.*

If TV is such a great educational tool, why are mutant turtles making the headlines?

It's a typical weekday afternoon. Shadows lengthen as weary neighbors return home from work and my wide-eyed son is perched inches from the television set, a backwards baseball cap over his disheveled blond hair. When I announce I'm fixing dinner, he waves me off, eager to hear the next pearls of wisdom from Bert and Ernie's Muppet mouths. A few minutes later, I return. He has changed the channel. Now, he is transfixed by the five-o'clock news. His face is placid as he watches tapes of the day's lead story: Body bags are being carried out of a crack house. I'm frightened—Seth is only two and a half years old. What's all this television doing to my kid?

Clearly I'm not the only one worried. Currently there are three bills floating in the House and Senate pertaining to children and television. The first—passed by both bodies last year but bogged down, at press time, in technicalities—provides an antitrust exemption for network and cable TV broadcasters to discuss the escalating level of violence on television. Another bill that has already passed the Senate would award a $10,000,000 national endowment to the Public Broadcasting System (PBS) for creating new educational programs for youngsters. This would enable PBS to air an entire library of quality shows for three years. After that, other broadcasters could purchase and air the shows.

The third bill, awaiting passage in both the Senate and House, would place a nine- to 12-minute cap on total commercial messages aired during each hour of kids' programs. But even that number can have a powerful impact. "Children are more accepting because they don't understand the persuasive intent of commercials," says Brian Wilcox, Ph.D., director of public interest legislation for the American Psychological Association. "They see it all as loud, exciting, short and well-produced shows."

The Electronic Sitter

Like most moms, I'm guilty of having the TV on more than I'd like. Television serves as my au pair, keeping Seth out of mischief and allowing me to meet deadlines, do chores or take a breather. In the morning, *Sesame Street* and *Mister Rogers' Neighborhood* let me dress without having vital pieces of clothing snatched away. During the day, I slap a kiddie tape into the VCR when I'm working. Dinner is courtesy, again, of *Sesame Street.*

"If you don't have help, what are you going to do?" asks Peggy Charren, founder and president of Action for Children's Television, a Cambridge-based organization pushing for quality TV. "If you work at home, you may only be able to work, and ultimately get paid, if your child is distracted by the television set. And the only way to get your kid out of the kitchen when you cook dinner may, again, be with TV. You have to work out a balance." Sometimes the balance seems off in my house, but I tell myself all this TV-viewing is harmless—until I catch Seth watching something he shouldn't, like a graphic news segment or the tail end of a cop show or even certain cartoons.

Naturally I'm worried about the effects of these images on my son. True, I've witnessed what good programming can do. Thanks to *Sesame Street,* Seth knows the alphabet, can count to 10 and identify words he recognizes. But he also whacked me over the head with an empty paper towel roll one day, explaining that he was "playing hockey." I was speechless until I realized that news footage on hockey games is rarely about scoring goals but rather about high-sticking and fights. Seth also pretends to be Jeff Smith of *The Frugal Gourmet* by dumping his food from bowl to bowl and, eventually, on the floor. "I'm cooking," he'll solemnly announce.

"Never assume that a young child can distinguish between fantasy and reality," warns John Condry, Ph.D., professor of human development and family studies at Cornell University in Ithaca, New York, and author of *The Psychology of Television*

(Lawrence Erlbaum Associates, 1989). "The line between what's real and what isn't is easily blurred. Even adults can have trouble if they watch a lot of TV."

Even adults? Though we don't admit it, we too are swayed by the power of the flickering screen. Who hasn't overheard a conversation that included a rehash of Jay Leno's monologue or a discussion about whether *thirtysomething*'s Nancy could survive both ovarian cancer *and* marriage to Elliot? But adults can usually shrug off television as a mindless diversion. Young children don't possess the knowledge or experience base to place what they see in perspective.

"We now have 25 years of solid research to back up the theory that violent television has negative effects on our children," says Wilcox. The American Academy of Pediatrics (AAP) recently issued a strong warning about how television violence makes children more aggressive and prone to fighting. That's just the tip of the iceberg. While sexual encounters on TV are not necessarily explicit, they can still appear mysterious and confusing to a child. And the consumption of alcohol is often depicted as glamorous—not as a major social problem. "It's usually not linked to violence," says Thomas E. Radecki, M.D., chairman and research director, National Coalition on Television Violence. "In real life, more than 50 percent of violent crimes occur while individuals are under the influence."

Also, many so-called children's programs help create and perpetuate sexual and racist stereotypes. Shows that target boys, like *G.I. Joe, Teenage Mutant Ninja Turtles* and *He-Man*, all have similar plots, points out Petra Hesse, Ph.D., assistant professor of psychology at Wheelock College in Boston and a research associate at the Center for Psychological Studies in the Nuclear Age at Harvard Medical School. "The heroes are usually white, blond and blue-eyed; the enemies are non-Caucasians with thick accents." The heroes are generally attacked for no apparent reason and must resort to violence to repel the enemy. While the "good guys" ultimately triumph, the "bad guys" always threaten to return. This type of scenario "teaches white children that the world is a frightening place, that they must not trust anyone who looks different or has an accent and that there is no such thing as peaceful compromise," says Hesse.

"For nonwhite children, the underlying message seems to be that darker skin and accents are undesirable, even evil. This gives kids a conflicting view of themselves. They want to be good and a part of their family, but TV indicates that you cannot be good if you're different. We're just beginning to explore what this confusion is doing to them."

Girls, on the other hand, tend to watch *The Smurfs* and *Care Bears,* in which "characters can tame anyone with simple sweetness,"continues Hesse. "So little girls conclude that they should always be passive and never fight back." Ideally, says Hesse, television should offer a balanced programming menu, featuring "androgynous characters who assess every situation differently."

Merely parking in front of the television can be detrimental, according to William H. Dietz, M.D., Ph.D., chairman of the AAP's subcommittee on children and television and director of clinical nutrition at the Boston Floating Hospital of the New England Medical Center. "Not only are kids inactive while watching TV, but they're usually being bombarded with commercials for high-calorie, low-nutrition foods," says Dietz, who pioneered research linking childhood obesity with television viewing. Evidence also suggests that energy not used while watching TV may make kids behave wildly once the set is off. "All that contained energy has to go somewhere," says Dietz.

There are other concerns, as well. "Every hour a kid spends in front of a TV represents an hour he's not reading books, exploring the world and, most important, socializing with other kids," says Condry. Hesse agrees: "By adolescence, the average child has spent more hours in front of a television than in a classroom. Any one source that has so much influence should be monitored."

Which is why current legislation is aimed at upping TV standards for children. As Charren says, "The competitive nature of the television business makes it tough for the good guys to get ahead unless they have some help." Many experts I talked to agree that even the good broadcasters need guidance. Because children between two and 12 are a diverse group—what interests a four-year-old would bore a 10-year-old and vice versa—they're difficult to program for. Only a mandate from Washington can help the industry get its act together and ensure that there will be something for everyone.

If Not TV, What?

Quality television, in sane amounts, allows children to peek at other cultures, be exposed to art and music and even travel to the moon and beyond. That's why it's important to read newspapers and magazine columns that review programs and let kids watch only the best. If you own a VCR, you can tape these shows for repeat screenings or rent movies that receive favorable reviews.

However, it's possible for youngsters to overdose on good TV. And just what is a "sane amount"? Is it practical for parents to limit the amount of time a child spends in front of the set? The AAP says two hours per day should be the cutoff. But there are other markers. "If a child can only act out fantasies about television characters, if all his or her play is centered on cartoons, the child is probably watching too much TV," says Hesse. The challenge is to limit viewing without making it seem like punishment. Condry says it can be done and that it may teach kids to be more selective about what they watch.

Once you turn off the TV, however, you have to serve up alternative activities. "Saying no to television means you have to say yes to something else," adds Charren. "Otherwise, you're going to have a very fussy child on your hands." An older child has to be encouraged to read, play games or visit a friend's house—where one hopes the TV won't be on. Younger kids need a grown-up who will read them stories, sing them songs or take them to the playground. My parents unplugged the television on Saturdays and took my brother and me to the zoo and to museums. I never felt deprived and was always eager for the weekend.

My own son is still young and it's easy to plop him in front of the television. It's not fair, I know; but I also know television is an indelible part of life. I've decided not to drive myself crazy thinking about it. Instead, I'll try to ensure that my own ideas—religious, ethical and moral—get more airtime than those of a mutant turtle.

SCARED SERIOUS

26,900 Teens Respond to Our 3rd Annual Survey

In our exclusive reader survey, 3 of 4 kids ages 12–16 worry they won't find a good job when they grow up. They 'latchkey generation' is knuckling down for the future.

Mary Ellin Barrett

They may shred their jeans with razors, mouth off like sassy Bart Simpson and hoot approvingly when singer Tracy Chapman talks about a revolution. A few daring ones may sport tattoos. But today's teenagers aren't building a counterculture to rival that of the '60s.

Forget those youthquake, generation-gap clichés. The 26,946 adolescents who answered USA WEEKEND's survey are striving for the bottom line. The responses to our full-page questionnaire, which ran in late May, topped the 23,300 mailed in last year.

These future Doogie Howsers and L.A. lawyers want to bank their baby-sitting earnings, enroll in top colleges and land lucrative jobs. They pick pay over satisfaction or challenge when it comes to what they hope for in a career.

But these material girls and boys don't lust after bucks alone. They yearn for security.

True, they're '80s babies. They grew up watching J.R., Alexis and the Rich and Famous consume conspicuously on the tube. But TV also brought them news of drugs, the deficit, homelessness and crime.

Sure, their working parents sprang for $68 Nikes and $69 Guess? jeans. But two-job families also meant "latchkey" syndrome and stressed-out moms and dads.

Our teenagers of the '90s don't want to get caught in their parents' grind. For them, wealth and success are a refuge in a worrisome world.

As Stephanie Wills, who's pictured on our cover, puts it: "With the homeless situation, I think people are really striving to be rich more these days. Because of all the dangers in the world like drugs, AIDS, the homeless, the starving, we're really waking up and realizing that we have to be more serious about life."

"I want to be rich," says the South Bend, Ind., 16-year-old, who wants to be a doctor. "I want to be rich more than anything in the world. I'd love to be able to buy myself a pair of jeans, a sweater and shoes that match. I want to be able to buy my mom a house in Connecticut. If I were rich, it would be easier to pay the bills. I want to be rich so that, if someday I get married, I can give my kids all the things they want. I want to be able to support myself, not rely on a husband."

Angie Ho, 13, of North Aurora, Ill., wants to be an architect and is equally blunt: "With pay, I can have more things. It allows you to live more comfortably." How does she define the swell life? "I've always dreamed of living in a six-bedroom house on the beach in North Carolina or California and having a Maltese dog, two children and a Mercedes."

Teens' password: security

Imagine beaded, bell-bottomed teens of the '60s laying this rap on their friends. They would have been branded as squares. How did the flower children's children learn such values?

Joan Anderson, who has written several books on family life, including *Teen Is a Four-Letter Word,* thinks that, when '60s rebels grew into '80s working couples, many abandoned their dreams for the daily grind. And their children took notice. "When the Woodstock generation came out of its coma and collided with the real world, it became more conservative," Anderson says. "The concern about financial security is something these kids are picking up from their parents. They are growing up in two-income families where there is a lot of concern about whether the bills will be paid."

Teens know it won't be easy holding on to what they have. They've watched their parents struggle to meet mortgages—even with two paychecks.

Particularly troubling is that nearly three of four couples with children in 1988 had two incomes. One parent worked full time; the other, at least part time. And almost half of the USA's households were making less than $25,000 in 1988; 13 percent were living under the poverty level of $12,092 for a family of four.

As Josh Salmons, 12, of Elbert, Colo., explains: "What happened to the homeless might happen to you. You're worried that if you don't get a job right after college, you're going to be in trouble later on."

Aspiring pediatrician Melissa Dubitsky, 15, from Riverdale, Md., exemplifies the new clean-and-sober attitude: "I don't really think college should be fun. College is the next step in your career, so I'm going to take it very seriously." LaMar Byron, 12, of Rochester, N.Y., who has his eye on a career in aeronautics, sums it up: "The more you know, the better you can become."

It fits, then, that traditional professions are top career choices in our survey, with doctor at 11 percent, teacher at 8 percent and lawyer at 8 percent. Still, 10 percent—most of them boys—want to be pro athletes. Pei Lun Shan, 13, from Redmond, Wash., wants to be a professional tennis player or an engineer. Either way, he figures, he'll bring in the bucks. "If I get paid well, then I can support my family and have a lot more vacations."

And although more than a third of our teens choose themselves, their parents or no one in particular as role models, those who do idolize the famous pick stars who are in the money. Favorite heroes include Donald Trump, basketball player Michael Jordan and pop hit-maker Paula Abdul.

From *USA Weekend,* August 17-19, 1990, pp. 4-5. Reprinted by permission.

3. PROBLEMS INFLUENCING PERSONAL GROWTH

'Life is one big test'

While adolescents are materialistic, Judy Blume, author of popular books for teens, believes that underneath it all teenagers would rather have better parenting and fewer possessions. "They'd rather have less and live in a happy, healthy family situation. They certainly wish that their parents would spend more time with them."

This concern surfaces in the survey. Though 31 percent of our teens plan to raise their children in much the same way they were raised, 19 percent want to spend more time with their kids, and 11 percent want to be parents who listen more.

Anderson, the family-life author, thinks today's conservative, money-oriented teens are insecure. She blames it on the latchkey syndrome. With working moms and dads absent so much of the time, adolescents don't feel like rebelling. They want to get closer. "These children are really the first generation to grow up without a consistent care-giver in the home."

Anderson also sees "a tendency (among parents) to provide things because they cannot provide time. The children get into the habit of equating stuff with love. What does love feel like to these children? Nintendo and tickets to the hockey game."

Teenagers agree that they're playing it safe because they're fearful about the future. They fret about finding a good job (74 percent) and about supporting a family 67 percent), and around half are even worried about dying.

Tracy Zuber, 15, from Troy, Pa., says, "There is a lot more crime and there are drugs—and we have to grow up faster." She is wary of adulthood. "Kids have lots of tests. But as an adult, life is one big test."

Idealism survives

Benjamin Spock, 87, the granddaddy of pediatricians, takes teens' angst in stride. "One of my conclusions is we are a naturally materialistic society . . . and, like rubber bands, kids snap back to a materialistic outlook unless something is pulling them away from it."

As Spock remembers it, the boys at the top of his college class (Yale, '25) wanted to be bankers and brokers. During the Great Depression, young people flirted with radical ideals. In the booming postwar '50s, college grads went for the house, the car and the best job they could find. The late '60s brought back rebels with causes. By the '80s, the pendulum had swung back to a materialistic mood.

Spock is nostalgic for the rebels of the '60s. "I learned a lot from them when they said, 'Why strain all your life to accumulate money and possessions? Why not live simply?' "

Spock should take heart. Despite their doubts and anxieties, kids still cling to ideals. Janice Hansen, 15, of Croton-on-Hudson, N.Y., wants to save the rain forests and oceans of the world as an environmentalist. Mellisa Dubitsky, who wants to heal children as a pediatrician, says: "I just love working with people. I don't care about the pay."

And they still crave adventure. John Felter, 15, from Arnold, Md., dreams of flying faster then warp speed. "I want to explore the galaxy, see what's out there," says the *Star Trek* fan, who has a 3-foot model of the starship Enterprise on a bedroom shelf.

As for money, that comes second to his quest for excitement. "In my first semester in 10th grade, I was in an English course called 'The American Dream.' The teacher asked, 'What is our American dream?' Most people said it was to be a millionaire. I think a lot of people nowadays want to have that million dollars, be set for life, not have to work. If I can make that million while I'm building a plane that goes Warp I, that would make me happy. I want it all."

ON THEIR MINDS NOW

More results from USA WEEKEND's survey of teen readers about the future:

JOBS

40% rate pay tops; 37% say satisfaction; 23%, a job's challenge. . . . $50,000 is the median salary expected by age 30. . . . What do the kids want to be when they grow up?
Physicians (11%), pro athletes (10%), lawyers (8%), teachers (8%). And 2% dream of being elected president of the United States.

WORRIES

What worries kids about the future? 74% are concerned about finding a good job; 67%, about supporting a family; 51%, about dying.
. . . And today's teenagers expect to be careful with money as adults: 68% plan to be savers, not spenders.

SCHOOL PLANS

98% are set on finishing high school; 83% want a college education. Boys (77%) are less likely than girls (86%) to want college.

FAMILY

70% say marriage is in their future. . . . 56% say divorce is not. . . . How do today's teens want to raise their own kids? 19% would spend more time with their kids than their parents have spent with them; 11% would really listen; 19% would be less strict; 2%, stricter; 31% would raise their kids the same way their parents raised them. . . . Most important in a marriage: 75% cite trust/communication (86% of the girls, 62% of boys).

SOCIAL ISSUES

34% predict that the environment will be the No. 1 problem by the time they reach 40; 24% say drugs and crime; 19% AIDS and other diseases. Only 2% expect racism to be the top problem. . . . 77% expect a black president by the time they reach 40 (no later than 2018); 72% overall say a woman will be elected president (80% of girls, 60% of boys).

AND FURTHERMORE . . .

67% want to stay young forever. . . . Half think you're over the hill at 50. . . . 28% say they'll be grown up when they get their own place to live; 18%, when they get a driver's license. . . . 70% want children. . . . 52% think the USA will have been at war by the time they reach 40 (10% think it'll be nuclear). . . . 68% think there will be a 51st state. . . . 50% of boys believe life will be discovered in space.
Not all kids have their noses to the grindstone. Here are some desired jobs: Club Med bartender, beach volleyball star, monkey trainer, record-album illustrator, karate instructor, baseball-card dealer, *National Geographic* deep-sea explorer, pro skateboarder.

26,946 KIDS COMPLETED OUR MAIL-IN SURVEY; 59% ARE GIRLS

A Much RISKIER PASSAGE

DAVID GELMAN

There was a time when teenagers believed themselves to be part of a conquering army. Through much of the 1960s and 1970s, the legions of adolescence appeared to command the center of American culture like a victorious occupying force, imposing their singular tastes in clothing, music and recreational drugs on a good many of the rest of us. It was a hegemony buttressed by advertisers, fashion setters, record producers suddenly zeroing in on the teen multitudes as if they controlled the best part of the country's wealth, which in some sense they did. But even more than market power, what made the young insurgents invincible was the conviction that they were right: from the crusade of the children, grown-ups believed, they must learn to trust their feelings, to shun materialism, to make love, not money.

In 1990 the emblems of rebellion that once set teenagers apart have grown frayed. Their music now seems more derivative than subversive. The provocative teenage styles of dress that adults assiduously copied no longer automatically inspire emulation. And underneath the plumage, teens seem to be more interested in getting ahead in the world than in clearing up its injustices. According to a 1989 survey of high-school seniors in 40 Wisconsin communities, global concerns, including hunger, poverty and pollution, emerged last on a list of teenage worries. First were personal goals: getting good grades and good jobs. Anything but radical, the majority of teens say they're happy and eager to get on with their lives.

One reason today's teens aren't shaking the earth is that they can no longer marshal the demographic might they once could. Although their sheer numbers are still growing, they are not the illimitably expanding force that teens appeared to be 20 years ago. In 1990 they constitute a smaller percentage of the total population (7 percent, compared with nearly 10 percent in 1970). For another thing, almost as suddenly as they became a highly visible, if unlikely, power in the world, teenagers have reverted to anonymity and the old search for identity. Author Todd Gitlin, a chronicler of the '60s, believes they have become "Balkanized," united less by a common culture than by the commodities they own. He says "it's impossible to point to an overarching teen sensibility."

But as a generation, today's teenagers face more adult-strength stresses than their predecessors did—at a time when adults are much less available to help them. With the divorce rate hovering near 50 percent, and 40 to 50 percent of teenagers living in single-parent homes headed mainly by working mothers, teens are more on their own than ever. "My parents let me do anything I want as long as I don't get into trouble," writes a 15-year-old high-schooler from Ohio in an essay submitted for this special issue of NEWSWEEK. Sociologists have begun to realize, in fact, that teens are more dependent on grown-ups than was once believed. Studies indicate that they are shaped more by their parents than by their peers, that they adopt their parents' values and opinions to a greater extent than anyone realized. Adolescent specialists now see real hazards in lumping all teens together; 13-year-olds, for instance, need much more parental guidance than 19-year-olds.

These realizations are emerging just when the world has become a more dangerous place for the young. They have more access than ever to fast cars, fast drugs, easy sex—"a bewildering array of options, many with devastating outcomes," observes Beatrix Hamburg, director of Child and Adolescent Psychiatry at New York's Mount Sinai School of Medicine. Studies indicate that while overall drug abuse is down, the use of lethal drugs like crack is up in low-income neighborhoods, and a dangerous new kick called ice is making inroads in white high schools. Drinking and smoking rates remain ominously high. "The use of alcohol appears to be normative," says Stephen Small, a developmental psychologist at the University of Wisconsin. "By the upper grades, everybody's doing it."

Sexual activity is also on the rise. A poll conducted by Small suggests that most teens are regularly having sexual intercourse by the 11th grade. Parents are generally surprised by the data, Small says. "A lot of parents are saying, 'Not my kids . . .' They just don't think it's happening." Yet clearly it is: around half a million teenage girls give birth every year, and sexually transmitted diseases continue to be a major problem. Perhaps the only comforting note is that teens who are given AIDS education in schools and clinics are more apt to use condoms—a practice that could scarcely be mentioned a few years ago, let alone surveyed.

One reliable assessment of how stressful life has become for young people in this country is the Index of Social Health for Children and Youth. Authored by social-policy analyst Marc Miringoff, of Fordham University at Tarrytown, N.Y., it charts such factors as poverty, drug-abuse and high-school dropout rates. In 1987, the latest year for which statistics are available, the index fell to its lowest point in two decades. Most devastating, according to Miringoff, were the numbers of teenagers living at poverty levels—about 55 percent for single-parent households—and taking their own lives. The record rate of nearly 18 suicides per 100,000 in 1987—a total of 1,901—was double that of 1970. "If you take teens in the '50s—the 'Ozzie and Harriet' generation—those kids lived on a less complex planet," says Miringoff. "They could be kids longer."

The social index is only one of the yardsticks used on kids these days. In fact, this generation of young people is surely one of the most closely watched ever. Social scientists are tracking nearly everything they do or think about, from dating habits (they prefer going out in groups) to extracurricular activities (cheerleading has made a comeback) to general outlook (45 percent think the world is getting worse and 62 percent believe life will be harder for them than it was for their parents). One diligent prober, Reed Larson of the University of Illinois, even equipped his 500 teen subjects with beepers so he could remind them to fill out questionnaires about how they are feeling, what they are doing and who they are with at random moments during the day. Larson, a professor of human development, and psychologist Maryse Richards of Loyola University, have followed this group since grade school. Although the results of the high-school study have not been tabulated yet, the assumption is that young people are experiencing more stress by the time they reach adolescence but develop strategies to cope with it.

Without doubt, any overview of teenage problems is skewed by the experience of the inner cities, where most indicators tilt sharply toward the negative. Especially among the minority poor, teen pregnancies continue to rise, while the institution of marriage has virtually disappeared. According to the National Center for Vital Statistics, 90 percent of black teenage mothers are unmarried at the time of their child's birth, although about a third eventually marry. Teenage mothers, in turn, add to the annual school-dropout rate, which in some cities reaches as high as 60 percent. Nationwide, the unemployment rate for black teenagers is 40 to 50 percent; in some cities, it has risen to 70 percent. Crack has become a medium of commerce and violence. "The impact of crack is worse in the inner city than anywhere else," says psychiatrist Robert King, of the Yale Child Study Center. "If you look at the homicide rate among young, black males, it's frighteningly high. We also see large numbers of young mothers taking crack."

Those are realities unknown to the majority of white middle-class teenagers. Most of them are managing to get through the adolescent years with relatively few major problems. Parents may describe them as sullen and self-absorbed. They can also be secretive and rude. They hang "Do Not Disturb" signs on their doors, make phone calls from closets and behave churlishly at the dinner table if they can bring themselves to sit there at all. An earlier beeper study by Illinois's Larson found that in the period between ages 10 and 15, the amount of time young people spend with their families decreases by half. "This is when the bedroom door becomes a significant marker," he says.

Yet their rebelliousness is usually overstated. "Arguments are generally about whether to take out the garbage or whether to wear a certain hairstyle," says Bradford Brown, an associate professor of human development at the University of Wisconsin. "These are not earth-shattering issues, though they are quite irritating to parents." One researcher on a mission to destigmatize teenagers is Northwestern University professor Ken Howard, author of a book, "The Teenage World," who has just completed a study in Chicago's Cook County on where kids go for help. The perception, says Howard, is that teenagers are far worse off than they really are. He believes their emotional disturbances are no different from those of adults, and that it is only 20 percent who have most of the serious problems, in any case.

The findings of broad-based studies of teenagers often obscure the differences in their experience. They are, after all, the product of varied ethical and cultural influences. Observing adolescents in 10 communities over the past 10 years, a team of researchers headed by Frances Ianni, of Columbia University's Teachers College, encountered "considerable diversity." A key finding, reported Ianni in a 1989 article in Phi Delta Kappan magazine, was that the people in all the localities reflected the ethnic and social-class lifestyles of their parents much more than that of a universal teen culture. The researchers found "far more congruence than conflict" between the views of parents and their teenage children. "We much more frequently hear teenagers preface comments to their peers with 'my mom says' than with any attributions to heroes of the youth culture," wrote Ianni.

For years, psychologists also tended to overlook the differences between younger and older adolescents, instead grouping them together as if they all had the same needs and desires. Until a decade ago, ideas of teen behavior were heavily influenced by the work of psychologist Erik Erikson, whose own model was based on older adolescents. Erikson, for example, emphasized their need for autonomy—appropriate, perhaps, for an 18-year-old preparing to leave home for college or a job, but hardly for a 13-year-old just beginning to experience the confusions of puberty. The Erikson model nevertheless was taken as an across-the-board prescription to give teenagers independence, something that families, torn by the domestic upheavals of the '60s and '70s, granted them almost by forfeit.

In those turbulent years, adolescents turned readily enough to their peers. "When there's turmoil and social change, teenagers have a tendency to break loose and follow each other more," says Dr. John Schowalter, president of the American Academy of Child and Adolescent Psychiatry. "The leadership of adults is somewhat splintered and they're more on their own—sort of like 'Lord of the Flies'."

That period helped plant the belief that adolescents were natural rebels, who sought above all to break free of adult influence. The idea persists to this day. Says Ruby Takanishi, director of the Carnegie Council on Adolescent Development: "The society is still permeated by the notion that adolescents are different, that their hormones are raging around and they don't want to have anything to do with their parents or other adults." Yet research by Ianni and others suggests the contrary. Ianni points also to studies of so-called invulnerable adolescents—those who develop into stable young adults in spite of coming from troubled homes, or other adversity. "A lot of people have attributed this to some inner resilience," he says. "But what we've seen in practically all cases is some caring adult figure who was a constant in that kid's life."

Not that teenagers were always so dependent on adults. Until the mid-19th century, children labored in the fields alongside their parents. But by the time they were 15, they might marry and go out into the world. Industrialization and compulsory education ultimately deprived them of a role in the family work unit, leaving them in a state of suspension between childhood and adulthood.

To teenagers, it has always seemed a useless period of waiting. Approaching physical and sexual maturity, they feel capable of doing many of the things adults do. But they are not treated like adults. Instead they must endure a prolonged childhood that is stretched out even more nowadays by the need to attend college—and then possibly graduate school—in order to make one's way in the world. In the family table of organization, they are mainly in charge of menial chores. Millions of teenagers now have part-time or full-time jobs, but those tend to be in the service industries, where the pay and the work are often equally unrewarding.

If teenagers are to stop feeling irrelevant, they need to feel needed, both by the family and by the larger world. In the '60s they gained some sense of empowerment from their visibility, their music, their sheer collective noise. They also joined and swelled the ranks of Vietnam War protesters, giving them a feeling of importance that evidently they have not had since. In the foreword to "Student Service," a book based on a 1985 Carnegie Foundation survey of teenagers' attitudes toward work and community service, foundation director Ernest Boyer wrote: "Time and time again, students complained that they felt isolated, unconnected to the larger world . . . And this detachment occurs at the very time students are deciding who they are and where they fit." Fordham's Miringoff goes so far as to link the rising suicide rate among teens to their feelings of disconnection. He recalls going to the 1963 March on Washington as a teenager, and gaining "a sense of being part of something larger. That idealism, that energy, was a very stabilizing thing."

Surely there is still room for idealism in the '90s, even if the causes are considered less glamorous. But despite growing instances of teenagers involving themselves in good works, such as recycling campaigns, tutorial programs or serving meals at shelters for the homeless, no study has yet detected anything like a national groundswell of volunteerism. Instead, according to University of Michigan social psychologist Lloyd Johnston, teens seem to be taking their cues from a culture that, up until quite recently at least, has glorified self-interest and opportunism. "It's fair to say that young people are more career oriented than before, more concerned about making money and prestige," says Johnston. "These changes are consistent with the Me Generation and looking for the good life they see on television."

Some researchers say that, indeed, the only thing uniting teenagers these days are the things they buy and plug into. Rich or poor, all have their Walkmans, their own VCRs and TVs. Yet in some ways, those marvels of communication isolate them even more. Teenagers, says Beatrix Hamburg, are spending "a lot of time alone in their rooms."

Other forces may be working to isolate them as well. According to Dr. Elena O. Nightingale, author of a Carnegie Council paper on teen rolelessness, a pattern of "age segregation" is shrinking the amount of time adolescents spend with grown-ups. In place of family outings and vacations, for example, entertainment is now more geared toward specific age groups. (The teen-terrorizing "Freddy" flicks and their ilk would be one example.) Even in the sorts of jobs typically available to teenagers, such as fast-food chains, they are usually supervised by people close to their age, rather than by adults, notes Nightingale. "There's a real need for places for teenagers to go where there's a modicum of adult involvement," she says.

Despite the riskier world they face, it would be a mistake to suggest that all adolescents of this generation are feeling more angst than their predecessors. Middle-class teenagers, at least, seem content with their lot on the whole: According to recent studies, 80 percent—the same proportion as 20 years ago—profess satisfaction with their own lives, if not with the state of the world. Many teenagers, nevertheless, evince wistfulness for what they think of as the more heroic times of the '60s and '70s—an era, they believe, when teenagers had more say in the world. Playwright Wendy Wasserstein, whose Pulitzer Prize-winning "The Heidi Chronicles" was about coming of age in those years, says she has noticed at least a "stylistic" nostalgia in the appearance of peace-sign earrings and other '60s artifacts. "I guess that comes from the sense of there having been a unity, a togetherness," she says. "Today most teens are wondering about what they're going to do when they grow up. We had more of a sense of liberation, of youth—we weren't thinking about getting that job at Drexel." Pop-culture critic Greil Marcus, however, believes it was merely the "self-importance" of the '60s generation—his own contemporaries—"that has oppressed today's kids into believing they've missed something. There's something sick about my 18-year-old wanting to see Paul McCartney or the Who. We would never have emulated our parents' culture."

But perhaps that's the point: the teens of the '90s do emulate the culture of their parents, many of whom are the very teens who once made such an impact on their own parents. These parents no doubt have something very useful to pass on to their children—maybe their lost sense of idealism rather than the preoccupation with going and getting that seems, so far, their main legacy to the young. Mom and Dad have to earn a living and fulfill their own needs—they are not likely to be coming home early. But there must be a time and place for them to give their children the advice, the comfort and, most of all, the feelings of possibility that any new generation needs in order to believe in itself.

With Mary Talbot *and* Pamela G. Kripke

Ambitious Bulimics

THINNESS MANIA

For high-achieving young women, thinness has become a symbol of success. Result: Millions diet their way to eating disorders.

Susan Wooley, Ph.D., and O. Wayne Wooley, Ph.D.

Susan Wooley *and* **O. Wayne Wooley** *are associate professors in the psychiatry department at the University of Cincinnati Medical College. They are founding directors of its eating disorders clinic.*

"Every time I lose a pound, I lose a pound for my mother. Every time I vomit, I vomit for my mother."

Irrational words. But they make perfect psychological sense to the speaker. She's a victim of bulimia, a compulsive cycle of starving, binge-eating and vomiting in the quest for thinness. And she's learning—as we, her therapists, have—that her problem stems from her self-image as a woman and her relationship with her mother. Though she's surprised to hear herself say it, she magically feels her bulimia will somehow rescue her mother from her burdens.

Her mother, of course, doesn't want such "help." Most parents of bulimics are terrified by their daughters' condition. Though bulimics often *look* normal—unlike anorexics, who can starve themselves into emaciation—they exhaust their bodies, binging on thousands of calories at a time, several times a day, and then using laxatives or vomiting to purge. The roller-coaster can be life-threatening—and feel virtually impossible to stop.

As therapists, we've worked with hundreds of bulimics at the Eating Disorders Clinic of the University of Cincinnati Medical College—one of the first few such specialized clinics in the country, founded in 1974. But in 1983, we realized that many of our patients weren't helped by regular therapy. So we began a three-and-a-half-week Intensive Treatment Program where six to eight women can go through focused individual and group treatment.

From *American Health Magazine*, October 1986, pp. 68-74.

The average patient is 24, 5′5″ and 123 lb., and a bulimic for eight years—though some in their late 30s have been bulimic for much longer.

After three years and more than 100 patients, we've found that the intensive program works. A year after treatment, some graduates still binge and purge occasionally, but only 15% as often as before. For the first time in years, they're able to eat normally for several months at a time. Virtually all say the program helps them feel better about their bodies, their families, their friends, their careers. Psychological tests show clear improvement.

But the intensive program hasn't only helped these bulimic women. It's also helped us, their therapists, explore the causes of bulimia in unusual depth. And our patients' stories show clearly that bulimia is a product of modern conflict over women's social roles—much as the hysteria Freud saw in his female patients symbolized Victorian conflicts.

Our patients have also shown us that women with special backgrounds and conflicts face the greatest risk. We've found, for example, that:

- Less than 9% of our patients had mothers who had jobs that required a college education—and could provide the role models their daughters want.
- Two-thirds of our patients, though already in their 20s, still had not chosen careers.
- And a frightening number—*almost half*—had suffered sexual abuse.

HOW DO YOU SEE YOURSELF?

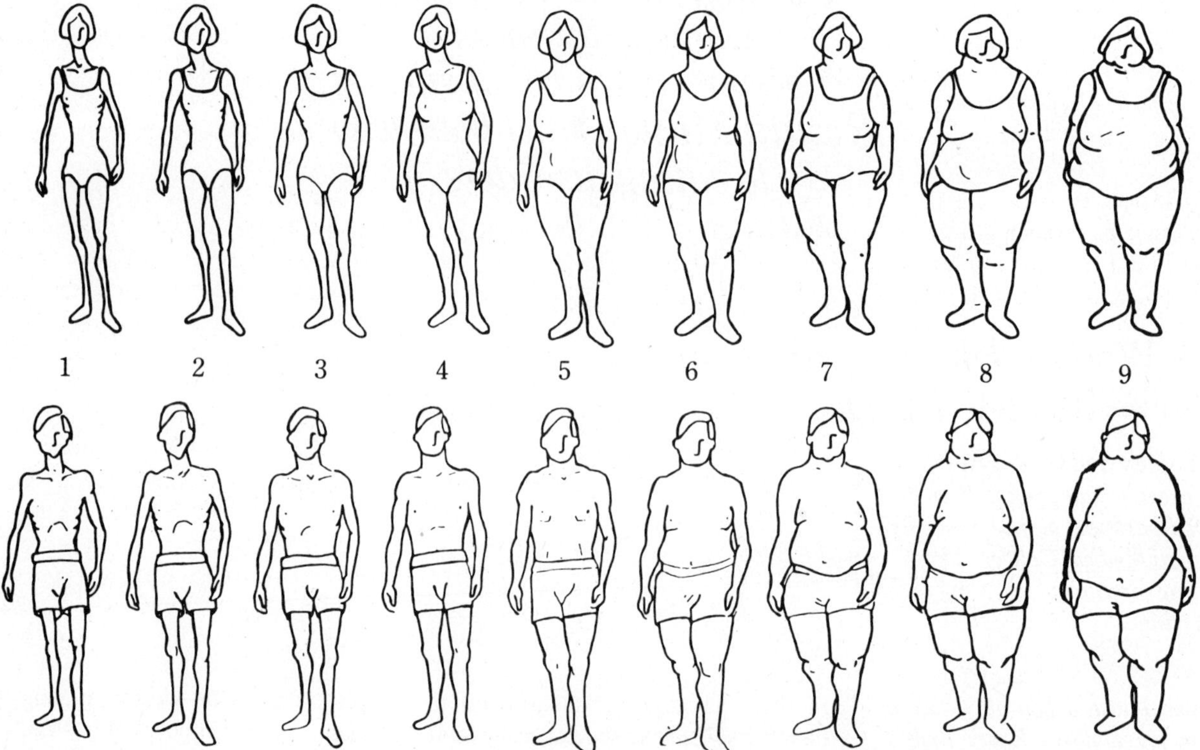

Look at the people above. Then, without thinking about it too much, pick the body that you think:

- Is closest to what you look like.
- Is closest to how you *want* to look.
- Is the body type that's most attractive to the opposite sex.

At the University of Pennsylvania, psychologists Paul Rozin and April Fallon tried this test on college students. The students' answers showed that men and women view their own bodies in dramatically different ways.

Men are satisfied with their looks. The average man says his ideal is body number 4—that's what he'd like to weigh—and he thinks he actually looks like that. He also thinks women are most attracted to that type—though *women* say they like their men leaner.

College women, in contrast, think pounds of fat lie between them and their ideal. They think, on the average, that their bodies are somewhat slimmer than woman number 4. But they think men would be most attracted to a number 3 body (when men actually say they like women a little *plumper* than that). And finally, these women want to be *even thinner* than that number 3 standard—significantly thinner than they think would be attractive to men. *—Joel Gurin*

Thinness symbolizes independence—not just being attractive.

Far from being unrelated, these clues have been crucial to understanding why these women became bulimic—and why bulimia has become epidemic in the '80s.

"New" Women, New Problems

Eating disorders can be so baffling that some researchers, despairing of psychological explanations, have suggested biochemistry is at fault. As evidence, they point to the fact that antidepressant drugs can help some bulimics. And research at the National Institute of Mental Health suggests hormonal abnormalities may be at work in some eating disorders.

But the sudden increase in bulimia makes it clear that it has social and psychological causes. Bulimia, a condition seen by most therapists only in the last decade, is spreading fast. A 1983 survey in *Glamour* magazine, conducted with our assistance, found that only 7.6% of women respondents over 30 had ever vomited for weight control—but a disturbing 20% of women under 20 had done so. Other surveys of high school and college age women have consistently found high rates of binging.

A recent Gallup Poll shows one reason the vast majority of bulimics are women: They're much more concerned with weight. About a third of women 19 to 39 diet at least once a month. Women learn early to fear fat; 59% of teenage girls would like to lose weight, while 52% of teen boys think their weight is fine—and 28% would like to *gain*. (See "How Do You See Yourself?")

Why are women in their teens and early 20s obsessed with weight, and at risk for bulimia? For starters, they are the daughters of the Weight Watchers generation—the first generation to be raised by highly weight-conscious mothers. Many, in adolescence, felt their mothers were critical of their own developing bodies. Such women have a higher risk of bulimia, according to a Miami University study.

So do women who, often learning from their mothers, start dieting early. Dieting is, in fact, almost a prerequisite for developing bulimia. Most people regain the weight they lose on a diet. The body eventually adjusts to a low-calorie intake: Metabolic rate slows down and it becomes easier to add more pounds. So the more times a woman diets, the more desperate she's likely to become—and the more likely to go beyond calorie counting to binges and purges.

But bulimia is more than dieting gone haywire. It comes from an obsession with thinness so intense it becomes the core of a woman's identity.

For '80s women, thinness is weighted with meaning. It's become symbolic of strength, independence and achievement, as well as attractiveness. And we think bulimia is surfacing now, not only because young women are under great pressure to be thin, but because they're pressured to be "strong" in other ways. For the first time in memory, young women are expected to grow up to be more like their fathers than like their mothers. Those new expectations can make the transition from adolescence to adulthood excruciating, and bulimia can become a way of dealing with the pain.

Before adolescence, girls and boys grow up in very different ways. Boys are encouraged to compete and achieve, while girls are raised to value relationships—and usually form strong emotional bonds with their mothers.

But with rapid social change, girls are being asked, in adolescence, to become suddenly like boys: to break the ties and become independent high achievers. To aspire to be a mother and homemaker is no longer enough. They must succeed on male terms, landing important jobs and becoming self-reliant. For these women, the passage from adolescence to adulthood has involved problems unknown to earlier generations. Many of them rage inside at their mothers for not offering an example they can follow.

And they equate their mothers' problems with their mothers' bodies. When we ask our patients to remember how they felt about their own bodies at various points in their lives, they remember being revolted by the changes of puberty. They were not disgusted because they were becoming sexual people, but because they were becoming like their mothers. For a bulimic, to have womanly curves is to be like her mother—powerless.

Most young women in the '80s face conflicts over their social roles. But only some become bulimic. Why?

Our work suggests, first, that the more traditional a woman's family, the greater her risk. Few mothers of bulimics work outside the home. Their fathers tend to be "old-fashioned" men: independent, powerful, successful—and emotionally distant.

Within the family, the bulimic daughter is usually a mediator and caretaker. Sometimes she tries to hold the family together in the face of overwhelming problems—angry divorces, extramarital affairs, alcoholism, illness. Or she responds to more subtle signs of stress, serving as her mother's confidante, "making up" for the failures of siblings. She may unconsciously try to keep her father at home by pleasing him with her accomplishments or charms. One patient realized she became a world-class athlete mainly because it forced her parents to go together to her games.

But the new script for adulthood calls on a woman to break her ties with her mother, and identify with her father. Autonomy and success are pitted against dependence and failure. To become like their fathers, our patients feel compelled to be thin—not just to minimize their womanliness, but also because thinness, in this culture, is a sign of achievement and mastery. The bulimic woman's thin body proclaims that she is as strong and lean as a man.

Being plump, on the other hand, symbolizes being a "traditional"

Those who want to be "superwomen" have the greatest risk.

woman, the family caretaker—exactly what the bulimic woman fears. "When I pictured myself the thinnest I could be, I saw myself alone," said one of our patients when we asked her to imagine her body changing in different ways. "And when I pictured myself the fattest I could be, there were lots of people around and I had to take care of them." Psychologist Catherine Steiner-Adair has found that girls who accept the "superwoman" ideal uncritically—wanting to grow up to be high-achieving *and* caretaking women —risk real conflict. They're the most likely to have disordered eating.

Ashamed to Have Needs

In her effort to be different from her mother—and separate from her—a young woman can be unaware of what she's losing. Her ambition to be "more like a man" can make her conceal her needs and feelings. She may equate her mother's emotional vulnerability with her apparent "failure" in modern terms, and her father's emotional detachment with his worldly "success."

Repressed emotional needs, though, don't disappear. Our bulimic patients are outwardly friendly, competent and in control. But beneath that facade, they are angry, hurt, lonely, needy. They may swing between stubborn independence and neediness much as they alternate between binging and purging.

Some learned to deny their emotions early in childhood when it became clear their needs would not be met. Many bulimic women, as children, had parents who were unusually stressed—for example, by the serious illness of a younger child. The daughter may have learned to be strong when she sensed that others needed help more than she.

A surprising number of our patients, too, shut down emotionally as a result of sexual abuse. Fully half of the women we've treated have been victims of incest, sexual molestation in childhood or rape. Often they blame themselves: "If I hadn't been so needy, if I hadn't needed my father's (. . . uncle's . . . neighbor's) affection, this wouldn't have happened to me." So they try to need no one at all.

The shame over sexual abuse also makes these women hate their bodies even more. For relief, they turn to self-purification: They avoid food and they exercise obsessively, trying almost to demolish their bodies. "I felt dirty and ashamed," said one patient whose brother had molested her as a child. "I started a diet and became obsessed with controlling my body. I wanted to make my body sacred—but instead ended up bulimic."

Breaking the Bulimic Cycle

Physically as well as emotionally, bulimia is based on self-denial. Although bulimics do binge, their disease is primarily one of self-starvation, a "part-time" anorexia. The starvation required to achieve a thin, boyish look plunges them into such hunger that they inevitably lose control over their eating. So they binge on enormous quantities of food—then try to undo the damage with laxatives, vomiting, compulsive exercise or more starvation. But such purging only leaves them hungry again.

To break the cycle, bulimics have to understand their bodies as well as their minds. Most are terrified that they'll gain weight if they start eating modest, regular meals. Also, the starve-and-binge pattern distorts bodily hunger in a way that makes it hard to return to normal eating. Since many women vomit soon after binging, only a fraction of the food is digested. They grow conditioned to eat large amounts before they feel satisfied.

As a woman recovers from bulimia, her body may take months to readjust fully, though improvement starts within weeks. During this time she will struggle with hunger, bloat and many gastrointestinal symptoms.

TO BE SURE YOU'RE NOT AT RISK

Try this self-test to see if you may need help

How do you think about eating, dieting and your body? To find out, see if these statements are true for you:

1. A day rarely passes that I don't worry about how much I eat.
2. I am embarrassed to be seen in a bathing suit.
3. There are many foods I always feel guilty about eating.
4. Most attractive people I see are thinner than I am.
5. I usually begin the day with a vow to diet.
6. My thighs are too fat.
7. I feel uncomfortable eating anything fattening in front of people.
8. It makes me nervous if people can watch me from behind.
9. After I eat a lot, I think about ways of getting rid of or burning up calories.
10. I hate seeing myself in a mirror.
11. I feel terrible about myself if I don't do a lot of exercise every day.
12. I find my naked body repulsive.
13. If I eat too much, I sometimes vomit or take laxatives.
14. My worst problem is the appearance of my body.

The odd-numbered questions tell whether your eating and exercise patterns have gone awry. The even ones tell if you're overly critical of your body. Add up the number of "true" answers. If your score is:

2-4: You're typical, and probably not at risk.

5-8: You're overly concerned with your weight. Watch your attitudes and behavior carefully.

9-14: You may well be developing an eating disorder. Consider professional psychological help. —*Eds.*

Two women said they were willing to die to become thin.

While we help our patients with the practical problems of eating, we focus on the psychological conflicts that led them into bulimia and now keep them there. Powerful techniques are required to get behind the facade the bulimic usually wears. Dramatic re-enactments of past events uncover painful issues and bring the group closer together. To recover, the women must become less absorbed in the problems of their families and more involved with their peers—in an open, "real" way. As therapists we have learned that we must be real ourselves, showing our own feelings, actively challenging any emotional whitewashing, and finding ways to break down the barriers that keep these women emotionally isolated.

Recovery also requires a change in the way a woman views her body. Psychologist Ann Kearney Cooke has developed new techniques for change. In one exercise, patients lie on the floor and picture their bodies in different ways—older, younger, taller, shorter, fatter, thinner—seeking important emotional associations to body size. In another, they sculpt their bodies in clay as they remember them at different points in their lives. In still others, a woman enters into her mother's body, exploring the influence of her life. And, of particular importance, psychological exercises help to master the trauma and shame connected with sexual abuse.

Sometimes we use an indirect, paradoxical approach to break through the resistance to change. When one group complained repeatedly of feeling fat—a fear that keeps many women bulimic—therapist Cooke suggested they use the therapy group to exercise and burn off calories. She asked group members, by turns, to lead the exercises, being as tough on the others as they were on themselves, and joined the chorus of orders and criticisms: "Move that leg! How do you ever expect to be thin if you're so lazy?" As the group approached total exhaustion, she asked, "Who really wants to be thin? How many of you are willing to do what it takes?" Finally, she said, "How many of you are willing to die?" When two members said they *were* willing to die, the others began to back off. "No!" said one. "This is crazy."

Learning New Strength

We gear many of our therapy techniques to resolving family issues. To deal with the difficulty of separating from one's mother, we'll ask one patient to play the mother and physically hold another, who literally has to struggle to be free. But family conflicts can't just be worked out in the safety of the group: A woman eventually has to face her family. So in the middle of our treatment program, all the members of our patients' families come for a two-day session. For many parents, it's the first time they've felt free to express their fury and pain over their daughter's binges and purges.

Out of these two days—stormy but always fascinating—come many revelations. One father, sensitized to the problems of incest in the high school where he worked, had backed away from his daughter at adolescence. His wife, herself a victim of incest, interpreted his aloofness as evidence of foul play and pushed him even further away from their daughter. The daughter had no idea why her father had abandoned her emotionally. Her self-hatred, previously aimed at her "fat," eased with this understanding.

Many bulimics are shocked to find their mothers are not weaklings. In family sessions, they feel their mothers fight them, hear them say "No." Seeing the mother's power may free the daughter to be powerful herself.

The message learned in family therapy, though rarely put into these words, is that the family (including the mother) can survive the daughter's passage into a life of her own. They'll be there to return to when she needs them. And it's okay to need: to need one's family, to need others. A vision of the future marked by emotional isolation—the male myth—is replaced by one populated by family and friends ready to respond to her true needs.

Recovering from bulimia does involve loss: To pass into womanhood is to give up the comforts of childhood. It is to leave one's mother behind—her life, perhaps, a series of unfulfilled promises—and cross a generational barrier greater than it has ever been. It's hard to move away from a mother who is truly a victim of a sexist culture.

If they are lucky, though, the mother can affirm her life has been worthwhile to her, and her daughter can believe it. And the daughter may be able to use her mother's skills—of caring and responsibility for others—as well as her father's independence.

Even with support from her immediate family and understanding from those around her, her passage into true adulthood will be hard. But if she can make it successfully, her own daughter may be spared the voyage through the agony of bulimia.

FOR MORE INFORMATION . . .

To learn more about eating disorders—and treatment programs in your area—contact any of the following national organizations.

■ American Anorexia/Bulimia Association, 133 Cedar Lane, Teaneck, NJ 07666. (201) 836-1800.

■ ANAD—national association of Anorexia Nervosa & Associated Disorders, P.O. Box 7, Highland Park, IL 60035. (312) 831-3438.

■ ANRED—Anorexia Nervosa & Related Eating Disorders, P.O. Box 5102, Eugene, OR 97405. (503) 344-1144.

■ Center for the Study of Anorexia and Bulimia, 1 West 91st Street, New York, NY 10024. (212) 595-3449.

■ National Anorexic Aid Society, 5796 Karl Road, Columbus, OH 43229. (614) 436-1112.

Understanding and Preventing Teen Suicide:

An Interview with Barry Garfinkel

Over the past 30 years, the number of U.S. youngsters who kill themselves has jumped 300%. Psychiatrist Barry Garfinkel and PDK Senior Fellow Jack Frymier explore appropriate responses by the schools to this growing problem.

JACK FRYMIER

JACK FRYMIER (Indiana University Chapter) is senior fellow at Phi Delta Kappa International Headquarters, Bloomington, Ind.

BARRY GARFINKEL, M.D., is director of the Division of Child and Adolescent Psychiatry at the University of Minnesota Hospital and Clinic in Minneapolis. Dr. Garfinkel is an authority in the areas of mental health, learning disorders, psychopharmacology, and child and adolescent suicide and has published extensively in these fields. He also headed the Phi Delta Kappa Task Force on Adolescent Suicide. Born in Winnipeg, Manitoba, Dr. Garfinkel has worked in the Departments of Psychiatry at the University of Toronto, Brown University, and the University of Minnesota.

Frymier: To some people, the problem of adolescent suicide seems to have sprung up from nowhere. Just how bad is the problem?

Garfinkel: In understanding teenage suicide today, we have to explain a number of specific concerns that have emerged over the past 30 years. First, the total number of youngsters who kill themselves has increased 300% during this time. What's more, suicide attempts have jumped between 350% and 700%. Clearly, one of the questions we must try to answer is, What has caused these increases? At the same time, there has been a dramatic rise in the number of severely and profoundly depressed high school students, amounting to between 6% and 8% of junior and senior high schoolers at any point in time.

Frymier: Can you tell us anything about who these young people at risk of suicide are, and how parents and educators might identify them?

Garfinkel: Researchers have been working to develop a profile of the young person likely to become involved in self-destructive behavior. Unfortunately, we haven't completely succeeded in our attempts to identify such individuals. We know that the three strongest social correlates of suicidal behavior in youth are family breakdown, a youth's unemployment, and the decreasing religious observance among the young. However, we have been more successful in identifying some characteristics of those least likely to commit suicide.

For instance, we know that girls kill themselves much less often than do boys – at a rate somewhere between one-third to one-quarter that of boys. We also know that race is a factor. The rate of suicide for black youth is about one-

From *Phi Delta Kappan*, December 1988, pp. 290-293.

fifth that for whites, while Native Americans kill themselves 10 times more often than whites. Geography seems to play a role, as well. Rural youth kill themselves at a much higher rate than do urban youth.

Then there are the factors associated with family life. Family breakdown is associated with higher rates of suicide among young people, and a family history of chemical dependency or of completed or attempted suicide is also associated with higher rates among young people. Thus it appears that suicide runs in families, though it's not possible to say precisely whether social learning and modeling of such behaviors as substance abuse is at work or whether some sort of genetic link exists. We also know that religion is a factor. The traditional conservative religions seem to have some preventive effect; Catholic and Jewish young people commit suicide less often than do Protestant youth.

Frymier: You say that researchers have not been wholly successful in describing individuals who are apt to commit suicide, but can you give us the best profile researchers have been able to develop?

Garfinkel: We see four specific patterns in youngsters who do engage in self-destructive behavior. First, we see the youngsters who are isolated and who passively avoid issues and demands placed on them. Signs of this pattern might be deteriorating academic performance, trouble complying with rules in school or at home, and, generally, avoidance of association with one's peer group.

Second, we see youngsters who are highly irritable, who seem to have a chip on their shoulder. These youngsters tend to push people away and prevent others from being effective helpers. Whether consciously or not, the result is that these young people are alone.

Third, we see a tendency to exhibit aggressive behaviors. These young people engage in petty crime and vandalism, but they are more nuisances than delinquents or dangerous criminals. On the surface, they tend to look like the truly antisocial youngsters who normally go through the juvenile justice system. But it is important that their needs be addressed by the mental health system rather than the courts.

Finally, we see youngsters who use maladaptive coping strategies to deal with their problems. Rather than resolve their difficulties, they'll pick up methods that give them temporary relief, e.g., experimentation with alcohol and other drugs or engaging in thrill-seeking behavior. In the end, however, these behaviors do not resolve the difficulties these young people face.

Frymier: Clearly, these young people have trouble dealing with the difficulties of growing up. Are the stresses teenagers face today, both in the family and in school, greater than they were previously? Are we placing more demands on young people than ever before?

Garfinkel: It is apparent that those youngsters who commit suicide or who attempt to do so are experiencing significant stress in their lives, including failing grades, difficulties with peers, trouble at home, and so on. But the stressors themselves are not, by and large, unique to suicidal individuals. Rather, an accumulation of various stresses ultimately overwhelms these youngsters and leaves them believing that suicide is the only solution available to them. Now we have found a few stressors that stand out as very difficult to adjust to and accept. One such is a history of physical and sexual abuse. The abuse of teenagers, boys and girls alike, is associated with a higher rate of self-destructive behaviors.

One striking finding of the research on teenage suicide is that, while some of the stresses that youngsters face do seem to cause suicidal behavior and depression, a whole set of stressors are a consequence of already being depressed. Thus deteriorating school performance and a drop in the level of participation in sports or in social activities are characteristics of a young person who is already depressed. Additional stresses simply compound and worsen the already-existing depression.

Frymier: What can we hope to do to prevent suicidal behavior in our young people?

Garfinkel: One of the things that we would like to achieve is for youngsters to be able to monitor themselves, to recognize when they are under stress or when they are beginning to feel depressed. Instead of letting the pressure build until they need massive amounts of help – possibly even hospitalization and medication – young people could then seek help sooner. In other words, we want youngsters to learn to recognize and admit to being troubled. We have found that girls are more willing than boys to say that they're depressed and to seek help. Perhaps boys are culturally conditioned to view this as unmasculine, as an acknowledgment of weakness, but for every adolescent boy who seeks help, three girls do so.

Frymier: Are there some other things that mental health professionals would

The student who cleans out a locker on Friday afternoon and gives away all of his or her possessions must be taken seriously.

like to see young people doing for themselves?

Garfinkel: Yes, we would like to help youngsters understand coping styles and coping mechanisms. We would like them to be better able to adapt to stress and feelings of depression. We would like to teach them to replace ineffective coping styles with more effective ones.

Frymier: What are some of the ineffective coping styles that young people resort to?

Garfinkel: Among the most common ineffective coping styles in this age group are experimentation with alcohol, the use of illicit drugs, promiscuity, delinquency, and school failure. Through such coping behaviors young people may find temporary social approval in certain peer groups, and this in turn may yield temporary relief from the discomfort of depression. But in the long run these behaviors only worsen the existing depression.

Frymier: What about more effective ways of coping with stress and depression?

Garfinkel: The effective coping styles all relate to an area in which we would like to educate our young people, and that is the importance of communication. Assertive, direct, and clear communication when one is troubled is a central goal of those of us who are trying to help troubled youth. Of course, this kind of communication depends on whether a troubled youngster knows and can trust specific adults or peers. Many troubled youngsters feel that they alone are burdened with a specific problem, when many young people probably share similar problems.

Once youngsters are able to communicate their feelings and are willing to share them, we would like them to become logical problem solvers, so that, when personal problems arise with their families or peer groups, they can sort them out logically and try to arrive at a reasonable solution. They can then try to find real solutions, rather than resort to the temporary relief offered by such artificial ways of handling stress as the use of illicit drugs and alcohol.

Frymier: Let me move to some more specific questions. Do depression and suicidal tendencies develop slowly over an extended period of time? And what behaviors might a teacher observe that would suggest seeking professional assistance for a child?

Garfinkel: First, there's a group of young people, mostly boys, who act impulsively and kill themselves in response to their very first bout of depression. One-fourth of all adolescent suicides fall into this category, and that number is growing. In such cases, there's very little planning involved, no suicide note, and no indicators.

As far as the rest of the potential teenage suicides are concerned, there are three clusters of identifying symptoms that I've referred to obliquely before. First, look for any signs of academic deterioration: grades falling from A's and B's to C's and D's, tardiness, incomplete assignments. Second, at-risk youngsters seem to slow down physically. They may have trouble staying awake, or they may suddenly drop out of athletic activities. Third, they may withdraw from other kinds of involvement with their peers. They may drop out of the drama club or the band and begin to seem socially isolated. These three clusters of symptoms are almost universal, but other symptoms may also appear.

Themes of suicide may appear in student writing or artwork. A youngster may begin to give away possessions. The student who cleans out a locker on Friday afternoon and gives away all of his or her possessions must be taken seriously. Finally, talking about suicide can be a sign that a young person is in trouble. Such pessimistic and self-deprecatory remarks as "I'm dead meat" or "I'm not worth a plug nickel" are not by themselves surefire signs of trouble, but they do occur at a much higher rate among youngsters who are suicidal.

Frymier: The subject of suicide is not one that teachers can easily broach with parents. If a teacher has serious concerns about a youngster, what would be some appropriate ways to bring up the topic and encourage the parents to seek help for their child?

Garfinkel: A teacher can take a number of steps. First, a teacher should not try to handle such a burden alone. Even in the best medical centers, in which handling suicidal youngsters is practically routine, we involve a network of people. Teachers in schools must tell the guidance counselor, the school social worker, or the school psychologist. Establishing that support network within the school is the first thing the teacher should do.

Second, with one of these other people, the teacher should confront the student to discuss what is causing him or her to contemplate suicide. If the student recognizes the need for help, that's when the family should be alerted. And it's important that the mental health professionals in the school, perhaps in conjunction with the principal or another administrator, should sit down with the family and discuss the concerns of the school staff about the child.

But the school's efforts shouldn't stop there. It's essential for the school to maintain a policy of monitoring and following up on youngsters who have been identified as suicidal. Just asking how things are going, just showing interest and concern, may be all that is required. Youngsters routinely get over periods of depression. But if things aren't getting better, then the school officials must once again alert the family.

Frymier: Let me follow up on the development of depression in young people. Is there a particular length of time that it takes for depression to develop in adolescents? Might a teacher become aware of it gradually? How long might a depression last?

Garfinkel: There has been a lot of research on this subject recently. Untreated depression appears to last anywhere from 6 months to 18 months. Because depression lasts a long time, a great many bad things can happen to young people while they're depressed.

When should a teacher begin to worry? Well, I don't have to tell teachers that adolescents are moody by definition, so every time students look grumpy or seem irritable doesn't mean that they're clinically depressed. But if that moodiness, grumpiness, or irritability persists and is generally consistent for longer than two weeks, then I would say it's time to get the school mental health network involved, meet with the student, and alert the family.

Frymier: I've heard that peer counseling is popular in high schools today. Does this offer some hope for dealing with suicidal youngsters?

Garfinkel: Peer counseling is something of a two-edged sword. Certainly, when they're depressed or are contemplating suicide, teenagers routinely seek out their peer group. But what this means is that the people who are most able to help, who have the expertise, and who have a mature perspective on the problem are not being asked to help. Our research has shown that 75% of teenagers who are severely depressed or suicidal turn to their peers, about 18% turn to their parents, and only 7% turn to mental health professionals. While peers offer what support they can, their limited perspective on the emotional problems of their agemates usually won't help to resolve the difficulties.

Teenagers make good diagnosticians, but they make terrible therapists — because they don't have the mature perspective.

We present teenagers with something of a puzzle. We tell them that they must become more independent and develop autonomy when they go off to high school or college or join the work force. Unfortunately, we don't often remind them that it's okay to ask for help when they're in trouble. Turning to someone for help isn't a sign of weakness or of being effeminate; it's a sign of good judgment, if you turn to the right person.

One final point about peer counseling: teenagers make very good diagnosticians, but they make terrible therapists. They're very good at recognizing issues that trouble members of their peer group, but they simply don't have the mature perspective to provide the most effective help.

Frymier: We've been talking almost exclusively about teenagers. Are depression and suicidal tendencies simply less of a problem in the elementary grades?

Garfinkel: Yes. There are a few epidemiological studies, both in the U.S. and in New Zealand, that have shown that depression isn't a major problem before puberty. The rate of depression in 10-year-olds, for example, is around 1.5%. Yet, as I mentioned before, in the high school years it runs to between 6% and 8%. Something happens during and following the onset of physical maturation that is associated with a greatly increased rate of depression.

Frymier: Are there certain people in

the school who, by virtue of the roles they play or the skills they have, would be most likely to be particularly aware of and helpful to young people who are depressed? Guidance counselors seem like the obvious candidates, but in many schools guidance counselors are so overburdened that they aren't able to spend much time with each student.

Garfinkel: First, anyone who has the opportunity to hear what young people are thinking and feeling is in a position to help by alerting others to a potential problem. And that means any teacher. What we have found is that physical education teachers and health teachers are often the first ones to become aware of a student's problem. They may notice that a student lacks energy or doesn't seem able to put forth as much effort as before. After them, we have found that those who work with mental health care, including school nurses, guidance counselors, school social workers, and school psychologists, are often in a position to learn of a problem firsthand, and, of course, they are often the people who can be of most help. After them, English teachers and art teachers get the opportunity to hear or see students' artistic expressions, which sometimes include themes of death and self-destruction.

Frymier: Is there anything you would like to leave with *Kappan* readers, any kind of closing statement that you would like to offer?

Garfinkel: I think that the most important thing to do is to recognize that we have a problem and that we must take action. The situation is worsening, and we aren't changing course. Moreover, I think that the school district is the appropriate level for action. Superintendents are the ones who must take the lead in raising the level of staff awareness and in committing the school district to respond with the appropriate resources and policies. Without their efforts to control and direct school policy, the needed changes will never occur.

Publications on Suicide Available

Phi Delta Kappa has available a number of printed resources dealing with the problem of adolescent suicide. A 32-page report, *Responding to Adolescent Suicide*, written by the Phi Delta Kappa Task Force on Adolescent Suicide (the group headed by Dr. Barry Garfinkel), provides policy guidelines and step-by-step procedures for schoolpeople who must handle the trauma of a student's suicide. The price is $2 (PDK members $1.50).

Single copies of the Phi Delta Kappa *Current Issues Memo* on "Responding to Student Suicide: The First 48 Hours" are free of charge. Additional copies of this three-page newsletter are 50¢ apiece (25 copies for $5).

The Phi Delta Kappa Center on Evaluation, Development, and Research has a volume in its Hot Topics series titled *Adolescent Suicide*. This 251-page volume, which contains articles that have been selected to reflect the best of current research, sells for $20.

For any or all of these publications, write to Phi Delta Kappa, P.O. Box 789, Bloomington, IN 47402-0789.

Not Past Their Prime

As women of the baby boom head into their 40s, menopause is losing its embarrassing stigma, and gaining recognition as a critical health issue

For women who came of age during the 1960s and later, the intricacies of their reproductive lives are as familiar and comfortable as the layout of their homes. But one room has remained shadowy and unexplored: menopause. "Mothers do a good job teaching little girls about menstruation," says Dr. Cynthia Stuenkel, medical director of the Comprehensive Menopause Program at the University of California, San Diego. "But they don't talk to their daughters about menopause." It's the only phase of the female cycle that chatty women rarely chat about—even among themselves. And with good reason: what little they know of it sounds pretty grim. Hot flashes, the weeps, chin whiskers—who would *want* to discuss it?

Hot topic: These days the answer is, suddenly, everyone. Menopause, which refers to a woman's final menstrual period, usually arrives between 45 and 55; the average age of onset is 51. In the next two decades, more than 40 million American women will enter their 40s, and already menopause is emerging as *the* woman's health topic of the '90s. "It's finally coming out of the closet," declares Sonia Hamburger, founder of the Menopause Clinic in San Diego. The cast of "The Golden Girls" can be seen in a public-service TV spot describing the first major government-funded study of this middle-aged rite of passage. Just launched by the National Institutes of Health, the three-year, $10 million Postmenopausal Estrogen-Progestin Intervention trial will chart the effects of various hormone treatments on menopausal women. In recent years, a dozen menopause clinics have sprung up around the country, and Dr. Wulf Utian of Cleveland's Case Western Reserve University has founded the North American Menopause Society. A cluster of fact-packed new books has appeared, from the feminist-oriented "Menopause, Naturally: Preparing for the Second Half of Life" by Dr. Sadja Greenwood, to "Managing Your Menopause," a sensible guide by Utian and Ruth Jacobowitz.

"The change" has always been a frightening topic. Before the 20th century, shorter life spans meant that menopause was usually followed in fairly short order by death. But today, most women can expect to spend fully a third of their lives postmenopausally. And though many suffer physically and emotionally, others sail through the transition with minimal angst. "Contrary to myth, menopause is a natural event in a woman's life," says Diana Laskin Siegal, 58, feminist coauthor of "Ourselves, Growing Older; Women Aging With Knowledge and Power."

In fact, a body of new research indicates that contemporary women don't find menopause the soul-wrenching experience it was for their mothers. A study reported last month by University of Pittsburgh psychologist Karen A. Matthews found that women who had recently gone through menopause did not have higher levels of depression, anxiety or stress than women of the same age who were still menstruating. Sonja and John McKinlay, epidemiologists at the New England Research Institute in Watertown, Mass., conducted a five-year study examining the health of midlife women. In a random sampling of 2,500 Massachusetts women, age 45 to 55, they found that three quarters of the participants felt either relieved or neutral about menopause. Only 3 percent viewed it negatively. "For the majority of women," says John McKinlay, "it's no big deal."

And yet, biologically, menopause is a very big deal. The drop in the body's production of the female hormone estrogen affects some 300 different body functions. The hormonal decline usually begins gradually, at 35 or 40, but women at any age can undergo an instant and especially intense menopause as the result of chemotherapy or surgical removal of the ovaries. About 1 percent of women have a natural menopause before the age of 40.

Whether it happens early or later, many clinicians consider menopause a potential disease state. "The ovary is an endocrine gland, and when you lose the function of that gland, problems develop," says Utian, who is chairman of reproductive biology at Case Western Reserve University School of Medicine and director of two Cleveland menopause clinics. Most menopausal women face two serious health hazards: increased risk of heart disease and the rapid bone loss that leads to osteoporosis and hip fractures. Then there are the immediate and tangible symptoms that range from the mildly annoying to the devastating. The list is headed by the notorious hot flashes, often resulting in disturbed sleep patterns; 67 percent of women experience them for more than a year, and 25 percent for more than five years. Other distressing occurrences include thinning and drying of the skin (which, in the vagina, can make intercourse painful), incontinence and urinary infections, deepened voice and facial hair, impaired touch perception, loss of libido, reduced short-term memory, mood swings and sadness.

In a small percentage of women, estrogen levels taper off quite slowly after menopause. Their bodies partially compensate for the loss by converting the male hormone androgen (present in all women) to estrogen. And because the conversion takes place in the fat cells, many—but not all—overweight women are at an advantage. "A woman who is a little Rubenesque is less likely to get estrogen-deficient osteoporosis than a skinny woman," says Utian.

Hormonal help: For the vast majority of menopausal women who have a more rapid decline in estrogen, several kinds of help are available. The most effective treatment is hormone-replacement therapy (HRT), usually given as a regimen of estrogen and progestin, a synthetic form of another female hormone. Studies show decisively that estrogen, both with and without progestin, can stave off the ravages of osteoporosis—an important benefit, since one of every five older women with a fractured hip dies from complications within a year. Other research suggests that HRT can cut the rate of female coronary heart disease in half.

HRT is also the only really effective treatment for hot flashes. Dr. Lila Nachtigall, director of the Women's Wellness division in New York University's department of obstetrics and gynecology, tells of a patient who had 40 hot flashes a day. With her hair and clothes disheveled from her repeated sweats, "she looked like a bag lady," says Nachtigall, until hormone therapy dramatically improved the woman's appearance and spirits.

As many as 70 percent of menopausal women could benefit from HRT, but federal health officials estimate that physicians are prescribing it for less than half of them.

Signs of the Time

The decline of estrogen levels in middle age can affect some 300 different body functions.

How Women Change

No More Periods: For many women, the cessation is a welcome relief.

Hot Flashes: These telltale bursts of perspiration can last from a few seconds to 15 minutes.

Dry and Thinning Skin: When it affects the vagina, this symptom can make intercourse painful.

Sleep Disturbances: Because hot flashes often happen at night, they can interfere with adequate rest.

Psychological Effects: Depression, anxiety and emotional fragility can occur, but may be due to the many other stresses of middle age.

How Women Cope

Hormone-Replacement Therapy: The treatment relieves hot flashes and reduces the risk of osteoporosis and heart disease.

Support Groups: Sharing common concerns can be reassuring.

Diet and Exercise: Calcium-rich foods and exercises like jogging and cycling help prevent bone loss.

Vaginal Lubricants: Estrogen creams and a new nonprescription product keep dry tissues moist.

Many women shy away because of the ongoing medical debate over whether HRT may increase the risk of breast cancer. The issue is not entirely resolved, but most well-regarded studies have shown either no link or a lower cancer risk in women on HRT. (A 1989 Swedish study that did find an increased risk has been criticized for imprecise methodology.) Some breast cancers are estrogen-dependent, Nachtigall notes, and thus could be stimulated by HRT. But she does not believe the therapy initiates the development of new tumors. The risk is negligible in women who take the hormones for 10 years or less, says Dr. Brian Walsh, director of the menopause clinic at Brigham and Women's Hospital in Boston.

Still, HRT isn't for everyone. Women with uterine or breast cancer, for example, shouldn't take it—and others don't want to because it brings back their monthly periods. Some doctors think HRT is overprescribed. But most women who try it are enthusiastic. Joan Karol, 58, of Brookline, Mass., had severe hot flashes, night sweats and depression. She has been on HRT for 14 years and says, "If anybody told me I had to go off it, I'd be totally devastated."

For women who can't take estrogen, there are some new alternatives. Recently, researchers reported in The New England Journal of Medicine that a drug called etidronate can dramatically reduce the incidence of vertebral "compression" fractures that commonly result from osteoporosis. There's also an over-the-counter vaginal gel called Replens that creates a film of moisture when inserted with an applicator every three days.

More physicians now realize that the menopausal woman needs to be treated holistically—not, says Utian, "just as a failed ovary." In midlife, says San Diego's Sonia Hamburger, women "usually do not get seen above the navel." But at the Comprehensive Menopause Program in San Diego, Stuenkel provides total medical care, spending an hour with each patient, evaluating her history, symptoms and psychological status. Hamburger runs four-hour workshops and encourages women to phone her on what she calls the "hot flash line." She gets a dozen calls a month, mostly from frantic patients struggling with a new symptom or the decision whether to take HRT. About 15 percent of her clients are premenopausal and simply want to be prepared for what to expect.

Early age: Premenopausal preparation is one innovative approach to postmenopausal health. In 1985 Dr. Morris Notelovitz, a gynecologist specializing in what he refers to as "adult women's medicine," founded one of the first menopause clinics to include premenopausal women: the Women's Medical and Diagnostic Center in Gainesville, Fla. Ideally, he believes, a woman should have a thorough medical evaluation at 35, including screening for cardiovascular disease, instruction in breast self-examination and a baseline mammogram.

The transition from premenopause to postmenopause is receiving serious attention from the National Institute of Mental Health. Dr. Peter Schmidt and Dr. David Rubinow, psychiatrists in NIMH's section on behavioral endocrinology, are looking at the effect of menopause on the emotions in a group of women who have recently begun to experience menstrual irregularities. They are also examining the impact of "negative life events" that often occur during middle age, such as the empty-nest syndrome and the demands of aging parents.

Inevitably, the feelings a woman brings to her menopause influence how she experiences it. Hot flashes and the other unpleasant changes are absolutely real, and the tangible signs of growing older are little cause for rejoicing. "It's tough to admit that you're aging in a society that demands that you look young and be useful," says Stuenkel. But the subject is now getting a welcome airing. The middle-aged women of the '90s have neither the time nor the inclination to let menopause confound them or slow them down. So, they'll read books about menopause, and some of them will *write* books about it. They'll ask their doctors for the help they need—and then they'll get on with the rest of the prime of their lives.

JEAN SELIGMANN *with*
DEBORAH WITHERSPOON *in New York,*
NADINE JOSEPH *in San Francisco and*
LAUREN PICKER *in Boston*

Meet the people who never quit learning

You name it. You can learn it. No age limit. Sound exciting? Read on!

The average man who retires at age 65 today is apt to live to be 80, and the average woman to be 84. As Dr. John Merritt, chief of geriatric medicine at the Hospital of Saint Raphael says, "That's a lot of life to do a lot of things with. If it's approached positively, it can be a great experience." Lifelong learning is one of the ways older people can keep growing.

Learning isn't just "the three R's." And it's not just teachers, textbooks, and tests. Learning can take place on a nature trail, at an overseas resort, in a classroom, or in a favorite armchair.

But wherever it happens—and whatever its subject—learning is strong medicine.

According to Dr. Harvey Rubin, a member of Saint Raphael's attending staff in psychiatry, lifelong learning can lead to long life.

"The more you do, the better you'll feel and the longer you'll live," he says.

Dr. Rubin points out that continuing learning can "counteract depression, the number-one problem among the elderly. It also counteracts anxiety, boredom, and a preoccupation with physical complaints."

David A. Goldberg, 82, says, "When I'm driving home from my classes at Southern Connecticut State University (SCSU), I see men and women, 65 and older, sitting on the bench, depressed, without a mission, without hope, without a goal. And it's sad. There's so much available to take advantage of, and they miss that."

Mr. Goldberg has firsthand knowledge of the value of lifelong learning: Next May he will receive his B.A. degree in political Science from SCSU.

"Education promotes social interaction," explains Dr. David Peterson, professor of gerontology at the University of Southern California. "Usually you get educated in groups, and, for older people, getting out and seeing other people seems to be about as important as the particular content of the course. Just by participating in an activity, you're likely to be more social, happier, and better integrated."

Keeping in touch. Opportunities for social contact are especially important for older persons, who may feel cut adrift due to age-related changes. "Some societal structures drop away after age 65," explains Dr. Carol Dye, a gerontologist at the Veterans' Administration Medical Center in St. Louis, Missouri. She adds that, as older family members and friends die, additional social support networks are lost. Declining physical powers or ill health may also necessitate a change in activities. "Continuing education programs can lessen the negative impacts of these changes," Dr. Dye says.

Diane Gibralter, 74, is a case in point. Before beginning art classes at SCSU seven years ago, Mrs. Gibralter was sure she could never be an artist. But now she has two paintings displayed in her grandson's dorm at Yale University, with a commission to complete a third.

Her art work has become so important to her that when she underwent open-heart surgery and was told the operation had not gone as well as expected, she "sat down and started painting, and I got so involved, I didn't even think about it."

Physical health can even get a boost from learning that involves activities such as folk dancing, tennis, walking, or anything else that, as one retiree puts it, "gets the old body moving."

Lifelong learning can be found in many places, though it's not always officially labelled as such. Churches and synagogues, public school systems, community organizations such as the Red Cross and the YMCA — all sponsor classes for adults.

Many colleges and universities have developed special programs for adults beyond typical college age. In Connecticut, for example, the state university system offers tuition-free classes for those 62 and older. Another notable college-based program for older people is the Elderhostel program.

There's a continuing-education topic to suit just about everyone's taste. A small sampling includes:

- Self-protection
- Money management
- Exercise
- Preventive health care
- Modern languages
- Yoga
- Macrame
- Cooking
- American history
- Needlepoint

MedTerms

Activity theory: The theory that older people should remain as active as they can as long as they can. When certain activities and associations must be given up (employment, for example), substitutes should be found.

Health: According to the World Health Organization, health is a state of physical, mental, and social well-being, *not* merely the absence of disease or infirmity.

Life expectancy: The number of years of life expected for an individual or a group. Life expectancy is rising rapidly in most countries.

Life span: The biological limit to the length of life. Each species has a characteristic average life span. For humans, it is over 100 years.

Reprinted by permission from *St. Raphael's Better Health,* November/December 1988, pp. 27-32.

- Mathematics
- Art appreciation
- Speed-reading
- Folk music
- Chess
- Car care and repair.

Today, adult learners are one of the fastest-growing segments of the population.

One reason is that people are living longer. Another is the growing number of people in the United States who have completed high school or college.

By 1990, an estimated 50 percent of the population over 65 will be high school graduates. And that, says Dr. Peterson, is one of the most important factors influencing a person's participation in continuing education.

But that doesn't mean only high-school or college graduates are eager to learn. Many older people who had to forgo an education due to the Depression or World War II are making up for lost time. So are women who interrupted or postponed their education because of childrearing responsibilities.

Aliss Cunningham, for example, was unable to attend college in her youth because of family finances, but enrolled at SCSU under its tuition- free program for senior citizens. She'll receive her B.A. degree in English next spring — at the age of 82. "Should I survive after I graduate, and if I'm on my feet, I'll probably audit some more classes," she says.

Unfortunately, getting older doesn't automatically lead to knowing the facts about aging. Many older people believe that loss of their learning ability is inevitable. They interpret the physical signs of aging, such as fatigue or failing vision, as indications that their intelligence is deteriorating as well. Popular culture — with its stereotypes and jokes about the elderly — reinforces these beliefs.

When surveyed, old and young people alike are apt to agree with the myth that "You can't teach an old dog new tricks." The idea that older people lose their ability to learn is one of the most pervasive — and harmful — myths about older people.

Even worse, the myth is self-perpetuating: Younger people assume that older people can't learn, and relegate them to insignificant roles on the sidelines, where there are few opportunities to learn.

According to Saint Raphael's Dr. Merritt, there is no basis for the myth that older people can't learn. "Except for people who have strictly neurological problems, an older person can assimilate as much overall as a younger person can in the same situation," he says.

In a Duke University Medical Center study of people aged 60 to 94, there was no demonstrable decline in overall ability to learn. The primary change in learning capacity noted in older people is that they take longer to learn something new, compared with their own ability when they were younger or with that of younger people.

According to Dr. Dye, "the hallmark of aging is the slowing of function. The brain is less responsive and less retentive as you grow older. Some of the best memories we have are old memories, because they were put into the brain at a

The Elderhostel program

Outer space. Watercolor techniques. Pioneer life. Computer technology. These are just a few of the subjects offered by Elderhostel, a continuing education program for people age 60 or older.

In all, Elderhostel offers over 3,500 programs, ranging from "Fun with the Dictionary" to "Predicting the Weather" to "Exploring the Okefenokee Swamp."

In 1987 the program had 142,000 enrollments—two of whom were Ruth and Wolfgang Wenten, a Fairfield couple who have participated in Elderhostel programs for more than nine years.

"It's a great thing because you learn something that you haven't learned before," says Mr. Wenten. "And the speakers are always experts in their fields.

"It's not just 'high-brow' courses, either. It could be tennis, it could be golf, it could be folk dancing," adds Mrs. Wenten. She says people shouldn't be afraid they'll have to face "really scholarly things. It runs the gamut." The Wentens, for instance, recently chose courses on art appreciation and on the politics of the family. Last year they traveled to Brazil to study its culture and history.

In the U.S. and Canada, Elderhostelers live on the campus of one of 1,200 colleges and universities for a week or more while participating in up to three classes. International programs in more than 40 foreign countries last two to four weeks, each week at a different institution.

According to Mrs. Wenten, the programs provide a "fantastic low-cost vacation." The average cost in the U.S. is $225 per program, which includes tuition, room, board, recreational facilities, and extracurricular activities. Courses abroad include these features as well as airfare and land travel to and from the host country. Prices vary according to destination and place of departure; a trip to Great Britain and Ireland is listed in the current Elderhostel at $1,689 to $2,100. Some scholarships are available.

No prior knowledge or training in the subject is required. Some participants have advanced degrees; others never graduated from high school. "We all have something to contribute," says Renee Dubina of New Haven. Now almost 80, she started working toward an associate degree while in her early 70s, and has participated in the Elderhostel program for more than five years.

Though Elderhostel traditionally uses university campuses and other educational facilities, programs are also held in national parks and environmental education centers. In the far north, for instance, hostelers at Arctic College in the Canadian Northwest Territories can study Indian and Inuit cultures while taste testing partridge and caribou. Elderhostel also sponsors rafting excursions in Oregon and cruises of Alaskan waterways.

The program is open to anyone over age 60 and spouses or companions age 50 or older. Three new intergenerational Elderhostel programs are now available at Warren Wilson College in North Carolina, the University of Michigan at Flint, and the University of Southern California at Catalina. In these programs elders participate with their own grandchildren or with high school students from the community.

Depending on the facility, Elderhostel accommodations range from the luxurious to the spartan, with shared bathroom facilities and cafeteria food the norm. But dedicated hostelers seem to be more concerned about their mental environment than their physical comforts. And when it comes to mental stimulation, Elderhostel gets an A+.

As Renee Dubina says, "It keeps the brain from getting rusty."

time when it was operating better. As you get older, the things that you put into the brain aren't kept there as well and they're more difficult to get to.

"But that doesn't mean older people can't learn," Dr. Dye hastens to add.

Older people *can* learn, and specific conditions can make learning easier for them.

For one thing, learning is a matter of "using it or losing it," Dr. Dye says. "If you have a lifestyle in which learning and reading and keeping up with current events is the norm, then your ability to learn will be much better than that of a person whose lifestyle is more mentally passive."

Dr. Dye suggests the following practical strategies for older learners:

- Take your time learning the information.
- Take your time "retrieving" or remembering information.
- Break learning into small parts. Learn a little, practice what you've learned, then learn a little more.
- Create a stress-free setting for learning.
- Allow yourself time to sit and think about what you've just learned, without interruptions or distractions.
- Participate actively in learning. Allow time to practice what you've learned. Repeat what you've just heard, and repeat the steps you've just been shown.
- Use rhymes or slogans to help jog the memory.
- Organize what you've learned in ways meaningful to you — through outlines, for example.
- Take notes on what you've heard or read and leave yourself notes about things to do or where to go.

Natalie Felske can attest to the value of these suggestions. Mrs. Felske's hopes for a college education were stymied first by the Depression, then by the beginning of World War II, and then again by her husband's illness. A determined lifelong learner, she is now working toward a degree in English at SCSU.

But first she has to complete a language requirement. Her slight hearing impairment has made it difficult to understand her language instructor and, at age 68, she finds that her retention of new information isn't as sharp as it once was, which makes it difficult to learn new vocabulary words in a foreign language. To conquer these problems, she has devised a system of flash cards for vocabulary words, and she fully intends to receive her degree in 1990.

These learning aids are important not just for older people themselves, but for people who interact with older people in a professional capacity.

For example, physicians who take their fast-paced, stressful work for granted may be frustrated when older patients can't remember information about medications when it's been given to them hurriedly in a busy clinic and without time to ask questions. But the same individual might have little or no trouble remembering instructions if he received them in a quiet room, was given written notes, allowed to repeat back the information, and encouraged to practice carrying out the instructions with supervision.

Because of the differences in their learning styles, many older learners prefer what is known as "age-segregated" learning where participants are about the same age, and the specific needs of adult learners can be addressed. Others deliberately seek the challenge of an age-integrated setting.

One such learner is Martha Caesar, who in 1978 became one of the first to take advantage of the free tuition program at SCSU. Mrs. Caesar finds that "one of the really exciting aspects of taking courses is the young people." At 81, Mrs. Caesar boasts, "some of my best friends are 18."

Like many older learners, Mrs. Caesar has found learning is more fun the second time around. She finds that "today, the classroom is freer. There's more give and take. I remember my professors as very austere, maybe because I was young and revered them. Now they are much more approachable."

Lack of pressure is another bonus from learning in later life, since courses can be audited without exams or grades. Mrs. Caesar had vowed, "never, as long as I lived, would I write another paper." She now takes classes that strike her fancy, starting off with geography classes and now exploring Asian religions.

Some older learners find that learning is in some ways easier later in life. David Goldberg notes, for example, that older people may be able to pay more attention in class because they aren't looking at classmates and thinking, "Am I going to be dating her?" or worrying about the college football team. Finding a job after graduation also needn't be a concern, although Mr. Goldberg teases his younger classmates that "when I graduate, you better watch out!" since he might look for a job as a political scientist.

Of course, it's not just the older learners who benefit from "age-integrated" learning. Young students benefit from their older colleagues' years of experience.

Frank Trangese, who has taken classes at SCSU since 1980, finds that, at 73, he can offer a unique perspective in history courses, since he has actually lived many of the events being discussed.

Having resolved that "when I retire, I'm not going to let my brain go blank," Mr. Trangese now takes classes at SCSU, is a coordinator for the campus Elderhostel program, and helps register others in the free-tuition program.

In a similar way, Natalie Felske thinks her age allowed her to serve as a "catalyst for discussion" in her creative writing class. Being older, she could "let her hair down" and share personal stories about her life and family, something the younger students were reluctant to do until she served as a role model.

By sharing ideas, strengths, and experiences, lifelong learners end up teaching as well as learning. And that's an important lesson in itself.

Melanie Scheller

Melanie Scheller, of Durham, North Carolina, frequently writes about health and wellness.

Reaching the child within us

ASHLEY MONTAGU

The truth about the human species is that we are intended to remain in many ways childlike; we were never intended to grow "up" into the kind of adults most of us have become. We are designed—in body, spirit, feeling, and conduct—to grow and develop in ways that emphasize rather than minimize childlike traits. By learning to act more like a child, human beings can revolutionize their lives and become for the first time, perhaps, the kinds of creatures their heritage has prepared them to be—youthful all the days of their lives.

What are those traits of childhood behavior that are so valuable yet tend to disappear gradually as human beings grow older? We have only to watch children to see them clearly displayed: Curiosity is one of the most important; imaginativeness; playfulness; open mindedness; willingness to experiment; flexibility; humor; energy; receptiveness to new ideas; honesty; eagerness to learn; and perhaps the most pervasive and the most valuable of all, the need to love. Children ask questions endlessly: "Why?" "What is it?" "What's it for?" "How does it work?" They watch, and they listen. They want to know everything about everything. They can keep themselves busy for hours with the simplest toys, endowing sticks and stones and featureless objects with personalities and histories, imagining elaborate stories about them, building sagas that continue day after day, month after month. They play games endlessly, sometimes carefully constructing the rules, sometimes developing the game as they go along. They accept changes without defensiveness. When they try to accomplish something and fail, they are able to try it another way, and another, until they find a way that works. They laugh—babies smile and laugh before they can even babble—and children laugh from sheer exuberance and happiness. Unless they fear punishment, they tell the truth; they call the shots as they see them. And they soak up knowledge and information like sponges; they are learning all the time; every moment is filled with learning.

Most adults draw back from the unfamiliar.

How many adults retain these qualities into middle age? Few. They tend to stop asking those questions that will elicit information. Not many adults, when confronted with something unfamiliar, ask, as children do: "What is it?" "What's it for?" "Why?" "How does it work?" Most adults draw back from the unfamiliar, perhaps because they are reluctant to reveal ignorance, perhaps because they have become genuinely indifferent to the interesting experiences of life and consider that absorbing something new is simply too much trouble.

Nor can most adults content themselves with simple playthings enriched by the imagination. Witness the enormous growth of industries that cater to the "leisure-time" and "recreational" activities of adults, that manufacture the toys grown-ups need to play: boats, cars, trailers, equipment for camping, hiking, running, tennis, and golf. The list seems endless.

Most adults have lost, too, the ability to laugh

From *Utne Reader,* January/February 1990, pp. 87-90. Abridged from Ashley Montagu's *Growing Young,* 2nd edition (Bergin & Garvey Publishers, an imprint of Greenwood Press, Inc., New York, 1989).

from sheer happiness; perhaps they have lost happiness itself. Adulthood as we know it brings sobriety and seriousness along with its responsibilities. Most adults have also lost the ability to tell the simple truth; many appear to have lost the ability to discern a simple truth in the complex morass they live in.

Perhaps the saddest loss of all is the gradual erosion of the eagerness to learn. Most adults stop any

Celebrate midlife with a ritual

As part of my work as a learning consultant, I have held ritual ceremonies for people who were concerned about reaching midlife. Like many in their 40s and 50s, these people are regretful about losing opportunities and youthful energy, worried about bodily changes, and fearful of losing influence as they grow older. The ritual's purpose is to create a vehicle for expressing concerns and regrets, in the process releasing some of the pain caused by midlife worries as well as moving toward acceptance of growing older, and ultimately gaining new-found peace and empowerment.

I've found rituals to be a very moving experience for participants, and I encourage readers to try their own. Any imaginative person with good listening skills, compassion, experience with symbols, and guidance from resource materials can serve as facilitator. A partial list of resources includes Nancy Cunningham's book *Feeding the Spirit* (Resource Publishing, 160 E. Virginia St., #290, San Jose, CA 95112), Penina Adelman's *Miriam's Well* (Biblio Press, 27 W. 20th St., Room 1001, New York, NY 10011), and Gertrud Nelson's *To Dance with God* (Paulist Press, 997 Macarthur Blvd., Mahwah, NJ 07430).

The following is a brief description of a ceremony for a group of women who recently turned 40. In this particular ritual, the participants were six women who had been friends since high school and who got together a few times a year. We started the evening with a potluck dinner, which allowed people to shed the day's stresses and to renew their bonds. Since it was fall, we celebrated the concept of harvest with each person bringing a dish made from local produce.

We began the ceremony sitting in a circle, stretching and breathing deeply as one by one each woman spoke of a frustrating experience of the day she wanted to release: a fight with a child, arriving late for a meeting. We passed a sprig of sage—which in Indian rituals is used as a purifier—to signify the start of a special event in which we would speak from a deeper, more poetic place in ourselves. I talked about the emotional stages we'd explore (ones similar to those experienced with loss) of grieving, acceptance, and empowerment.

Then the women named all the things they disliked about being 40—varicose veins, wrinkles, needing to go to bed earlier—while tossing a ball to each other. The ball game brought a lightheartedness to the heartfelt disclosures. Ready now to go deeper, we made a centerpiece out of a circle of gray fabric, on which each woman placed a stone she had brought. The women took turns being storytellers, slipping on a full-length black coat to symbolize loss and grieving. I asked them to dive deep inside themselves to find what it was that pained them most about aging, and to begin a story about what they discovered with the phrase "I never thought ________ would happen to me." Their stories revealed the feelings of betrayal midlife can bring. One spoke of priding herself on never needing glasses; yet a doctor recently suggested that "it's not too early to consider bifocals." Another said that she "feels so young, and yet two of my teeth have already died." Another lamented the fading of the passion that formerly inspired her to stay up all night to know its mystery and then to greet the dawn. And as each woman finished her lament, there was a chorus of, "Oh no! Not you, too!" We pounded the floor and wailed and laughed as these common experiences comforted us.

After some time spent writing in journals, which helped everyone process and pay tribute to the losses of midlife, each woman held the stone she had brought. I led a meditation on the agelessness and endurance of the stones, which have witnessed so much on the planet since their creation, and asked people to imagine that they could send their pain into their stone.

Next we changed the centerpiece to a cloth that symbolized harvest, and each woman added the ripe fruit or vegetable she had brought—a metaphor for the bounty that comes with aging—and commented on it. As an example, one noted that her ripe peach would have been hard and tasteless before; now its fragrance fills the air and it is lush and flavorful. Then each added a photo of a woman in her 40s whom she admired. Many photos were of women older than us, and we mused on how our sexist society is slow to recognize a woman for her accomplishments. One photo showed the wizened face of a native woman, another the mother of a participant who continued to have zest for life at 70.

Next we passed around an ear of corn—a symbol of physical nurturing for humans in almost every culture—as each woman told of something she was passing on to the next generation. Each reflected on the experiences and wisdom the years had brought: love of music, the ability to read a story aloud with drama, pride in ethnic heritage, helping people to believe in themselves.

Then, as the women laid on their backs listen-

conscious efforts to learn early in their adulthood, and thereafter never actively pursue knowledge or understanding of the physical world. It is as if they believed that they had learned all they needed to know by the age

The later years can be the happiest of one's life.

of 18 or 22. At this time they begin to grow a shell around their pitiful store of knowledge; from then on they vigorously resist all attempts to pierce that shell with anything new. In a world changing so rapidly that even the most agile-minded cannot keep up, the effect of this shell building on a person is to develop a dislike of the unfamiliar. This hardening of the mind—psychosclerosis—is a long distance from a child's acceptance and flexibility and open-mindedness.

But the qualities of the child are ours to express for all time. Genius, said Baudelaire, is childhood recaptured. The fables we have inherited concerning aging are so old that many accept them as truths beyond refutation. Such myths constitute striking examples of the self-fulfilling prophecy. Senility is a disease, not an inevitable consequence of aging. Physical,

We are intended to remain childlike–curious, flexible, imaginative, playful, honest, open-minded.

physiological, and psychological changes do occur with aging. There is, however, no necessary connection between the aging of the body and the aging of the mind.

Recent research indicates that intellectual ability does not decrease through the eighth decade and that with exercise and training significant gains can be achieved. To remain intellectually active, intellectual stimulation is necessary, and that is what the quality of youthfulness is constantly encouraging: to remain in touch with reality, to soak up from the environment that for which the mind hungers.

The later years can be the happiest of one's life. Many of those who have achieved what others call old age have confessed to feeling embarrassingly young, as if such feeling were something anachronistic, an unexpected freshness. It is the kind of freshness that the long-distance runner experiences when at the peak of fatigue he experiences a second wind that takes him on to the finish line. This kind of freshness can be maintained throughout life; it is not too late to achieve it in one's later years. The earlier one has been encouraged in one's childlike qualities, however, the more likely is one to realize that feeling of unadulterated joy in being alive that the romping child so gloriously feels—perhaps without the physical romping, but with that gaiety of spirit that has enabled one to grow young more effectively and more happily than was ever before possible—the last of life, for which the first was made.

ing to soothing background music, I led a meditation that reflected on each part of the body, thanking it for its gifts, e.g., strong arms and legs that take us on journeys, hands that carry out the creativity borne in the heart and mind.

Next, we reflected on other gifts that years and personal growth had brought: As we focused on one woman, each of her friends in turn held a mirror up to her, saying, "I see that the years have given you the gift of ________," gifts such as a great sense of humor, endurance, self-confidence, courage, and patience.

Finally, each woman shared some of the wisdom she had gained from life that could be helpful to others, and then we closed by taking hands and sending a squeeze around the circle, reminding everyone that she could reach back through time to get sustenance from this evening any time she encountered the turning-40 blues.

Rituals for people turning 50 have a different flavor. At this stage, people are generally more accepting of the aging process and more interested in sorting through the emerging patterns in their lives and celebrating the richness of the journey. Ritual components vary: One woman gathered friends and family and described how each person had been instrumental in her life. She made a hoop from the two ribbons each guest brought—one representing a quality they loved in her and the other representing a funny memory they shared. We talked about the three phases women pass through—maiden, creator/mother, and crone—and conjured up images of those in each of us through guided imagery. Another chose to reconnect with the child in her and thank that child for helping her become who she was, and we made masks to invite our own child out. Guests brought a poem or picture that reminded them of the woman who was having her 50th birthday.

Rituals offer a means of viewing life as a journey that offers us many opportunities for transformation. Any moment or event of importance to someone can be acknowledged and explored in a personalized ritual—spontaneous or planned. Thus, if someone you know wants to mark her midlife, consider going beyond those black balloons that say, "You're over the hill now."

—Kaia Svien
Special to Utne Reader

Life in the not-so-fast lane

The middle-aging of society will affect the way all Americans live—from the television they watch and the food they eat to the way they spend their precious free time. Here are some statistics to help you chart the course for this coming cultural revolution.

Percent growth in the number of Americans aged 35 to 44 between 1987 and 2000: 27%
Percent growth in the number of Americans aged 45 to 54 between 1987 and 2000: 59%
Percent growth in the number of Americans aged 25 to 34 between 1987 and 2000: -16%
Median age of the U.S. population in 1965: 28.1
Median age in 1985: 31.5
Projected median age in 2005: 37.8
Projected median age in 2030: 41.8
Projected median age in 2080: 43.9
Average annual expenditures for households in 1986: $24,000
Average annual expenditures for households whose head was aged 45 to 54 in 1986: $32,000
Number of companies offering long-term care insurance policies in 1984: 20
Number of companies offering long-term care insurance policies in 1987: 73
Percent of daily newspapers that assigned a reporter to an "aging" beat in 1987: 38
Percent of daily newspapers that carried a regular column on aging in 1987: 47
Number of subscribers to cable TV's Nostalgia Channel since 1985: 5 million
Percentage of luxury car owners who are aged 35 to 54: 41
Percentage of American Express gold card holders who are aged 35 to 54: 42
Number of people in work force per each retiree in 1985: 3.4
In 2030: 2.0
According to the Social Security Administration's intermediate forecast:
The year that Medicare will slip into deficit: 1993
The year that Medicare reserves will be depleted: 1998
The year the federal Social Security disability fund will be exhausted: 2034
The year the federal Social Security pension fund will go broke: 2050
Cost of the nation's disability fund, Medicare, and pension fund as a percent of the nation's taxable payroll in 1985: 14 percent
In 2055: 42 percent
Percent of 18- to 29-year-olds who prefer to spend their leisure time at home: 28
Percent of 30- to 44-year-olds who do: 45
Percent of 45- to 59-year-olds who do: 53
Percent of 18- to 29-year-olds who went to bed before midnight on New Year's Eve 1988: 13
Percent of 30- to 44-year-olds who did: 20
Percent of 45- to 59-year-olds who did: 26
Percent of women aged 18 to 34 who used hair coloring in 1986: 17
Percent of women aged 35 and over who did: 26

—Compiled by Blayne Cutler

Statistics taken from a variety of sources, including Roper Organization polls and Interep Research. For a list of citations, send an SASE to Aging Facts, Utne Reader, 1624 Harmon Pl., Minneapolis, MN 55403.

THE PLOWBOY INTERVIEW

ELISABETH KÜBLER-ROSS ON LIVING, DYING . . . AND BEYOND

Elisabeth Kübler-Ross is best known for her work with death and dying, and her fame is well earned. More than any other individual in the Western world, she has helped shatter the taboo that—as recently as 20 years ago—isolated the terminally ill in an atmosphere of nervous silence. Meanwhile, the Swiss-born physician devised her celebrated five-stage (denial, anger, bargaining, depression, and acceptance) model of the dying process . . . authored the classic book On Death and Dying *(as well as a number of other volumes on the subject) . . . sparked the hospice movement in the United States . . . and helped millions of people learn to see dying as "the final stage of growth": an integral part of life itself.*

Most people would agree that the lessons that Kübler-Ross has learned while aiding thousands of terminally ill patients can have meaning for everyone . . . because we all have to deal with others' deaths and—ultimately—with our own. But her teachings have a broader relevancy as well. From her work with the seriously ill, Elisabeth has gained a great deal of practical wisdom about how to live *more fully and positively. Indeed, a good portion of her work now consists of running intensive, five-day "Life, Death, and Transition" workshops (given through her service organization, Shanti Nilaya) . . . in which she attempts to help people express, and then get rid of, internal hostility, fears, and guilt.*

When, years ago, several of her patients told her that they'd traveled in spiritual form during near-death experiences, Elisabeth's work took on a further *dimension: The previously* nonreligious *physician-scientist set upon an investigation of the nature of death itself* and *of the reality of an afterlife. Subsequently, in keeping with the openness that helped make her a successful healer and counselor, Kübler-Ross has publicly described many of her own perceived out-of-body experiences and spirit-guide encounters. (She gained some notoriety for this aspect of her work when she supported, and was subsequently duped by, a pair of self-styled—and apparently unscrupulous—psychic healers. Kübler-Ross has since severed all connections with the couple.)*

And while (as Elisabeth herself suggests in the following interview) the reader can make up his or her own mind about the validity of Kübler-Ross's personal religious beliefs, we hope that no one will dismiss her more "down to earth" wisdom . . . because this short, hardworking ("If you had 50 parents of murdered children to contact, would you *watch TV?"), and plain-spoken woman has been, in many ways, a healer of the human heart.*

Recently, staffer Pat Stone took one of Kübler-Ross's "Life, Death, and Transition" workshops, then followed her to Washington, D.C. and—later on—to her home in Escondido, California . . . in order to get enough time alone *with Elisabeth to complete this interview. He remarks: "The workshop I attended was a theater of catharsis, a moving lesson to me in the pain, and potential, of human existence. The majority of our 70-member group was motivated by Elisabeth's 'externalization of negativity' techniques to share and, in many cases, to positively* resolve *deep personal hurts and shames. And, although Elisabeth feels there* are *some advantages to working through painful personal issues* at *one of her workshops, she has willingly related many of her methods here . . . so that people who wish to do so can use them on their own.*

"Kübler-Ross herself was clearly one of the most intuitive, empathic, and loving people I've ever met. However, she was definitely not *a mild-mannered 'softy'. This often very blunt woman* demanded *honesty from her workshop participants. On the other hand, though, she typically stayed up until the wee hours with needy individuals and, whenever I was with her, never failed to respond to the people who seemed to be* constantly *approaching her with appeals for help. Even during the last portion of our interview—when we were in the secluded privacy of her mountain home (where she* somehow *finds time to tend her garden and goats)—she was often interrupted by the telephone. (After advising one such caller, a woman whose brother had just been killed, how to deal with her own grief, Elisabeth suggested that the woman attempt to contact the* murderer *as well. 'That poor man's whole life will now be ruined. Try to have compassion and see whether you can help him with* his *pain.')*

"And, amazingly enough, she expends all this energy on a diet that generally consists of less than one full meal a day, attributing her tirelessness to the fact that she loves her work and to her belief that once an individual cleans the negative emotions out of him- or herself, he or she will discover an abundance of energy. Without meaning to say that she's faultless, I have to conclude that, in my opinion, Elisabeth Kübler-Ross is a saintly woman."

We hope you enjoy, and gain from, what she has to say.

PLOWBOY: Elisabeth, you're credited with breaking through our culture's reluctance even to *consider* death, and with helping people learn to accept the end of life openly, but I'd have to say—after spending a week in your seminar—that the emphasis of your work is really on *living*!

KÜBLER-ROSS: Of course. It's *living* that's difficult. People who have lived fully are never afraid of death. So it's much more important for me to teach people how to live than it is to help them to accept death.

In fact, when I started what has since become my life's work, I wasn't even *concerned* about how to deal with death and dying. No, when I first left home, a Swiss girl hoping to do relief work in Germany and Poland at the end of World War II, I wanted to learn what could cause people to kill hundreds of thousands of children in concentration camps. How could normal, average men and women—who were mothers and fathers themselves—do that without any qualms . . . and then go home and worry when *their own* children caught chicken pox?

PLOWBOY: But how does that experience tie into the work you're doing now?

KÜBLER-ROSS: At Maidanek—a concentration camp where 960,000 children were killed—I met a Jewish girl whose grandparents, parents, *and* brothers and sisters had all died in the gas chamber. She was saved from dying with them only because there was no room left in the chamber to squash in another person. As a result of that horror, she became determined to survive . . . so she could tell the world about all the atrocities committed by Hitler's Germany. Yet she told

From *Mother Earth News,* May/June 1983, pp. 17-22.

me that when the liberating army finally arrived, she suddenly realized that—if she did what she'd intended—she'd be no better than Hitler himself . . . because she, too, would be spreading hate and negativity.

This young girl touched my life more than anybody ever had, by teaching me that there's a "Hitler" in every human being. My first reaction to that concept was, "Oh no . . . not in me! I'm a very nice person. I want to help the world." But soon after meeting her, I left Germany and headed toward Poland, where a typhoid epidemic was in progress. At that point I hadn't had any food for three days, and I suddenly realized that if a child had walked by with a piece of bread, I would have *stolen* it!

Then I began to understand what my Jewish friend had been saying. As a result, when I went back home, I studied medicine and tried to figure out how to help people to eliminate some of the *negativity* from their lives. When I married and came to America, I began working—quite successfully—with chronic, supposedly "hopeless" schizophrenics, and then with multiple-handicapped children. And, as time went on, I started slipping into death-and-dying work, because I found that the terminally ill patients in institutions were just as neglected as were the schizophrenics or the handicapped children. Hospital personnel didn't even refer to them by name . . . they'd talk about "the pancreas in Room 17" when they meant a person, a human being with a family and children, who had terminal pancreatic cancer!

PLOWBOY: You seem to have been drawn to the most seriously ill or disturbed patients.

KÜBLER-ROSS: I guess that's because I grew up in a *very* nice, affluent home . . . but I was a triplet, and felt I had no real *identity*. Do you understand? Among the earliest memories of one of my sisters is the time my father gave her a bath twice and skipped me. People called us combination names because they couldn't be bothered to tell us apart. Even our teachers didn't know who was who, so they gave us all average grades whether we did good work or lousy! Why, once one of my sisters planned to go on a big date but got sick, so I went in her place . . . and the boy never knew the difference!

Naturally, then, when a person grows up without having an identity—without ever receiving real, *personal* love—he or she begins to be attracted to others who have no identity . . . people like "the pancreas in Room 17". And through this work, I began to see that these three groups of people—the multiple-handicapped, the chronic schizophrenics, and the dying—are perhaps the only individuals left on the planet who are intuitively honest (if they don't like you, they say it and get it over with), and that most so-called healthy people are really phony baloneys, who live their lives with double faces.

These patients became my teachers. They taught me how to communicate with others. And, listening to them, I learned a lot . . . not about dying, but about living.

PLOWBOY: What do you mean?

KÜBLER-ROSS: Well, when you visit an old man who's confined to a hospital bed—actually such a person could be old *or* young, but I started my work with grown-ups—you'll often find an individual who receives absolutely no stimulation. All people ask is that he swallow his pills, let somebody take his blood pressure, and so forth . . . that's all the communication he receives. That man lies there with nothing to do, *knowing* his days are numbered, and he begins to think back on his life.

Then you sit with that man and let him know you care about him. You're not coming to lecture him, or give him a guilt trip about accepting a particular set of religious beliefs. You make *no* demands . . . you're simply willing to sit and listen should he decide to share some of the lessons he has learned in his life. Well, he tells you how he tried to double his income, to get a bigger house, to send his kids to the best colleges . . . but he never *ever* took the time out to get to know his children. He never worked in the garden with them, maybe, or went fishing with the family.

And now, he's dying . . . but his son and daughter don't sit and listen to him as you're doing, because he never developed a close relationship with them. This man realizes that he's spent his whole life chasing a fallacy, pursuing the most irrelevant things in the universe. He sums up his life by saying, "I made a living, but I never really lived."

Don't you see? Most people never learn what's really important in life until tragedy strikes. A mother loses a child, for instance, and *then* thinks, "Why did I scream at her all the times she came home from school with dirty shoes? Why didn't I say, 'Take your shoes off, and we'll clean them,' instead of getting us both so angry, ruining our evening and our meal . . . for nothing?"

Believe me, it would be *impossible* to work in this field, and listen to some 20,000 patients approaching death, as I have, without being altered by their philosophy of life, without realizing how lucky you are and coming to believe that you shouldn't hold grudges or waste time on petty concerns.

PLOWBOY: Elisabeth, you obviously know how to relate to terminally ill patients, so let me ask you this: How *should* people act toward a friend or relation who's dying?

KÜBLER-ROSS: There's no cookbook recipe for what one "ought" to do or say. Every individual is going to have a different reaction to being in the room with a terminally ill person, so the only thing you *can* do is stay constantly aware of how you feel about being there. Your dying friends or relatives won't pick up on what you *say*—the superficial words from your head—but instead will instantly recognize how you *feel*. If you're genuinely glad to see them and you hug them and really mean it (not hugging too hard, naturally, if the person has lots of physical pain), they will *feel* that love.

PLOWBOY: What if you're nervous about being in a hospital, or upset about seeing the person seriously ill?

KÜBLER-ROSS: Just *talk* to him or her honestly about the situation, and admit that coming there isn't easy for you. This will show the person how much you care for him or her, that you've come to visit in spite of the fact that the experience is nerve-racking for you. Then your friend or relative may well help *you* by saying something like, "It's not really bad for me. I have this one doctor I care for" . . . to let you see that dying is a human experience, not an unmentionable nightmare.

PLOWBOY: I can remember a time when my own wife was very ill . . . I'd always cry on my way to her hospital room, and then act strong and supportive when I was with her.

KÜBLER-ROSS: That's phony. To be strong is to be honest, not to be a phony baloney. If you love somebody and are concerned that he or she may leave you soon, naturally you're sad. It's much more real to come in and shed a few tears and say, "It's very hard for me to see you lying there like that." Once that's out in the open, you'll have a chance to help each other.

PLOWBOY: But how do you learn *how* to help someone in that situation?

KÜBLER-ROSS: You *ask*. For example, I first tell the patient, "I can only stay for so long"—I always have to say that because my time is so limited—then I say, "What is it that I can do for you? What is it that you need to share? How can we be of help to each other?" I always say "each other", too, because patients need to know that they can still contribute something, and don't have to lie there completely dependent on someone else's services.

Sometimes such a person might say, "I have this horrible itch, and I can't reach it" . . . so you scratch it, which can be a greater service than you might imagine. Then again, some people don't want to talk at all. They just want somebody to be there and watch television with them. But if you *do* that for a while, suddenly the patient—perhaps without even turning away from the TV screen—may say, half aloud as if he or she is testing you, "How long do you think it's going to be?"

And then you're forced to check out your *own* feelings again. Are you frightened to discuss that person's death, and do you actually *know* about how long this patient has to live?

Of course, you can answer the person only by saying what you really feel. I'd start to talk about that person's chances honestly—admitting that there are always miracles, that nobody can ever predict exactly *what* will happen—but I wouldn't say too much at once . . . because a patient might *sound* as if he or she wants to hear the truth but really *not* want to face it. So after a sentence or two, I'd stop. If the person then said, "And . . ." to encourage me to keep on talking, I'd go on. If he or she didn't want to hear any more, though, the individual would probably change the topic, saying something like, "Oh, did you see what just happened on the television?"

There are no golden rules, you see, except you can *never* go wrong if you listen to the cues of the patient. He or she will always tell you how far to go, what to talk about, and when to stop. If you're sensitive to the patient's communication—whether it's verbal or nonverbal—you can't make a serious blunder.

PLOWBOY: What exactly do you mean by verbal and nonverbal communication?

KÜBLER-ROSS: Dying people communicate in three ways. First, they may talk directly to you. In plain English they'll say something like, "I'm dying. I'm not going to be here at Christmas anymore." These people are the easiest to deal with . . . as long as *you* can be honest, too. Of course, if you respond by saying, "Oh come on, don't talk like that," you'll shut them up. If, instead, you say, "Well, is there anything I can do for you?" or "Do you have some people you want me to send something to for Christmas?" . . . you can help such individuals get their affairs in order.

I call the second language of dying people *symbolic verbal.* For example, I had a young woman patient who was full of cancer. She was probably going to die soon, yet when I visited her, all she could talk about was how the radiation treatments she was receiving in her lower abdomen would make it impossible for her to have children. "Dr. Ross," she said, "I want to understand why I won't be able to have children. I absolutely want children."

Of course, she was *really* asking me about her illness, but she phrased it in symbolic language by talking about her inability to have children. So we talked about that for a good while, and *then* I said to her, "This is hard to accept, but your life may soon be over, and you'll never have experienced being a mother." And at that point she was able to say, "Yes, *that's* what I'm talking about."

You see, you have to let people who are using that symbolic language know that you understand what they're *really* talking about . . . and then play the situation by ear, seeing how honest they actually want to be. The third language of dying patients is that which I call *symbolic nonverbal.* A simple example of that would be a case when *you* want to talk about death, but the patient turns his or her back to you. That's symbolic nonverbal language. There are other types besides body language, though. Why, people can show their feelings in their spontaneous drawings or in things they make out of clay, for instance.

If you understand these three languages, you cannot go wrong in dealing with the dying, because the patients will tell you [1] *when* they need help, [2] *from whom* they need help, and [3] *what* this help should be. If you are ever picked to help someone complete his or her unfinished business, it'll be a blessing for you . . . and an experience that you will never forget.

PLOWBOY: Is it sometimes best for terminally ill people to die at home?

KÜBLER-ROSS: I'm very much in favor of letting patients die at home. When you've done all you can to prolong or save life, you should then let people spend at least their last few weeks in a familiar environment . . . a place where they can have unrestricted visits or smell the aroma of soup or coffee in the kitchen, and where they can have their favorite dog or cat on their knees or see their children or grandchildren at play.

PLOWBOY: How can you tell *when* someone should be allowed to go home to die?

KÜBLER-ROSS: A good doctor has to be able to judge when further medical treatment is unpurposeful. And the family needs to listen to the patient to know whether, for emotional reasons, taking him or her home is the right thing to do.

I can remember telling an old man how hard we were trying to save him, and he said, "Could you try a little *less* hard?" After we laughed over that remark, he added, "All I want is to be left in peace. I've lived a long life and think I'm entitled to stay home." And he was right. On the other hand, though, a depressed cancer patient who has a good chance to make it into remission, but is so discouraged that he or she just wants to give up and go home, may need to be told to wait until the potentially helpful treatment is over.

PLOWBOY: I imagine many *families* are overwhelmed by the thought of caring for terminally ill relatives.

KÜBLER-ROSS: Yes, families often need help. Frequently, they'll need an "outside" person to assist in caring for a patient, so—for example—the wife of a dying man can still get to the hairdresser, or a teenager can go out on a date. It's important not to make the house into a morgue in such a case, because the other people living there still have to *continue* to lead normal lives: If they're *not* allowed to, those individuals will quickly become exhausted, and *very* bitter.

PLOWBOY: How does a family *find* such a helper?

KÜBLER-ROSS: If they really look, they'll find someone—perhaps a neighbor or friend—that they and the patient feel comfortable with. As an example, I once paid a house call to a young Swedish lawyer who had ALS, Amyotrophic Lateral Sclerosis disease. He was paralyzed from the neck down and couldn't talk. His wife and two small children were totally worn out from caring for him, and they were about ready to give up and send him to the hospital. The man sensed his family's desperation, and with the help of a speakingboard—a wonderful tool that helps such paralyzed people communicate—had begged to see me.

After visiting him, I asked his wife exactly what kind of assistance she'd need to be able to continue keeping her husband at home. She said, "I need someone who can take care of my husband from 8:00 p.m. to 8:00 a.m. every day, so I can go to bed and not have to worry all night." Well, I went on to teach my scheduled workshop and met a wealthy American there who had "workshopitis" . . . that's what I call the attempt to grow and become spiritual by attending lots of these sessions. When this man told me that he really wanted to help humankind as I had, I informed him that his first job was going to start that Friday night, and would entail 12-hour shifts with no pay.

That workshop member reported to the needy family on Friday, stayed with the ALS lawyer until he died, and everyone involved was immeasurably happy about the arrangement!

PLOWBOY: But the average family doesn't have Elisabeth Kübler-Ross around to hunt up idle, noble-minded helpers for them.

KÜBLER-ROSS: You don't have to be Elisabeth Kübler-Ross to do it! Ask around! Spread the word to church groups, the scouts, or whatever organization you're affiliated with. There are always people who want to do some service work and be needed. *Look* . . . you'll find the help you seek.

PLOWBOY: Elisabeth, what should people do for *themselves* once they've lost a loved one?

KÜBLER-ROSS: First, you should prepare *before* the person dies. Face the fact that you won't have your next of kin forever, and realize that now is the time to say the things you want to say before it's too late.

To put it simply, if you love somebody, tell them . . . then you can skip those schmaltzy eulogies! When the person dies, you will have *grief*, but not *grief work.*

PLOWBOY: What's the difference between those two emotions . . . and how does a person deal with each one?

KÜBLER-ROSS: Grief is simply natural sorrow, and the way to deal with that is to let yourself cry. Eventually, you'll heal . . . *if* you give yourself the time you need to be sad and remember and mourn.

Grief *work*, on the other hand, involves the fear, guilt, and shame you have if there are things you think you should have done for the dead person but never did. The only way to get rid of those feelings is to share them with somebody you really trust. If you discuss the shame and guilt honestly, it will likely be followed by a tremendous flood of tears. *Then* all you have to do is to forgive yourself, and you'll be able to let go of the feelings. If you *can't* get rid of that emotional pain, though, you probably have a need to continue punishing somebody . . . most of the time, yourself. And that wasted energy will eventually make you ill.

PLOWBOY: In the "Life, Death, and Transition" workshop I attended, you helped people to deal with their grief work, to learn to forgive themselves. Could you explain what, for you, the overall purpose of those workshops is?

KÜBLER-ROSS: I am trying now to show people how to diagnose the Hitlers inside them and to become, symbolically speaking, Mother Theresas . . . so that they can live fully and pass love, instead of negativity, down to their children.

Healthy people, you see, don't *react* . . . they *act.* They're in control of their lives. But if you spend your whole life reacting to others, you never live your own life. You become a cripple. The fastest, easiest way to become emotionally healthy is to diagnose your own unfinished business, to admit the existence of those negative feelings that block you from acting in positive, constructive ways.

PLOWBOY: Are there other negative feelings besides what you call grief work?

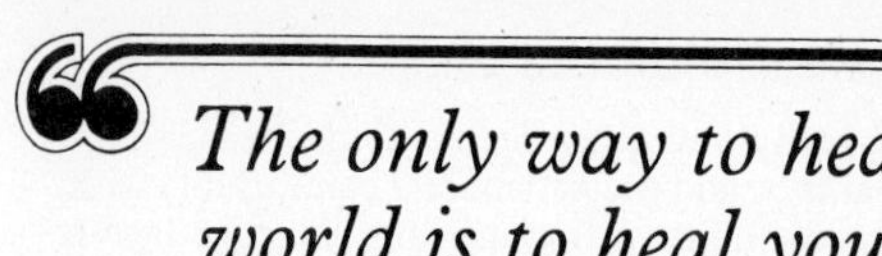

The only way to heal this world is to heal yourself.

KÜBLER-ROSS: As I see it, there are five natural emotions . . . and each one has a negative, *unnatural* counterpart. The first basic positive emotion is *fear* . . . which is a gift from God that helps preserve our lives. However, I believe that the only two natural ones are fear of falling and fear of loud noises. All the rest—including concern about what your neighbors think of you, being scared of your boss, and other phobias—are unnatural. They only drain your energy and lead to ill health.

PLOWBOY: How can a person get rid of such unnatural fears?

KÜBLER-ROSS: *Scream.* If you live in the country, go out in the forest. If you live in an apartment in New York City, get in your car, close the windows, drive down the highway . . . and scream at the top of your voice. When you do that, you can get in touch again with all the horrors you've repressed. It will feel really good, and provide you with relief.

Grief, the second natural emotion, is *also* a God-given gift, and it helps us deal with all the thousand little deaths in life. And tears are the blessing that helps us get rid of grief. The unnatural corollary to grief is, of course, guilt . . . and I've already mentioned some ways to deal with that.

The third natural emotion is anger. This, too, is a God-given gift. It's my opinion, though, that natural anger lasts only 15 seconds. Whenever you're mad for longer than that, it's because you're full of leftover, unfinished anger from something else. If you don't get rid of that, you will end up becoming a bucket full of rage, hate, and lust for revenge, and you'll eventually get very sick.

PLOWBOY: How do you get rid of anger or repressed rage?

KÜBLER-ROSS: The best way is to take a piece of rubber hose and beat all your hate and anger against an old mattress or pillow. You have to verbalize your feelings while you do this . . . you can't just beat in silence until your muscles are tired. And don't be afraid to *act* excited or violent while striking the pillow, because you're not hurting anybody. Instead, you're probably *preventing* yourself from hurting somebody in the future.

Now *all* of these techniques work better if—at least, at first—you have someone to *help* you get your feelings out. It has to be a person who has compassion, someone who won't preach to you and make you feel more guilty.

PLOWBOY: How can we figure out what might be *causing* our repressed anger?

KÜBLER-ROSS: Keep a diary and note anytime that you get overly upset by somebody. After a while, you'll begin to see the pattern of what bothers you and be able to deal with it. You see, whenever you react strongly to people, when someone is able to "push your buttons", it's a gift from the Creator . . . in the form of a signal to you to get in touch with your own unfinished business.

Let me tell you what happened to me once. I had to do a workshop one year in Hawaii . . . and it was scheduled over Easter, a time when I really wanted to be with my family. The man who organized it was a tightwad. He charged us extra for every little service . . . 50¢ for each sheet of paper we used for our spontaneous drawings and 10¢ more for each crayon . . . 25¢ for the little cups we used for coffee. He could have simply asked for $200 more for expenses, and I wouldn't have minded, but his string of tiny fees just kept making me angrier and angrier.

By the last day of the workshop, I was so incensed by this man that if he had asked for one more quarter, I would literally have *killed* him, right then and there. I mean it. And here I am such a "good" person, someone who goes around the world teaching unconditional love!

When I arrived back home, I was so drained by my anger that I was almost physically sick. I didn't know why I was so upset, except that I felt maybe I was "allergic" to cheap men. At any rate, my coworkers from my Shanti Nilaya organization met me and asked how the workshop went. I didn't want to talk about it, so I said, very curtly, "Fine." They asked again, and I said, "Fine, fine. G.D. fine."

Now one of our rules at Shanti Nilaya is that we all have to get rid of our unfinished business—our repressed negativity—but *another* rule is never to ask anything more than three times, because by doing so we may deprive someone of their choice to avoid the subject. I knew if I could last through one more question, they couldn't bother me with it anymore. However, instead of asking me about the workshop, one of my associates said, in a sickeningly sweet voice, "Well, tell me of your visit from the Easter Bunny, then."

That let the cork out of the bottle . . . I *exploded.* After eight hours of crying and talking with my friends, I was able to empty a whole pool of negativity and get in touch with something from way back in my childhood.

You see, as I've indicated before, my parents never gave me much affection, so eventually I rejected them and lavished all my love on some pet bunnies I had. Every once in a while, though, my father—who was a thrifty Swiss—would get a taste for rabbit meat . . . and order me to carry one of my bunnies to the butcher shop. The clerk there would slaughter and process the animal, and then I'd have to walk all the way back home, carrying a bag filled with the warm meat of my dead pet.

Finally, I had only my favorite bunny, a black one, left . . . and eventually my father told me I had to sacrifice him. Oh, I let that rabbit out of his cage and *tried* to get him to run away, but he loved me too much to flee. So I had to carry *him* all the way down to the butcher shop. That man cut up my animal and came back to me and said, in a matter-of-fact voice, "It's a pity you killed this one. She was pregnant. In another week she would have had babies."

I didn't say a word—or eat a bite—at supper that night . . . because I was determined not to let my family see the deep pain I felt. And I continued to repress my anguish over that childhood sorrow so completely that I eventually forgot it . . . until the actions of that cheap man in Hawaii brought back my angry feelings. Then, through my intense work with my friends, I was able to release that negativity, so I'm not likely ever to murder a man for miserliness! In fact, I can now bless that individual for what he helped me learn about myself.

And that's why I've said that every man and woman in every one of our prisons is there because of his or her own "black bunny". So I believe that if someone else is a criminal, then I am a criminal, too.

PLOWBOY: Let's move on now to the other two natural emotions. What are they?

KÜBLER-ROSS: Jealousy, the fourth natural emotion, is a healthy urge to improve, to be able—for example—to read or roller-skate as your big sister does. When it's repressed, though, it turns into envy and harmful competitiveness . . . and is often associated with a lot of shame and guilt. To get rid of those unnatural feelings, you have to be able to *recognize* when you act out of envy and then try to connect that feeling to its origins—likely from your childhood—so you can understand how you became that way. Once that's done, you can look at your own gifts, see the ways in which you are special and unique, and let go of the old envy.

The last, and most important, emotion is love. It has two aspects. One is the need to hold and hug, to feel very secure and wanted and physically close. And the other aspect of love is the ability to say "no", to provide firm, consistent discipline.

Most of us are raised with "I love you *ifs*". I love you *if* you become a doctor, *if* you do well in school, *if* you clean up your room. We try to buy people's love with compliance, by doing things to get it. Well, that's not love, that's prostitution. Real love has no claims or expectations. It doesn't judge: It listens and respects the individual *as* he or she is. Real love is *unconditional* love.

I had a case where an 11-year-old boy came home from school with one bad grade on his report card. His father saw that, and said, "So you don't care. Well, if you don't care, *we* don't care." He ordered the rest of the family to ignore the boy that night. The mother didn't even tuck him in bed. The following morning the child was dead. He had committed suicide. The lack of unconditional love *killed* that 11-year-old.

And he's not alone. Suicide is the third most common cause of death among American children today.

PLOWBOY: Children are very important to you. Do you feel that people can apply the lessons you're teaching—about dealing with negativity—to parenting?

KÜBLER-ROSS: Yes, they can if they keep in mind that children who grow up with unconditional love and firm, consistent discipline —both in equal measures—have few problems dealing with life. You can love a youngster and hate some part of his or her behavior. You don't belt or spank or beat the child for it, though. Kids don't learn from harsh words or beatings. Instead, every time a child does something wrong, try to turn your response into a firm expression of love by meting out an appropriate consequence, immediately.

PLOWBOY: Could you give me some examples of "appropriate consequences"?

KÜBLER-ROSS: If your three-year-old boy—for instance—acts up too much when you go to a restaurant, don't take him the next time you eat out. Show him that he has to stay home with a babysitter until he is ready to behave in a restaurant. If your little girl misuses or carelessly ruins a toy, don't replace it. Tolerate her pain and crying, *and* the guilt trip she'll try to put on you, and say, "That's terribly sad. Next time you have something you love, don't let that happen to it."

Or if, when it's time for your son to go to bed, he gets angry for more than 15 seconds or tries to hit you, give him a rubber hose and tell him to go beat his mattress . . . let his anger out . . . and *then* go to bed. If he sees you're not screaming at him or spanking him for expressing his natural anger, he'll learn that there's a certain time when he has to go to bed, and that there's a safe place for him to get mad . . . and that will be that.

Naturally, you also have to serve as a living example of all these ideas. If you go around screaming and yelling and hitting, you can't honestly expect your children *not* to learn that from you. In fact, a parent's *greatest* gift to a child is simply to work on his or her *own* unfinished business. If you want to raise healthy children, you first have to heal the child inside of you. If you were beaten by your parents, instead of doing that to *your* offspring—imposing your physical power on totally helpless children and calling it authority—find an outlet for your rage and anger. Go chop wood or beat a rug and curse whatever you need to curse. Then you can come back and deal with the problem *without* overreacting. Remember, though, that children should always know they're loved, even though they also know that you may not, at times, love their behavior.

In addition, watch your own actions, and—especially—see how consistent you are in your punishment. Children get very confused if one day everything is fine because a parent comes home in a good mood, but the next day they do the same things they did the day before and suddenly get slapped for it. If you come home grouchy from work, try saying, "I've had a terrible day, so you'll probably have to be twice as quiet as usual, but I hope I'm not often like this." The children will learn to adjust to that quickly. And then, if—someday—one of them tells *you* that he or she is in a bad mood, you should respect the child's feelings, too.

Last, don't go overboard in protecting your children from the hardships of life. If you raise your young ones like plants in a greenhouse, sooner or later, when those plants have to come out into the open, they won't be able to stand the cold. To put it another way—as one of my favorite sayings goes—"Should you shield canyons from the windstorms, you would never see the beauty of their carvings."

PLOWBOY: Elisabeth, as you've portrayed it, getting rid of one's own negativity sounds like a lot of work.

KÜBLER-ROSS: It is, but if you want to weed your garden, you have to bend. You have to get your hands dirty. Yet, in America, working to *promote* one's emotional health is a completely neglected concept. Instead, *after* a person has become seriously disturbed, he or she is given tranquilizers or locked up. That's horrible. What I practice and teach is simply preventive psychiatry . . . and we need much more of it. We should have screaming rooms in every hospital, staffed by people who've lost loved ones themselves, so families can have a place to unload their grief after someone dies. Schoolteachers should use the technique of interpreting spontaneous drawings of children as a screening tool to learn, early on, which ones need help.

PLOWBOY: What happens if a person *is* able to get rid of his or her negativity?

KÜBLER-ROSS: As you work on your emotional quadrant—on your unfinished business—your own intuition will grow and bloom, and you will become more and more spiritual. You see, you don't have to go to school or meditate to develop your spirituality. It's been with you since birth, and it just has to evolve. If you can get rid of the weeds that are strangling your ability to get in touch with your intuitive, spiritual self, that part of you will grow naturally.

Look at me. I'm a Swiss hillbilly. I come from a background that's almost *opposite* to that of a stereotypical Californian. I can't sit still and meditate. I've never been to India or had a guru, yet I've had about every mystical experience there is. And it's important that you *know* that will come . . . that you can see what's in store for you if you weed your garden.

PLOWBOY: Elisabeth, let's talk about the moment of death itself. Based on your experience and research, what would you say happens when a person dies?

KÜBLER-ROSS: There are three stages of dying. The first occurs at the physical level, the one that concerns your normal consciousness and your body . . . which is like a cocoon. When you are mortally injured, in a coma or whatever, and you lose consciousness, your brain ceases to function. The real you then emerges from your physical body and moves to the second, psychic, level . . . like a butterfly emerging from a cocoon. At that point you have what I call *all-awareness*: Your body feels whole, and you are completely and totally aware of everything going on around you. Blind people can even see when they enter the psychic stage of dying.

And—though it may *sound* strange—all this is quite easy to verify. I've studied thousands of cases of out-of-body and near-death experiences in which people traveled to the psychic level. In many instances, when these patients regained consciousness, they could tell everything that had been going on around them. The blind ones could tell me what color ties their doctors had been wearing. An old woman who had been in a complete coma told me that the nurse had said, "That old bag . . . I hope she takes off." Many researchers have noted this sort of thing.

After hearing about these experiences, one begins to realize that no human being can die alone, for three reasons. For one thing, once you're out of your physical body, time and space do not exist, so you can travel to your living loved ones at the speed of thought. Second, you will see your family and friends who *preceded* you in death. You will meet them, you will recognize them, and you will be surrounded by more love than you can imagine.

And this, too, is easy to verify. I checked it out by collecting cases of tragedies in which a seriously injured child regained consciousness a good while after an accident had claimed the lives of other members of the family. Such youths would talk about what happened while they were unconscious . . . saying something like, "I saw Mommy and Peter waiting for me," thereby identifying those people who had died.

The third reason why you cannot die alone is that you have a guardian angel. This spiritual guide—who's assigned to you and to you alone—helps you during your life, trying every means he or she can to keep you on course, so that you will do what you've committed yourself to do in this lifetime. When you die, you'll meet this guardian angel and experience instant recognition along with the greatest love you've ever felt.

PLOWBOY: But how can one scientifically verify the existence of these spirit guides?

KÜBLER-ROSS: You or I can *know* these things from personal experience, but right now, science cannot verify them . . . because our technological knowledge doesn't yet have tools, or even a language, to deal with them. That doesn't mean that the things I tell you are not scientific or true, though . . . the fact is that science is still in its baby shoes!

However, our technological capabilities *are* improving, and I'm absolutely sure that, in the next decade, we'll be able to take an energy photograph of the separation of the "butterfly" from the "cocoon"—the severing of the cord that connects the spiritual and physical—that occurs at death.

PLOWBOY: But is it possible to reach, or contact, this level *without* dying or having a near-death experience?

KÜBLER-ROSS: The psychic level can be reached, and manipulated by humans, but I'm *very* opposed to teaching such things, *including* techniques that help one autogenically induce an out-of-body experience. Now I don't feel this way because psychic energy is, in itself, bad. It is *not* bad, but people misuse it dreadfully. I'd say that anybody who fools around with psychic energy has a 90% chance of becoming a phony. But, you understand, I am also a burned child. I've *seen* people misuse their psychic gifts.

Besides, what's the point of deliberately trying to bring about such experiences? As long as you do only work that you really *love* to do, and do your job with faith and trust, you will *always* get whatever experiences you need for your own evolution. So why sidetrack yourself by spending years "shopping" for some psychic or spiritual event that's not meant for you yet? That's like trying to study high-school math before you learn any arithmetic in elementary school.

PLOWBOY: Let's move back to dying. What's the third stage of death?

KÜBLER-ROSS: At the end of the second stage, the person goes through something that—for him or her—represents *transition* to the third, or the spiritual, level. That symbol may be a mountain pass, the Ganges river, a tunnel, the pearly gates . . . every individual's perception of the transition will be culturally determined. At any rate, at the end of that tunnel or whatever, you will see a light. Once you have a glimpse of it, you'll have no fear of dying . . . *no way.* In fact, experiencing that light will give you an overwhelming feeling of love and bliss.

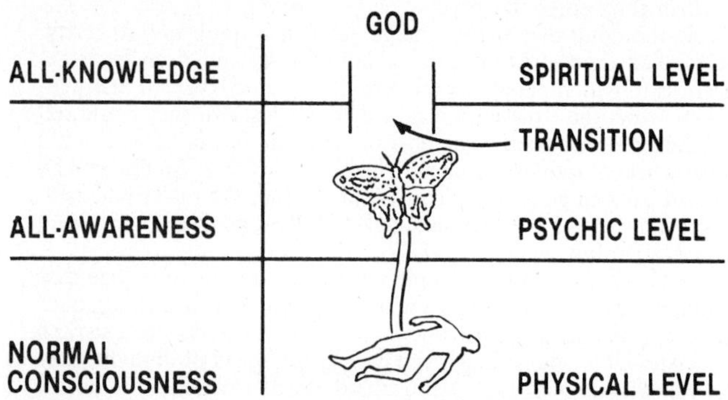

KÜBLER-ROSS'S THREE STAGES OF DYING

Then when you finally die, the invisible energy cord that connects the cocoon to the butterfly is severed . . . and you complete your journey to the spiritual level. This level is in the realm of God. It can't be manipulated in any way by humankind.

Once there, you realize what humanity *could* be. You review all the words, thoughts, and deeds of your life and know how they've affected others. You learn that the summation of your life is the consequence of every single choice you've made. You see whether you've learned the lessons you promised yourself to learn in this lifetime so you can "graduate" . . . or whether you will need to come back to earth to try again. You see, you cannot return to God with dirty hands, because you're responsible for your actions. You cannot kill, for example, and then think you can sit in heaven for eternity. You have to come back and make good for all your mistakes.

PLOWBOY: Elisabeth, I don't mean to deny any of what you are saying—actually I feel unqualified to judge any of it—but it does seem clear that our discussion has now moved into the realm of personal religious beliefs. Do you have a name for your spiritual views?

KÜBLER-ROSS: Yes, practicing Christianity.

PLOWBOY: I'm sorry, but I never thought of Christianity as including reincarnation and spirit guides.

KÜBLER-ROSS: Oh yes. Reincarnation was taught in Christianity for hundreds of years. The teaching of it was eventually forbidden by the First Ecumenical Council, for purely political reasons. And the Bible is full of references to guardian angels!

PLOWBOY: But most orthodox Christians also have a vision of damnation in their picture of the universe. In fact, Jesus himself referred to the fires of hell.

KÜBLER-ROSS: I believe that was symbolic language! It was meant to describe the fact that you will be so *sorry* when you review your life and see how many times you were given chances to live, to give, to share . . . but looked away. It's my contention that God is *all* love, made up of so much love you cannot even conceive of it.

Yet many so-called Christians judge other people. And many churches use fear and guilt to fill their pews. Why? Christianity teaches us to love our neighbors as ourselves. It does not discriminate or condemn. Christ, by his example, was the best teacher of unconditional love *imaginable.* He accepted and loved and healed and worked . . . everywhere he went. He didn't ask people whether they attended such and such a church before helping them!

PLOWBOY: I'm sure you've taken abuse from many people, religious and otherwise, for some of your spiritual views.

KÜBLER-ROSS: Oh yes. But I remember that, back in 1968, I was spat at in the hallways of hospitals for helping dying patients . . . that my work was considered "horrible" then. And look how that's changed . . . there are now more than 100,000 courses being taught on death and dying!

PLOWBOY: Does it bother you that some people may reject your insights about living and dying because of your unusual opinions concerning an afterlife?

KÜBLER-ROSS: Let people believe what they're ready to believe. It's not my place to tell them what to think. I have a practical mission in life to love my neighbor as I do myself . . . and by my example, I try to teach that. If people can't accept something I say, they can throw it out and claim, "It's a pity she became kooky later on." They'll know the truth, anyway, when they make the transition themselves!

In addition, I believe that the fact that I'm willing to discuss my psychic and spiritual happenings and beliefs in front of crowds of 15,000 people also helps *others* get the courage to share their experiences. Now, I can go to Southern Baptist country and hear a minister who attempted suicide describe how he can no longer be the minister of his church because he was enveloped in such total love upon encountering the divine light that he can no longer teach condemnation.

More and more people today are having experiences similar to what I've had and describe. In fact, I believe this is going to develop exactly as did my early work in death and dying. Twenty years from now, *everybody* will know these things . . . everybody.

PLOWBOY: You're saying that, in just two decades, everyone will see the importance of getting rid of his or her negativity and of practicing unconditional love . . . *and* will agree with your views concerning an afterlife?

KÜBLER-ROSS: Oh yes. I can see the changes taking place—and at a rapid rate—right now. Everywhere I go, I'm seeing more and more people who care, who have compassion, who are able to face their own negativity honestly and do something about it. Also, many organizations in which people try to help each other rather than simply make profits are beginning to spring up.

This doesn't mean that the road ahead is going to be easy, though. But the tide has turned since the war-torn days of Vietnam and Kent State. Indeed, I hope I live to about the year 2004. I think by then the big changes will have occurred, and I'll be able to retire.

PLOWBOY: What sort of changes do you foresee?

KÜBLER-ROSS: Primarily, I see growth in human awareness . . . including our finally learning who we really are, and I also see us beginning to put our energy into constructive projects—growing vegetables, trees, and flowers, say—instead of creating military machines. I think we're approaching a time when the world is going to be much, much more fair. I truly believe that, within four or five generations, we'll ultimately outgrow war and hate and weapons.

PLOWBOY: What do you see as your part, your mission, in bringing that change about?

KÜBLER-ROSS: I see myself as a translator and a catalyst. I can help trigger reactions, but then the reactions develop by themselves. I'm here to help people get rid of fear and guilt, so they can live fully and not be afraid of living *or* dying . . . to help people to know what it means to love thy neighbor as thyself . . . and to convey to people that death, as an *end* to things, does not exist.

PLOWBOY: And what is the main piece of advice you have for others?

KÜBLER-ROSS: The only way to fight negativity is not to curse the darkness or the Hitlers—because that is, itself, negativity—but to look at the Hitler inside of you. The only way to heal this world is to heal yourself. So with every choice you make, try to take the highest choice, the one that helps the most people.

Let me put it this way: Just ask yourself, each day, "If everybody would live as I have today, would the world be a better place?"

EDITOR'S NOTE: Elisabeth Kübler-Ross's books are available from Shanti Nilaya, Dept. TMEN, P.O. Box 2396, Escondido, California 92025. Some of the best are On Death and Dying *($2.95), her first . . .* To Live Until We Say Goodbye *($5.95), a series of portraits of Elisabeth's work with dying patients . . .* The Dougy Book *($2.95), a hand-colored letter to a child with cancer . . . and* Working it Through *($15.95), a volume about Kübler-Ross's "Life, Death, and Transition" workshops. Shanti Nilaya sells several other related materials, including tapes and videotapes of Elisabeth . . . and* Quest *($3.95), Derek Gill's biography of Kübler-Ross's early years. Please include $1.00 shipping and handling for one book, and 50¢ for each additional volume.*

You can also write Shanti Nilaya to obtain a schedule, with locations, of upcoming "Life, Death, and Transition" workshops . . . a listing of workshops that teach the psychological interpretation of spontaneous drawings . . . and information about "Never PRN", an oral medication that can help seriously pained patients be alert and pain-free.

A FEW HELPFUL RESOURCES

There are many hundreds of self-help and service organizations related to the field of death and dying today. Here are just a very few of the available resources (as always, MOTHER asks that you send a dollar or two with any request for information, to help cover these people's expenses):

Candlelighters Foundation
Dept. TMEN
2025 I Street N.W.
Washington, D.C. 20006
An international organization for parents of children with cancer

Compassionate Friends
Dept. TMEN
P.O. Box 1347
Oakbrook, Illinois 60521
A self-help group for parents who have experienced the loss of a child

Make Today Count
Dept. TMEN
P.O. Box 303
Burlington, Iowa 52601
A national group concerned with improving the quality of life for persons (and their families) facing a serious illness

Parents of Murdered Children
Dept. TMEN
1739 Bella Vista
Cincinnati, Ohio 45237
A self-help group for those who have survived the death of someone close

Children's Cancer Research Institute
Dept. TMEN
2351 Clay Street, Suite 512
San Francisco, California 94115
A family-oriented center for the care of children and young adults with cancer, including medical treatment and support services

Speakingboards Information
Dept. TMEN
c/o Janet and Bill Raven
31 Ilex Drive
Newbury Park, California 91320
How to learn about three tools that help paralyzed people (who still have mental alertness and the ability to move their eyes) communicate

Exceptional Cancer Patients
Dept. TMEN
2 Church Street
New Haven, Connecticut 06519
A psychological support system helping people learn to live in the face of catastrophic illness

Relating to Others

People in groups can be seen everywhere: couples in love, parents with their children, teachers and students, gatherings of friends, church groups, theatergoers. People have a great influence on one another when they congregate in groups. Groups spend a great deal of time communicating with members and nonmembers. The communication can be intentional and forceful, such as when protesters demonstrate against an oil spill or other environmental disaster. Or communication can be more subtle, such as when college classmates guzzle large quantities of beer, and a new friend conforms, perhaps drinking to the point of illness.

In some groups the reason a leader emerges is clear—perhaps the most skilled individual in the group is appointed leader by a higher power. In other groups—for example, during a spontaneous nightclub fire—the rapidly emerging, perhaps self-selected, leader's qualities are less apparent. In most groups there is bound to be occasional lack of cohesiveness, and increased competition between members. At other times, friendliness may prevail. And, of course, both good and bad decisions can be made in any group.

Some groups such as corporations issue formal rules in writing; discipline for rule-breaking is also formalized. Other groups such as families possess fewer or less formal rules and disciplinary codes, but the rules are quickly learned by their members nonetheless.

Some groups are large, yet seek more members—for example, large, nationalized labor unions. Other groups seek to keep their groups small and somewhat exclusive—such as fraternal orders. There are groups that are almost completely adversarial with other groups. Conflict between youth gangs is receiving much media attention today. Other groups pride themselves on their ability to remain cooperative with similar groups, such as families that band together in a neighborhood crime watch.

Psychologists are so convinced that groups are important to the human experience that they have intensively studied interpersonal relations. There is ample evidence that contact with other people is a necessary part of human existence. Research has shown that most individuals do not like being isolated from other people. In fact, in laboratory experiments where subjects experience total isolation for extended periods, some subjects begin to hallucinate the presence of others. In prisons, solitary confinement is often used as a form of punishment because it is so aversive. Other research has shown that people who must wait under stressful circumstances prefer to wait with others, even if they are total strangers, rather than wait alone.

This unit explores relationships between people, especially interpersonal relations in small groups and dyads. The first three articles reveal how people typically communicate with each other. "A Theory of Success and Failure," describes why minority children fail in school and what can be done to improve their success rate. "Art of Anger Difficult for Women to Master," pertains to women who sometimes feel powerless in society and might not express anger as much or as assertively as men.

The next series of articles describe general problems in interpersonal relationships. In "The Language of Persuasion," David Kipnis and Stuart Schmidt discuss persuasive styles individuals utilize to influence others. In the following article, "They Have Ears, But Hear Not," Gail Gregg describes the art of listening—really listening—to others.

Continuing this series of article on interpersonal relations is "Beyond Selfishness," which describes the "when" and "who" of altruistic or helping behavior. "The Dance of Intimacy," by Harriet Goldhor Lerner, relates to intimate relationships. The author contends that we need to feel comfortable with ourselves first and then, and only then, can we be involved in or improve an existing relationship.

Looking Ahead: Challenge Questions

Do you agree with the premise in the article on minority children and schools that minority children have to give up their own cultures and adopt middle class culture to do well in our schools? Do you think schools are feminine in that they require children to learn passively, be cooperative and quiet, and taught by a largely female staff? If yes, what effect does this have on all children, black and white, male and female?

Are there other interpersonal processes besides persuasion, listening, and helping that would be important to study in society? Do you think social processes are operative in all societies, or do societies differ greatly?

Unit 4

From where do you think altruism originates? Why is control so related to helping behavior? Do you think age is related to altruism the way research suggests it is?

Do you think group dynamics are the same or different from group to group? Do you think groups can reverse processes (such as decision-making) that go awry?

Why do men play the dominant role in many relationships? When do women dominate couples or groups? Can this universal phenomenon of culture be changed? If so, how can we change it? Can women change their relationships with others by expressing anger? If not, why not? If yes, how so?

Have you visited other cultures where the rules for communicating verbally and nonverbally were at variance with America's culture? Why is touch so closely controlled by society? Between which kinds of people is touch an important means of communication? Describe several different cultures you have studied or visited, and compare and contrast them on a variety of dimensions with our own.

Do you think it is possible to find happiness by oneself (without an intimate partner)? How so? What are the benefits of a relationship? What are the disadvantages?

Can opposite-sex friends relate as well as same-sex friends? Have you adopted any strategies for making and keeping friends you should share with others?

A Theory Of Success And Failure

Berkeley anthropologist John Ogbu asks why some minorities do better in school than others. More and more educators are talking about his controversial conclusions.

David Hill

Like a brave tourist in an unfamiliar city, John Ogbu has never been afraid to ask "stupid" questions. While conducting extensive ethnographic research on minority students in Stockton, Calif., in the late 1960's, Ogbu says, "I could ask any stupid question to any group: white, black, Chicano, Chinese, Filipino." More recently, he has become well known for asking a simple question that goes to the heart of the thorny issue of race and achievement in America: Why are some minorities successful in school while others are not, even though they may face similar barriers of culture, language, and poverty?

Ogbu, 51, an anthropologist at the University of California-Berkeley, is the leading proponent of a controversial school of thought that holds that there is a critically important difference between immigrant minorities—people who have moved to the United States because they seek a better life—and nonimmigrant, or "castelike," minorities—people whose status in American society is the result of slavery, conquest, or colonization.

Immigrants—Southeast Asians, Chinese, or Filipinos, for example—may face seemingly insurmountable barriers once they arrive, Ogbu says, but they tend to see those barriers as temporary, and they tend to share with the white middle class certain "folk theories" of getting ahead.

Castelike minorities, he argues, not only experience discrimination from the dominant white culture, but they also are caught in a web of inferiority and self-defeat that discourages them from living up to their potential.

Ogbu's work got a lot of ink—not all of it favorable—several years ago, when he and fellow anthropologist Signithia Fordham found that many bright black students at a Washington, D.C., high school did not live up to their academic potential for fear of being accused of "acting white."

Floretta McKenzie, D.C. school superintendent at the time, endorsed the study (published in an academic journal called *The Urban Review*), telling *The Washington Post*: "As we seek to improve achievement of urban blacks, there's only so much you can do with more teachers and books and so on. We're going to have to deal with the value structure, with youngsters who don't see the reward for achieving." Other blacks weren't so thrilled by Ogbu and Fordham's analysis. In a letter to the *Post*, Reginald Wilson, then-director of the Office of Minority Concerns for the American Council on Education, wrote: "It is astonishing that an allegedly responsible educational study can conclude, and the D.C. superintendent reportedly affirm, that the reason black children do not learn is simply because they believe academic achievement means 'acting white.' Blaming the victim for his condition is a very old and tiresome game."

Ogbu now says the study was blown out of proportion. Fear of "acting white" is one reason why some black students fail to achieve, but it isn't the only reason. "It's one thing in a complex series of

Reprinted with permission from *Teacher Magazine*, Vol. 1, No. 9, June/July 1990, pp. 40-45.

factors," he says. Still, the controversy over the "acting white" article isn't surprising, given the raw emotions just beneath the surface of any discussion of race and education.

Long before the "acting white" controversy, Ogbu was well known for his work in the hybrid field of educational anthropology. Currently holding the title of "distinguished alumni professor" at U.C.-Berkeley, he has received numerous grants, awards, and honors throughout his career, including the prestigious Margaret Mead Award, given by the Society for Applied Anthropology. His *curriculum vitae* runs a hefty 40 pages long. If John Ogbu still isn't a household name among educators and policymakers, at least in the way that James Comer is, it's probably because Ogbu does not prescribe concrete solutions. "That's not my job," he says. "I want to provide information so that others can design effective programs."

Ogbu's current project, a comparative ethnographic study of four Bay-area minority neighborhoods (low-income black, middle-income black, Hispanic, and Chinese-American) and their schools, could very well put the anthropologist in the national spotlight and give his work wider influence. With more than $500,000 in funding from the Carnegie Corporation of New York, the Exxon Education Foundation, the William T. Grant Foundation, the Russell Sage Foundation, the John D. and Catherine T. MacArthur Foundation, the Rockefeller Foundation, and the State of California, Ogbu and his team of researchers are trying to pinpoint the factors that influence minority students to be more or less successful in school. Ogbu intends to produce a report on his findings, to be disseminated to policymakers and school officials.

"There are very few people who are asking the questions that he is," says Barbara Finberg, executive vice president of the Carnegie Corporation, which contributed $100,000 to the project.

Although the differences have narrowed since the mid-1970's, black and Hispanic students continue to lag well behind whites in key measures of academic achievement, including SAT scores, reading proficiency, dropout rates, and college enrollment. Many social scientists attribute the persistent gaps to differences in culture and language; minority students, they argue, are "culturally deprived" or "disadvantaged" compared with white middle-class students. If the term "cultural deprivation" is rarely used now because of its negative connotation, the theory still carries weight among educators and policymakers. In particular, it continues to be the basis for most compensatory-education programs designed to help at-risk students.

Ogbu was one of the first social scientists to challenge the cultural deprivation theory. He argues that it doesn't go far enough because it fails to explain why some minorities do better in school than others. Why, for example, do Asian-Americans produce an average combined SAT score nearly 200 points higher than blacks? Why, in 1982, did a higher percentage of Asian or Pacific Islander high school graduates receive A averages than students from any other racial background, including white?

The answer, Ogbu believes, is that not all minorities are alike. Castelike minorities—blacks, Native Americans, or Mexican-Americans, for example—don't see their situation as temporary. "On the contrary, they tend to interpret the discrimination against them as more or less permanent and institutionalized," says Ogbu. "Although they 'wish' they could get ahead through education and ability like white Americans, they know they 'can't.' "

Immigrants, Ogbu says, see education as a golden opportunity to get ahead, and they embrace that opportunity. "Immigrant parents and communities seem to emphasize for their children the importance of acquiring job-related skills, proficiency in the English language, and basic skills in reading, writing, and math," he says. "They also emphasize that to succeed in these things children must follow the advice of teachers, school counselors, and other school personnel about rules of behavior and standard practices for academic success."

To blacks and other nonimmigrant minorities, the American educational system isn't such a panacea. "Blacks more or less believe that the public schools cannot be trusted to educate black children in the same way as they educate white children," Ogbu says. "We find a similar sense of distrust among American Indians and Mexican-Americans."

And there's good reason for that distrust, Ogbu argues. He points out that blacks in the United States have historically been excluded from the high-quality education received by whites, and this exclusion—plus ongoing subtle devices of exclusion within schools today—has hampered the academic performance of black children. In addition, minorities—particularly nonimmigrant minorities—have consistently been denied access to desirable jobs. Ogbu says this has discouraged whole generations of caste-like minorities from investing time and effort in education and may have prevented them from developing a strong tradition of striving for academic achievement.

As a result, Ogbu argues, many blacks see education as a "subtractive process," one that forces black students who do well in school to give up their minority culture in exchange for the dominant white culture. In short, blacks who achieve in school are considered to be "acting white."

In their study of the Washington, D.C., high school (fictitiously called "Capital High School"), Ogbu and Fordham found that to "act white" isn't merely to do well in school; the concept incorporates a variety of attitudes and behaviors. Among them: speaking standard English; listening to white music and white radio stations; going to the opera or ballet; spending a lot of time in the library studying; working hard to get good grades in school (those who get good grades are labeled "brainiacs"); going to the Smithsonian Institution; doing volunteer work; going camping, hiking, or mountain climbing; having a cocktail party; being on time; and reading and writing poetry.

Ogbu and Fordham found that students who *did* get good grades tried to hide their intelligence from their peers. One student told them: "In the 6th grade, it was me and these two girls; we used to hang together all the time. They used to say we was brainiacs, and no one really liked us. . . . It's not something—well, it's something that you want to be, but you don't want your friends to know. . . . Because once they find out you're a brainiac, then the first thing they'll say is, 'Well, she thinks she's cute, and she thinks she's smart, she thinks she's better than anyone else.' So what most brainiacs do, they sit back and they know an answer, and they won't answer it."

Black students, then, are caught in a bind: If they work hard in school, "they may indeed succeed academically but suffer peer criticism or ostracism as well as suffer from affective dissonance [identity conflict]," Ogbu says. "The dilemma is that nonimmigrant minority students have to choose between academic success and maintaining their minority and cultural frame of reference."

Ogbu argues that immigrant minorities succeed, in part, because they do not equate hard work, good behavior, and success in school with the dominant white culture. Immigrants, Ogbu says, "make a clear distinction between adoption of attitudes, knowledge, and behaviors that enhance academic success for future employment on the one hand and adoption of attitudes, knowledge, and behaviors that lead to loss of cultural identity and to assimilation into white American culture on the other hand." He adds: "Maybe if blacks can find a way of thinking in the same mode, they will avoid a number of problems."

Is Ogbu, in fact, "blaming the victims for their condition"? It is true that blacks who blame racism for all their ills will find only partial solace in Ogbu's work. Yes, he admits, blacks and other minorities encounter racism all the time. Yes, they constantly come up against a "job ceiling" that prevents them from entering the economic mainstream. And yes, reforms aimed at eliminating those barriers are vital. "But minorities cannot simply rely on public policies," he says. "They have to accept some responsibility if they want to succeed."

At the same time, Ogbu does not offer much comfort to conservatives who argue that only by changing black attitudes will black achievement improve. "To change this situation—to eliminate black academic retardation—requires . . . a total destruction of the caste system, that is, the creation of a new social order in which blacks do not occupy a subordinate position vis-à-vis whites," Ogbu has written. "If we destroy the caste system, both schools and blacks will begin to manifest changes compatible with the new social order, and academic retardation will disappear."

Some critics say the distinctions Ogbu draws between castelike and immigrant minorities are oversimplified and unfair. Bart Landry, a sociologist at the University of Maryland and author of *The New Black Middle-Class* (University of California, 1987), points out that, unlike American blacks, immigrants are a self-selected, highly motivated slice of a much larger population. Moreover, he argues, blacks who migrated north in the 40's and 50's, to places like Chicago and New York, were just as highly motivated as immigrants to the United States. "In those days," he says, "blacks had hopes of bettering themselves." But the problems of poverty and low achievement among the black underclass remain and, Landry argues, Ogbu's approach does not explain why.

When Ogbu began studying the schools in a Stockton neighborhood in 1968, he was, in a sense, turning the tables. After all, countless American anthropologists had gone to Africa to conduct ethnographic research. Why shouldn't an anthropologist from a small village in Igboland, Nigeria, use the same tools to study an ethnic neighborhood in America?

Ogbu went to Stockton's Boggs Tract neighborhood (called "Burgherside" in his study), where 92 percent of the elementary school students were either black or Mexican-American, as part of a bilingual demonstration project. He interviewed teachers, school board members, counselors, students, parents, and concerned citizens. "As an African, I could not claim to know from the start what American education is or should be nor the appropriate behavior that leads to success in school," he wrote in his study, published in 1974 as *The Next Generation: An Ethnography of Education in an Urban Neighborhood.* Instead, he set out to study education "as a cultural institution. . . to study how the people in Stockton, including Burghersiders, conceptualize their educational system and their place in it, and how these conceptualizations influence the way they behave within the institution." One of his goals was to understand why Burghersiders had such a high rate of academic failure.

Ogbu's work in Stockton led to many of the ideas he now holds about the school performance of minorities. It cast doubt on the theory that minority children are prone to failure simply because they are born into poverty. Poverty is a factor, he concluded, but cultural and historical factors must be taken into account. Because blacks have been denied good education and economic opportunity throughout their history, Ogbu contends, they have "responded, more or less unconsciously, partly by reducing their efforts in school tasks to the level of rewards they expected as future adults of American society."

In Stockton, Ogbu found that blacks and Mexican-Americans were caught in a vicious circle of failure. He found a high level of absenteeism among students and a lack of seriousness about their work when they did attend class. He concluded that blacks and Mexican-Americans do not try to perform and compete academically because they believe strongly that they have very "limited opportunity to benefit from their educations. And lack of competitiveness ensures that they will not do well in school, that many of them will fail."

Ogbu's later research helped him to understand the difference between castelike minorities and immigrant minorities. He found that castelike minorities in other cultures also lag behind the dominant culture in school performance. One such group Ogbu writes about in his book *Minority Education and Caste* are the Burakumin, a pariah caste in Japan who were once called *Eta*, meaning "full of filth." Although racially the Burakumin are no different from the dominant Ippan Japanese, significant differences exist between them in literacy rates, truancy rates, school dropout rates, and performance on standardized tests of scholastic achievement and IQ. Yet studies show that no such differences in achievement exist between members of the Burakumin and the Ippan who have migrated to the United States. The reason? "The outcast immigrants and their children are no longer overwhelmed by the traditional prejudice and discrimination associated with caste status per se," Ogbu says.

Ogbu's reluctance to provide detailed prescriptions for change and his view that improving black academic performance requires "a total destruction of the caste system" have led some educators to label his work as overly pessimistic. In an article critical of Ogbu's work, Frederick Erickson, director of the Center for Urban Ethnography at the University of Pennsylvania, wrote: "As an educator, I cannot accept the premise that there is nothing we can do to improve the educational situation of domestic minority students in the United States. I am not simply willing to wait for a revolution in the general society."

Yet, neither is Ogbu, it seems. "While I believe that school reforms and the elimination of caste barriers will eventually influence blacks to develop a new set of attitudes, self-conceptions, learning habits, and other skills that promote success in school, I also believe that it is necessary to develop programs that will speed up the process," he says.

When it comes to programs, however, Ogbu is short on specifics, and that frustrates some educators and policymakers who—understandably—want answers. But Ogbu offers no apologies. "The current mood in America is to find answers. But, as an anthropologist, I'm interested in knowing why some minorities are able to cross cultural boundaries and others are not. Why in Stockton do the Chinese continue to do well? Why in New Zealand do Polynesians coming from other islands continue to do well while the native Maoris, who come from the same language and cultural background, fail? Why is it that in Britain, West Indians, whose language and culture most resemble the British, do so poorly, whereas East Indians, whose culture is very different, do well? Why is it that the Burakumin do so poorly in Japan, but in this country they are shining students? Those are the questions that interest me. So I am not asking how to solve the problem, and that's where I get into a lot of arguments with people who don't like my work."

Ogbu wants educators to use his work as a starting point for programs and policies aimed at helping minority students achieve. Principals and teachers, he says, must recognize the strong influence of cultural perceptions on minority students' academic attitudes and efforts. Programs that encourage racial pride are on the right track, but they should also encourage nonimmigrant minorities to adopt the immigrant minorities' successful model of "accommodation without assimilation."

"I would like to see the time when blacks are not overrepresented among kids who have academic problems," says an optimistic-sounding Ogbu. "I don't think you need to have a group that is so dependent on a remedy to achieve a significant success." Is that possible? he is asked. "That's my hope."

A Plan That Works

By bringing together parents, mental-health specialists, and school staff, Yale child psychiatrist James Comer helped turn around the troubled New Haven schools. Now he's taking his ideas nationwide.

Daniel Gursky

James Comer is convinced.

"All kids can learn regardless of their income and their background," says the Yale University child psychiatrist. "They can learn at the level needed to be successful in society."

His conviction is based on the most personal kind of evidence—his own childhood in East Chicago, Ind. Comer tells how he and three friends started out at an integrated school in one of the more comfortable parts of town. All of them were as intelligent and capable as anyone at the school. Yet, Comer sadly reports, he was the only one of the four to "survive" school and succeed in life; one friend died young from alcoholism, another has spent much of his life in jail, and the third has been in and out of mental institutions.

Comer believes that the only difference between him and his friends was their family experience. Although his parents had little education—Comer's father was a steel-mill laborer with a 7th grade education and his mother was a domestic with no formal schooling—they gave their children the clear, consistent message that school was the ticket to a better future. The five Comer children went on to earn 13 college degrees between them, thanks, Comer says, to that unwavering encouragement and support.

"That experience made me aware that we were losing too many bright, able people" because they lacked family support, Comer says. "All of those young people could have been successful, and yet they all went on a downhill course because of something that didn't happen at home and something that didn't happen at school."

Most of Comer's career has been a search for ways to provide children with the support they need and are not getting at home. After earning a doctorate of medicine from Howard University, Comer returned to East Chicago as a general practitioner. But he became frustrated because what he had in his medical bag could not relieve the problems that afflicted the black community—depression, drug abuse, unstable families, poverty, and perhaps most damaging, hopelessness. Comer concluded that psychiatry might help him prevent other children from ending up like his elementary school friends.

So, in 1964, he came to Yale University for training in psychiatry, and the more he worked with children, the more he came to believe that the school was the only place where children who were stuck in poverty and failure could receive the support their families could not give them. When the Yale Child Study Center received a grant for a school-intervention project in 1968, Comer jumped at the offer to direct what was to become the School Development Program. It gave him exactly what he was looking for—a chance to apply principles of child development and behavior to schools.

Comer has focused on schools ever since, drawing from his experience to refine an approach to education that has come to be known as the "Comer process." His school-reform model emphasizes the social context of teaching and learning. No academic progress is possible, Comer argues, until there is a positive environment at the school where teachers, students, and parents like each other and work together for the good of all the students.

The process is built around three elements: a school-governance team, a mental-health team, and parental participation. The basic goal is to create schools that offer children some of the same stable support and role models that Comer looks back on

Reprinted with permission from *Teacher Magazine*, Vol. 1, No. 9, June/July 1990, pp. 46-54.

fondly from his own childhood. That may be why Comer's model—unlike countless other disappointing attempts to help low-income, urban students—has been remarkably successful.

When Comer first started working with two predominantly black New Haven, Conn., elementary schools more than 20 years ago, students, teachers, and parents were frustrated, angry, and disappointed. The schools were stuck at the bottom of the city rankings in achievement and attendance. Today, they are at or near the top in both those categories, and serious behavior problems have been all but eliminated. Some 35 schools in New Haven and more than 70 in other communities across the country, from Lee County, Ark., to Prince George's County, Md., have now adopted the Comer process, and many of them report equally impressive results. Every week, schools and districts from all over the nation call Comer to learn more about the School Development Program. Teachers, parents, and administrators are enthusiastic.

Comer's program will soon have an even wider, national impact. Because of his success at overcoming the "culture of failure" that afflicts many schools, the Rockefeller Foundation recently launched a huge, long-term, multimillion-dollar initiative to spread Comer's ideas to teachers, principals, parents, and child-development specialists around the country. (See box.) "Comer's work is reflective of the most powerful intervention for at-risk kids that we've encountered," says Hugh Price, vice president of the foundation. "His record in turning around failing schools holds enormous promise."

Why has Comer succeeded where many other well-funded programs have failed? Comer says reforms are doomed if they focus solely on academics without considering the crucial relationships between people in schools. Academic reforms are fine for the 20 percent or so of students who already thrive in school. But for the huge numbers of disadvantaged students who eventually lose interest and drop out, such reforms may do more harm than good.

"Kids are very much affected by the way they are treated by staff," Comer explains. "If you ask most kids why they drop out, they don't tell you about money or those sorts of things. They say, 'Nobody cares.' It's this impersonal environment they're in. They have no way of knowing if their teacher cares about them. So you have to create an environment where all the kids feel like they belong and have a right to be there and are cared for."

Ann O'Connell is the sort of teacher who makes Comer's ideas work. She serves on the governance team at Martin Luther King Jr. Elementary School in New Haven, she has a good rapport with the parents and welcomes their help in her 2nd grade class, and she constantly strives to see that her students do more than just study textbooks and worksheets. She says she can't imagine teaching any other way.

"The Comer program creates a climate in the school as a whole that's conducive to learning," O'Connell says. "A lot of what individual teachers do [in the classroom] would be negated if things outside the room were done in a different way. But we have a good climate."

The group charged with creating that good climate is the governance team, one of the three key elements of the Comer process. Teachers such as O'Connell—usually chosen to represent their grade level or discipline—play a major role on the team at every Comer school. But Comer stresses that all the "stakeholders" should have a voice on the team. At a large middle school or high school, teachers might be joined on a 20-person team by the principal, parents, a curriculum specialist, a union representative, a counselor, and a custodian. At a small elementary school like King, the team would be much smaller but would also include teachers, administrators, and parents.

"We realized many of the problems in school were growing out of the fact that people weren't talking with each other, they didn't trust each other, and they didn't like each other," Comer says. "We had to create something that brought all those warring and potentially warring people together so that they could work in a cooperative, collaborative way."

That's exactly what has happened at New Haven's Roberto Clemente Middle School, according to Theresa Kazmaier, a music and life-skills teacher who serves on the governance team. "It changes the interactions from being very difficult to being very positive," she says. "Everybody is involved in decisionmaking, everybody is informed about what's going on in the community and in the school. There's a feeling that everybody's thoughts count."

Whether the topic is parent-teacher conferences or the latest standardized test scores, the governance team makes decisions by consensus. This can be time-consuming, Comer admits, but it avoids the winner-loser mentality that formal votes can produce. Equally important, team members need to spend their time solving the schools' problems rather than blaming each other for those problems.

Because the principal remains the school's final authority, much of a team's success depends on the principal's willingness to cooperate. Carl Babb, assistant principal at Clemente Middle School, says the governance team makes his job much easier. "If you don't look at it as threatening, this team works," he says. "It helps me to know that I've got a team that is doing things for the building, for the students, for the school system in general."

In current school-reform jargon, the governance

Spreading The Word

James Comer's success in educating poor, minority children in New Haven, Conn., has attracted attention and praise for quite a few years. Now, the Rockefeller Foundation is providing the money needed to encourage the adoption of his ideas far beyond New Haven and the seven other districts Comer works with directly. Rockefeller officials expect to spend roughly $3 million a year over the next five years on the project, according to foundation Vice President Hugh Price.

This year, the foundation will provide $1.39 million for the first part of the initiative, which focuses on teaching teachers, administrators, and teacher educators about Comer's approach. The initial money will be used to:

• Form a consortium on urban education that will include Comer and representatives from the Yale Child Study Center, the New Haven school system, and Southern Connecticut State University. The group will design and field-test a teacher-preparation curriculum based on Comer's ideas, covering such topics as the unique needs of urban students, parental involvement, collaborative school management, and problem-solving. Once developed and tested, the curriculum will be offered to urban school systems and schools of education.

• Allow Comer himself to train education school faculties and officials in his methods. Those who receive the training will then work directly with school districts. Comer's first stop will be the District of Columbia, where he will work with Howard University and the D.C. Public Schools. Ten D.C. schools will adopt his model this year; eventually it will be in every elementary school in the city.

• Produce a series of detailed "how-to" videos and accompanying manuals to acquaint educators and parents with the Comer process. Featuring commentary by Comer, the videos will cover much of the same subject matter as the proposed teacher-training curriculum and present case studies from schools that use the process.

Rockefeller also will fund some other activities that are "philosophically consistent" with Comer's approach. For example, it will create leadership academies beginning this summer at Michigan State University and the University of New Mexico where teachers, principals, parents, and child-development specialists will learn more about urban children's developmental needs and collaborative school management.

In addition, the foundation will support local Urban League efforts to mobilize community support for school reform. This initiative was inspired by the experience of the league's Rochester, N.Y., affiliate, which played a central role in rallying support for the district's widely publicized reform program.

—D.G.

team is Comer's version of school-based management. But he and others on his project staff are somewhat uncomfortable with the term, which in some cases has come to mean more power for teachers without considering the needs of the students. "The battle cry shouldn't just be teacher empowerment," says Ed Joyner, a coordinator for the School Development Program, "because parents, social workers, students, and support-service people all need to be empowered."

O'Connell offers a similar assessment. Serving on the governance team does give her a say in policy decisions at Martin Luther King, but the bottom line is that the team's decisions are "always for the good of the children," she notes. "If you keep that in mind, you can't go wrong."

One of the team's main tasks, after members consult with the entire staff, is to create a comprehensive school plan. Ideally, Comer believes, the plan should encourage as many school activities as possible—inside and outside the classroom—that develop both social and academic skills.

"Middle-income children from better-educated families gain what is necessary to succeed in school simply by growing up with their parents," Comer says. "We want to provide some of those experiences in school for inner-city children."

James Comer's background as a child psychiatrist is evident throughout his model, but perhaps no place more than in its second major element: the mental-health team that is assembled at each school. "When we went into the schools," he says, "the psychologists, social workers, special-education teachers, and others all worked separately and not around a plan. We found one child who was being seen by seven different people, and none of them talked to each other."

Why not have all these specialists meet as a team? Comer thought. In addition to eliminating duplication and fragmentation of services, the group could look at the entire school to find the general causes of the problems they were seeing among individual students. Most importantly, the team could help prevent problems. "In many schools, you wait until there is a problem and then you try and treat the child as if the child is the sole source of the problem," Comer says. "We focused on prevention because it became apparent that many of the problems of individual children were due to procedures and processes within the school as a whole."

Comer offers the example of an 8-year-old who transferred to New Haven from rural North Carolina. When the child was brought into his new class the first morning, the teacher—who had already three transfers the week before—rolled her eyes and offer a nonverbal message of "Oh no, not another one." The new student picked up that negative message, looked around at all the strange faces, and panicked; he kicked the teacher and ran out of the room.

"In most schools, that kid would be sent to the principal," Comer says, "The principal would punish him and then send him back to the classroom. Some kid will laugh at him or they'll give him the business in some way, and he'll punch somebody out and be sent back. And he goes around and around until he's labeled as disturbed. Then he's sent off to somebody like me to have his head fixed."

Instead, the school's mental-health team discussed how stressful it must have been for the boy to endure such a radical change in setting. Rather than punish the child, the team worked with the teacher, encouraging her to welcome him back into the class, pair him with other successful students, and generally make him feel welcome in his new school. "We didn't stop with the classroom," Comer adds. "Now we don't introduce kids right into a new classroom. We give them an orientation session and let them know how the school functions, what to do if they have a problem."

The mental-health teams, which typically meet every other week, do deal with individual students. At a recent meeting at Jackie Robinson Middle School, team members discussed a boy who was expelled for bringing an air gun to school and a girl who had recently attempted suicide. In both cases, the group talked about the student's problems at home and at school, as well as the actions they had taken to help the child and the family. But the teams also keep an eye out for problems throughout the school that may demand a more comprehensive approach. One school, for example, has formed a group for children of single parents to discuss their special concerns.

Teachers say it helps to know they can turn to the mental-health team for advice when they have a particularly troublesome student. "If we bring it up to the whole team," says O'Connell, the 2nd grade teacher, "we stand a better chance of getting down to what the problem might be sooner."

Other school practices are a direct result of Comer's knowledge of child development. O'Connell, for instance, is one of many 1st and 2nd grade teachers in New Haven who keep the same students for two years. Comer and other mental-health specialists were searching for ways to provide continuity and stability for the many children whose family lives were anything but stable when they came up with the two-year idea. The practice has brought spectacular results: Some children who made no academic gain in their first year progressed two years in their second year, in part, Comer believes, because of the trusting relationship they were finally able to establish with a caring, predictable teacher.

These efforts to give students emotional and psychological support extend throughout the school. As Roberto Clemente teacher Kazmaier puts it: "We're constantly telling the kids, 'We care about you, you're valuable, we're here to help you.' "

But Comer isn't trying to create schools that replace the family. Schools can be improved without the help of the parents, he argues, but they can be much more effective with the third element of his model: parental involvement. "You want parents involved," he says, "because it's not enough just to have the kids raise their grades. You're really preparing them for the long-run—for jobs and for life after school."

In the best of circumstances, it's not easy to involve parents in their children's schooling. In the inner city, it's a massive challenge. "When you ask low-income children to do well in school," Comer points out, "you're asking them to aspire to positions in life that are different than their own parents, and you've created a conflict between home and school for the child. So you've got to involve parents in a program at the school in ways so they will support the program and not view it as antagonistic."

Comer's model includes three levels of parental involvement. The smallest and most active group of parents are those who serve on the school's governance team. They are often people, like Deborah Smart, who are active in their parent-teacher group. "I like being involved and knowing what's going on, not only for my kids, but for all the kids in the neighborhood," says Smart, president of the Clemente Middle School Parent-Teacher Organization. Smart keeps the PTO members informed about school activities, but she also raises issues at governance-team meetings that first come up in the PTO. When parents expressed concerns about school safety because of unauthorized

When parent Olivia Teague first went into King 10 years ago, she helped the kindergartners get their coats off. Today, she's a computer assistant.

visitors, for example, the governance team devised a system for having visitors check in and out of the building.

"The school has really been working on getting parents involved," Smart says. "They really want us to have a say in what goes on."

Parents at the second level of involvement help out in the classroom. "I was one of those parents that when I brought my child to school, I used to wait outside," recalls Olivia Teague, whose daughter attends Martin Luther King Jr. Elementary School. "One day the principal came outside and invited me in. So I went inside, and in kindergarten I saw a lot of children with one teacher, and they were all asking for help: 'teacher, teacher, teacher.' I stood there and thought, 'Oh, my goodness.' So I offered my help, and then she invited me back the next day."

Teague kept coming back to help out, and eventually she did everything from leading reading groups to planning parties. She even substituted at times for the regular teacher. She's now an aide in the school's computer-based "Writing to Read" program. "It makes you feel like you're doing something," she says. "And they make you feel welcome."

O'Connell certainly welcomes help from parents; Teague worked in her room for 10 years. "If parents would like to come into the school and just sit in the classroom and watch, they know they can do it," O'Connell says. "By coming in they see that you don't need to have a teaching degree to be able to contribute to the school or the classroom."

The students also benefit from good parent-teacher relationships, O'Connell adds. "When there's a problem with a child, it's not me against them," she says. "It's us working together for the good of the child."

Parents who want to volunteer are offered a variety of workshops to match their interests and capabilities with available tasks at school, such as tutoring, clerical work, or cafeteria help. Other workshops teach parents how to help their children with homework, as well as offering advice on topics such as nutrition, finance, and substance abuse. Comer has also visited schools to talk about parenting skills.

But even in New Haven, where there is a strong commitment to parental involvement, volunteers like Smart and Teague are sometimes hard to find; most parents don't have the time or interest to get involved. That's where the third level of Comer's parents program comes in. The school makes a concerted effort to organize activities that entice parents into the building. So, for the majority of mothers and fathers, participation means attending the numerous events that appear on each school's social calendar—everything from Black History Month dinners and Halloween parades to book fairs and student concerts.

"You'll never be satisfied with parental participation," admits Kazmaier. "We still work on that. Any kind of activity that involves youngsters, we always try to have parents attend. And any time a parent walks into the building, you have some parental contact. We try to get the parents in on a comfortable level."

Some of Comer's schools boast of parental-involvement levels that would be the envy of even the most stable, affluent community. Take Katherine Brennan Elementary School in New Haven, a predominantly black school that serves a housing project: Last year, more than 90 percent of the parents visited the school at least 10 times.

Every school in New Haven and elsewhere that has adopted the Comer process uses its basic elements—the governance team, the mental-health team, and parental participation. But there's plenty of room for variation from school to school.

"In all of the schools and districts we are in, you will find many, many different things that grow out of the comprehensive school plan," Comer says. "Those things are not the program, per se, but they are what the program makes possible because people are able to work together in a cooperative, collaborative way, and the creative energy of everybody in the building comes together."

Prince George's County, in suburban Washington, D.C., has attracted national attention for its success in raising the performance of minority students. Jan Stocklinski, who supervises the Comer program there, credits part of that success to the implementation of Comer's ideas. She says his model is especially well suited for a place like Prince George's, where many of the teachers come from a different racial and socio-economic background than their students. The emphasis on communication between teachers and parents, she says, helps overcome the mutual suspicion and lack of trust that often exist.

Stocklinski says that there has been some resistance to the program among teachers and other staff members who think it adds to their already-heavy workloads. That may be true in the short term, she notes, because it often takes time to reach consensus and develop comprehensive plans for an entire school. "But the long-term result," she says, "is that the children's behavior is better in class, so teachers can spend more time on the academic tasks." And when schools are struggling with the model, she adds, it's usually because the staff hasn't learned how to work together for the good of the students.

Comer maintains that schools shouldn't need much extra money to make his program work, an important factor that could make his model even more attractive to districts, especially in a time of tight budgets. "It's the way you use what you have that is most important," he says. "We're asking people to work differently. Our approach asks social workers, psychologists, and special-education teachers to use the one-on-one approach less and to apply their knowledge of child development and relationship issues to the entire program of the school and to share their knowledge with their colleagues in general education who do not have that knowledge."

And, he adds, there's no time to waste: "We've got to make it possible for all of the children to succeed so they can meet the expectations of school and the expectations of society. If we don't do that, our country is on a downhill course in 20 or 30 years. So we've got to make a difference, and we've got to make a difference very quickly."

Comer understands this daunting challenge as well as anyone, but he remains optimistic about the future. "Things can be turned around," he says. "But enough people need to understand that education really has to be based on what kids are like and what kids need. If we can get the bureaucracy and processes in education really designed to address the needs of children, then we can turn education around."

Art of anger difficult for women to master

Barbara Sullivan

Chicago Tribune

CHICAGO—Patricia Adams, a reporter for a news magazine, could feel the rage rising as she started reading an article she had written. Although the article had her byline, it had been rewritten by her editor in such a way that it bore little resemblance to her original. Worse, the editing had made the article inaccurate.

"First, I felt disbelief and then I was absolutely furious," she said. "I could not believe he had done this. But I knew I could not call him right away because I had to sort out the emotionalism. I didn't want to cry.

"It was two days before I talked to him. My anger by that time had not diminished one whit, but it was a cold anger as opposed to the hot anger.

"I knew exactly what I wanted to say and I said it. At first, he kept trying to justify his actions, and then he tried to get off the track. But I kept getting right back to it (the subject). I did not cry and I did not get emotional. Our relationship since then has been fine, and it hasn't happened again."

By almost any measure, Adams is a successful woman and has much in her life to feel good about. But her ability to get angry that week—to recognize her anger and then clearly express it without tears and without emotion—filled her with an intense feeling of accomplishment.

It was a breakthrough because she was aware that it's difficult for herself and most women to even allow themselves to get angry in the first place, much less use that anger constructively as a powerful tool to get their point across.

Uncomfortable with anger

Anger is not an emotion most women feel comfortable with or handle well.

Women traditionally have been raised not to feel or express anger. They are the pleasers, the peacemakers, the guardians of the home. Conversely, men are raised to know it's OK to get angry, to be aggressive.

Historically, said Chicago therapist Jo Lief, "men were given permission to go out and shoot the beasts, and women were objects, wearing their housedresses and girdles and accommodating (male) authority."

But as difficult as it is, anger is increasingly being recognized as the force that will allow women to become successful in the workplace and to improve their personal relationships.

Well-used anger is power, and that power can change not only women's lives but, obviously, the lives of the people they work with and live with as well.

Well-used anger is not temper-tantrum anger, in which people fling objects through the air or yell and scream at each other, or become fragmented and tearful. Well-used anger is anger that's recognized and acted upon. It's used to state and possibly change a situation that is unacceptable.

"There's been a taboo against women's anger," says Menninger Foundation therapist Harriet Lerner, author of the best-selling *The Dance of Anger* (Harper & Row, $8.95).

"Women can become angry for other causes, such as against drunk drivers, but there has been a powerful taboo against women using their anger on behalf of their own self.

"But never, never will a woman be successful, either in the workplace or in her relationships, if she's not able to feel her anger, speak to important issues and take a clear position."

A stereotypical response

Although women are making strides toward channeling anger, they are still newcomers to it, and the stereotype of the angry woman is of a woman who has succumbed to negative, non-rational emotions and has thus become ineffectual.

It's a stereotype that has been prevalent both in the workplace and in personal relationships.

For example, picture this real-life scenario of a couple driving down a road.

He's driving, and another driver, a woman, refuses to make room for him to change lanes. He rolls down the window and yells, "You dumb broad, move over."

His female companion is enraged. She grabs the closest available object, which happens to be a box of tissue, and throws it at him while yelling at him to never use the term "dumb broad" again.

He gives her a long, appraising look, and then comments that if there's one thing he dislikes, it's women who lose their tempers. Of the two of them, he continues, he is the stable one.

The more emotional she becomes at

HOW TO CHANNEL ANGER, MAKE USE OF IT

Chicago Tribune

Anger is a powerful emotion. Likewise, it can be a powerful tool for achievement, both in the workplace and in personal relationships.

But learning to channel anger into appropriate, powerful behavior is a skill that doesn't always come naturally. Here is a set of recommendations compiled from comments made by Menninger Foundation therapist Harriet Lerner, who has written extensively on anger, and Evanston psychologist Robert Mark, a corporate consultant on matters of executive development and corporate conflict.

- Don't react quickly. Slow down when a situation arises that makes you angry. Be sure the anger is justified for that particular situation and isn't related to a prior situation.
- Give yourself time to determine what you want to accomplish by communicating your anger. Move from anger to a clear plan of what you want, and when you are ready to speak up, talk specifics, not generalities.
- Shift from feeling to doing. You may feel that you've been hurt, but the point is to use that awareness of being hurt to do something about it.
- Don't accuse. It's better to say something like "I don't like the way things are going," rather than "Why are you doing this to me?" People don't want to hear blame being cast on them, and doing that will raise the intensity level rather than accomplish a change.
- Know what your bottom line is. Are you prepared to negotiate or compromise, or is the situation that has provoked your anger intolerable to the degree you are ready to walk if changes aren't made?
- Don't cloud the issue with emotionalism.
- It's important, especially in personal relationships, to focus on what is needed to change a situation rather than focusing on guilt.
- Be prepared for countermeasures when you express anger.
- And finally, some specific advice for men, according to Robert Mark: "They need to develop their facility for listening and responding. They need to broaden their perspective and reconnect to the emotional part of themselves. Men have these abilities, but, until now, they haven't had to use them in the workplace."

this assessment, the cooler and more calculating he becomes.

Finally, she actually finds herself wondering if she is, indeed, wrong, and her anger becomes suffused with self-doubt and guilt.

Going along to get along

"It's very hard for women to clarify their anger," said Lerner. "Often a woman will go along with a situation for a long time, and then she'll explode, blow up. But too often exploding is just part of a repetitive, unproductive pattern, and then business goes on as usual.

"Anger should be used to define a new position in a relationship pattern, a position that does not mean self-betrayal."

Psychologists such as Lerner stressed the importance of understanding the real source of the anger.

For example, the car passenger was angry at the immediate situation. More important, she had a deep, long-felt but never-expressed anger at what she perceived as the man's hostility toward all women, both in his professional and personal life.

She could not use her anger to change him.

But, by stating clearly and unemotionally how she felt about the situation, she could change her role in the relationship. In time, she did this; the relationship ended.

Anger creates separation

That might not be a so-called "happy ending," and it's one of the reasons women so often sit on their anger or fail to even recognize it. Women have traditionally identified themselves through their relationships, their connections with other people. Expressing anger creates a separation—even if it's only temporary—between themselves and the other person. The result of anger can be aloneness.

"Many women go right from sadness to forgiveness, skipping anger completely," said Evanston clinical psychologist Robert Mark. "And the reason they skip anger is because they're afraid of abandonment.

"Being assertive and expressing anger has its costs. One cost is that the culture we live in still wants to see women as sweet and nice.

"Second, just because a woman is capable of expressing anger—of knowing where she stands and what she wants and asserting herself—doesn't mean that the other people in her world are going to like it."

So to get ahead and feel good about themselves professionally and personally, women must feel and use anger, but they have to do it carefully. It's like walking on eggshells.

On top of that, there are few role models. Past generations of women turned anger inward; depression, sadness and guilt were the unhappy results. And finally, women's anger, even when expressed appropriately, is viewed far more critically than men's anger.

"People react very differently to men's anger and women's anger. Imagine the Boston Tea Party, if it had been women who threw that tea overboard. They would have been written up as a group of hysterical, strident, immature women in the throes of PMS (premenstrual syndrome)," Lerner said.

"It's a big problem for women," acknowledged Wilma Smelcer, the first female senior vice president at Continental Bank. "They can't let their emotions show because that's unprofessional. This probably applies to men, too, but I think women have to be more careful."

A learned expression

"Anger—how to express it—is something I've learned," Smelcer said. "I had to learn it. And when I feel anger, I step back and say, 'All right, what is the real reason why I'm feeling angry?'

"Because sometimes it has to do with other things that have gone on during the week rather than what's happening right now. Once I get through that process, I have to decide whether it's appropriate to react strongly to the situation. You have to stay calm, but you cannot be a wimp."

Smelcer talked about a woman she knew several years ago, who held a high-pressure managerial job.

"She was seen crying one day. No one knew what the reason was, why she was crying, but (the crying) took on a life of its own.

"Every time her name came up about something, there was the impression that this was an emotional, mercurial woman rather than a professional."

Roadblocks exist even when women transform teary anger into lucidly expressed anger. The status quo has a habit of being comfortable, and when women start expressing anger, they are changing that status quo.

"Say you're in a relationship and you want to make a change," Lerner said. "So you, the woman, make it clear you are not going to continue in a certain pattern any longer.

"There is almost certainly going to be a countermove. The other person probably won't want that change. And when there's a countermove, the anger is probably going to intensify."

Finding the bottom line

"So women have to know what their bottom-line position is," Lerner said. "The bottom line is using anger to make very clear what the acceptable limits are, and saying, 'I can no longer tolerate this in the job or in the marriage.' If you know you cannot survive without the job or marriage, you have to navigate within the situation."

Such a bottom-line position—the possibility of anger ending a relationship or job—can strike fear in the strongest of women.

"Women are still terrified—they want approval and love, and they fear that they'll lose that if they get angry," said Evanston, Ill., therapist Linda Randall. "I still hear women saying, 'I'm afraid to be angry.' "

Betty Cook (not her real name) was desperately afraid of that bottom-line position.

The suburban homemaker was afraid, and she also had trouble feeling any anger. She got depressed and sad, but not angry. For most of her 26 years of marriage, she negotiated carefully, trying to change abusive situations without drawing the final line.

"I had always felt that he was right, that he was smarter—I was raised like that. I would think, 'All right, I'll try this for one more year and see if things change.'

"Then the year would be over and I'd just keep rolling along. We kept going in the same circle. It's hard to break out of that.

"He was verbally abusive and physically abusive at times to the boys. He would order me to leave the room (when he became physically abusive to the sons), and I would."

Counseling helped

They started family counseling, but he participated for only a short time. She continued by herself.

"It gave me strength. I started taking stands. Quiet stands, but stands. He (her husband) had problems when I didn't agree with him. He said he was uncomfortable and wanted things back the way they had been. I could not go back."

After 26 years, she got to the bottom line. She told her husband she wanted a divorce.

But she said she still isn't sure what anger is all about. She understands guilt and sadness, she said, but she still doesn't understand anger, or particularly feel that anger is a good thing.

"I defused things and I walked away a lot. But I always felt, and still do, that getting angry would be losing control. I don't want to ever lose control."

It may be a matter of definition, of semantics. Anger was never part of her vocabulary. But, call it what you will, she channeled her emotions into an understanding of what she wanted—and didn't want—and clearly stated that understanding to her husband.

Complicated emotion

"Expressing anger doesn't mean a hysterical, histrionic display of rage," said Robert Mark. "It means going up to someone and saying, 'This is what I want.'

"It's complicated—anger is very complicated," Lerner said. "But women are learning about anger and how to use it. It's changing the way all of us live."

The Language of Persuasion

HARD, SOFT OR RATIONAL: OUR CHOICE DEPENDS ON POWER, EXPECTATIONS AND WHAT WE HOPE TO ACCOMPLISH.

DAVID KIPNIS AND STUART SCHMIDT

David Kipnis is chairperson of the psychology department, and Stuart Schmidt is professor of human resources administration in the School of Business Administration, both at Temple University. Their survey, "Profiles of Organizational Influence Strategies," is published by University Associates, San Diego.

"I had all the facts and figures ready before I made my suggestions to my boss." (Manager)

"I kept insisting that we do it my way. She finally caved in." (Husband)

"I think it's about time that you stop thinking these negative things about yourself." (Psychotherapist)

"Send out more horses, skirr the country round. Hang those that talk of fear. Give me mine armour." (Macbeth, Act 5)

These diverse statements—rational, insistent, emotional—have one thing in common. They all show people trying to persuade others, a skill we all treasure. Books about power and influence are read by young executives eager for promotion, by politicians anxious to sway their constituents, by lonely people looking to win and hold a mate and by harried parents trying to make their children see the light.

Despite this interest in persuasion, most people are not really aware of how they go about it. They spend more time choosing their clothes than they do their influence styles. Even fewer are aware of how their styles affect others or themselves. Although shouts and demands may make people dance to our tune, we will probably lose their goodwill. Beyond that, our opinion of others may change for the worse when we use hard or abusive tactics (see "The View from the Top," *Psychology Today*, December 1984).

Popular books on influencing others give contradictory advice. Some advocate assertiveness, others stealth and still others reason and logic. Could they all be right? We decided to see for ourselves what kinds of influence people actually use in personal and work situations and why they choose the tactics they do.

We conducted studies of dating couples and business managers in which the couples described how they attempted to influence their partners and the managers told how they attempted to influence their subordinates, peers and superiors at work. We then used these descriptions as the basis for separate questionnaires in which we asked other couples and managers how frequently they employed each tactic. Using factor analysis and other statistical techniques, we found that the tactics could be classified into three basic strategies—hard, soft and rational (see the "Influence Strategies" box).

These labels describe the tactics from the standpoint of the person using them. Since influencing someone is a social act, its meaning depends upon the observer's vantage point. For example, a wife might ask her husband, "I wonder what we should do about the newspapers in the garage?" The husband could consider this remark nagging to get him to clean up the garage. The wife might say her remark was simply a friendly suggestion that he consider the state of the garage. An outside observer might feel that the wife's remark was just conversation, not a real attempt to influence.

As the box illustrates, hard tactics involve demanding, shouting and assertiveness. With soft tactics, people act nice and flatter others to get their way. Rational tactics involve the use of logic and bargaining to demonstrate why compliance or compromise is the best solution.

Why do people shout and demand in one instance, flatter in a second and offer to compromise in a third? One common explanation is that the choice of tactics is based upon what "feels right" in each case. A more pragmatic answer is that the choice of tactics is based strictly on what works.

Our studies show that the reasons are more complex. When we examine how people actually use influence, we find that they use many different strategies, depending on the situation and the person being influenced. We gathered information from 195 dating and married couples, and from 360 first- and second-line managers in the United States, Australia and Great Britain. We asked which influence tactics they used, how frequently and in what conditions.

The choice of strategies varied predictably for both managers (see the "Bystanders" box) and couples. It de-

From *Psychology Today*, April 1985, pp. 40-42, 44-46. Copyright © 1985 by PT Partners, L.P. Reprinted by permission.

INFLUENCE STRATEGIES

Strategy	Couples	Managers
Hard	I get angry and demand that he/she give in.	I simply order the person to do what I ask.
	As the first step I make him/her feel stupid and worthless.	I threaten to give an unsatisfactory performance evaluation.
	I say I'll leave him/her if my spouse does not agree.	I get higher management to back up my request.
Soft	I act warm and charming before bringing up the subject.	I act very humble while making my request.
	I am so nice that he/she cannot refuse.	I make the person feel important by saying that she/he has the brains and experience to do what I want.
Rational	I offer to compromise; I'll give up a little if she/he gives up a little.	I offer to exchange favors: You do this for me, and I'll do something for you.
	We talk, discussing our views objectively without arguments.	I explain the reason for my request.

WHY PEOPLE CHOOSE EACH STRATEGY

Hard tactics are normally used when:
Influencer has the advantage.
Resistance is anticipated.
Target's behavior violates social or organizational norms.

Soft tactics are normally used when:
Influencer is at a disadvantage.
Resistance is anticipated.
The goal is to get benefits for one's self.

Rational tactics are normally used when:
Neither party has a real power advantage.
Resistance is not anticipated.
The goal is to get benefits for one's self and one's organization.

WE FOUND THAT PEOPLE USE MANY DIFFERENT STRATEGIES, DEPENDING ON THE SITUATION AND THE PERSON THEY WANT TO INFLUENCE.

pends on their particular objectives, relative power position and expectations about the willingness of others to do what they want. These expectations are often based on individual traits and biases rather than facts.

Objectives

One of our grandmothers always advised sweetly, "Act nice if you want a favor." We found that people do, indeed, vary their tactics according to what they want.

At work, for instance, managers frequently rely on soft tactics—flattery, praise, acting humble—when they want something from a boss such as time off or better assignments. However, when managers want to persuade the boss to accept ideas, such as a new work procedure, they're more likely to use reason and logic. Occasionally, they will even try hard tactics, such as going over the boss's head, if he or she can't be moved any other way.

Couples also vary their choice of tactics depending upon what they want from each other. Personal benefits such as choosing a movie or restaurant for the night call for a soft, loving approach. When they want to change a spouse's unacceptable behavior, anger, threats and other hard tactics come into play.

Power Positions

People who control resources, emotions or finances valued by others clearly have the advantage in a relationship, whether it is commercial or personal. In our research with couples, we discovered which partner was dominant by asking who made the final decision about issues such as spending money, choosing friends and other

GETTING PERSONAL BENEFITS, SUCH AS CHOOSING A MOVIE OR RESTAURANT FOR THE NIGHT, CALLS FOR A SOFT, LOVING APPROACH. BUT TO CHANGE A SPOUSE'S UNDESIRABLE BEHAVIOR, THREATS AND OTHER HARD TACTICS COME INTO PLAY.

family matters. We found that people who say they control the relationship ("I have the final say") often rely on hard tactics to get their way. Those who share decision power ("We decide together") bargain rationally and often compromise. Partners who admit that they have little power ("My partner has the final say") usually favor soft tactics.

We found the same patterns among managers. The more one-sided the power relationship at work, the more likely managers are to demand, get angry and insist with people who work for them, and the more likely they are to act humble and flatter when they are persuading their bosses.

The fact that people change influence tactics depending on their power over the other person is hardly surprising. What is surprising is how universal the link is between power and tactics. Our surveys and those conducted by others have found this relationship among children trying to influence younger children or older children, and among executives dealing with executives at other companies more or less powerful than their own, as well as among spouses and business managers dealing with their own subordinates and bosses.

There seems to be an "Iron Law of Power": The greater the discrepancy in clout between the influencer and the target, the greater the likelihood that hard tactics will be used. People with power don't always use hard tactics as their first choice. At first, most simply request and explain. They turn to demands and threats (the iron fist lurking under the velvet glove of rea-

THE SHAKESPEARE CONNECTION

The best art is life condensed, with its truths shown clearly and accurately. One of us (Kipnis) decided to test what has been learned about tactics of influence by comparing this understanding with how two of William Shakespeare's most famous characters go about persuading others. Each time King Lear and Macbeth try to influence someone in the play, successfully or not, the attempt was coded as hard, soft or rational. For example:

Hard tactic

"Kent, on thy life, no more."
(*Lear*, Act I, Scene 1)

Soft tactic

"Pray do not mock me. I am a very foolish fond old man."
(*Lear*, Act IV, Scene 7)

Rational tactic

"Think upon what hath chanced; and . . . the interim having weighed it, let us speak. . . ."
(*Macbeth*, Act I, Scene 3)

Both Macbeth and Lear consistently attempt to influence others throughout the plays, more in the last act than earlier. This finding is particularly interesting in regard to Lear, since he is thought of as an increasingly feeble, dying old man. Yet, when you analyze his words, he tries to exercise influence more frequently in the fifth act than at any other time in the play.

But the methods Lear and Macbeth use change dramatically during the five acts. As the table below indicates, Lear's tactics become increasingly soft, while Macbeth's become harder and harder.

Art, then, imitates life. Both Lear and Macbeth choose their tactics in relation to their power. Since Lear has given up his major base of power (his kingdom) in Act I, he must plead and use soft words. Macbeth, who has gained a kingdom, turns increasingly to tough tactics.

Influence Tactics* in *King Lear* and *Macbeth*

	King Lear					Macbeth				
Tactic	Act I	Act II	Act III	Act IV	Act V	Act I	Act II	Act III	Act IV	Act V
Hard	64	57	13	14	0	33	36	44	75	77
Soft	16	38	25	79	100	33	36	9	19	4
Rational	20	5	63	7	0	33	27	47	6	19

*Expressed in percentages. Some columns don't add up to 100 because the figures are rounded off.

THERE SEEMS TO BE AN IRON LAW OF POWER: THE GREATER THE DIFFERENCE IN CLOUT BETWEEN TWO PEOPLE, THE GREATER THE LIKELIHOOD THAT HARD TACTICS WILL BE USED.

son) only when someone seems reluctant or refuses to comply with their request.

In contrast, people with little power are likely to stop trying or immediately shift to soft tactics when they encounter resistance. They feel the costs associated with the use of hard or even rational tactics are unacceptable. They are unwilling to take the chance of angering a boss, a spouse or an older child by using anything but soft methods.

Expectations and Biases

We have found that people also vary their strategies according to how successful they expect to be in influencing their targets. When they believe that someone is likely to do what is asked, they make simple requests. When they anticipate resistance and have the power, they use hard tactics.

This anticipation may be realistic. Just as a robber knows that without a gun, a polite request for money is unlikely to persuade, a boss knows that a request for work on Saturday needs more than a smile to back it up. But less realistic personal and situational factors sometimes make us expect resistance where none exists. People who are low in self-esteem and self-confidence, for instance, have difficulty believing that others will comply with simple requests.

We found that lack of confidence and low self-esteem are characteristic of managers who bark orders and refuse to discuss the issues involved, of couples who constantly shout and scream at each other and of parents who rely on harsh discipline. These hard tactics result from the self-defeating assumption that others will not listen unless they are treated roughly.

Social situations and biases can also distort expectations of cooperation. Misunderstandings based on differences in attitudes, race or sex can lead to hard tactics. Our research, and that of others, shows that orders, shouts and threats are more likely to be used between blacks and whites or men and women. The simple perception that "these people are different than I am" leads to the idea that "they are not as reasonable as I am" and must be ordered about.

The reasons shown in the "Why People Choose" box are generalizations. They don't necessarily describe how a particular person will act in a particular situation. People may use influence tactics because of habit, lack of forethought or lack of social sensitivity. Most of us would be more effective persuaders if we analyzed why we act as we do. Simply writing a short description of a recent incident in which we tried to persuade someone can help us understand better our own tactics, why we use them and, perhaps, why a rational approach might be better.

People who know we have studied the matter sometimes ask, "Which tactics work best?" The answer is that they all work if they are used at the right time with the right person. But both hard and soft tactics involve costs to the user even when they succeed. Hard tactics often alienate the people being influenced and create a climate of hostility and resistance. Soft tactics—acting nice, being humble—may lessen self-respect and self-esteem. In contrast, we found that people who rely chiefly on logic, reason and compromise to get their way are the most satisfied both with their business lives and with their personal relationships.

BYSTANDERS, TACTICIANS AND SHOTGUN MANAGERS

When we analyzed data from our study of managers, three distinct types emerged:

Shotgun managers use any and all means to get their way. Compared with the others we studied, they have the least managerial experience, hold staff rather than line positions and express the greatest number of personal needs (to receive benefits) and organizational needs (to sell their ideas) that require them to exercise influence. Shotgun managers are young, ambitious and unwilling to take no for an answer.

Tacticians rely heavily on reason to influence others. They usually have considerable power in an organization, direct units that do technologically complex work and feel they influence company policy.

Bystanders are the timid souls of the sample. They seldom use their managerial power to persuade others. Bystanders usually direct units that do routine work and have been in the same job for more years, on the average, than the other managers. Our impression is that they are marking time and feel it is futile even to try to influence others.

'They Have Ears, But Hear Not'

Would a course in listening help?

Gail Gregg

Gail Gregg is a New York-based freelance writer. She has been a reporter for UPI and Congressional Quarterly, *and in 1981–82 held a Walter Bagehot Fellowship for business and economic reporters at Columbia University.*

Readers: please assume the proper listening mode. Slow down and concentrate. Look interested. Try to identify with me. Ask pertinent questions, but don't interrupt. Control your emotions. Don't let ringing telephones or headaches distract you. Take notes if you think it will help you remember. Make a brief mental summary as you go along. And keep asking yourself, "What's the point here?"

Ready? My name is Gail Gregg. I'm a reporter. Along with 19 other students, I've just spent two balmy days closeted in a windowless midtown Manhattan conference room learning how to listen and how to remember what I've heard. Not too long ago, many companies would have laughed off such a $675 minicourse that promised to teach managers a skill that nearly everyone is born with. If you can hear, you can listen—right?

Wrong, say the American Management Associations (AMA), the sponsor of the course, along with listening instructor Robert L. Montgomery and the 19 firms that paid for my middle-manager classmates to attend two days of listening study. They are among many American businesses that now believe the human problems they once dismissed as irrelevant to profitability do affect the bottom line. And foremost on nearly every firm's list of human problems is communications.

"When employees become effective listeners, you'll see people working together to get projects completed, production speeded up, mistakes reduced or eliminated, sales increased and reports expedited as profits soar," claims Madelyn Burley-Allen, author of *Listening: The Forgotten Skill* (John Wiley & Sons). Dr. Anthony J. Alessandra, a nationally known listening consultant, writes, "It would not be wrong to suggest that ineffective listening contributes to the majority of the problems we now face in our business and personal relationships." And the Sperry Corporation, a firm that has made a name for itself as "the company that listens," said it even more simply in a newspaper advertisement that told readers, "It pays to listen."

Though such observations sound obvious today—and they did to our AMA seminar of hopeful world-class listeners—it is less apparent that listening is an acquired skill. But Montgomery and other professional speakers who make their livings teaching listening systems maintain that people need to be taught how to listen in much the same way that they are taught to speak, read or write.

That need is what prompted Martin M. Coyne II to register for the AMA program. Coyne was recently promoted to head Winthrop Laboratories' marketing division and discovered that communicating with his employees was a major part of the new job—and a part he wasn't trained for. "I figure I have no place to go but up," he said. Like Coyne, most of the participants enrolled in the AMA seminar at their own request. Most were not quite middle-aged, and many had just been moved to jobs that required that they now be on the listening end of things. They included: Daniel Dacres, a labor-relations officer for the New York City Transit Authority; Mary Fennell, public-

From *Across the Board,* September 1983, pp. 56-61. Reprinted by permission of the author and The Conference Board.

relations manager for Monsanto Fibers; Tom Mansmann, a senior planning advisor for the Postal Service; and William Benko Jr., a systems designer for AT&T.

Although a few members of our group already had participated in some of the dozens of other seminars the AMA offers each year, most of us had little idea of what to expect from instructor Montgomery, described as a Ph.D. in "communication arts." What we hadn't anticipated from the man who was to teach us how to slow down and really listen to people was a nonstop torrent of words that lasted almost the entire 13 hours we spent in his class. As Tom Mansmann described Montgomery's "outstanding" lecture style, "He doesn't teach—he performs."

A tall man with well-coiffed dark brown hair, Montgomery roamed the classroom tirelessly as he talked, sprinkling his lectures with such Dale Carnegie-like counsel as, "Positive thoughts bring positive results," and, "You will succeed if you are vital, enthusiastic, alive." Sounding at times like a smooth-talking television game-show host, Montgomery frequently recalled anecdotes from his own life; cited unsourced statistics to back up his lecture ("The average person spends 45 percent of his communication time listening and 30 percent talking."); and quoted such experts as "the greatest teacher of them all," Jesus Christ. ("If any man has ears to hear, let him hear." St. Mark.)

Montgomery's commandments for better listening began with a full day of memory practice, "so you can remember what you learn tomorrow." "Everything you ever learned is in your brain, even if you can't get it out," Montgomery told us. "How many of you went to kindergarten?" he asked, as hands shot up almost instantly. "No computer could do it that fast!" he said, tapping his head. "This is an amazing contraption."

Giving our minds better clues when we commit something to memory makes it easier to retrieve the information later, Montgomery continued. The best clues, he said, are associations and mental pictures. And we can make those clues even more powerful by bringing them to life with action, color and exaggeration (ACE).

To demonstrate his technique, Montgomery led us through the name-recall method that has helped many a politician on the stump or many a minister in his parish. As we introduced ourselves, we learned to make an association and a visual image for each name, to anchor it in our memory. We remembered Carlos Confresi, a technical writer for Equitable Life, as a carload of cold Fresca; Ginny Zumpano, accounts payable supervisor for Coopers and Lybrand, as gimme some pano; Jean Nadort, a financial analyst for the Postal Service, as a blue-jeaned postwoman who no longer—nay—delivered dort to dort. (Readers: I introduced myself to you in the second paragraph of this story, but can you still remember my name? Try to picture a reporter taking shorthand notes in the middle of a gale. . . .)

Once we had mastered names, Montgomery showed us how to use associations and mental pictures to stack and link items in a long list. Then he followed with a third system in which the numbers 1 through 10 are assigned a visual value that also happens to rhyme with the number: One is bun; two, glue; three, key; four, store; and so on. If you want to remember a grocery list that includes bread, milk, coffee and potatoes, imagine a loaf of bread between a bun; a milk carton glued to your hand; pounds of coffee cascading from the closet you opened with your key; and a store full of nothing but potatoes.

Although most of us were still having trouble remembering the picture-rhyme system itself—let alone our shopping lists, Montgomery then showed us how to use the technique to memorize entire magazines. If the page-1 ad is a Chrysler car, put it between a giant hamburger bun in your memory; if page 2 is the index, glue it to you, and so on. It's a good way to impress strangers in doctors' waiting rooms, Montgomery assured us. Earlier he had promised, "We can save so much time with productive memories—and be more popular and happy."

> "Giving our minds better clues when we memorize something helps to retrieve it. In a picture-rhyme system, one is bun, two glue, three key."

To remember numbers, Montgomery taught us yet another system, which consists of translating numbers into certain consonants. That allows you to make words out of numbers, to remember the area code 212 as "ntn" or "notion," for example. But by the time the numerical system was introduced, many of us found that those "amazing contraptions" of ours were overloading. We told ourselves we'd study our free copies of Montgomery's *Memory Made Easy* at home—and moved on to the topic of listening with great relief.

"Listening is essential for our business, social and personal success," Montgomery reminded us. Rather than define good listening for us, he let us do it for ourselves. And he wisely had us start the other way round, by describing the worst listeners we each knew.

That simple exercise provided dramatic proof for his

theory that poor listening is a serious problem, for each of us was only too happy to complain about an unnamed bad listener—perhaps a boss, friend, or spouse—with whom we disliked conversing as a result. We recalled worst listeners, who didn't make eye contact, never changed facial expression, interrupted, completed our sentences for us, jumped to conclusions, gave only monosyllabic answers, became emotional or changed the subject.

Not nearly as cathartic was the group exercise to define good listeners. We had no trouble describing someone we'd enjoy talking with: he or she was patient, looked us in the eye, was alert, interacted with us, asked pertinent questions, helped focus the conversation and didn't hurry us. Montgomery then shaped our observations into what he calls his "ladder" system (Alessandra calls his system the seven "screams."):

- Look at person you're talking with.
- Ask questions.
- Don't interrupt.
- Don't change the subject.
- Emotions—control them.
- Respond.

Finally, Montgomery told us, enhance LADDER with AIM, and your listening will improve manyfold. AIM stands for anticipate, identify the evidence, and mentally summarize.

People with Type-A personalities have the hardest time learning to listen, Montgomery told us. Such people are always in a hurry, frequently are dissatisfied with their co-workers or acquaintances, lose their temper often, rarely take vacations, and crowd too much into their days. For such hyper people, just learning to relax can make a dramatic difference in how well they listen. Montgomery gently poked fun at the coin jinglers in our seminar as likely Type A's—though most of us admitted openly we all had "hurry-itis" to some degree.

Admonishing us that "it's not going to be easy, it's going to be hard work," Montgomery assigned us to small groups to practice what he had preached. One member of each group talked for a few minutes while a second member listened and a third member graded the listener. Then we all switched roles. We discovered that Montgomery was right: it was hard work. Some of us just couldn't bite our tongues and injected ourselves into the conversation when we shouldn't have. Others were too passive. Some had trouble maintaining eye contact or what Montgomery calls an "active listening posture." Even those who performed well found that the task had taken a lot of concentration.

In my group, Marty Coyne talked for five minutes about his commuting "buspool"—a topic he admitted wasn't easy to listen to. I graded Robert Shydo, a systems analyst for New York Telephone, as a superb listener. He kept his eyes on Coyne, had a sense of humor, and followed up with questions even when it appeared there wasn't another thing that possibly could be said about the commuter bus. Coyne, in turn, listened well to my monologue about the problems of working mothers; and I had the good fortune to play listener to Shydo's interesting description of his hobby—playing the stock market. We all congratulated ourselves on our impressive listening skills before rejoining the full group, though it's likely none of us has listened as well since.

That was it. Montgomery had "come in for a landing," as he called it. It was time for us to file our new listening skills into our new memory systems and go back to our workplaces to try them out. ("How do you get to Carnegie Hall?" Montgomery reminded us. "Practice. Practice. Practice.") But before we left, we were instructed to make a listening resolution which we jotted on oversized index cards that would not be easily forgotten in a handbag or shirt pocket.

"Love people," wrote one of our classmates. That was not a bad summation for much of what Montgomery had been trying to tell us, in his show-biz way. He had explained early in the course that he believes there are three prerequisites for being a good listener: desire, concentration, and love of people. No amount of eye contact or sympathetic head nodding can substitute for caring about the speaker.

"I haven't heard anything new," commented Douglas Kenyon as he left the seminar for Pittsburgh, where he is associate director of the V.A. medical center. "But having it put together in a form like this gives it focus. Now I have a formula."

Many other participants noted that although much of what Montgomery had taught had been "commonsense kind of stuff," he had forced them to take a hard look at their listening and memory skills and had given them a system for improvement.

"I'll stop and think now," said Jean Nadort. "This was an excellent course."

Seminar participants polled several weeks after the course reported that they were putting Montgomery's lectures to use—particularly the memory skills. "I don't want to sound like a walking advertisement," said Carlos Confresi, "but I thought it was great. I've even used the memory system to remember lists." Gerard Smith, training supervisor for General Cable Corporation of Greenwich, Connecticut, noted: "Just to sit around and talk about these things is almost like relearning them."

Newsweek subscription-fulfillment director Vincent M. Pace said he wished Montgomery had gone beyond the listening basics and given him more practice and advanced listening skills. Nevertheless, Pace felt that on balance, "He gave me what I needed—desire. I wouldn't hesitate to send a subordinate who wasn't a good listener to this course."

Whether the two days of memory/listening drill was worth $675 is a judgment only each participant and his or her company could make. Judging by the size of the booming listening business, though, it appears many firms are willing to reach deep into their pockets to help their employees improve communications skills. Montgomery is only one of nearly 100 listening instructors who travel the country helping people willing to listen to them. Several publishing firms have brought out multimedia listening "modules" that companies can purchase for in-house training programs. And the nonfiction section of any good bookstore boasts at least a half-dozen volumes for do-it-yourself listeners.

But just as listening is one of the least taught skills, it is also one of the least studied. In the mid-1920s, Dr. Paul T. Rankin, director of research for the Detroit school system and one of the earliest researchers in the area of communication, looked at how much time people spent reading, writing, speaking and listening. He found that listening was by far the most time-consuming type of communication but the one we're least trained in. Subsequent studies have confirmed his findings that most of us spend approximately 50 percent of our communication time listening—and that we remember only about a quarter of what we listen to. But there is little known about why some people are better listeners than others. And though listening lecturers often report "positive feedback" from seminar participants, no one has done follow-up studies of listening-course graduates to determine whether their listening habits changed significantly—and over the long term—as a result of their training.

If my own experience is any guide, I would need follow-up training to help me really change my listening habits. I learned in Montgomery's class that while I'm a relatively good listener in professional situations in which I'm conducting an interview or taking notes during a speech, I'm less effective in other instances. In particular, so-called "emotional triggers" trip me up: I often listen poorly to people whose appearance is strange, who have an abrupt or awkward manner, or who use such phrases as "you girls." And in personal encounters I frequently thwart the communication process by injecting my own opinions and concerns into a conversation before hearing the other person out. An occasional refresher course might provide me with the incentive and opportunity to practice controlling these bad listening habits.

Dr. Lyman K. Steil, the former University of Minnesota professor who developed the Sperry Corporation's listening program, notes that how much is retained after a "staged, one-stop" listening seminar depends both on the individual and on his or her firm. Good listening does take a lot of practice, he stressed—and it also takes reinforcement. While most Sperry employees attend only one listening seminar, the subject is discussed regularly in department meetings or in the in-house newspaper. Sperry workers simply aren't permitted to forget about good listening.

Steil, who wrote his doctoral dissertation on listening, uses a different teaching approach than such professional speakers as Montgomery, who teach a simplified, broad-brush course. He says he tries to: increase his students' knowledge about listening in general; increase their knowledge about themselves as listeners, and change their behavior through self-analysis, exercises and other techniques.

Steil stresses that our listening abilities change dramatically depending on who is talking—boss, spouse, co-worker, child—and depending on the topic of conversation. Some people are bad at chitchat but listen well to technical information. Others respond well in business conversations but not in emotional conversations. Steil uses exercises to help his seminar participants discover their listening strengths and weaknesses. His students might be asked, for instance, to identify factors in a conversation that raise their emotions. And once they know what "flash" words or attitudes offend them, they can listen more objectively.

Steil, who now heads his own Communications Development Inc. consulting firm, warns potential listening-seminar students to heed caveat emptor when approaching this newly popular field: Many of the nearly 100 lecturers on the subject in the U.S. today don't have any special listening training. He encourages individuals or corporations interested in listening to check the educational backgrounds, seminar outlines and references of listening instructors they are considering. Still, he notes that almost any course is better than no course at all. "Anyone who spends anytime focusing on listening is better off than the person who doesn't," Steil said.

According to Montgomery, perhaps engaging in a bit of flattery, my 19 classmates and I number among an elite of 2 percent of American adults who are graduates of a formal listening course. But if listening stays in fashion, there will be many more of us assuming the active listening posture and recalling LADDER and AIM. I think most of my classmates would agree that this would be a positive development.

"I *feel* so much better," was how Vince Pace, who is happier now that he's able to communicate better both at the office and at home, summed up the payoff from learning to listen. Maybe it was that feeling the Sperry Corporation had in mind when it counseled in one advertisement that "Closing the mouth helps open the mind."

DOING GOOD

BEYOND SELFISHNESS

We start helping others early in life, but we're not always consistent. What makes us helpful sometimes and not others?

Alfie Kohn

Alfie Kohn, a contributing editor, is the author of No Contest: The Case Against Competition *(Houghton Mifflin).*

You realize you left your wallet on the bus and you give up hope of ever seeing it again. But someone calls that evening asking how to return the wallet to you.

Two toddlers are roughhousing when one suddenly begins to cry. The other child rushes to fetch his own security blanket and offers it to his playmate.

Driving on a lonely country road, you see a car stopped on the shoulder, smoke pouring from the hood. The driver waves to you frantically, and instinctively you pull over to help, putting aside thoughts of your appointments.

Despite the fact that "Look out for Number One" is one of our culture's mantras, these examples of "prosocial" behavior are really not so unusual. "Even in our society," says New York University psychologist Martin Hoffman, "the evidence is overwhelming that most people, when confronted with someone in a distress situation, will make a move to help very quickly if circumstances permit."

Helping may be as dramatic as agreeing to donate a kidney or as mundane as letting another shopper ahead of you in line. But most of us do it frequently and started doing it very early in life.

Psychologists have argued for years about whether our behavior owes more to the situations in which we find ourselves or to our individual characteristics. Prosocial behavior seems to be related to both. On the situation side, research shows that regardless of your personality, you'll be more likely to come to someone's aid if that person is already known to you or is seen as similar to you. Likewise, if you live in a small town rather than a city, the chances of your agreeing to help increase dramatically. In one experiment, a child stood on a busy street and said to passersby, "I'm lost. Can you call my house?" Nearly three-quarters of the adults in small towns did so, as compared with fewer than half in big cities. "City people adjust to the constant demands of urban life by reducing their involvement with others," the researcher concluded. You are also more likely to help someone if no one else is around at the time you hear a cry for help. The original research on this question was conducted by psychologists Bibb Latané and John Darley. They offer three reasons to account for the fact that we're less apt to help when more people are in the area: First, we may get a case of stage fright, fearing to appear foolish if it turns out no help was really necessary. Second, we may conclude from the fact that other people aren't helping that there's really no need for us to intervene either. Finally, the responsibility for doing something is shared by everyone present, so we don't feel a personal obligation to get involved.

But some people seem to be more other-oriented than others regardless of the situation. People who feel in control of what happens in their lives and who have little need for approval from others are the most likely to help others. Similarly, people in a good state of mind, even if only temporarily, are especially inclined to help. "Feel good, do good" is the general rule, researchers say, regardless of whether you feel good from having had a productive day at the office or, say, from finding money in the street. In one study, people got a phone call from a woman who said the operator had given her their number by mistake, and she was now out of change at a pay phone. The woman asked if the person who answered would look up a number, call and deliver a message for her. It turned out that people who had unexpectedly received free stationery a few minutes before were more likely to help out the caller.

But some investigators aren't satisfied with knowing just when prosocial acts will take place or by whom. "Why should we help other people? Why not help Number One? That's the rock-bottom question," says University of Massachusetts psychologist Ervin Staub, who's been wrestling with that problem since the mid 1960s.

Obviously we do help each other. But it's equally obvious that our motives for doing so aren't always unselfish. Prosocial behavior, which means behavior intended to benefit others, isn't necessarily altruistic. The 17th-century political philosopher Thomas Hobbes, who believed that we always act out of self-interest, was once seen giving money to a beggar. When asked why, he explained that he was mostly trying to relieve his own distress at seeing the beggar's distress.

His explanation will ring true for many of us. But is this always what's going on: helping in order to feel good or to benefit ourselves in some way? Is real altruism a Sunday school myth? Many of us automatically assume so—not because there's good evidence for that belief but because of our basic, and unproved, assumptions about human nature.

New research describes how we feel when helping someone, but that doesn't mean we came to that person's aid in order to feel good. We may have acted out of a simple desire to help. In fact, there is good evidence for the existence of genuine altruism. Consider:

■ **Do we help just to impress others?** "If looking good were the motive, you'd be more likely to help with others watching," says Latané. His experiments showed just the opposite. More evidence comes from an experiment Staub did in 1970: Children who voluntarily shared their candy turned out to have a lower need for approval than those who didn't share. "If I'm feeling good about myself, I can respond to the needs of others," Staub explains. So helping needn't be motivated by a desire for approval.

■ **Do we help just to ease our own distress?** Sometimes our motivation is undoubtedly like that of Hobbes. But the easiest way to stop feeling bad about someone else's suffering is "just to ignore it or leave," says Arizona State University psychologist Nancy Eisenberg. Instead we often stay and help, and "there's no reason to believe we do that just to make ourselves feel better."

When people are distressed over another person's pain they may help—for selfish reasons. But if they have the chance simply to turn away from the cause of their distress, they'll gladly do that instead. People who choose to help when they have the opportunity to pass by, like the biblical Good Samaritan, aren't motivated by their own discomfort. And these people, according to C. Daniel Batson, a psychologist at the University of Kansas, describe their feelings as compassionate and sympathetic rather than anxious and apprehensive.

Older children can feel for another person's condition, understanding that distress may result from being part of a class of people who are oppressed.

Batson explored this behavior by having students listen to a radio news broadcast about a college senior whose parents had just been killed in a car accident. The students who responded most empathically to her problem also offered the most help, even though it would have been easy for them to say no and put the whole thing out of their minds.

■ **Do we help just to feel pleased with ourselves or to avoid guilt?** The obvious way to test this, Batson argues, is to see how we feel after learning that "someone else" has come to a victim's aid. If we really cared only about patting ourselves on the back (or escaping twinges of guilt), we would insist on being the rescuer. But sometimes we are concerned only to make sure that the person who needs help gets it, regardless of who does the helping. That suggests a truly altruistic motivation.

Pretend you are one of the subjects in a brand-new study of Batson's. You are told that by performing well on a game with numbers, you might be able to help someone else (whose voice you've just heard) avoid mild but unpleasant electric shocks. A little later, you're informed that the person won't be receiving shocks after all. How do you feel? Batson found that many subjects were pleased even though they personally didn't get the chance to do the good deed.

Batson, incidentally, used to assume that we help others primarily to benefit ourselves. But after a decade of studying empathic responses to distress, he's changed his mind. "I feel like the bulk of the evidence points in the direction of the existence of altruism," he says.

■ **If we're naturally selfish, why does helping behavior start so early in life?** At the age of 10 to 14 months, a baby will often look upset when someone else falls down or cries. Obviously made unhappy by another person's unhappiness, the child may seek solace in the mother's lap. In the second year, the child will begin comforting in a rudimentary way, such as by patting the head of someone who seems to be in pain. "The frequency (of this behavior) will vary, but most kids will do it sometimes," says Eisenberg.

By the time children are 3 or 4, prosocial behavior is common. One group of researchers videotaped 26 3-to-5-year-olds during 30 hours of free play and recorded about 1,200 acts of sharing, helping, comforting and cooperating. Children can be selfish and mean, too, of course, but there's no reason to think that these characteristics are more common or "natural" than their prosocial inclinations.

Psychologist Hoffman points to two studies showing that newborns cried much more intensely at the sound of another baby's cry than at other, equally loud noises. "That isn't what I'd call empathy," he concedes, "but it is evidence of a primitive precursor to it. There's a basic human tendency to be responsive to other persons' needs, not just your own."

Hoffman rejects biological theories that claim altruism amounts to nothing more than "selfish genes" trying to preserve themselves by prompting the individual to help relatives who share those genes. But he does believe "there may be a biological basis for a disposition to altruism. Natural selection demanded that humans evolve as creatures disposed toward helping, rescuing, protecting others in danger" as well as toward looking out for their own needs.

According to Hoffman, the inborn mechanism that forms the basis for altruism is empathy, which he defines as feeling something more appropriate to someone else's situation than to your own. The way he sees it, empathy becomes increasingly more sophisticated as we grow. First, infants are unable to draw sharp boundaries between themselves and others and sometimes react to another's distress as if they, themselves, had been hurt.

By about 18 months, children can distinguish between "me" and "not-me" but will still assume that others' feelings will be similar to their own. That's why if Jason sees his mother cry out in pain, he may fetch his bottle to make her feel better. By age 2 or 3, it is possible to understand

t appears that caring about others is as much a part of human nature as caring about ourselves. Which impulse gets emphasized is a matter of training.

that others react differently and also to empathize with more complex emotions.

Finally, older children can feel for another person's life condition, understanding that his or her distress may be chronic or recognizing that the distress may result from being part of a class of people who are oppressed.

Other psychologists, meanwhile, believe that you are more likely to help others not only if you feel their pain but also if you understand the way the world looks to them. This is called "role-taking" or "perspective-taking." "When people put themselves in the shoes of others, they may become more inclined to render them aid," according to Canadian researchers Dennis Krebs and Cristine Russell.

When they asked an 8-year-old boy named Adam whether that seemed right to him, he replied as follows: "Oh yes, what you do is, you forget everything else that's in your head, and then you make your mind into their mind. Then you know how they're feeling, so you know how to help them."

Some people seem more inclined than others to take Adam's advice—and, in general, to be prosocially oriented. Staub has found that such people have three defining characteristics: They have a positive view of people in general, they are concerned about others' welfare and they take personal responsibility for how other people are doing.

All these, but particularly the first, are affected by the kind of culture one lives in. "It's difficult to lead a competitive, individualistic life"—as we're raised to do in American society—"without devaluing others to some extent," says Staub. So raising children to triumph over others in school and at play is a good way to snuff out their inclination to help (see "Raising a Helping Child," this article).

It appears, then, that caring about others is as much a part of human nature as caring about ourselves. Which impulse gets emphasized is a matter of training, according to the experts. "We fundamentally have the potential to develop into caring, altruistic people or violent, aggressive people," says Staub. "No one will be altruistic if their experiences teach them to be concerned only about themselves. But human connection is intrinsically satisfying if we allow it to be."

Raising a Helping Child

HOW DO YOU BRING up a child who will be more inclined to help than to hurt? For starters, if you believe aggressive behavior is natural or even desirable—or find it amusing even while telling a child to stop—you are unlikely to curb such behavior. But if you communicate a deeply felt disapproval of hurting, you will be far more effective at discouraging children from doing so.

The intensity of the disapproval is not enough, however. Rather than simply restraining children or punishing them or yelling "No!" you should make the consequences of hurting clear. Children who are plainly told about the effect of aggression on the victim are more likely to refrain from such acts. Of course, helping is more than just the absence of hurting. Those who study child development recommend the following for encouraging specifically prosocial behavior:

- **Focus on the positive.** Help a child to understand how (and why) to help; telling him or her what not to do isn't enough. "A focus on prohibition may also promote self-concern, thereby diminishing attention to others' needs," Ervin Staub says.
- **Explain the reason.** Just as children ought to be told why aggression is bad, so they should hear why altruism is desirable: "When you share your toys, Diane gets to play, too, and that makes her feel good."
- **Set an example.** Particularly before the age of 3, children are powerfully influenced by how adults conduct their own lives. A parent who normally responds to another's distress is teaching a child to do likewise. In general, showing seems to be more effective than telling.
- **Let them help.** Give children the opportunity to try out what they've learned about being sensitive to others. A child who has taken care of a younger sibling or a pet, for example, has experienced first-hand what it means to be prosocial.
- **Promote a prosocial self-image.** Children should be encouraged to think of themselves as caring people even though their prosocial tendencies were initially shaped by a parent. "You want them to start thinking of themselves as the kind of people who help," says psychologist Nancy Eisenberg.
- **Be a warm, empathic parent.** Children who can form a secure attachment to Mom or Dad feel that the world is a basically safe place. They also feel good about themselves and well-disposed toward other people. Such children are more likely to respond to the needs of others than are those raised by parents who emphasize power and control. Responsiveness to children's needs — which includes respecting their occasional preference for distance from you—is also recommended.

The Dance of Intimacy

A relationship is like a dance: to stay close without stepping on each other's toes takes practice. To make real music takes finesse. With insights from a renowned psychologist, you can bring out the best in each other and make your partnership soar.

Harriet Goldhor Lerner, Ph.D.

What does an intimate relationship require of us to be successful? For starters, intimacy means that we can be who we are in a relationship and allow the other person to do the same. By "being who we are," we can talk openly about things that are important to us, we can take a clear position on where we stand on significant emotional issues, and we can clarify the limits of what is acceptable and tolerable to us. If we allow the other person to do the same, we can stay emotionally connected to that other party, who thinks, feels, and believes differently, without needing to change, convince, or fix him.

An intimate relationship is one in which neither person silences, sacrifices, or betrays the self, and each expresses strength and vulnerability, weakness and competence, in a balanced way. Truly intimate relationships do not operate at the expense of the self, nor do they allow the self to operate at the expense of the other. This is a tall order, or, more accurately, a lifelong challenge. But it is the heart and soul of intimacy.

Only when we stay in a relationship over time—whether by necessity or choice—is our capacity for intimacy truly put to the test. Only in a long-term relationship are we called upon to navigate that delicate balance between separateness and connectedness, and only then can we confront the challenge of sustaining both, without losing either, in a way that works for each partner.

When Relationships Are Stuck

All of us develop our identities through emotional connectedness to others, and we continue to need close relationships throughout our lives. We get into trouble when we distance ourselves from friends, lovers, and kin; pretend we don't need people; ignore a relationship that begins to go badly; or put no energy into generating new options for change.

The challenge of change is greatest when a relationship becomes a source of frustration and our attempts to fix things only lead to more of the same. These stuck relationships are often "too distant," and/or "too intense," precluding real intimacy. Intense feelings—no matter how positive—are hardly a measure of true and enduring closeness. In fact, intense feelings may *prevent* us from taking a careful and objective look at the intimate dance we carry on with significant people in our lives. Intense togetherness can easily flip into intense distance—or intense conflict, for that matter.

Too much intensity means one person overfocuses on the other in a blaming or worried way or in an attempt to fix him. Or each person may be overfocused on the other and underfocused on the self.

Too much distance indicates there is little togetherness and real sharing of one's true self in the relationship. Important issues go underground rather than get aired and worked on. Many distant relationships are also intense, because distance is one way we manage intensity. If, for instance, you haven't seen your ex-husband in five years and can't talk with him about the kids without clutching yourself inside, then you have a *very* intense relationship.

Once a relationship is stuck, the motivation to change things is not enough to make it happen. For one thing, we may be so buffeted by strong feelings that we can't think clearly and objectively about the problem or our own part in it. When intensity is high we *react* rather than observe and think, we overfocus on the *other* rather than on the self, and we find ourselves in polarized positions where we are unable to see more than one side of an issue (our own) and find new ways to relate. We may navigate relationships in ways that lower our anxiety in the short run but diminish our capacity for intimacy over the long haul.

In addition, we may have a strong wish for change in a relationship but be unaware of, or unwilling to confront, the actual source of anxiety that is fueling a problem and blocking intimacy. How can we gain the courage to discover and confront the real issues? How can we unblock our intimate relationships?

Naming the Problem

A couple of years ago my sister came to me with a problem that illustrates this situation. Susan called me one day and confessed she was having a very rough time with her boyfriend, David. Although she felt entirely committed to the relationship, David said he needed more time to work through his own issues in order to make a decision about their living together. Susan and David lived in different cities, making for long and tiring weekend trips; however, this long-distance arrangement (and David's indefiniteness) was nothing new—it had been going on for quite some time.

What was new was my sister's sudden feeling of panic, resulting in her pressuring David for a decision he was not yet ready to

From *New Woman*, April 1989, pp. 66-68, 71-72. Excerpt from *The Dance of Intimacy*, by Harriet Goldhor Lerner.

make. Because Susan had been working for some time on altering her pattern of pursuing men who were distancers in romantic relationships, she was able to see her behavior like a red warning flag. She was unable, however, to tone down her reactivity and stop pursuing. By the time Susan called me, she was feeling terrible.

While thinking about my sister's situation, I was particularly struck by the *timing* of the problem. Susan's sense of desperation and her heightened reactivity to David's wish for more time and space followed a trip we took to Phoenix to visit our parents and to see our uncle Si, who was dying from a fast-moving lung cancer. Si's diagnosis had been a shock to us—he'd always been such a vibrant, active man. Seeing him sick reminded our family of past losses, impending losses, and some recent health scares on the family tree. Of all these stresses, the closest to home for Susan and me was the earlier diagnosis of our father's rare, degenerative brain disease. Because our father surprised everyone by regaining his functioning, this devastating diagnosis was replaced with a more hopeful one—but the experience had been very hard on our family.

During our phone conversation, I asked Susan if there might be a connection between her anxious focus on David and all the emotions that were stirred up by our recent visit to Phoenix. This made intellectual sense to her, but it also seemed a bit abstract, since Susan did not feel any connection at a gut level.

A few weeks later Susan visited me for a long weekend and decided to consult a family systems therapist. Afterward, she began to more fully appreciate the link between recent health issues in our family and her anxious pursuit of David. Simply *thinking* about this connection helped Susan to de-intensify her focus on David and reflect more calmly and objectively on her current situation.

Only when we stay in a relationship over time—whether by necessity or choice—is our capacity for intimacy truly put to the test.

Susan was also challenged to think about the pursuer-distancer pattern she was stuck in. It was as if 100 percent of the anxiety and ambivalence about living together was David's. And as if Susan was just 100 percent raring to go—no worries at all, except how they would decorate the apartment. Such polarities (she stands for togetherness, he for distance) are common enough, but they distort the experience of self and other and keep us stuck.

Finally, Susan confronted the fact that she was putting so much energy into her relationship with David, she was neglecting her own family and her career. On the one hand, Susan's attention to this relationship made sense because insuring its success was her highest priority. On the other hand, focusing on a relationship at the expense of one's own goals and life plan overloads that relationship. The best way Susan could work on her relationship with David was to work on her own self. This kind of self-focus is a good rule of thumb for all of us. While Susan's energy was overfocused on David, another woman might find herself overfocusing on another kind of relationship; she might dwell too intensely on a co-worker who undermines her or on a troubled sibling.

Breaking the Pursuit Cycle

Susan had gained insight and understanding of her problem, but her next challenge was translating what she had learned into action. What could she do differently when she was back home to lower her anxiety and achieve a calmer, more balanced relationship with David? By the time Susan left, she had formulated a plan. Whenever we are feeling very anxious, it can be enormously helpful to have a clear plan, one based not on reactivity and a reflexive need to "do something—anything!" but rather one based on reflection and a solid understanding of the problem.

Susan enacted her plan. First, she shared with David that she had been thinking about their relationship during her trip and had gained some insight into her own behavior. "I came to realize," she told him, "that the pressure I was feeling about our living together had less to do with you and our relationship and more to do with my anxiety about some other things." She filled David in on what these were—family issues related to health and loss. David was understanding and clearly relieved.

Susan also told him that perhaps she was letting him express the ambivalence for both of them, which probably wasn't fair. She reminded David that her own track record with relationships surely provided her with good reason to be anxious about commitment, but she had avoided this pretty well by focusing on *his* problem and *his* wish to put off the decision.

This statement was the hardest for Susan, because when we are in a pursuer-distancer polarity, pursuers are convinced that all they want is more togetherness, and distancers are convinced that all they want is more distance. Sometimes only after the pursuit cycle is broken can each party begin to experience the wish we all have for both separateness and togetherness.

Finally, Susan told David that she had been neglecting her work projects and needed to put more time and attention into them. "Instead of driving up next weekend," Susan said, "I'm going to stay at home and get some work done." For the first time in a while, Susan became the spokesperson for more distance, *not in an angry, reactive manner but as a calm move for self.*

The changes Susan made were successful in breaking the pursuer-distancer pattern, which was bringing her pain. If we are pursuers, such moves can be excruciatingly difficult to initiate and sustain in a calm, nonreactive way. Why? Because pursuing is often an unconscious reaction to anxiety. If it is our *usual* reaction, we will initially become *more* anxious when we keep it in check.

From where, then, do we get the motivation and the courage to maintain such a change? We must get it from the conviction that the old ways simply do not work.

Before Susan returned home, she considered another option aimed at helping her to calm things down with David. Whenever she found herself feeling anxious about the relationship and slipping back into the pursuit mode, she would contemplate sitting down and writing a letter to our father instead, or calling home.

This may sound a bit farfetched at first, but it makes good sense. If Susan managed her anxiety about family issues by distancing, she would be more likely to get intense with David. If, instead, she could stay connected to the *actual source of her anxiety,* she would feel more anxious about our parents' failing health, but the anxiety would be less likely to overload her love relationship. Indeed, learning how to stay in touch with our relatives and working on key emotional issues at their source lays the groundwork for more solid intimate relationships in the present or future.

A Postscript on Partners Who Can't Make Up Their Minds

What if *your* partner can't make a commitment? What if he's not ready to think about marriage, not ready to give up another relationship, not sure he's really in love? He may or may not be ready in two years—or 20. Does Susan's story imply that we should hang around *forever,* working on our own issues and failing to address our partner's uncertainty? Does it mean that we should never take a position on our partner's distancing or lack of commitment? Certainly not. A partner's long-term ambivalence *is* an issue for us—that is, if we really want to settle down.

We will, however, be *least successful* in

An intimate relationship requires a level of communication that allows each person to be comfortable with who they are and not feel it necessary to sacrifice their own identity.

addressing the commitment issue, or any other, when we feel reactive and intense. Working to keep anxiety down is a priority, because anxiety drives reactivity, which drives polarities. (*All* he can do is distance. *All* she can do is pursue.) The more we pay attention to the different sources of anxiety that affect our lives, the more calmly and clearly we'll navigate the hot spots with our intimate other.

A Calm Bottom Line

Let's look at a woman who was able to take a clear position with her distant and ambivalent partner, a position relatively free from reactivity and expressions of anxious pursuit. Gwenna was a 26-year-old real estate agent who sought my help for a particular relationship issue. For two and a half years she had been dating Greg, a city planner who had had disastrous first and second marriages and couldn't make up his mind about a third. Gwenna was aware that Greg backed off further under pressure, yet she didn't want to live forever with the status quo. How did she ultimately handle the situation?

As a first step, Gwenna talked with Greg about their relationship, calmly initiating the conversation in a low-keyed fashion. She shared her perspective on both the strengths and weaknesses of their relationship and what her hopes were for their future. She asked Greg to do the same. Unlike earlier conversations, she conducted this one without pursuing him, pressuring him, or diagnosing his problems with women. At the same time, Gwenna asked Greg some clear questions, the answers to which exposed his own vagueness.

"How will you know when you *are* ready to make a commitment?" she asked. "What specifically would need to change or be different than it is today?"

"I don't know," Greg responded. When questioned further, the best he could come up with was he'd "just feel it."

"How much more time do you need to make a decision one way or another?"

"I'm not sure," Greg replied. "Maybe a couple of years, but I really can't answer a question like that. I can't predict or plan my feelings."

And so it went.

Gwenna really loved this man, but two years (and maybe more) was longer than she could comfortably wait. So, after much thought, she told Greg that she would wait until the fall—about ten months—but she would move on if he couldn't commit himself to marriage by then. She was open about her own wish to marry and have a family with him yet equally clear that her first priority was a mutually committed relationship. If Greg was not at that point by fall, then she would end the relationship—painful though it would be.

Having set up a waiting period, Gwenna was able *not* to pursue Greg, and *not* become distant or otherwise reactive to his expressions of ambivalence. In this way, she gave him emotional space to struggle with his dilemma, and the relationship had its best chance of succeeding. Her bottom line position (a decision by the fall) was not a threat or an attempt to rope Greg in, but rather a true definition of self and a clarification of the time limits she could live with. Gwenna would not have been able to proceed this way if the relationship were burdened with baggage from her past and present that she was not paying attention to.

Unfortunately, doing our part right does not insure that things turn out as we wish. While my sister and David now live together happily, Gwenna's story has a different ending.

When fall arrived, Greg told Gwenna that he needed another six months to make up his mind. Gwenna deliberated a while and decided she could live with that. But when the six months was up, Greg was still uncertain and asked for more time. It was then that Gwenna took the painful but ultimately empowering step of ending their relationship.

Getting to the Source

We all know that anxiety impacts on everything from our immune system to our closest relationships. How can we identify the significant sources of emotional intensity in our lives? How can we know when anxiety from source *A* is causing "stuckness" in relationship *B*?

Sometimes it's obvious: there may be a recent stressful event, a negative or even positive change we can pinpoint as a source of the anxiety that is overloading a relationship. If *we* miss it, others may see it for us ("No wonder you've been fighting with Jim—you moved to a new city just three months ago and that's a major adjustment!").

Sometimes we think that a particular event or change is stressful, but we aren't fully aware just how stressful it really is. Our narrow focus on one intimate relationship obscures the broader emotional field from our view. For example, we may downplay the emotional impact of significant transitions—a birth, wedding, job change, promotion, graduation, child leaving home, ill parent—because these are just normal things that happen in the course of the life cycle. We fail to realize that "just normal things," when they involve change, will profoundly affect our closest ties.

Paradoxically, couples become less able to achieve intimacy as they stay focused on it and give it their primary attention. Real closeness occurs most reliably not when it is pursued or demanded in a relationship, but when both individuals work consistently on their own selves. By working on the self, I do not mean that we should maintain a single-minded focus on self-enhancement or career advancement; these are male-defined notions of selfhood, which women would do well to challenge. Working on the self includes clarifying beliefs, values, and life goals; staying responsibly connected to people on one's own family tree; defining the self in key relationships; and addressing important emotional issues as they arise.

The Challenge of Independence

For women, this presents an obvious dilemma. Only a few of us have been encouraged to put our primary energy into formulating a life plan that neither requires nor excludes marriage. In fact, we may have received generations of training to *not* think this way. Yet this kind of self-focus not only insures our well-being, it also puts us on more solid ground for negotiating in our intimate relationships. *We cannot navigate clearly within a relationship unless we can live without it.*

Having a life plan means more than working to insure our own economic security. It also means working toward clarifying our values, beliefs, and priorities and then applying them to our daily actions. It means thinking about what talents and abilities we want to develop over the next two—or 20—years. Obviously, a life plan is not written in stone but is instead open to constant revision over time.

Finally, having a life plan does not mean adopting masculine values and pursuing goals single-mindedly. Some of us may be striving to lighten our work commitments so we can spend more time with our friends and family or in other pursuits, such as spiritual development or the world peace movement. What *is* significant about a life plan is that it can help us live our own lives, not someone else's, as well as possible.

When we do not focus our primary energy on working on a life plan, our intimate relationships suffer. We begin to look to others to provide us with meaning or happiness, which is not their job. We seek a partner who will provide self-esteem, which cannot be bestowed by another. We set up a situation in which we are bound to get overinvolved in the other person's ups and downs because we are underfocused on ourselves.

Intimate relationships cannot substitute for a life plan. And, to have any meaning at all, a life plan must include intimate relationships. Only through our connectedness to others can we really know and enhance the self. And only through working on the self can we begin to enhance our connectedness to others. There is, quite simply, no other way.

Dynamics of Personal Adjustment: The Individual and Society

The passing of each decade brings changes to society. Some historians have suggested that changes are occurring more rapidly. In other words, history appears to take less time to happen. How has American society changed? The inventory is long. Technological advances, for example, can be found everywhere. A decade ago few people knew what "user-friendly" or "64K memory" signified. Today these terms are readily identified with the rapidly expanding computer industry. Ten years ago Americans felt fortunate to own a thirteen-inch television that received three local stations. Now people feel deprived if they cannot select from 100 different worldwide channels for their big, rear-screen sets. Today we can "fax" a message to the other side of the world just as quickly as we can propel a missile to the other side of the world.

In the Middle Ages, Londoners worried about the plague. Before vaccines were available, people worried about polio and other diseases. Today much concern is focused on the transmission and cure of AIDS, the discovery of more carcinogenic substances, and the greenhouse effect. In terms of mental health, psychologists see few hysterics, the type of patient seen by Freud in the 1800s. Depression, psychosomatic ulcers, and alcohol and drug addiction are more common today. In addition, issues about the changing American family continue to grab headlines. Nearly every popular magazine carries a story or two bemoaning the passing of the traditional, nuclear family.

This list of societal transformations, while not exhaustive, reflects society's continual demands for adaptation by each of its members. However, it is not just society at large that places stress on us. Smaller units within society, such as our work group or family, also demand continual adaptation by individuals. Families change as children leave the proverbial nest, as parents divorce, and as adoptions occur or new babies are born. Work groups expand and contract with economic fluctuations. Even when group size remains stable, new members come and go as turnover takes place, and, in turn, change the dynamics of the group that shifts in response to the new personalities. Each of these changes, whether welcome or not, places stress on the individual who needs to adjust to or cope with the change.

This unit of the book addresses the interplay between the individual and society in producing the problems each creates for the other. The first series of articles are about selected individuals in society. "The Indispensable Woman," explores the dual roles of career women, the roles of employee and of homemaker, which can place stress on women who feel that they must excel at both. "The American Man in Transition," examines how the model of the ideal man has changed from aggressive and tough to sensitive and family-oriented. The last article in this series on special individuals is about people who use a peculiar strategy called self-defeating behavior. These individuals often sabotage their own behavior so that they fail. A supportive environment, the author reminds us, can often reverse this behavior.

The second set of articles describes social conditions related to couples and small groups that may need to be changed if we are to be a happier and more egalitarian society. In "Getting Better—Together," you will learn that even happily married couples often face the problem of stagnation and what they can do about it—together. In the article, "No Life To Live," codependency, a new buzzword for the 1990s, is described. Codependent individuals are often too involved in salvaging the life of an addicted loved one to live their own lives. Again, therapy can help.

The next series of articles describe what happens to individuals in society when they are not treated well by society at large. Lance Shotland, in "When Bystanders Just Stand By," discusses our usual practice of avoiding the giving of aid to crime victims rather than assisting them. Finally, in "Psychologists Find Ways to Break Racism's Hold," Daniel Goleman asserts that prejudice need not rear its head in schools since cooperative team learning decreases prejudice of school children. Victims of crimes and of prejudice would fare better if others around them would step in and reverse the victimization, but often no one is willing to take the first step.

Unit 5

Looking Ahead: Challenge Questions

Is society today more stressful than it was a century ago? How so? Are there changes from a decade ago that make our living easier? Harder? Can and should anything be done to slow change, or should the focus be on new methods for adapting to change?

Do you think men's and women's roles have changed in the last few years? How so? For better or worse?

Do you think individuals sabotage their own behavior? What are some of the ways mentioned in the article on self-defeating behavior that individuals handicap themselves? Can you think of any other self-handicapping strategies? If you had a friends who did this, what could you do about it?

Are Americans insensitive to each other? Can a person be "alone" in a crowd? Are there methods for psychologically adapting to crowding so that it is not as deleterious a phenomenon?

What problems do unhappily married couples face? Happily married couples? Do you think that marital problems need to be corrected by both individuals; that is, is couples therapy always the answer?

Describe the co-dependent's life. Codependency is usually described in relationship to an addicted spouse. Can codependency occur in families with other types of problems? What can a codependent do to stop living someone else's life?

Why don't people readily come to the aid of others? Can people be trained to be more altruistic? Should helping behavior be legislated; that is, should it be against the law to ignore a victim? What motivates volunteerism? What do you accept as your civic responsibility? If you are not now a volunteer, why not?

Against what other people does the average American hold prejudices? Are Americans the most prejudiced group of citizens? If American prejudice is so ubiquitous and undesirable, how can children be raised to be prejudice-free? What harm comes to the victim of prejudice? Does the bigot ever suffer?

The Indispensable Woman

She always says yes. She never asks for help. And she thinks that without her, things would all fall apart. But how does she stay together?

ELLEN SUE STERN

A FEW YEARS AGO, HAD SOMEone called me an "indispensable woman," I would have considered it a compliment. Today, I know better.

As an indispensable woman, I ran myself ragged. And I was proud of it. I stacked one career challenge on top of another, regardless of whether time and energy allowed. When I wasn't racing around filling each minute with activity, I turned my attention on the other people in my life, with or without an invitation.

I applied the same perfectionism to my family and friends. I presided over my husband Gary's involvements, criticizing him when his pace or productivity lagged. When his share of responsibilities wasn't completed on *my* timetable, I'd simply take over, adding to my already teeming pile of demands. I treated my children like projects, efficiently orchestrating their lives, often at the expense of their feelings.

At 2:00 a.m. one morning, as I was working frantically at my computer, my 3-year-old son, Evan, appeared in the kitchen bleary-eyed, thumb in mouth, clutching his beloved Raggedy Andy.

"What's wrong, honey?" I asked, one eye on the screen.

"Nothing. I'll just lie on the floor next to you until you're done," he replied. I felt guilty. But I still couldn't make myself stop.

Deep inside, though I never would have admitted it, I sensed something had to change. And slowly, eventually, it did. I learned, both from my own experience and the experience of women I spoke with in an effort to understand my dilemma, that it *is* possible to be productive, successful, and fulfilled without making yourself indispensable.

THE PERFECTION TRAP

Although my story and the stories of women I spoke with were unique, the theme, *If I don't hold it together, it will all fall apart,* played over and over until it started to sound like the female battle cry of the eighties. It was clear to me that, regardless of how many of us bemoaned the pressures of our lives, we were reluctant to let them go—because *having* them reassured us that we were wanted and needed. Instead of accepting that our best would be good enough, nothing less than perfection reassured us that we were valued.

We all know that no one is perfect. And yet who doesn't have an image of the ideal mother, infallible friend, perfect partner, or ultimate professional? Our definition of perfection is highly personal and rooted in the positive images we've internalized from childhood. One woman may have absorbed the ideal of the "good mother"—gracious, accommodating, sacrificing her needs to make others' lives more comfortable; another woman may strive to attain the traditionally male ideals of independence, financial success, and prestige in the workplace; a third woman may seek to emulate *both* her parents, expecting herself to create a perfect home and maintain trouble-free intimate relationships while making her mark professionally.

When we measure ourselves against any of these ideals, believing in them as reachable goals, we set ourselves up for frustration and disappointment.

WHO IS THE INDISPENSABLE WOMAN?

The indispensable woman adopts one or more of the following behavior patterns. Do any of them sound similar to your own experience?

Overcommitment. There are only 24 hours in a day, but the indispensable woman tries to squeeze in more. Consequently, she's impatient, often in the position of having to apologize, and almost always running behind time. While at first glance being overextended seems ag-

From *New Woman*, April 1989, pp. 74–76. Excerpt from *The Indispensable Woman.* Published by Bantam Books, a division of Bantam Doubleday Dell Publishing Group, Inc.

gravating and exhausting, it appeals to the indispensable woman's sense of urgency and drama. Having a tight schedule makes her feel important. When faced with the choice of cutting back or accelerating, she inevitably steps on the gas pedal.

The woman who is overcommitted keeps herself so busy *doing* that she has little time for *feeling*. The rush of perpetual motion creates a convincing illusion of purpose, but in truth she barely has time to get where she's going, much less know if it's the right place to be.

Fragmentation. The indispensable-woman's life is compartmentalized. She lives by a list, with each moment accounted for. When something goes wrong or the unexpected occurs, it becomes nearly impossible to keep everything straight. And she leaves herself little, if any, room for error. Each aspect of her identity must be synchronized, like so many parts of a watch.

Women who are fragmented say that at best they are in a constant state of anxiety; at worst, they feel as if they are on the verge of a nervous breakdown.

An Unbalanced Picture. Regardless of how high the indispensable woman climbs, it only takes one minute for her to fall off the mountain. Since her identity is based on multiple roles (friend, employee, wife, mother, lover), it might seem that the potential for positive self-esteem would be great. But that's not so for a woman determined to prove herself in *every* area. Taking on more roles can simply raise the stakes for failing to live up to high expectations. She winds up feeling haunted by her incompletes rather than heartened by her successes.

Confidence Swings. The indispensable woman shifts back and forth between diminishing her own worth and presenting an inflated image of her importance.

Lisa, 31, takes pride in her ability to handle 12 different things at once. But when the weekend for her tenth-year college reunion comes around, her normally smooth demeanor shows a crack. "How can I go anywhere?" she asks bitterly. "Without me, the kids would eat Froot Loops for dinner and the laundry hamper would burst before anyone thought to empty it."

Lisa has made herself feel so essential to others that it seems impossible to extricate herself, even for a weekend. What's more, the very idea that her absence *would not* automatically signal a disaster makes her terrified to leave.

The Inability to Ask for Help. The indispensable woman perpetuates an image of self-sufficiency, rarely asking for help and refusing it when offered. While there are times when depending on yourself *is* the simplest solution, more often self-sufficiency becomes a smoke screen for feelings of vulnerability. The woman who does it all needs and deserves all the support she can get—if only she'd accept it.

BREAKING THE PERFECTION CYCLE

No one can make you stop trying to be indispensable; you have to want to. Remember, changing destructive behavior is a gradual process that requires making a long-term investment. The following steps will help you alter your perfectionist pattern.

Do You Take On Too Much?

The Oxford English Dictionary defines someone who is "indispensable" as a person who *can't be done without.*

To learn if you are making yourself indispensable—and forfeiting the chance to enjoy your own life—answer yes or no to the following questions:

1. Do you typically take on more in a day than you can *comfortably* handle?

2. Does the idea that you can give up any of your responsibility strike you as ridiculous?

3. Is it hard for you to ask for and accept help and support?

4. Are you typically rushing and late for appointments?

5. Do you live by a list?

6. Do you secretly believe that no one can do it as well, as fast, or as efficiently as you?

7. Do tight deadlines and extra responsibility make you feel challenged and exhilarated?

8. Do you hide your insecurities behind a veil of competence?

9. Do you believe that other people don't appreciate how hard you work and how much you do?

10. Do feelings of accomplishment in one part of your life *not* necessarily carry over into another?

11. Do you become so wrapped up in a project that you lose sight of what else is happening around you?

12. Are you extremely goal oriented?

13. Do you find yourself resenting how much responsibility you have and wondering how you got it?

14. Are you chronically tense, frazzled, and exhausted?

15. Is it hard for you to relax and enjoy yourself because you're worrying about what isn't being done?

16. Is there a gap between what you *are* responsible for and what you *feel* responsible for?

17. Do you experience a constant need to prove yourself?

18. When your demands pile up, do you snap into action and come up with more efficient and organized means of handling them?

19. Do you find it difficult to sit still and do nothing?

20. Do you feel your best isn't enough?

If you answered yes to more than five of these questions, you are in some stage of becoming or being an "indispensable woman." Take some time out to evaluate how much you do and how much would be enough. Chances are, that extra load you've taken on is sabotaging your satisfaction in life. Now it's time to let go.

Accept Personal Responsibility. Take *more* responsibility? The operative word is *personal.* You accept responsibility when you quit blaming others for the pressures in your life and when you stop viewing yourself as a victim. You need to see that you are the source of your pressures and that you play a large part in perpetuating this pattern.

Taking responsibility involves accepting consequences. Once you recognize the connection between your perfectionism and the resulting problems in your career or relationships, you can begin to make changes.

Simplify. No matter how much you talk about slowing down, nothing will change until you act. If you complain more vigorously about doing most of the housework, for example, but continue to do it, nothing will change. Stop performing and start negotiating.

Simplifying restores balance. Relinquishing some of your responsibilities frees you to cultivate other aspects of your life—activities and interests that nurture you and give you greater perspective.

Let Go of Guilt. Guilt is the punishment we mete out to ourselves for not being perfect; by hanging on to it we remain mired in our indispensability. Letting go of guilt doesn't mean abdicating responsibility or no longer caring. It *does* mean giving up responsibility for things that are beyond our control.

Create Reachable Goals. Perfectionists are overly optimistic about what can be accomplished in a day, forever playing catch up and feeling inadequate when anything is left undone. It is essential that you create reachable goals based on both your strengths and weaknesses. Reachable goals are ones that protect your energy, establish healthy boundaries, and do not promise more than you can deliver. When you set your sights on what is achievable, you vastly increase your likelihood of success, which, in turn, increases self-esteem.

Beyond perfectionism is something better, something healthier and more satisfying. Instead of squandering our energy and running around in circles, we're able to focus on the things that are really important. When we shed our indispensability, we rediscover ourselves.

STUBBORNLY ▲ FOLLOWING ▲ WOMEN'S ▲ EXAMPLE, ▲ MEN

THE AMERICAN MAN IN TRANSITION

ARE ▲ CHANGING. ▲ THEY ▲ HAVE ▲ NO CHOICE.

PROJECT EDITOR MICHAEL SEGELL

Men are doing a lot of soul-searching these days. The old role models—taciturn John Wayne, macho Stallone, sensitive Alda, workaholic Iacocca—simply have no relevance now. Inspired by women, who have radically redefined their roles in America, men are casting about for an identity that is comfortably, and truly, masculine. They're in transition, and they're finding it a wrenching, lonely business.

One thing is certain. American men must do something to change—and women have to help them, or risk losing them. On average, men die seven years younger than women. Biology isn't the full explanation—the gap used to be smaller. By one estimate, only two of those years can be clearly attributed to hard-wired differences in male and female biology. The traditional male sex role, characterized by a roll-with-the-punches stoicism and isolation, fraught with stress, anxiety and ambivalence, is hazardous to men's health. The body, that exacting taskmaster and teacher, is telling men to find a new way to be. It's a matter of life and death.

The American man's emotional life is crying out for change, too. Just as feminism encouraged women to enrich their lives by looking outward, the gains women have achieved have indirectly suggested to men the benefits of looking inward. Not only is the old male model physically destructive, it's emotionally stultifying—and unacceptable to many women. The sorry condition of men's interpersonal skills is reflected in a few telling data: At no time in history have there been so many divorced men, so many single fathers—and this at a time when men claim to cherish family and home life more than any other facet of their lives. That they are so inept at it is tearing them apart.

Their current failure to integrate their lives, though, may be temporary—a transition before they reach their ultimate transformation. A new *American Health*/Gallup survey has turned up a remarkable finding: Men and women are in very close agreement on the characteristics that make up an ideal man (see "Perfection Incarnate"). Does this signal an end to the battle of the sexes? Maybe, suggest some of the authors on the following pages. Many men, by changing themselves, are at least moving toward a rapprochement. Like the early feminists, these men herald a shift, however gradual, in the American male psyche. Some—optimistically, perhaps—are calling the trend a men's movement.

Our survey documented not only evidence of that shift, but the ambivalence, reticence and discomfort accompanying it. Both men and women agree, for instance, that it's most important for an "ideal man" to be a good husband and father, have a sense of humor and be intelligent. That ideal traveled well even with single people, particularly men, who also rated qualities associated with being a family man near the top of the list.

The rise of this new ideal may signal the demise of the old: Both married and single men and women feel that conventionally "male" attributes like physical strength, aggressiveness, toughness and earning power are no longer as important as they once were.

Our poll did, however, highlight

their best friend understands them better than their husband or boyfriend.)

The isolation our poll found may be rooted in men's earliest, most primary male relationship. Most sons—daughters, too—feel closer to their mothers than to their fathers. On average, both men and women rate their relationship with their father a 7.5, on a 10-point scale, while mom rates almost a full point higher. The American man may cherish his family, but his children are more attached to his mate.

Perhaps that's one reason why more than half the fathers we polled (51%) would quit their jobs and stay home with their children, if money were not a problem. Clearly, men feel torn between being able to provide their families with more of themselves and being, simply, good providers. The pressures of a two-career family are especially disturbing—70% of married men would prefer that their wives not work, despite the many proven benefits to health and self-esteem that a job provides.

The American male, in short, is in flux. He's trying to shake the old rigid macho values, but he'd still like to be the sole breadwinner and keep his wife in the kitchen. Some college-educated trendsetters think men should feel more emotion, but the rest of the population—particularly men, and to a lesser degree, women—is terrified by the idea. Men still can't share their feelings with other men, preferring to rehash ball games or dissect the nuances of office politics with their best friends rather than reach for what really matters. The "lonely guy" is real.

WHAT MEN—AND WOMEN—TOLD US

When It Comes to Defining the Ideal Man, Men and Women Largely Agree; the Characteristics They Choose, and the Percentage Choosing Each, Are Shown in "Perfection Incarnate." But When They're Talking With Friends of the Same Sex, Men and Women Differ Tremendously, as "Shop Talk and Jock Talk" Makes Clear.

PERFECTION INCARNATE

Qualities of an "Ideal Man"

Quality	%
Being a good husband and father	68%
Intelligence	48%
Sense of humor	46%
Emotional sensitivity	31%
Ambition	30%
Rationality, not being overly emotional	17%
Earning power	17%
Being a good lover	11%
Aggressiveness	9%
Physical strength	7%
Physical attractiveness	5%
Toughness	4%
Sports ability	4%

(Total is more than 100% because respondents could give more than one answer.)

SHOP TALK AND JOCK TALK

Men talk with best friends about:

Topic	%
Work issues	43%
Sports	42%
Goals for the future	28%
Their children	26%
Personal problems and self-doubts	23%
Politics	21%
Books, movies, cultural activities	14%
Romantic relationships	13%
Religion	2%

(Total is more than 100% because respondents could give more than one answer.)

Women talk with best friends about:

Topic	%
Their children	47%
Personal problems and self-doubts	41%
Work issues	27%
Books, movies, cultural activities	23%
Goals for the future	22%
Romantic relationships	15%
Politics	10%
Sports	8%
Religion	2%

(Total is more than 100% because respondents could give more than one answer.)

some differences of opinion among various segments of the population. 45% of college graduates, for instance, think it's good for a man to be emotionally sensitive, compared with only 23% of non-college-graduates. The finding suggests that even though men know they have to abandon their old distant, authoritarian style, they're not quite ready to adopt a demeanor that could label them as wimps.

Men are lonely, too, our poll found. We asked men what they talk about when they get together with their closest friends (see "Shop Talk and Jock Talk"). **In contrast to women, who talk mostly about their children and personal problems, men talk about work and sports. Men *say* their families are the most important things in their lives, yet seem unable to talk about them with their best friends. In that sense, men truly may be isolated from sharing what they really care about.**

Men may also be more isolated from their families—or more specifically, their wives—than they would like. Our poll found, for instance, that 29% of men think their best male friend understands them better than their wife or girlfriend. (High as that figure may seem, it falls short of its counterpart among women: 39% of women say

But some men are breaking down the old models and reconstructing the male role. Men are seeking each other's counsel, healing wounded relationships with their fathers, and exploring, with the help of poetry, myths and fairy tales, what it means to be masculine. Finally, men's groups are meeting with women's groups—a summit of sorts of the sexes—in an effort to raise everyone's consciousness and understanding.

It's an effort to go beyond feminism, beyond "masculinism," toward humanism—a noble direction, whatever your gender.

SUCCESS AT FAILURE: UNDERSTANDING SELF-DEFEATING BEHAVIOR

People with self-defeating behavior "are afraid of failure as well as success. . . . Their strategy allows them to do well, but not so well that they hurt or offend others."

Rebecca Curtis

Dr. Curtis is professor of psychology, Adelphi University, Garden City, N.Y. This article is adapted from her book, Self-Defeating Behaviors, *published by Plenum Publishing.*

WHY would someone get so intoxicated the night before an important job interview that he would sleep through his alarm? Why would an athlete fail to practice before crucial meets and tournaments, but practice regularly before unimportant events? Why would a woman act in a manner to make another dislike her for no apparent benefit? These are some of the questions psychologists recently have attempted to answer in studies about self-defeating behaviors.

This conduct is defined as a behavior which leads to a lower reward/cost ratio than is attainable by another behavior, and includes negligence of health maintenance, underachievement, self-handicapping, learned helplessness, self-defeating excuse-making, anxiety about success, avoidance of accurate information, and procrastination.

Researchers have found that men who were told they were successful with tasks regardless of their actual performance later chose to take a drug described as "debilitating" as opposed to a "facilitating" drug before performing similar tasks again. The psychologists conducting this experiment theorized that the men chose the debilitating drug to protect their favorable, but fragile, self-image. If they performed poorly on the subsequent task, they could attribute poor performance to the drug, not their lower ability.

Self-handicapping is one type of sabotage behavior which occurs after people have experienced successes seemingly independent and unrelated to a person's actual behavior. Other studies found that both animals and humans could become helpless when unpleasant events or, in some cases, pleasant ones happened, regardless of what the animal or person did. This type of "learned helplessness" in humans is related to depression and pessimism regarding the future.

The people most at risk for helplessness

Reprinted from *USA Today Magazine* (Society for the Advancement of Education), March 1990, pp. 66–67.

as a self-defeating behavior following uncontrollable events are those who explain them using internal, stable, and global causes. For example, they might attribute failure to their lack of ability ("a stable and internal" characteristic), and this was due to a "global" quality, such as their lack of intelligence or unlikability. College students with this explanatory style usually have poor grades. Those who obtain higher grades attribute their failures to a lack of effort (an "unstable" quality) or to the difficulty of the material (an "external" explanation). Fortunately, considerable research, including my own, indicates that training people to attribute their failures to a lack of effort leads them to try harder, perform better, be more optimistic about the future, and reward themselves more.

Studies also have been conducted upon a phenomenon called "choosing to suffer." In my laboratory research, experimental volunteers who were expecting that they *probably* would be asked to taste unpleasant foods (such as fried grasshoppers, caterpillars, and a worm) gave themselves more self-administered electrical shocks than participants who *definitely* were expecting to taste unpleasant or pleasant foods. People given an opportunity to do something unpleasant often have been shown to expect better outcomes in the future than those not given such an "opportunity." A general conclusion from the many studies of masochistic-like behavior in animals and humans "choosing" to suffer is that both animals and people chose to suffer to escape or avoid situations they expected to be even more anxiety-provoking. Clinical impressions of people in therapy bear out similar findings. People learn behaviors that are ultimately harmful to themselves to avoid worse situations.

Another type of self-defeating behavior is the fear of success. Originally discussed by Sigmund Freud, a motive to avoid success once was postulated to account for the poor performance of women in the presence of men. One study found that women who scored high on a measure of fear of success performed better alone, whereas women who scored low in the fear of success performed better in a mixed-sex situation. Although various controversies ensued over these conclusions, subsequent investigations were conducted.

One researcher found that students with a high fear of success are likely to procrastinate and less likely to choose any special assignments required to obtain an A in a course. They have greater indecisiveness and conflict, find it more difficult to choose a major, are more dissatisfied with their majors and change them more often, and are more likely to take leaves of absence from school.

People who fear success are more likely to miss meetings in weight-reduction workshops and alcohol-detoxification programs. They have performance decreases after success and performance increases after failure, whereas the reverse is true for those who do not fear success. After good accomplishments, success-fearers can perform well again if they are given an opportunity to read self-derogating, but not self-affirming, statements. People who do not fear success perform better after reading self-affirming statements.

Are these people simply neurotic or does the fear of failure explain their behavior as well as the idea of fearing success? Many studies have found that success-fearers are not generally neurotic, but do have unstable self-esteem and conflicts with their motivation to achieve. They are afraid of failure as well as success. Less likely to sabotage success in cooperative, as opposed to competitive, situations, their strategy allows them to do well, but not so well that they hurt or offend others. On three athletic teams, all of the best "clutch players" named by the coaches had a high fear of success. In the "clutch," their fear of success or out-starring their teammates is neutralized by the cooperative structure of the team, and their motive to avoid failure is at its strongest.

Origins

Where does the fear of success come from? Some research indicates that parents of children who have a high fear of success were found to criticize their offspring more in experimental tasks, give more hints and instructions, make comments about the child to the experimenter, and be more active and intrusive. On a word construction test, only parents of success-fearing children moved their child's letters, gave the youngster words, and, in several instances, pushed the child away and made the words themselves. In contrast, parents of children with a low fear of success sat quietly and calmly. Parents of success-fearers preempt their child's independence, apparently made anxious by it.

In my book, *Self-Defeating Behaviors*, I propose a theory of the situations leading to them. This research confirms the emerging models of behavior developed by both therapists and cognitive experimental psychologists. When people perceive a discrepancy between the outcomes they obtain and those they desire, they act to reduce this discrepancy by engaging in expectancy-confirming behaviors. First, they may attempt to alter the outcomes they have obtained—if they differ from those they had expected. If they fail to obtain their desired outcomes, they either may retain their expectations and make excuses for the failure or consider changing their expectations.

Considerable research has shown that people frequently engage in behaviors which confirm their expectations. Erroneous presumptions, once established, can be quite resistant to change in spite of contradictory evidence, as found in numerous experiments. In order for people to change their views about themselves and others, they must risk abandoning their belief systems. This means they must test their old beliefs. If their hypotheses as to what will happen are not confirmed, they will develop new beliefs about themselves, others, or the relationships between actions and the consequences of those actions. For example, people hold beliefs not only about themselves and their abilities, but also about how others see them. Although many appear to seek out accurate information about their abilities much of the time, my research has demonstrated that people avoid accurate information about their abilities when these are very important and when they expect that the evaluation may be unfavorable.

The first step people need to take to change their maladaptive beliefs is hearing the evaluations of family members, friends, co-workers, and others who are in a position to provide accurate information about their abilities. The next is to engage in the new behaviors necessary to obtain the desired outcomes, regardless of the amount of anxiety generated. People must fail some of the time to know the limits of their abilities.

When failures occur, thoughts such as "I am incompetent at everything" or "I am unlovable" must be avoided. Fortunately, people can learn to behave differently. Human behavior differs from other species' acts in that it is determined more by learning and less by genetic endowment. We are very adaptable and can change. Because overcoming self-defeating behaviors involves accepting negative as well as positive information, the process can be painful. Although there are many useful techniques which can increase self-enhancement, a thorough investigation of a person's self and social theories sometimes requires addressing the fundamental belief systems and meanings people make of their existence. A safe, supportive atmosphere with a friend or a professional is helpful in providing the setting necessary for such a thorough examination to take place.

Getting Better —Together

Bruce A. Baldwin

Dr. Bruce A. Baldwin is a practicing psychologist and author who heads Direction Dynamics in Wilmington, North Carolina. This article has been adapted from Dr. Baldwin's book for busy achievers, It's All In Your Head: Lifestyle Management Strategies For Busy People.

Sooner or later in life, you meet that special person, you fall in love, and you marry. As the years pass, with hard work and great energy, you become established in your careers, purchase a home, and find yourself doing just fine economically. Ten years or so later, you live in a nice neighborhood, and you're part of a community. It's an American success story.

On the inside of that home, however, there's trouble brewing. There is a marriage that is stagnating and in trouble. Two people deeply in love in years past are living together but growing steadily apart. Ironically, they spend more time at home than ever before because there's so much to get done. However, the quality of that time decreases. They don't talk much anymore except about problems at work, issues with the kids, who's spending money on what, and schedules for today and tomorrow. They are making a good living, but they're not very fulfilled nor even happy.

That's exactly the scenario in millions of homes these days. A marital relationship that was to last forever has become shallow, strained, and unsatisfying for both partners. Deep down, neither spouse really wants the relationship to end, but the thought has sure crossed each one's mind. The marriage has reached an emotional crisis point.

How a couple handles this kind of very common but serious problem will determine whether the relationship will be renewed or continue to deteriorate. On the negative side, the options range from affairs, burying yourself in more work, excessive drinking or drug use, physical separation and divorce, or just continuing the status quo in a relationship that has little substance. Most of the time, however, these choices just create more interpersonal problems and unhappiness.

A far better option is for a couple in this situation to reverse this negative trend in their lives and recover the closeness and intimacy they once had. Couples who are motivated to do that must first understand four points:

Most marital problems slowly grow over long periods of time. By almost imperceptible increments, a marital relationship can easily erode over years. Typically, it takes from five to 15 years for the distance to become acutely felt and the lack of personal fulfillment to create a painful void within. The root cause is those thousands of little decisions, made daily, that slowly but surely diminish the importance of the marital relationship.

Marital problems are often closely correlated with an increase in responsibility. Early in a marriage, there is one precious commodity that helps ensure closeness and good times together, yet slowly but surely disappears over the years: time for one another. With the years come the responsibilities of children, busy careers, home maintenance demands, and community involvements.

Once-healthy priorities become inverted. Most marriages begin with the highest priority placed on being together and enjoying one another. As the years pass, two destructive priorities slowly take precedence: to make more money so there can be more and more "things," and to spend all available time getting chores done. The net result is that a marital relationship slips to the absolute bottom of the priority list.

A serious marital crisis develops. If couples who have been happily married for many years are questioned, the majority will mention a time when the marriage was in serious jeopardy. Perhaps there was even a separation or serious talk of it. Most of the time, these marital crises reflected priority problems that had developed. In these good marriages, a couple worked together to resolve the issues separating them and went on to live compatibly and happily for many years. Where problems could not be resolved, the marriage usually did not survive.

When life becomes difficult and a marriage begins stagnating, there is a very natural human tendency to blame something or someone external for the problem. Finding a scapegoat is easy. Closely examined, however, the reality is different. Most of the time, problems in a marriage reduce themselves to specific choices made each day by each partner. Seen from this perspective, each person must assume personal responsibility for the problems that are occurring.

The bottom line is simple: You can reverse the changes that have occurred in a marriage by changing the choices you make each day. And the very first choice you both must make is equally simple. Your marital relationship must be moved from the absolute bottom of the priority list to the absolute top. You must change the habit of giving one another only

From *USAir Magazine,* August 1990, pp. 30, 32, 34, 35–36. Adapted from Baldwin, B.A., *It's All in Your Head: Lifestyle Management Strategies for Busy People,* Direction Dynamics, 1985. Reprinted by permission.

what's left over, because usually there is nothing left over. Your marriage must take precedence over everything else: getting things done, making more money, even over the children. If you are each willing to make that single choice, you have already moved a long way toward resolving a serious problem that has been slowly developing for years.

Removing Myths About Marriage

Deep within most couples whose relationship drifts into trouble is a desire to make it good once again. In recent years, the throwaway mentality has been eroding as far as marriage is concerned. Thankfully, the "me" generation has evolved into the "we" generation of the '90s, holding a deeper and stronger commitment to making relationships work. Along with this underlying commitment are more realistic expectations of what it takes to keep a marriage viable and strong.

There are numerous erroneous beliefs, however, that either perpetuate or make worse many marriage problems. Eliminating these myths about marriage is actually the process of renewing it. It's a good idea for both partners to discuss each one of them and then to each take the necessary steps to reorient priorities in healthier directions.

Myth: The more you love someone, the better you treat him or her. Early in a relationship, couples are extremely responsive to one another in a positive way. As the years roll by and life becomes pressured, an irony develops. A work role demands that the individual be a kind, caring, courteous, and responsive individual. At home, however, positive attention once given to a spouse is replaced by irritability, avoidance, negative communication, and outright rejection.

Your first step is to recognize this sad state of affairs and then begin to modify how you respond to one another. Don't say those three or four negative things you'd love to say to your partner each day. And while you're chatting, completely eliminate as topics the children, what has to be done, money, schedules, and work. Good eye contact and taking the time to really listen to one another is mandatory. And remember that a compliment a day keeps marital trouble away.

Myth: Couples who spend a lot of time together usually have a good relationship. Early in a marriage, couples in love spend every spare moment together, really enjoying one another's company. Years later, however, overworked, chronically pressured, and burned-out couples still spend a lot of time together. It's usually at home, though, because there is either no time or they're too tired to go out. The quality of the time together is not good. Pressed a bit, these same men and women often admit to being painfully lonely while living together.

Making time for one another at home is an absolute key to a successful marriage. Begin by legitimizing this time together. To do so, you must both break two bad habits. The first one is looking around, seeing so much to be done, and deciding to do chores instead of spending time with your partner. Second, at all costs turn off the television set. Spend some time sitting and talking on the back porch or take a slow, leisurely walk together instead.

Myth: It's my spouse's role to make me happy. Rarely stated out loud, this is a common perception. In fact, couples must meet some basic needs in each other for a relationship to be good. In broader form, though, this idea reflects an avoidance of responsibility for personal contentment. The deep belief is, "It is up to someone else to make me happy, and that person is my spouse." When a spouse doesn't do just that, that partner becomes the object of blame.

Accepting responsibility for personal happiness is the first step when dealing with this myth. Taking positive action toward personal growth is the second one. It's up to you to break out of the rut. Bring back some variety to your life by taking time for things you enjoy, like beginning an interesting new hobby, starting a project you'd really enjoy, taking a short course, or seeing friends you've neglected for years.

Myth: If we have a good sexual relationship, everything else will fall into place. Early in a relationship, physically relating is extremely important. The chemistry is intense, and couples find this part of their relationship very fulfilling. With the years, sexual relating drops from a top priority to third or fourth. As a result, focusing only on renewal of a sexual relationship when there are marital problems is putting the cart before the horse.

To re-establish a healthy marital relationship, you must bring back into your marriage regular, spontaneous, sincere, nonsexual affection that has disappeared as responsibilities have grown. The fact is that sitting close, holding hands, snuggling on the couch, even horsing around in the kitchen are essential prerequisites for a healthy relationship. Also, bringing back nonsexual affection is one of the very best ways possible to rejuvenate a stagnating sexual relationship.

Complete absence of conflict is definitely not a sign of a good relationship.

Myth: Our relationship would be wonderful if there was never any conflict between us. This is a belief often held in marriages where there is too much emotionally destructive conflict. Complete absence of conflict is definitely not a sign of a good relationship. Indeed, the difference between a good and a bad relationship isn't the absence of conflict, but how that conflict is handled. Two mature individuals living together have differences and as they change with age, new differences are created. Learning to resolve those differences in mutually compatible ways is a major key to a good marriage.

The trick is to learn to fight fairly.

A few simple rules help immensely. First, strive for two winners, not a winner and a loser. Second, no name-calling or low blows to your partner's vulnerabilities. Third, stay with one issue to be resolved now, instead of referring to the past or other problems in the present. Fourth, agree to disengage and resume discussion later if relating becomes too heated or emotional. Finally, be willing to personally change to make things better for both of you.

Myth: We're so different from one another, it's no wonder we're having trouble. Early in a relationship, couples are prone to say that opposites attract. Later on, these same couples cite differences as a major source of their problems. The fact is that most couples have differences: in values, interests, recreational outlets, sociability, and backgrounds, just to name a few.

In good relationships, three qualities are almost always present. First, differences are accepted and accommodated between partners. There is no pressure for one to be a mirror image of the other. Second, the strengths of one are used to complement a weaker area of the other. For example, one who is good handling finances assumes responsibility in that area; the other may be better at dealing with household repairs and thus does that. Finally, the couple has at least one activity that they regularly enjoy experiencing together.

Myth: If we were only more economically successful, then we'd be happy together. Most men and women, now economically successful, define the "good old days" as their youth, when they had little money but plenty of time to enjoy life and one another. As demands mount, responsibilities increase, and life becomes extremely complicated, although there is a much higher income. It then becomes seductive to strive toward making even more money to bring happiness, because the financial resources available now just aren't doing it.

To get out of this rut, first stop defining yourself by how much you make and what you own, because you already have the basics. Do not let your ego drive you further into debt. Instead, for deeper personal fulfillment begin to define yourself in terms of your key relationship: husband or wife, friend, companion, lover. Put energy into experiencing life together. A bit of romance just like when you were young wouldn't hurt a bit, either.

Myth: If only our responsibilities were fewer, we'd have more time for one another. The parenting years are extremely busy, but at any age you can tie up your time getting things done instead of nurturing your marriage. It's easy to convince yourself that there's so much to do that you have no choice in the matter, and you put your marriage on the back burner. The result is that you take your marriage for granted, slipping into the belief that your partner will always be there, even though the relationship is being emotionally neglected. You may find yourself sadly mistaken.

The choice to mow the lawn, wash the dishes, or stay overtime at work are actually personal choices to postpone time together in lieu of chores. Start now to put your partner first. At all costs, grit your teeth and overcome the tendency to look around the house, see things that need to be done, and feel guilty about relaxing together. These healthy choices will help you reduce stress and increase your marital satisfaction.

Myth: If only my husband/wife would change, then we could really live the good life. An old adage states that when men and women talk about change in a marriage, they are usually talking about changing their partner. This projection of responsibility for renewing a marriage has within it a severe flaw: "I want you to be just what I think you should be." As this way of thinking about a partner grows, acceptance of your partner diminishes, and resentment builds.

The first rule of thumb is to change yourself, not your partner. Look deep within yourself for your contributions to a stagnating marriage. Then take the initiative to make key changes in your priorities and choices simply because they are the right and healthy things to do. You will become a positive model for your partner, and it will be easy to reciprocate. You will feel more in control, and more than likely your marriage relationship will become more personally fulfilling.

Myth: We have to work hard now, but there will be plenty of time for us later. Children are promised greener pastures if only they will study hard and sacrifice now. Young couples striving to become established do the same thing, so they can enjoy life later. To put aside personal pleasure to work for long-term goals is an essential skill for economic comfort. However, sacrificing a marriage relationship definitely isn't part of success.

For any couple who has reached the "thirtysomething" age, the future must be now, not later. Work hard, but make it a point to enjoy the present instead of habitually waiting for the future. To do so, you will have to face guilt for slowing down a bit, but you'll last longer. You will have to overcome your ego's need to build a personal empire, but what you gain will be personal satisfaction, emotional closeness, fun times together, and all the deeper fulfillments that elude so many.

The first rule of thumb is to change yourself, not your partner.

Other Marital Aids

It's togetherness that makes a good marriage personally fulfilling and a strength for both partners. If you are ready to renew your marriage, use as guidelines the four C's of marital communication: commitment, caring, compliments, and creativity. Keep in mind that communication is reflected both in what you say and in your actions.

Commitment is a basic, and it's the antithesis of the throwaway mentality of past decades. At its root, commitment is a solid underlying belief that marital problems can and will be worked out together. If at present you can't quite believe this, then assume it. With this underlying foundation, you never threaten to leave when the going gets rough. You think only in terms of a partnership.

Most men and women verbally profess to care about their spouses, but you'd never know it from their actions. Begin by communicating the most basic caring of all: "I love you." Follow it up with little expressions of these feelings. Take the initiative to help out. Make a call to say "hi" in the middle of the day. Plan a surprise lunch out. Take a walk hand in hand. The possibilities are endless.

It's easy to become so preoccupied with all you have to do that you don't compliment one another anymore. The fact is that everyone needs to hear nice things regularly, and there are many opportunities each day to do just that. Comments on a bright smile, how good clothes look, and the wonderful dinner prepared are just a few. It bolsters self-esteem and invites the same in return.

"Variety is the spice of life," and creativity is the essence of variety. That means keep your marriage interesting. Routines become monotonous, so break them at all costs for yourself and for your marriage. It takes a little planning, but only when you're out of the "routine rut" will you realize how deep it was. It's as simple as trying a new recipe or planning an afternoon alone together.

There is no doubt about it: To make a marriage work takes understanding, maturity, and persistence. But the satisfaction gained is well worth the problems that are part of every marriage relationship. The real payoffs in a good marriage take many years to accrue. Commitment, companionship, and quality communication will build deeper and more fulfilling bonds between you. As Mark Twain put it, "Love seems the swiftest, but it is the slowest of all growths. No man or woman really knows what perfect love is until they have been married a quarter of a century."

Fixing the 'Between'

Therapists are pushed to examine the roles of men and women in the family

DAVID GELMAN

When it first appeared three decades ago, the field of family therapy was considered revolutionary for its view of the family as a "system" in which members collide with one another in predictable ways. Today family therapy is undergoing a small revolution of its own. Spurred by feminists in its midst, the profession is being forced to re-examine its persistent sexual stereotyping of family members—a tendency all the more curious in a brand of therapy that places heavy emphasis on gender roles. One of the more familiar, and problematic, family constellations, for instance, is the so-called pursuer-distancer couple, consisting of an "overinvolved" mother and an "unavailable" father who, between them, stir up a witch's brew of family tensions. Such concepts have come under attack by feminists who believe that a mother's expressive ways are somehow being turned into a liability by therapists.

The family approach first came to prominence in the 1970s, a time of huge upheavals in the nuclear family. What made it seem such a radical departure from conventional therapy was that the system itself was the patient. Classically, parents come in with a troubled child as the "identified patient." But the child's symptoms usually reflect some hidden problem between the parents that reverberates through all the family relationships. So instead of focusing on any one individual, therapists concentrate on what happens between individuals. It is the "between" they try to change.

Like dominoes: But by the late '70s, female therapists had begun to realize something was missing from this revolutionary new theory. For one thing, therapists seldom seemed to factor in the profoundly different expectations placed on men and women in the family. Never mind, for example, that the mother had a job or a career to attend to these days. It was she who was still given almost total responsibility for the family's emotional life—only to be told she was overinvolved. It was as if the family system operated outside any context of place and time. "Until about a dozen years ago," says Betty Carter, director of the Family Institute of Westchester, in Mt. Vernon, N.Y., "we thought the system was all, uncomplicated by gender. Family members would simply fall into place like dominoes."

Today Carter is one of the women at the forefront of the new consciousness in family therapy. In 1978, she and three colleagues, Marianne Walters, Peggy Papp and Olga Silverstein, launched the Women's Project in Family Therapy, a series of lectures and workshops aimed at sensitizing the profession to the feminist critique. Among the immediate targets was the penchant for "mother-blaming." Therapists seemed always to be hitting on the mother and coddling the father. They spoke frequently of the need to "pull the mother out" so that distant, unexpressive Dad could become more involved.

In part, the women realized, the onus was on the mother because she was usually the one who sought help to begin with, and was therefore most "available" for change. But also, it seemed a result of blatant sexual stereotyping by people who should know better. "There is a common belief that couples share—often with the collusion of the therapist—that '[the mother] can and [the father] can't'," observes Walters, who heads the Family Therapy Practice Center in Washington, D.C. "In therapy, the person who needed to change was the mother," Walters notes.

Although the Women's Project had not intended to launch a movement, the workshops drew large crowds and ultimately have had a wide impact on the profession. The group's efforts also angered some of the older guard. "If we had realized the amount of anger and personal criticism to which we would be subjected by colleagues, we might have had second thoughts about setting forth on this new course," wrote Walters in "The Invisible Web," a 1988 book authored by the four Women's Project organizers. Resistance continues to this day among theorists who believe the gender issue creates what one of them calls "a needless distraction" from the issues of therapy. "It's very hard to discuss and everybody takes it personally," says a therapist who thinks it best to withhold her name. "Not with your patients—its among your colleagues that it can't be discussed."

The hostility merely strengthens the resolve of the feminists, who insist that family therapy must begin to take account of the cultural and social context in which families operate. Classically, they argue, women have carried much of the responsibility for making the family work. Women's attempts to shift some of the burden to their husbands in large measure account for the domestic havoc that has become part of the social climate of the '80s. "What we think of as the family," says Monica McGoldrick, a colleague of Carter's, "really had to do with the role that women always played—but now are not agreeing to play."

Interviewed jointly, Carter and McGoldrick provide a kind of impromptu workshop on the subject. In the past, they say, it was the wife-homemaker who held the strands of the family together, like Penelope weaving while Ulysses roamed. *McGoldrick:* "Women did whatever was done in terms of remembering, reinforcing and making connections happen." *Carter:* "It would be the woman who did all the shopping for gifts, who would remind her husband that it was his mother's birthday and 'Here's the present I bought for her,' and she would plan on having her over for dinner Sunday night." *McGoldrick:* "And now she says, 'Hey, you know, that's *your* mother, if you want to invite her over for dinner, go ahead, but don't invite her on Friday because I'm working all day and I work pretty hard'." *Carter:* " So you see, it's an enormous disruption in the old connectedness—and now we have the fragments."

Among these fragments are stepfamilies. Unfortunately, stepfamily members almost instantly get into trouble by falling back on the gender structure that got them in trouble in their original families. Says Carter, "The man assumes she will take care of his children. Or she assumes he has to support her and her children, and he ends up supporting two households. It pushes gender arrangements to their illogical conclusion."

When a couple divorces, they are perfectly capable of carrying gender stereotypes with them into single-parent households. Parents, especially the women who head most such households, generally feel insufficient for failing to provide a male role model. Single mothers typically worry their sons will turn into "mama's boys." Carter says her "gender red-alert flag goes up" whenever she hears that from women. "You run into a lot of social dogma, like, 'We all know women can't raise their sons without the strong hand of the father.' Well, of course they can. But mothers don't know that either—they have this gender-based mythology." As it happens, adds Marianne Walters, the mythology is supported by therapists themselves, most of whom feel two-parent families are best. But what is best, Walters argues, "is whatever family is working well."

'One down': As the feminist perspective asserts itself in family therapy, a reverse danger has begun to emerge: "father-blaming." In the process of emphasizing the strains on women, some therapists overlook the problems of men who are made to feel "one down," as husbands and fathers, says August Napier, director of the Family Workshop in Atlanta, Ga. Napier, author of the influential 1978 book "The Family Crucible," more recently wrote "The Fragile Bond," which draws candidly on his experiences with his wife (and cotherapist), Margaret. In therapy sessions, he and Margaret don't hesitate to talk about some of their own marital disagreements. They have come to believe gender issues are so crucial that the most responsible way to handle them is with a male-female therapy team.

Napier himself believes the focus of therapy now ought to be on showing men how to take a more equal family role, something extremely hard for them to do because their own fathers were so often emotionally unavailable to them. He encourages male patients to join support groups where they can help each other learn to be better parents. Many men genuinely want to change their role but don't have enough emotional underpinning, he says. "Women try to teach us and we get defensive."

Men and women are different, and perhaps at best their resulting difficulties can be ameliorated only a little. But something has certainly happened in the social order to make the effort more urgent. In nearly every couple he and his wife had seen, notes Napier, "the women were angry and resentful, the men were deeply—if often silently—threatened. 'Why,' I asked myself, 'are we men having so much difficulty dealing with the changes in our wives?' " It is just as well that a discipline called family therapy has begun to address such problems without the very biases that helped create them originally.

No Life to Live

Codependents take over other people and forsake themselves

Melinda Blau

Melinda Blau *is a New York–based writer who reports frequently on mental health and family issues.*

For the four years Laura* was involved with Mike, a verbally abusive heavy drinker, he kept telling her she ought to leave him. Rather than ending the relationship or even worrying about herself, Laura reassured *him* instead.

"I never got on him for his drinking," she says. "I used to excuse him a lot, apologize for his behavior. Some days I'd shave him. I'd let him hide out in my house. I wouldn't even tell his brother and his father." Her love and devotion didn't work. One night, after telling Laura he loved her, Mike hung up the phone and shot himself.

*Names have been have been changed to protect people interviewed about personal experiences.

Ellen spent 15 years preoccupied with her son's drug addiction, which began when the boy was in high school. Gradually, her life narrowed down to activities designed to keep her son from using. "I'd take him to the movies, even though it wasn't a movie I wanted to see—or even what I wanted to be doing with my time. I'd take him away on vacations—well into his 20s." All those years of turmoil and endless defeats only delayed her son's getting the kind of help he really needed—and kept Ellen from living her own life.

Laura thought her love could keep Mike alive, and Ellen sincerely believed she could stop her son from using drugs. Both examples illustrate behavior many mental health professionals have come to label "codependency." Countless others like Laura and Ellen spend years obsessing over a spouse, child, friend or co-worker—always worrying, manipulating, trying to control. They take over other people's responsibilities, clean them up when they get sick, make excuses for their behavior, even lie for them. These "codependents" don't realize that as the people they're trying to protect plunge deeper into their particular addiction, they, too, are traveling downward on a parallel and equally deadly path.

Codependency—actually an old concept adapted by the substance abuse treatment field—has become a buzzword for our times, not surprising in our addiction-ridden society. "There are 40 million codependents in the U.S.," estimates Aileen Clucas, nursing clinical coordinator at the Smithers Alcoholism Treatment and Training Center in New York City. This figure is extrapolated from frequently cited statistics that each of the 10 million alcoholics in the country affects at least four people.

Chances are, that estimate is low. Today codependency is recognized in families and relationships held in thrall to alcohol or drugs, chronic medical problems, mental illness, as well as other kinds of compulsive behavior, such as eating disorders, gambling, sex addiction, workaholism and compulsive spending. In fact, treating codependency has become a burgeoning industry. Self-help books stretch along bookstore shelves and two have been on *The New York Times*' best seller list; there are conferences, workshops, national organizations, rehabs, treatment centers and self-help groups, and 12-step recovery programs modeled after Alcoholics Anonymous (see "Help Yourself: A Guide to Peer Support Groups").

And with good reason. "Codependency is just as lethal as alcoholism or drug addiction," says Clucas. "You see hypertension, ulcers, drug and alcohol abuse, depression, suicide—all as a result of chronic codependency." Codependents use many of the same defense mechanisms as addicted people to excuse their own behavior—or ignore it. They rationalize: "I stayed home from work because I had housework to do, not because I was trying to keep an eye on Bill." And they deny both the addict's or drinker's problem and their own reaction to it: "He wasn't really that drunk or out of control—after all, it *was* his birthday."

Codependents even protect their "supply," much the same way an addict protects his supply of alcohol or drugs, Clucas explains. In this case, the "drug" is the other person. For example, a codependent will forgo dinner plans with a friend in favor of being with the addict. "The progression is similar to the addict's. In the end, the codependent's world becomes smaller and smaller as finally everything revolves around the addict."

Definitions of codependency abound. San Francisco psychiatrist Timmen Cermak, a pioneer in treating the adult children of alcoholics, sums it up: "When codependents die, they see someone else's life flash before them!"

Many experts refer to codependency as a "disease," like alcoholism, but Dr. Cermak says "it fits into the category we call 'personality traits disorders.' " He cites typical characteristics: Codependents change who they are and what they feel to please others; they feel responsible for meeting other people's needs; they have low self-esteem; they're frequently driven by their own compulsions—cleaning, eating, sex, sometimes substance abuse—as well as their partners'.

Cermak points out that the degree of codependency varies: "Just about everyone has some of it," he says. "It can be universal in its minor form, but it can also intensify and take over someone's life. The more thoroughly codependent a person is, the less they feel they have any choice."

Peter Topaz, a New York City family therapist who treats alcoholics and addicts, eschews the codependency label altogether and criticizes the great "marketing" effort alcoholic treatment providers have launched to promote it.

Definitions of codependency abound, but Cermak sums it up: "When codependents die, they see someone else's life flash before them!"

Of course, it exists, Topaz says, but he prefers to put the stress on the disabled family, not necessarily the codependent alone. Within the family system, Topaz asserts, "As one person becomes more dysfunctional or altered, it has an impact on all the other family members. It's a ripple effect.

"You can't just keep the focus on the drug," Topaz adds. "Everyone's bound up, and nothing is accomplished unless you get the whole system to change." He mentions a 38-year-old woman who called recently, wanting to know how to get her husband to stop using cocaine and alcohol. "She's tried the typical things—yelled at him, denied him sex. She makes threats but can't follow through."

Typically, codependents like this woman think one way of controlling another's substance abuse is by exerting pressure, nagging or getting angry. Instead, says Topaz, she should try to get him and the whole family in for treatment. "Provoking" behavior gives an addict reason to get high. I may make him feel rebellious, guilty, depressed or hopeless.

Most codependents are also "enablers." They support their partners in a number of ways: They accept excuses just to avoid conflict, fail to follow through on threats, and bail the person out of tough spots, both emotionally and financially. As a result, the addict is encouraged to continue indulging, and is also protected from the consequences of his or her actions. Meanwhile, the codependent, tangled in this disaster, gets sicker, too.

The good news is there *is* help out there—for codependents as well as addicts. In the last decade, as thousands of alcoholics, addicts and other people with compulsive behavior disorders have begun to fight their addictions, there is a new awareness of the need to treat the addict by looking at all the members of a family—an approach known as "systems" psychology. To help loosen the unholy bond that ties addict and codependent, the recovery industry has taken codependents under its wing. Certainly, one should assume a "buyer beware" attitude, but it's reassuring to know others are dealing with the same problem.

Fatal Distraction

It wasn't always that way. Pia Mellody, a nurse and consultant to The Meadows in Wickenburg, AZ, a treatment center for addicts and codependents, is the author of *Facing Codependency* (Harper & Row, $10.95). In her book she talks about wrestling with her own codependency during the late '70s, long before it was so fashionable—or even recognized. "In those days," she says, "the counselors blamed how I was feeling on being married to someone chemically dependent—but I knew my symptoms were too sick, sometimes sicker than the alcoholic's. While working with the family members of drug addicts and alcoholics, I discovered that they had the same symptoms as me."

The common thread in alcoholic and other dysfunctional families is that both spouse and children maintain a precarious balance, keeping the focus on the addicted person, unwittingly supporting the habit and ignoring their own needs. Codependents also breathe life into the illusion that all their problems are caused by the addict—and that if they could somehow "fix" the other person, everything would be fine. But it doesn't necessarily work that way. In fact, when the alcoholic or addict goes into recovery, that's when spouses usually have to start looking at their own problems.

Unless codependents get help by going into therapy themselves and attending support groups, the vicious cycle will continue. Children who come from alcoholic homes have a

HELP YOURSELF: A GUIDE TO PEER SUPPORT GROUPS

Since the first Alcoholics Anonymous group was founded in 1935, peer-supported, 12-step recovery programs have been formed for people with virtually every type of addictive and compulsive behavior and, like AA's companion program, Al-Anon, for family and friends affected by them as well. Such groups have no professionals to guide them, although someone "chairs" each meeting. A donation, a dollar or less, is requested but not mandatory.

Below are three major support groups that deal with general codependency issues. Many groups overlap; if you feel comfortable in a particular type of meeting, it's probably right for you. More specific programs, like Nar-Anon (people affected by drug abuse), O-Anon (eating disorders) or Gam-Anon (gambling) can be found by looking up their companion groups (Narcotics Anonymous, Overeaters Anonymous and Gamblers Anonymous) in local phone directories. Or send an SASE to the National Self-Help Clearinghouse, 33 W. 42nd St., Room 620N, New York, NY 10036.

■ Al-Anon: Established in 1951 for families and friends of alcoholics, the more than 30,000 worldwide groups now attract anyone affected by someone else's drinking as well as people not in relationships with alcoholics but who want to learn why they tend to seek such people out. Alateen is for young people affected by alcoholism. Contact: Al-Anon Family Group Headquarters, P.O. Box 862, Midtown Station, New York, NY 10018-0862; 800-356-9996.

■ Codependents Anonymous (CoDA): Founded in 1986, this relatively new fellowship, for "men and women whose common problem is an inability to maintain functional relationships," already has over 1,500 meetings in more than 48 states and six other countries. Contact: Codependents Anonymous, P.O. Box 33577, Phoenix, AZ 85067-3577; 602-277-7991.

■ Adult Children of Alcoholics (ACA): Though these groups theoretically are for children who've grown up in alcoholic homes, you'll hear "I'm a child of a dysfunctional home" in these meetings as well. Not surprisingly, some of the issues raised here are related to codependency. Contact: Adult Children of Alcoholics, P.O. Box 3216, Torrance, CA 90505 (send an SASE for a printed meeting guide in your area); 213-534-1815.

---

greater chance, some estimate as much as 50%, of marrying substance abusers. Their early experience leaves them tragically prepared to serve as someone's mirror image.

"Both my parents were alcoholic. Then I found out that in every relationship I was in, the man was an alcoholic too," says Maureen, a 29-year-old alcoholism counselor who has been dealing with her own codependency for the last eight years. "At first, I only went into therapy because I needed help coping; then I realized I had to look at some of my own behavior patterns." Today Maureen is in both group and individual therapy and goes to Al-Anon, a self-help group for families and friends of alcoholics, based on the same 12-step program AA follows.

The Three C's

"There's no recipe for recovery," says Melody Beattie, author of what has become the unofficial bible for self-help seekers, *Codependent No More* (Harper/Hazeldon, $9.95). "The key is to find your own healing process—and the proof is if it's working." Depending on the person's needs and what he or she can afford, some type of therapy may be in order. Beattie is also an advocate of programs like Al-Anon and believes recovery begins with step one: "We admitted we were powerless over alcohol and that our lives had become unmanageable." Paradoxically, power starts with admitting your are powerless.

At such support-group meetings there are no professionals. People talk about how hard it is to change time-worn habits of relating to the alcoholic or addict; how they're great at taking care of others, but don't have a clue about meeting their own needs. Hearing it all for the first time can be overwhelming, which is why it's wise to try at least six meetings before deciding you're in the wrong place.

Whether it's the solace of knowing others feel the same way, the vulnerability and honesty expressed in "the rooms," as many refer to the meetings, or the belief that "a power greater than ourselves could restore us to sanity," as the second step reads, few dispute the benefits of regularly attending a 12-step program.

One slogan reminds, "It works if you work it." That means using the "tools" of the program: going to meetings, reading all the literature, nourishing one's spiritual life. "Codependents need to learn how to stand still for a minute, instead of running to *do* or *control*, so they can determine what they're feeling—to learn to act instead of react," Aileen Clucas explains. Spirituality, she says, means "being loving to yourself and connected to your higher self—your intuition—and respecting it."

Which is why taking time for yourself—many do it through prayer and meditation—is recommended for quieting the obsessive chatter in the codependent's head. It's also why slogans like, "Easy does it" and "Think" are popular at meetings. And it's why the concepts of surrender, detachment and letting go are repeated constantly, reminding codependents that they can't control someone else's behavior, they can only deal with their own anxiety and fear.

Naturally, many codependents deny they need help. "I resented it," admits Jane, recalling the first time she was advised to go to Al-Anon. "Why should I go, I thought? I'm the one who's had to put up with all of this—all my life, in fact." Jane had a schizophrenic mother and married an alcoholic.

Al-Anon and other support groups encourage people like Jane to focus on their own behavior. These programs also exhort parents and spouses to remember the Three C's: You didn't *cause* it, you can't *control* it, and you can't *cure* it. However, you can change your own behavior so it no longer supports the addict's abuses. With an addicted person, there's almost nothing you can do until you get help yourself.

Caroline's route to Al-Anon was slightly different. In AA since her early 20s, she also joined Al-Anon because she was in a relationship with an alcoholic and her life was still unmanageable. "After I got sober my behavior was just as crazy," Caroline admits. "I was terrified of new situations. I had low self-esteem. I made people feel guilty or responsible for me." A self-described "people addict," Caroline feels Al-Anon has been the key to her recovery. She learned that her substance abuse was only a symptom of much more deeply rooted pain. "Today I realize I was trying to take care of my pain by taking care of other people," she says.

Breaking the Unholy Bond

Peer support programs aren't for everyone—nor are they necessarily all the help a person needs. Treatment facilities mandate sessions for the whole family, so that substance abusers and codependents can finally begin to see how they affect one another. Ongoing couple or family therapy is often advised as well. The idea is to help people recognize and then disrupt the unhealthy patterns that have developed as a result of years of adapting to someone else's disease.

In addicted family systems, Peter Topaz explains, roles get confused. If the substance abuser is an adult, he or she has been pushed out of the adult role—the codependent has literally taken control—so the balance has to be restored. When a child is addicted, parents have to reclaim their authority as adults, setting limits and offering loving guidance, but not trying to control the child's substance abuse.

It may be hard to accept the idea, but it's not the codependent's job to directly help the alcoholic stay dry, stop the overeater from eating, or keep the gambler from the gaming table. What's more, even if the addict is in treatment, if family members don't also change *their* behavior, there's a good chance the person will relapse and start using again because the system is still supporting it.

"When my son was 15, a psychiatrist told me I should help him out even more than I already was. That's the opposite of what he needed," says a rueful Ellen, who spent years buffeted by a mental health network woefully ignorant about addiction and codependency. Today, Ellen and her husband are in family therapy with their son, the young man is in a therapy group with other addicts, and all three work with individual therapists as well. Ellen now sees how her efforts to "keep my son straight" inadvertently prevented him from facing his drug abuse. "We've learned that although we didn't create the problem, we became a part of it—and until we were disentangled, there would be no solution."

Some codependents opt for more intensive help in the form of short-term inpatient programs. For example, the Caron Foundation, a comprehensive addiction treatment center in Wernersville, PA, offers two such packages, one for adult children of alcoholic or other dysfunctional homes and another for codependents who are in current relationships with alcoholics and are first beginning to accept that they too need help. In both groups, participants are led through various experiential techniques such as "family sculpturing," in which they reenact painful scenes from childhood.

"I can't tell you what in fact works," admits Ann Smith, corporate director of family services for the Caron Foundation, and author of *Grandchildren of Alcoholics* (Health Communications, $8.95). She suspects, however, "It's the safety and opportunity to vent old, repressed feelings and hook up with the past—the group experience is very nurturing, not confrontational."

Liz, a graduate of Caron's five-day Adult Children of Alcoholics program, remarks, "It changed my life. I could finally get angry about my childhood. I'd been programmed to believe I couldn't change things." The 36-year-old associate TV director recalls a former relationship so blatantly codependent that there were no mirrors in the house: "I'd get up in the morning and say, 'How do I look?' and if the other person hesitated for a second, I'd change my clothes and my whole

CODEPENDENCY CHECKLIST

If you identify with some of the following statements, you may wish to visit one of the self-help groups listed on the preceding page.

1. I find myself "covering" for another person's alcohol or drug use, eating or work habits, gambling, sexual escapades or general behavior.
2. I spend a great deal of time talking about—and worrying about—other people's behavior/problems/future, instead of living my own life.
3. I have marked or counted bottles, searched for a hidden "stash," or in other ways monitored someone else's behavior.
4. I find myself taking on more responsibility at home or in a relationship—even when I resent it.
5. I ignore my own needs in favor of meeting someone else's.
6. I'm afraid that if I get angry, the other person will leave or not love me.
7. I worry that if I leave a relationship or stop controlling the other person, that person will fall apart.
8. I spend less time with friends and more with my partner/child in activities I wouldn't normally choose.
9. My self-esteem depends on what others say and think of me, or on my possessions or job.
10. I grew up in a family where there was little communication, where expressing feelings was not acceptable, and where there were either rigid rules or none at all.

day would be ruined. Today I don't need someone else as my mirror."

To be sure, some short-term codependency programs can be catalytic, but recovery is a process, not an event. Several caveats are in order for those seeking help. Any program that doesn't provide referrals for after-care groups or individual therapy, suggesting that the work is over when you leave, is totally irresponsible.

"There's no panacea. You can't fix these kinds of problems in five or 10 days," Topaz maintains. He also points out that graduates of these programs—and people who attend support groups as well—may just learn to *talk* about what they do, while their *behavior* remains the same. Indeed, many people in recovery dot their conversations with phrases like, "I'm bottoming out on my control issues," meaning that focusing on other people is no longer staving off the pain. "The words become another form of relief," Topaz says. "These people refuse to look inside themselves."

Dr. Cermak, who is developing psychiatric criteria for the diagnosis and treatment of codependency, has other concerns: "I'm distressed by inpatient treatment programs that don't define codependency. How do they evaluate if the person has been helped?"

Many other experts agree with Cermak's belief that not all counselors who treat alcoholics are equipped to deal with codependency. Though knowledgeable about addictions, they often lack child development training and the expertise to understand, no less handle, transference and countertransference reactions. These can occur when the client's buried feelings are projected onto the therapist or when the opposite happens because the therapist hasn't dealt with those issues in his or her own life.

Above all, recovery is a complex process. "I didn't realize I had to work for it," admits 23-year-old Jennifer, whose penchant for unavailable men is linked to a compulsive-overeater father and a workaholic mother. Jennifer had been in therapy and then spent four weeks in a codependency treatment center. "When I came home, despite a new openness, I started repeating old behavior."

It takes what it takes. A year later, continuing with individual therapy and regularly attending Al-Anon, Jennifer is learning to share her feelings. She's also beginning to recognize her own needs and act for herself. Today she knows she has choices—and she dares to imagine what many recovering codependents hope for: "I can feel a healthy relationship coming!"

When Bystanders Just Stand By

WHY DO SOME PEOPLE HELP CRIME VICTIMS WHILE OTHERS WON'T LIFT A FINGER OR EVEN A PHONE?

R. LANCE SHOTLAND

R. Lance Shotland is a professor of psychology at Pennsylvania State University. He and Melvin M. Mark coedited the book Social Science and Social Policy, *published by Sage Publications Inc.*

Twenty-one years ago, Kitty Genovese was brutally murdered as her cries in the night went unanswered by 38 of her neighbors. That infamous incident riveted public attention on just how helpless and alone crime victims may be without the support of their fellow citizens.

In fact, bystanders often do play a crucial role in preventing street crimes when they serve as extended "eyes and ears" of the police. Arrests occur more frequently when bystanders are present than when they are not. More than three-fourths of all arrests result from reports by bystanders or victims, while relatively few come from police surveillance alone. In more than half of all criminal cases, bystanders are present when the police arrive. These citizens may be important information sources, potential witnesses and influences on the victim's decision to report the crime.

Bystanders can also help control crime directly. In some cases, they leap in and rescue crime victims, or even form spontaneous vigilante groups that catch and punish offenders. Yet at other times they are peculiarly passive, neither calling the police nor intervening directly. What accounts for these differences?

The death of Kitty Genovese intrigued the press, the public and social psychologists, all of whom wondered how 38 people could do so little. In 1968, psychologists John Darley and Bibb Latané started a torrent of research by discovering experimentally that a person is less likely to help someone in trouble when other bystanders are present.

As Latané and Steven Nida have noted, by 1981 some 56 experiments had tested and extended this observation. These studies examined the reactions of unwitting subjects who witnessed a staged emergency—either alone or in the presence of actors instructed to ignore the incident. In 48 of the studies, bystanders helped less when someone else was present. People who were alone helped 75 percent of the time, while those with another person helped just 53 percent of the time. After close to 20 years of research, the evidence indicates that "the bystander effect," as it has come to be called, holds for all types of emergencies, medical or criminal.

The effect occurs, the studies show, because witnesses diffuse responsibility ("Only one person needs to call the police, and certainly someone else will") and because they look at the behavior of other bystanders to determine what is happening ("If no one else is helping, does this person really need help?"). As a result, membership in a group of bystanders lowers each person's likelihood of intervening.

This phenomenon does not completely explain the behavior of bystanders, however. In the Genovese murder, for example, even if each bystander's probability of helping had dropped appreciably, with 38 witnesses we would expect several people to attempt to help. Other factors must be involved.

When the witnesses in the Genovese case were asked why they did not intervene, they said, "Frankly, we were afraid," or, "You don't realize the danger," or, "I didn't want to get involved," and even, "I was tired." In other words, in deciding whether to help, they considered the cost to themselves. When direct intervention might lead to physical harm, retaliation from the criminal or days in court testifying, consideration of such costs is understandable. However, the deterrent effects of other costs, such as intervention time, are more surprising. Some of my own work indicates that if helping is likely to take approximately 90 rather than 30 to 45 seconds, the rate is cut in half.

Ambiguity also lowers the intervention rate. In a simulated rape, many more bystanders intervene if they glimpse a struggle than if they only hear the incident. In a simulated accidental electrocution, researchers Russell Clark and Larry Word found that more people intervene if they see a victim being "electrocuted" than if they see and hear only the flashes and sounds of a presumed victim's electrocution.

At times, people misinterpret rare events such as crimes even if they see them. A young woman recently told me about an incident in which she had intervened. She and her friends had met three young men in a bar. After some friendly conversation, the young men left, and the women left shortly afterwards. From a distance, the woman saw her recent acquaintances in the parking lot and thought they were simply horsing around. It wasn't until she reached her car, which was closer to the scene, that she realized the young men were being assaulted in a robbery attempt.

Even if they interpret the situation correctly, bystanders may still be unsure about what they are seeing. People who see a crime, an accident or other unlikely event may wonder, "Did it really happen?" and freeze while they try to figure it out. Latané and Darley were the first to observe that if people are going to intervene, most do it in the first few seconds after they notice the emergency.

Certain types of crime, such as a man's attack on a woman, have unique features that may particularly invite misinterpretation and inhibit intervention. One Genovese witness said, "We thought it was a lovers' quarrel." Bystanders frequently reach similar conclusions when a man attacks a woman. Nine years after the Genovese incident, this story was carried by the Associated Press:

"A 20-year-old woman who works for the Trenton [New Jersey] Police Department was raped yesterday in full view of about 25 employees of a nearby roofing company who watched intently but did not answer her screams for help. . . . [One witness explained], 'Two people did that up there about a year ago but it was mutual. We thought, well, if we went up there, it might turn out to be her boyfriend or something like that.' "

IN 48 OF 56 STUDIES, BYSTANDERS HELPED CRIME OR ACCIDENT VICTIMS LESS WHEN SOMEONE ELSE WAS PRESENT THAN WHEN THEY WERE ALONE.

Some of my own research conducted with Gretchen Straw, a former graduate student, shows that bystanders behave very differently if they assume a quarreling man and woman are related rather than strangers. For example, bystanders who witnessed a violent staged fight between a man and a woman and heard the woman shout, "Get away from me, I don't know you!" gave help 65 percent of the time. But those who saw the fight and heard the woman scream, "Get away from me, I don't know why I ever married you!" only helped 19 percent of the time.

People interpret fights between married people and between strangers quite differently. In our study, the nonresponsive bystanders who heard the "married" woman scream said they were reluctant to help because they weren't sure their help was wanted. They also viewed the "married" woman as much less severely injured than was the woman attacked by the "stranger," despite the fact that the two fights were staged identically. Hence, a woman seen as being attacked by a stranger is perceived as needing help more than is one fighting with a spouse. Furthermore, people expect the husband to stay and fight if they intervene, while they expect a stranger to flee. This makes intervention with fighting strangers seem safer and less costly. Unfortunately, if bystanders see a man and a woman fighting, they will usually assume that the combatants know each other.

What role do individual characteristics play in bystander behavior? Researchers have identified only a few personality factors that differentiate helpers from nonhelpers. Psychologist Louis Penner and his colleagues at the University of South Florida have found that people with relatively high scores for "sociopathy" on a personality test (although not clinically sociopaths) are less likely to help and are less bothered by others' distress than are people with low scores. On the other side of the coin, Shalom Schwartz and his colleagues at the Hebrew University in Jerusalem have shown that people who have a sense of moral obligation to the victim are more likely to help than those who do not.

Psychologist John Wilson of Cleveland State University and his colleagues have found that those concerned with achieving a sense of security are less likely to help than those who feel secure but need to build their sense of self-esteem.

These personality characteristics, combined with all the situational factors described earlier, go a long way in explaining the behavior of bystanders. But there are other factors as well. Consider those rare individuals who intervene directly when a crime is in progress:

Psychologists Ted Huston of the University of Texas at Austin and Gilbert Geis of the University of California at Irvine and their colleagues, who interviewed 32 of these people, found them to be quite different from the ordinary person. Active interveners were very self-assured and felt certain they could handle the situation by themselves. Further, they were likely to have specialized training in police work, first aid or lifesaving, and almost all were male. These people were more likely to have been victimized themselves and to have witnessed

SHOULD HELPING BE LEGISLATED?

Given the important role of citizen participation in crime control, Vermont, Rhode Island, Massachusetts and Minnesota have attempted to compel "good samaritanism" through legislation. Other states are considering passing such laws. Under such legislation, citizens who do not respond after witnessing a serious crime against a person could be fined, jailed or sued, depending on how the law is written.

Such laws, if enforced vigorously, might make inaction more "costly" in bystanders' minds than involvement. They might reduce diffusion of responsibility by making bystanders realize that they will be held personally responsible for their inaction. The laws might also tip the balance toward intervention if bystanders find the situation ambiguous, since they may feel it is safer to guard against a penalty by intervening rather than walking away.

Whether these presumed benefits actually occur is unstudied and unknown. But since they require strong enforcement to occur at all, such outcomes are unlikely. In the four states with duty-to-assist legislation, enforcement seems minimal, and to my knowledge, only one person is being or has even been prosecuted.

If such laws were vigorously enforced, the disadvantages might well outweigh the benefits. Consider how bystanders in the Kitty Genovese case might have been affected: The first attack occurred sometime after 3 a.m. The neighbors were in their apartments when they heard the sounds of the struggle and went to their windows. Not all remained passive spectators; some were ineffective helpers, turning on their lights, opening their windows and shouting. They did scare the killer away—twice. But no one went down to rescue her, an act that might have saved her life. One person called the police after considerable soul-searching about what action to take. His response was too late, however. The remainder did nothing.

Would the law have changed anyone's behavior? Perhaps, but not necessarily for the better. These bystanders had an easy escape: the claim that they were sound sleepers and heard nothing. Research shows that a sizable percentage of bystanders will use such excuses. Would they have told the police what they saw and risk a fine, jail or a legal suit for their nonintervention? Will there needlessly be more victims of rape and murder and more criminals going free because witnesses, fearing legal reprisal, will not provide information? Unfortunately, intimidation through such a law seems as likely as enlisting greater bystander participation. In those rare cases having many witnesses, even if some are intimidated, others are likely to report, so little information is lost. But in cases with only one witness, can we afford the risks of intimidation and lost information?

I doubt that a citizen can be effectively prosecuted with such a law, because it has an implicit time frame within which the authorities must be notified. As an example, take the Genovese witness who finally did call the police. How soon should he have acted to avoid prosecution? We know—and a jury trying his case would know—that he did not call in time. But could he have known?

Laws might avoid the specific time question by specifying that a bystander must report the crime within a "reasonable" amount of time, leaving the definition of reasonable up to prosecutor, judge or jury. When did the Genovese helper first become aware of the attack? Could it ever be determined reliably without his cooperation?

A bystander would have to act very quickly to aid in apprehending a criminal. Research conducted in Kansas City suggests that if crimes are reported while in progress, an arrest related to the response occurs just 35 percent of the time. If bystanders report the crime in less than a minute after the event ends, the chance of capture drops to 18 percent. Waiting a full minute to report lowers the capture rate to 10 percent, and delaying by one to five minutes brings it down to 7 percent. Again, what is reasonable?

Or consider the case of the young woman, mentioned earlier, who thought at first that the parking-lot assault she saw was a case of highjinks by friends. Had her car been parked farther from the crime scene, she might have simply ignored it and gone home. With a duty-to-assist law in effect, she could have been fined, sued or jailed. Should there be a penalty for an innocent mistake, and how can it be distinguished from deliberate shirking of civil duty? Given the huge monetary and emotional costs of a trial, do we want to leave these decisions to a prosecutor? These are but a sampling of the questions raised by prospective duty-to-assist legislation.

I believe such laws will be unenforceable as part of the criminal code and will create a nightmare in civil court similar to the excesses that have accompanied auto-accident litigation. The basic benefit from such laws, then, is likely to be symbolic, pointing out what society expects of its citizens. But I believe that Americans already know that. Such an unenforced law does a disservice by making people believe that a serious problem has been solved when a viable solution is still desperately needed.

I believe that workable solutions are at hand, but they will take time to institute. Social psychologist Jane Piliavin and her colleagues at the University of Wisconsin suggest that school training at an early age may be part of the answer. We also need more effective strategies for reporting crimes. For example, we know that eyewitness identification has many shortcomings. In a property crime such as burglary, which is likely to have physical evidence, perhaps we should teach people to focus on and report characteristics of the getaway car instead of concentrating on the criminal. Whatever the details of the program, we do desperately need new approaches in order to return the balance of fear to favor the citizenry.

more crime in the prior 10 years than were people in general.

From other research, we know that when direct interveners were asked why they did not seek help, they answered that "there wasn't enough time" and boasted that they could "handle the situation." In addition, many either had training in physical defense or boxing or possessed—and were willing to use—a knife.

Not everyone is born or trained to be a hero. Some bystanders help indirectly, by reporting the incident to authorities and/or providing information concerning the crime. Unlike those who leap into the fray, these people do not feel competent to intervene. A typical comment: "I couldn't do anything myself so I went to get help." Such people may also see the potential cost of intervention—injury or death—as too high. A bungled rescue attempt may not help the victim and may harm the rescuer.

Even indirect intervention calls for a quick response. Otherwise the criminal act may be over and the attacker gone. But sometimes the crime happens too suddenly for anyone to comprehend and react in time. The *New York Daily News* reported an example a few years ago.

"A plumber was shot dead on a sunny Brooklyn street last weekend in full view of about 50 of his friends and neighbors. But not a single witness has come forward to tell the police exactly what happened.... Treglia was about to get into his truck when a car pulled up alongside him. A man in the car shot him four times and drove off, leaving him dead in the street."

The bystanders were willing to cooperate with the police, but there were no firsthand accounts. Almost every piece of information was based on what the bystanders had heard from others. The police found this hard to believe, but they did not interpret the behavior as a fearful coverup of mob murder. The bystanders' reactions are understandable if you look closely at how the situation probably developed:

The incident itself must have been over in seconds. Bystanders had no reason to look at the victim until they heard the shots. It would only have taken a second or two to realize that the man was shot, but by then, where was the gunman? Eyewitness testimony would have been impossible for most people. The great majority would not have seen the man fall, or been certain that shots were fired, or known their source. After talking to their neighbors, however, bystanders could have pieced the event together and told the police what they collectively knew.

Another response, a rare one, is spontaneous vigilantism, in which bystanders not only apprehend a criminal but mete out punishment themselves. For example, *The Washington Post* reported:

"... in the fashion of a Mack Sennett comedy, 29 cab drivers from the L&M Private Car Service and the No-Wait Car Service chased three men who had robbed and stolen one of No-Wait's taxis. Alerted over radio by their dispatcher, the cab drivers chased the suspects from 162nd Street and Amsterdam Avenue through two boroughs, finally cornering their prey in the Bronx. There, they collared two of the suspects, beat them and held them until the police arrived. Both were admitted to Fordham Hospital. One of the drivers, ..., a Vietnam veteran, said after the incident, 'We've got to stick together.' "

Research shows that spontaneous vigilantism happens only in response to certain types of crimes under definable conditions: First, the crimes generate strong identification with the victim (as in the case of the taxi drivers), leaving community members with a strong sense of their own vulnerability. Second, the crimes are particularly threatening to the local community's standards; bystanders would be especially motivated to prevent any recurrence. Third, bystanders are certain (even if sometimes mistaken) both about the nature of the crime and the identity of the criminal. Although people who resort to spontaneous vigilantism usually do not witness the incident directly, the details seem unambiguous because they are interpreted unambiguously to them by someone they view as credible. Fourth, spontaneous vigilantism usually occurs in neighborhoods that are socially and ethnically homogeneous, factors that enhance communication and trust as well as identification with the victim. Poor areas with high crime rates also breed vigilantes motivated by frustration with crime and by the apparent ineffectiveness of the legal system in deterring it.

When vigilantes join together to take illegal action, each person's share of the responsibility is proportionately lessened. Thus, unlike its usual effects in fostering inaction in bystander groups, the diffusion of responsibility in a vigilante group leads to action.

Bystanders can prevent crime by their very presence on the streets. Interviews with convicted felons confirm that, when planning a crime, they view every bystander as a potential intervener and take steps to avoid being seen by potential witnesses. For example, they avoid heavily traveled commercial districts and favor sparsely used residential streets where potential victims often park. Similarly, victimization on subways is highest when there are few riders, and crime rates are higher in areas that offer the greatest possibilities for concealment.

If bystanders decrease the likelihood of crime, then keeping pedestrians on the street should help to reduce it. Unfortunately, people who fear crime are likely to stay behind locked doors and avoid the streets. The greater their fears, the more they stay off the streets, thereby increasing the risks for those who do venture out.

The prevalence of crime in a community can be viewed as the result of a delicate balance between criminals' fear of bystander intervention and possible arrest and bystanders' fear of criminal victimization. To maintain social control effectively, the balance must strongly favor the citizenry. If fear of crime gains ascendance in a neighborhood, residents lose control of criminals, who then rule the streets.

Districts in which social control has been lost need not remain this way. A major item on the public agenda should be developing strategies to help community members exert social control (see box, "Should Helping Be Legislated?"), thus returning the streets to law-abiding citizens.

Psychologists Find Ways To Break Racism's Hold

Techniques work best in grade-school years, but some can be applied to adults as well.

DANIEL GOLEMAN

As racial violence continues to roll communities like Bensonhurst and more subtle prejudice permeates many American institutions, psychologists are refining their understanding of how bigotry develops and devising new ways to fight and prevent it.

Some of the most promising techniques are aimed at grade-school children, whose biases have not had time to harden. But research has also led to a range of principles that can be used by any organization, whether university or corporation or city government or armed service, to change the atmosphere that leads to racial incidents.

"There is no single cure for racism," said Dr. Robert Slavin, a psychologist at Johns Hopkins University. But he and other psychologists have used data from experiments to identify techniques and principles for reducing the hold of racism.

Interracial Learning Teams

One of the most successful methods is dividing students into interracial learning teams, which, like sports teams, knit members together in common purpose that can lead to friendship.

Such learning groups are widespread in the United States, especially in school districts with potential or actual racial problems. In Israel, they have been used to defuse tensions between Jewish students of Middle Eastern and European descent; in Canada between Canadians and immigrants, and in California between Hispanic and non-Hispanic students.

Such cooperative groups reduce prejudice by undercutting the categories that lead to stereotyped thinking, according to research published in the August issue of The Journal of Personality and Social Psychology.

"Once you categorize people into groups in any way, you tend to like people in your own group more than those in others," said Dr. Samuel Gaertner, a psychologist at the University of Delaware who conducted the research.

"It happens in many situations apart from race relations," he added. "You see it often, for instance, in a corporate merger, when people in the acquiring company continue to stereotype people from the acquired company with disdain, and those from the acquired company resent what they see as a favored status for those with the acquiring firm."

In Dr. Gaertner's experiment, volunteers were formed into arbitrary groups to work on a hypothetical problem about surviving after a crash landing. Once they had become a unified group, they began to like each other more than they liked people who were put in other groups, a simulation of the process that can lead to prejudice in other circumstances.

When the working groups were then mixed with others into a single unified group to work on another problem, their preferences shifted yet again.

"Cooperation widens your sense of who's in your group," Dr. Gaertner said. "It changes your thinking from 'us and them' to 'we.' People you once saw as part of some other group now are part of your own. That's why team learning groups can reduce bias."

The need for such efforts is as great as ever, psychologists say. Incidents like the killing of Yusuf K. Hawkins, the black teen-ager shot during an attack by whites in the Bensonhurst section of Brooklyn on Aug. 23, are only the most visible and public reminders.

Subtle Prejudice Persists

Although surveys show a decline over the last 40 years in the number of people who openly express bigotry, prejudice persists in more subtle forms. Dr. Howard Gadlin, a psychologist at the University of Massachusetts in Amherst, says the behavior of college students is a telling indication of racial attitudes. Campuses were in the forefront of the civil-rights movement in the 1960's; yet in the past two years, he notes, "racial incidents have been on the rise on campuses across the country."

In devising ways to combat racism, psychologists can turn to a strong body of research into the mental processes that lead to bigotry. Dr. Janet Schofield, a psychologist at the University of Pittsburgh, has demonstrated ways in which social barriers between racial groups can create suspicion and mistrust.

In one junior high school she observed, the students were split into hostile racial cliques. "A socially active black kid was more likely to be seen as aggressive than was a white kid doing exactly the same thing," Dr. Schofield said. "For instance, if he asked someone in the cafeteria, 'Can I have your cake?' or even if he happened to bump someone in the hall, that was interpreted as an aggressive act if it was done by a black kid, but not by a white."

That perception was part of a cycle in which the social distance between blacks and whites fostered stereotypes that could not be broken down even by positive experiences.

"Whites and blacks avoided each other," Dr. Schofield said. "Because the whites were prone to interpret even normal social activity by blacks as hostile and aggressive, they felt afraid of social contact. That made the blacks see the whites as stuck-up, which tended to actually make them hostile in response."

> Interracial learning teams knit members together and head off tension.

Pigeonholes of the Mind

The most widely used technique for promoting racial harmony, mixing racial or ethnic groups into teams where they cooperate for a common goal, is intended to break down just such barriers to understanding.

The growing consensus from psychological experiments is that racial and ethnic prejudices are an unfortunate byproduct of the way the mind categorizes all experience. Essentially, the mind seeks to simplify the chaos of the world by fitting all perceptions into categories. Thus it fits different kinds of people into pigeonholes, just as it does with restaurants or television programs.

That is where the problem begins, psychologists say. Too often people see the category and not the individual. Once these categories are formed, the beliefs and assumptions that underlie them are confirmed at every possible opportunity, even at the cost of disregarding evidence to the contrary.

David Hamilton, a psychologist at the University of California at Santa Barbara, has found in a series of experiments that people tend to forget facts that would change their assumptions about categories, while seeking and remembering information that would confirm those assumptions. When they meet someone who does not fit the stereotype, they tell themselves the individual is an exception.

The strength of stereotypes — both innocent and hostile — is attributed to the mind's natural bent to seek to confirm its beliefs. While several experiences to the contrary can challenge those beliefs, an isolated experience is unlikely to do so.

The Power of Teamwork

Such self-confirmation of stereotypes is especially likely when members of different groups have little contact with each other. Merely integrating a school, business or neighborhood may fail to change old stereotypes if the groups keep to themselves.

The learning-team approach was based on pioneering work on intergroup harmony in the 1950's by psychologists like Dr. Gordon Allport and Dr. Muzafer Sherif. It was given added scientific impetus by research on prejudice among high school students in the 1970's. That work, by Dr. Slavin and others, found that in mixed-race schools, students with the least prejudice and most friends from other races were members of sports teams or bands in which they had to work together.

The most widespread approach puts students together in four- or five-member "learning teams." The racial or ethnic makeup of each team reflects the overall makeup of the school. While members study together and are encouraged to teach each other, they are tested individually. But the team gets a score or other recognition of its work as a unit. Teams work together for about six weeks, and then students are reassigned to a new team to promote as many contacts as possible among students.

"No point is made of the fact that these are mixed racial groups," Dr. Slavin said. "The kids see nothing unusual; it seems random. The effects are very positive, especially in junior and senior high school, where the problem is greatest."

After the students work together in teams, Dr. Slavin and other researchers have found a significant increase in the number who say their friends are from other races or ethnic groups.

'Zero Tolerance' for Bias

"Even in cooperative groups, students may still carry biases into the sessions," Dr. Schofield said. "Blacks may expect that the whites will dominate, for instance. Sometimes you can combat these attitudes by giving minority kids a head start on a lesson, and having them teach it to the white kids."

Apart from engineering mixed-race working groups, psychologists say the overall social climate is also important in fighting racism. They say those in charge can establish a clear norm that racism will not be tolerated.

"Administrators and managers can show that they have zero tolerance for racial putdowns," Dr. Slavin said.

The psychologists say a sense of fairness is also important. If one group is perceived to be treated better or to have higher status than another, the situation is ripe for tensions. For that reason, psychologists stress the importance of openly acknowledging differences in the ways groups are treated.

"My research shows that when people try to act colorblind, as though there were no racial or ethnic differences, it backfires," Dr. Schofield said.

Dr. Slavin says school officials need to recognize and address such differences.

"If 90 percent of the kids suspended are black or Hispanic, or all the kids on the student council are Oriental or white, you need to bring that fact into the open before you can deal with it," he said. "The worst thing is for members of some group to feel, 'People like me have no chance here.'

"You need to pay careful attention to issues of equity. If it's a school, for instance, you need to be sure the cheerleading squad and student council are racially mixed in a way that represents the student body, even if that means a certain proportion are appointed."

Many universities are now appointing ombudsmen to deal impartially with complaints of racial, ethnic or sexual bias, among other grievances.

"It may seem obvious, but it's often overlooked," said Dr. Gadlin, who is the ombudsman at the University of Massachusetts. "You must have a system in place where those who feel racially harassed can lodge a complaint that will be acted on, not covered up.

"We need ways of dealing openly with the fears and resentments that breed racial tensions," he added. "We have no forums where you can do much more than talk around the problems in ways that are proper and polite but avoid the real issues. If you have to pretend that racial problems don't exist, the tensions will escalate until they explode."

Those in charge 'can show that they have zero tolerance for racial putdowns.'

Enhancing Human Adjustment: Learning to Cope Effectively

On each college and university campus a handful of students experiences overwhelming stress and life-shattering crises. One student learns her mother, living in a distant city, has terminal cancer and less than two months to live. Another receives the sad news that his parents are divorcing; the student descends into a deep depression that lowers his grades. A sorority blackballs a young woman whose heart was set on becoming a sister; she commits suicide. Now all of the sorority sisters sense the heavy burden of responsibility. Fortunately, almost every campus houses a counseling center for students; some centers even offer assistance to employees. At the counseling service, trained professionals such as psychologists are available to offer aid and therapy to troubled members of the campus community.

Knowing what assistance to provide is not the first step, however. The first difficulty with treatment or therapy is not *how* to intervene but *when* to intervene. There are as many definitions of mental illness and its reciprocal, mental health, as there are mental health professionals. Some practitioners define mental illness as whatever society cannot tolerate. Others define mental illness in terms of statistics: if a majority do not behave that way, then the behavior is deviant. Some professionals suggest that an inadequate self-concept is a sign of mental illness. And others cite a lack of contact with reality as an indicator of mental illness. A few psychologists claim that mental illness is a fiction: to call one individual ill suggests that the rest are healthy by contrast when, in fact, there may be few real distinctions between people.

Since mental illness is difficult to define, it is often difficult to treat. For each definition, each theorist concocts a different treatment strategy. Psychoanalysts press clients to recall their dreams, their childhoods, and their intrapsychic conflicts in order to empty and analyze the contents of the unconscious. Humanists encourage clients to explore all facets of their lives in order for the clients to become less defensive and more open to experience. Behaviorists are not concerned with the psyche at all, but rather are concerned with observable and, therefore, treatable symptoms or behaviors. No underlying causes such as intrapsychic conflict are postulated to be the roots of adjustment problems. Other therapists, namely psychiatrists who are physicians by training, may utilize these therapies and add somatotherapies such as drugs and psychosurgery as well.

This brief list of therapeutic interventions raises further questions. For instance, is one form of therapy more effective, less expensive, or longer-lasting than another? Should a particular diagnosis be treated by one form of therapy when another diagnosis is more amenable to a different treatment? Who should make the diagnosis? If two experts disagree on the diagnosis and treatment, who is correct? Researchers are studying these questions now. Some psychologists question whether therapy is effective at all. In a well-publicized but highly criticized study, researcher Hans Eysenck was able to show that spontaneous remission rates were as high as therapeutic "cure" rates. You, yourself, may be wondering whether professional help is always necessary. Can people be their own healers? Is support from friends as useful as professional treatment?

In this final unit, many of the problems of adjustment and several forms of treatment are examined in closer detail. "Psychotherapy's Value Becomes a Key Issue as More People Use It" evaluates whether or not today's psychotherapy works. The author ultimately gives therapy high marks in most instances. On the other hand, "Wounded Healers," will stimulate you to think about why counselors enter the helping profession in the first place. Are they, themselves, in need of help? Both articles will leave you healthily skeptical and should give you ample background for the rest of the unit.

The next set of articles deals with specific but common problems. Depression and its treatments are the topic of "Beating Depression." "The Trusting Heart," describes the Type A personality, which has been receiving much attention lately, and points to hostility as the major cause of subsequent coronary proneness. Of course, these selections would not be complete if an article on everyday stress was not included. "When Stress Becomes Distress" describes the commonplace problem of too much stress and imparts to the reader the various psychological services available in the community to assist in stress management. A final article in this series of articles on common problems of adjustment pertains to guilt. The author, Joan Borysenko, conveys to the reader the difference between a debilitating shame-based identity and everyday shame.

The last two articles highlight two important issues in contemporary psychology. In "Healthy Characters," world renowned authority Hans Eysenck details specific person-

Unit 6

alities that accompany specific illnesses; Eysenck reveals that physical well-being is underlaid by good mental health. Finally, in "Healthy Pleasures," Robert Ornstein and David Sobel chide the average American for forgetting that life's small pleasures, such as a good nap or fine food, bring large rewards in terms of physical and mental health.

Looking Ahead: Challenge Questions

There are a myriad of definitions for mental illness. Catalog and discuss the pros and cons of each one. Is it possible that mental illness is a fiction created by society to repress a minority? Is mental health the absence of mental illness?

Each profession (medicine, law, teaching, etc.) has its own code of ethics. What are the ethical guidelines under which psychotherapists should operate? Do you think some therapists are unethical or incompetent? How could a client prove malpractice?

Are adjustment problems such as depression, Type A behavior, and alcoholism forms of mental illness? Does everyone experience these problems? At what point should we determine that a person has adjustment problems?

Suppose an employee refuses treatment offered by her or his company. Should she or he be fired? Retained?

Do you think adjustment problems are exclusively the realm of mental health professionals? What do you think society at large should do about problems such as rape and alcoholism?

Marital problems, unfair labor practices, and substance abuse can cause distress. What other everyday situations are stressful, and how can people cope effectively with them? Is professional help the best answer?

Do you believe that the immune system is affected by the psyche? What other physiological mechanisms might the psyche affect? Do you believe that the route to better physical health is via better mental health?

Besides naps, good food, and other small pleasures mentioned in Ornstein and Sobel's article, how else can we enjoy life, remain optimistic, and cope with stress? What do you do to cope with stress?

Psychotherapy's Value Becomes a Key Issue As More People Use It

Studies Are Shedding Light On How and How Often The 'Talking Cure' Works

A Brief Regimen Gets a Test

Jerry E. Bishop

Staff Reporter of The Wall Street Journal

It was a terrible time in her life, the New York schoolteacher recalls. "I had just begun my first teaching job, and I was having difficulty in my relations with men," she says. "I had suicidal thoughts, constant depression, a feeling of deep despair." At the suggestion of a friend, she went to a psychotherapist.

That was 20 years ago. Almost every week since then, she has spent at least one and often two 45-minute sessions in therapy. The bill now tops $3,000 a year, and there is no end in sight.

Psychotherapy has "both saved and dramatically changed my life," she insists, noting that she now is in the seventh year of her third and happiest marriage.

But if psychotherapy is effective, why isn't she cured after 20 years? The teacher explains that she suffered severe parental abuse as a child. "The nature and depth of my problems is such," she says, "that counteracting them is a long-term thing, one that requires constant support. I don't think in terms of cure but in terms of managing my anxieties."

'TALKING CURE'

How well psychotherapy works has been debated almost from the day in 1893 when two Viennese physicians, Josef Breuer and his protege Sigmund Freud, first described the "talking cure" they used on five patients suffering from what was then called hysteria. For decades the question drew little attention outside the staid pages of academic journals and the inner circles of professional societies. But now it is flaring in a new quarter, with possible consequences for millions of Americans. Appalled at the surging cost of psychotherapy benefits and citing seemingly interminable cases like that of the New York schoolteacher, insurers, employers, union welfare funds and government agencies are starting to demand hard evidence that psychotherapy is effective.

Psychotherapy is beleaguered today as never before," says Hans Strupp, a professor of psychology at Vanderbilt University, in a widely reprinted lecture. "On the one hand, it has become a billion-dollar industry, a set of treatments compensable by the government and health-insurance companies. On the other hand, it is attacked by scores of critics who deny that there is such a thing as psychotherapy or who question its effectiveness."

In reaction, academics are undertaking broad research into psychotherapy's effects. They are doing controlled studies similar to evaluations of new drugs, and they are analyzing videotapes of hundreds of sessions for clues to what is going on between therapist and patient.

MOVING TARGET

An obstacle to these assessments is the great variety of theories and techniques, bearing names like dynamic-eclectic therapy, client-centered therapy, rational-emotive therapy, transactional analysis, interpersonal therapy, gestalt therapy and systematic desensitization. Another hitch is the slippery nature of the problems addressed by psychotherapy. Prof. Strupp has no doubt it can measurably reduce such things as anxiety and depression, "but," he says, "if you're interested in, say, how a woman relates to her children, how do you measure improvement or change?"

Early support for psychotherapy consisted mainly of case histories in which the therapist simply judged the patient improved. In the 1930s and 1940s some comparative studies appeared, but they were questionable; the field is still stung by an analysis in 1952 by Hans Eysenck, a London psychologist, who added up the data from numerous studies and could detect no greater improvement or deterioration in patients treated by psychotherapists than in those seen by ordinary medical doctors.

"Eysenck's study was the focus of a major storm, but it forced people to do more careful studies," says a psychologist who took issue with him at the time, Lester Luborsky of the University of Pennsylvania's Center for Psychotherapy Research.

Since then, many better-designed studies have been carried out. And recently three University of Colorado researchers did a statistical analysis of 475 of them, involving tens of thousands of patients. Their conclusion: "The results show unequivocally that psychotherapy is effective."

They found that the majority of patients undergoing psychotherapy end up better off than the majority of untreated patients. They calculated that if one took a large group of psychologically distressed persons, plucked out someone who was better off than half of the others and worse off than half, then put him through psychotherapy, the odds are he would end up better off than 80% of the group.

Controlled studies aren't easy to do in psychotherapy. Pairing of similar subjects, one to be treated and the other to get a placebo, is difficult, since every patient's mental situation is unique. The treatment given is never quite identical either; psychotherapy is an art and involves personalities, so there are bound to be variations from one practitioner to another and even among a given therapist's patients.

Researchers tried to surmount these problems in a study just being completed for the National Institute of Mental Health. They picked 18 psychotherapists and trained them for a year to reduce variations in how they treated people. Then they took 162 volunteers suffering moderate to severe depression, as measured by a standard test.

Half underwent 12 to 16 weekly sessions with the psychotherapists. Of the other half, some got a drug, imipramine, that is known to relieve depression, while the others got an inert pill and made weekly visits to a psychotherapist who asked them how they were feeling but didn't attempt any therapy.

After the experiment, more than half of those taking imipramine showed a sharp drop in their scores on the depression test, almost tantamount to remission. What is delighting psychotherapists is that more than half of those getting psychotherapy also showed such a drop in their depression-test scores. This radical improvement was seen in only 2% of those that got the placebo pill and visits. The greatest improvement came in the most severely depressed patients; for others, the benefits of therapy were less clear-cut.

Psychotherapy took about 12 weeks, and the drug about eight, to achieve roughly the same maximum benefit for the severely depressed. The crucial question the researchers are waiting to answer is whether, once treatment stops, the effects of psychotherapy last any longer than those from the cheaper drug treatment. Therapists long have contended that while a drug may relieve symptoms, only psychotherapy gets at the causes and produces lasting benefit.

TAKE YOUR PICK

But what counts as psychotherapy? The variety of techniques available today is daunting. One way to sort them out is to class them as either "dynamic" or "cognitive."

Dynamic therapies are rooted in Freud's theory that the unconscious is a kind of battleground where the rational part of the mind tries to control the instinctual urges, a struggle that is affected early in life by the child's relations with a parent or other significant person. If these ego-instinct conflicts aren't resolved in childhood, the theory goes, the person will go through life unconsciously reenacting them. A basic tenet of dynamic therapy is that as the sessions proceed, the patient unconsciously begins to view the therapist as the significant figure of his childhood and to repeat the troublesome patterns of behavior. The therapist then tries to get the patient to bring the conflicts to consciousness so they can be dealt with.

Cognitive therapies are based on various theories that have distress stemming not from ego-instinct conflicts but from false notions and perceptions learned in childhood. A child whose parents denigrated him might grow up with an unconscious feeling of worthlessness, for instance. The therapist tries to get the patient to become aware of misperceptions imbedded in the unconscious and to develop a more realistic view of himself and the world. In practice, what the various therapists do is often less different than theoretical underpinnings would suggest.

Although the original psychotherapy, psychoanalysis, may take years of several-times-a-week sessions, by the 1920s some practitioners were advocating shorter therapy, contending that the painstaking exploration of repressed childhood memories wasn't always necessary. Today most patients have one 45- or 50-minute session a week with a therapist, and the average length of therapy is only about a year.

BRIEF ENCOUNTERS

At Vanderbilt an experiment is under way to test a short-term approach devised by Prof. Strupp and a colleague, Jeffrey L. Binder. Instead of the usual "open-ended" therapy that lasts until the patient or the therapist judges it finished, they propose a limit of 25 sessions. The therapist would be more active and try to get the patient to focus on his problems sooner.

In the experiment 16 psychiatrists and psychologists are treating two patients apiece for 25 weeks with their usual approach. They then will be trained in the more active technique and use it to treat two more patients with problems similar to the first two. The researchers eventually will analyze tapes of the sessions to see how well the therapists followed the new technique and try to detect differences in how well the patients fared.

Although psychotherapy has long been racked with controversy over which theories and methods are best, study after study has shown them all to work about equally well, helping something like 75% of patients within a year. This result has led to efforts to find what the methods have in common.

HELPING ALLIANCE

It has traditionally been thought that success rests heavily on the therapist's skill in understanding the patient's unconscious conflicts and his ability to get the patient to recognize them. But today's research suggests a more basic factor: how well the therapist and patient "click."

In an experiment at the University of Pennsylvania, Prof. Luborsky and his colleagues found wide variations in the effectiveness of different therapists who treated drug addicts for anxiety and depression. After seven months, one therapist's patients showed an average 80% improvement in a psychiatric test, another's a 17% gain, and a third's patients a 1% deterioration, though all three had been carefully trained in the same procedure. Researchers found a clue to this result in questionnaires filled out after the third session. If by then the patient felt he and the therapist had reached a kind of mutual understanding that together they could work out the patient's problems, a good outcome more often followed.

This mutual understanding is usually called the helping alliance. Though the concept is an old one, this apparently is the first scientific evidence of its importance. The research indicates that the therapist's personality, or at least his ability to form a warm, supportive relationship with the patient, is critical.

This may explain why some people seem able to work through their emotional problems through long talks with a friend, says Prof. Strupp, though he adds that training enables psychotherapists to recognize the conflicts and "keep the patient on target, avoid digressions and keep the treatment from floundering."

The "helping professions," notably psychotherapy and the ministry, appear to attract more than their share of the emotionally unstable

WOUNDED HEALERS

"What asylum doctor has not had his own attack of madness by dint of continual association with madmen? . . . But before that, what obscure inclination, what dreadful fascination had made him choose that subject?"

—*Marcel Proust*

"I think that my parents were crazy, and I think that, somehow, being psychiatrists kept them in line. They used it as a protection. They're both *quite* crazy, but their job gave them a really good cover."

—*a child of psychiatrists*

THOMAS MAEDER

Thomas Maeder is a researcher, technical writer, and consultant in the biomedical field. Born in Philadelphia, Maeder graduated from Columbia University in 1973 with a B.A. in psychology and did graduate work in developmental neurobiology at the University of Pennsylvania. Maeder is the author of The Unspeakable Crimes of Dr. Petiot *(1980) and* Crime and Madness: The Origins and Evolution of the Insanity Defense *(1985). Maeder's article is adapted from his book* Children of Psychiatrists, *published by Harper & Row.*

ALFRED ADLER, ACCORDING TO HIS SON, ONCE SAID, "I think I could make out of a sadist a good butcher—perhaps even a good surgeon." He would need to imbue the sadist with social interest and modify certain patterns of behavior, and he would end up with a constructive member of society who nonetheless retained the sadist's underlying personality pattern and motivations. One might wonder what sort of pathological type Adler would have selected as raw material for a psychotherapist.

One does not need to search for pathology to explain career choice any more than one needs underlying scatological or sexual explanations to understand every innocuous bit of behavior. Altruistic people, who work hard to help others, should not be suspected *ipso facto* of harboring ulterior selfish motives. Nonetheless, the "helping professions," such as nursing, charitable work, the ministry, and psychotherapy, attract people for curious and often psychologically suspect reasons. Something is a bit odd about people who proclaim "I want to help other people"—the underlying assumption being that they are in a position to help and that others will want to be helped by them. Such people may be lured, knowingly or unknowingly, by the position of authority, by the dependence of others, by the image of benevolence, by the promise of adulation, or by a hope of vicariously helping themselves through helping others. Though some helping professionals have humbly and realistically perceived that they have something to offer and are willing to accept the responsibilities inherent in their calling, others use the role to manipulate their world in a convenient, simplistic manner, ultimately failing to take responsibility and using authority precisely to avoid it. For such people their job is not merely a way to earn a living: it is the essence of their lives.

It is a commonplace that psychotherapists are crazy, and that this is probably what led them to their jobs. "What still strikes me," one woman I interviewed said, "is I'll go to a party in New York, and inevitably the craziest person there is a psychiatrist. I mean the person who is literally doing childish, antisocial things, making a fool of himself and embarrassing everyone else. I just shrug. That's the way it is." A president of the American Academy of Psychotherapists once said, in an address to the members of his organization, "When I first visited a national psychiatric convention, in 1943, I was dismayed to find the greatest collection of oddballs, Christ beards, and psychotics that I had ever seen outside a hospital. Yet this is to be expected: psychotherapists are those of us who are driven by our own emotional hunger."

Psychotherapists often take a perverse delight in criticizing their peers, and the amount of abuse I have heard them heap upon one another is truly astounding. Psychiatrists often say that analysts are crazy. Analysts say that psychiatrists, being unanalyzed, are crazy. Both of them say that social workers and psychologists, whose training is more limited and subject to fewer quality controls, are crazy, and are particularly harmful because a little bit of knowledge is a dangerous thing. Social workers and psychologists accuse psychiatrists and analysts of being pompous asses—pompous *crazy* asses, so puffed up with theoretical abstractions that they are out of touch with the real world.

PSYCHIATRISTS SAY THAT ANALYSTS ARE CRAZY. ANALYSTS SAY THAT PSYCHIATRISTS ARE CRAZY. BOTH OF THEM SAY THAT SOCIAL WORKERS AND PSYCHOLOGISTS ARE CRAZY.

"I very rarely have found a healthy, well-integrated, happy person *seeking* this profession," one training psychoanalyst says. Another man, a clinical psychologist, told me, "I questioned your calling it a myth that therapists are crazy because the *fact* is that most of them *are.* If you need any proof, let me tell you that every patient who comes into this office who has had a previous experience with another therapist has some kind of horror story to tell, about some *major* failing on the therapist's part, including, quite often, sexual abuse, verbal abuse, things that cross the boundary of mere bad technique and come pretty damn close to the criminal."

Various statistical surveys of the psychopathology of therapists have been published, but this literature yields inconclusive results. In one study 91 percent of psychiatrists surveyed agreed that psychiatrists had "emotional difficulties that are special to them and their work as contrasted with non-psychiatrists." The psychiatrists said, however, that some of these problems were related to the personalities of people who went into the field, and others stemmed from the nature of the work. Few considered their "emotional difficulties" to be diagnosable clinical problems. But an interesting Swiss study compared the military-conscription records of people who subsequently became psychiatrists with the records of those who became surgeons and internists, and found that significantly more of the eventual psychiatrists were declared unfit for military service because of psychiatric disorders.

In another survey, this one of psychologists, social workers, counselors, and other nonmedical psychotherapists, 82 percent of respondents said they'd had relationship difficulties, 57 percent had experienced depression, 11 percent admitted to substance abuse, and 2 percent said they had attempted suicide. Again, the survey does not make clear how serious the relationship difficulties and depression were, nor does it give comparable figures for a non-therapist population.

With respect to alcohol and drug abuse, a concrete measure of emotional problems, physicians in general show a higher incidence than nonphysicians, and a study that examined ninety-eight physician members of Alcoholics Anonymous found that 17 percent were psychiatrists, who constituted only 8 percent of physicians at the time. Though this has been interpreted to mean that a disproportionate number of psychiatrists (among physicians in general) are alcoholics, it may also mean that out of the total population of alcoholic physicians, psychiatrists are among the most likely to seek help. Other studies have found that alcohol-abuse rates among therapists range from 6 to 11 percent, but in the absence of proper controls such studies seem inconclusive. When therapists are asked about themselves, 4 percent of them report drug or alcohol abuse serious enough to affect their work. When asked about their colleagues, these same therapists say that 18 percent of them are so impaired.

Studies of suicide among psychiatrists also furnish contradictory results. "Among the specialties, psychiatry appears to yield a disproportionate number of suicides," said an article on suicide among physicians which appeared in the *British Medical Journal* as long ago as 1964. "The explanation may lie in the choosing of the specialty rather than its demands, for some who take up psychiatry probably do so for morbid reasons."

Physicians in general do not seem to commit suicide at a rate significantly different from that of their nonmedical peers, although, perhaps because of their knowledge of drugs and access to them, their methods of choice are characteristically nonviolent: doctors poison themselves more than twice as often as the lay public, and shoot themselves less often. Psychiatrists, however, show a markedly greater tendency to commit suicide than the population at large or their medical peers. After several conflicting and methodologically flawed studies of suicide among psychiatrists were published, the Task Force on Suicide Prevention of the American Psychiatric Association instigated its own study of psychiatrists' suicides. Investigators examined the records on nearly 19,000 physician deaths from 1967 to 1972 and calculated the ratio of suicides to members for each medical specialty. They found that psychiatrists killed themselves about twice as often as other physicians. No other specialty showed a frequency significantly greater than average. Moreover, when individual years of the time span were examined, the rate was found to be constant, "indicating a relatively stable over-supply of depressed psychiatrists from which the suicides are produced."

Some people have argued that many psychiatrists who commit suicide have good reasons for doing so. One view is that psychiatrists are more likely to kill themselves when they are terminally ill than are most other people, because they take a more realistic and enlightened view of human life and suffering. Some of the prominent early analysts are examples: Paul Federn shot himself when he was dying of cancer, and Wilhelm Stekel, faced with declining health, poisoned himself.

Others suggest that the strains of the profession, whether practical or emotional, may drive practitioners to despair. Judd Marmor, a well-known professor of psychiatry, points out that the burden of constantly associating with depressed people, the stress of the transference-countertransference situation, the problems of role uncertainty, the burden of continuing education, and economic difficulties might be expected to take their toll on anyone. Fritz Wittels, originally an antagonist of psychoanalysis but later an ardent supporter, wrote of analysts who

> involve their own unconscious in the dreams of others as in a distorting mirror; so that a gremlin catches them and drives them to death. Weininger was one of those who became involved in a bit of self-analysis, saw a distorted image of his unconscious that pressed a revolver into his hand. I have known three brilliant analysts, Schrötter, Tausk, Silberer, who voluntarily ended their lives. And in Vienna alone. Others will follow.

After Wittels changed his opinion of psychoanalysis, he retracted this view, saying that Weininger was not really a qualified psychoanalyst, that the others had not been properly analyzed, and that these facts, in the end, were to blame. "An analyst who has not himself been analyzed is in danger, be it suicide or otherwise."

On balance, however, with the significant exception of an apparent high suicide rate, the evidence that psychotherapists are disproportionately *impaired* is slight, and to accuse them of pervasive gross psychopathology would be foolish. Therapists are not crazy. Nonetheless, in terms of personality types, emotional weaknesses, and psychological motivations, a substantial majority of them may differ from the general population in ways more subtle than full-blown pathology yet more important than mere style.

What factors lead people to become psychotherapists? On this, not surprisingly, such information as exists is poorly controlled, open to wide interpretation, and generally anecdotal, as is psychotherapy itself. A book by William Henry, John Sims, and S. Lee Spray, titled *The Fifth Profession*, presents statistics that are diverting but scarcely enlightening. Given a questionnaire asking why they had become interested in the field of psychotherapy, 15.8 percent of all polled therapists said they wanted "to help people," 14.4 percent wanted "to understand people," and 9.6 percent wanted "to gain professional status." Psychoanalysts and psychiatrists, which were considered separate groups, were more interested in "gaining an identity," whatever that means, than in any of the other possibilities, whereas this was of negligible concern to the clinical psychologists and social workers. And 24.4 percent of all therapists gave an "other" reason for their interest.

Once one gets past the responses that invoke benevolence and civic-mindedness, one finds reasons that tend to involve a search for compensations and cures for the therapist's personal unhappiness. Freud theorized that a strong desire to help others stems from longings that are the consequence of childhood losses. Indeed, several articles on related issues assert that many therapists grew up in rejecting or inadequate families and were thus led to what Karl Menninger has called a "professional interest in lonely, eccentric, and unloved people."

One book that examines the lives of twelve psychotherapists concludes that most of them felt responsible for maintaining family happiness during their youth. In the cases the authors studied, the mothers were seen as pallid or uninspired women, notably indifferent to their children except insofar as the children could be manipulated for the mothers' own gratification. The fathers were typically weak and estranged, though their children admired them. "Since every study shows that [therapists] mostly come from disrupted or disjointed families, often with the father physically or psychically absent, the therapists-to-be were delegated the task of assuring the fate and fulfillment of the family. They became, and are, the family nurturer."

Often the psychotherapist's secret goal is to continue in the role of family support. In analytic transference the analyst comes to represent aspects of the patient's parents, and the patient represents aspects of the therapist's earlier life. Unfortunately, however, patients are not trained to manipulate this curious relationship, nor is that what they have come and paid money to do. Meanwhile, the therapist treats a succession of patients not only for their own problems but also for other problems, belonging to another time and place in the therapist's life, that haunt his consultation room. One study describes several therapists who seem to have done this. A psychiatrist undergoing analysis became depressed when she realized that she would not be able to cure her mother, an idea that lay in the back of her mind and had been her most important motive for entering psychiatry. A psychiatrist who in childhood had been saddled with the burden of maintaining family harmony was found to harbor the fantasy that one day his father and mother would be happy together as a result of his efforts. Meanwhile, he had particular difficulty treating patients with severe marital problems, and his own marriage suffered from his tendency to treat his wife as if she were a patient. In a third case a medical student embarking upon his psychiatric residency broke under the strain of caring for his emotionally disturbed mother and dependent psychiatrist father; he had planned to work in child psychiatry, and was especially interested in helping doctors' families.

The children of psychotherapists seem to talk more than most people do about their parents' emotionally dismal childhoods. They portray their therapist parents as exceptionally lonely and unhappy, socially ostracized at school, and abused at home, either psychologically or physically. The parents were ill at ease with themselves and with others, and sought through association with the world of adults and a retreat into the world of the intellect, and ultimately through the field of psychotherapy, to understand and manage their misery and to protect themselves and, later, their families. In many cases, the therapist parents themselves had said that their unhappy early lives were the primary motivation for their choice of career. In others, the motive seemed so clear that the children drew the conclusion on their own.

A host of other less-than-selfless motives may enter into the choice of psychotherapy as a profession: sublimated sexual curiosity, aggression, the problem-solving pleasure of clarifying emotional confusions, and a voyeuristic interest in the lives of others. These factors, which have been discussed by other authors, are very likely important, but they seem to be secondary rather than determining characteristics and will be considered here only insofar as they enter into what I believe to be the primary one: that of the wounded healer.

The idea of the wounded healer has ancient roots. In Greek mythology, Chiron, the centaur who taught medicine to Aesculapius, suffered an incurable wound at the hands of Hercules. Saint Augustine was conspicuous but not alone among the Christian saints in using his own weaknesses and his struggle against them to help him find compassion and strength. Mythology and religion are fraught with figures who must learn to heal themselves before healing others—who must recognize and forgive their own sins before they can, with authentic humility and understanding, forgive anyone else. Many of Freud's significant early discoveries arose out of the scrutiny of his deeply buried memories and then heroic confrontations with the painful things he found. In case histories of his patients he drew upon his own experience often enough to show that he regularly put his own flaws at the service of the empathic process. Psychoanalysts in training are required to undergo analysis for two complementary reasons. First, they must try to rid themselves of their psychological problems, so that they will be less likely to project their preoccupations onto their patients and then mistake what they perceive in them for objective fact. Second, the painful analytic process is itself instructive: an analyst who ventures into the patient's world needs to know how analysis can hurt and how it can help, and to recognize that therapist and patient are made of the same mortal stuff. Having emotional problems may not actually be a prerequisite or an advantage for a psychotherapist, but, clearly, having had problems is not in itself a handicap, so long as these problems have been recognized, confronted, and successfully resolved.

The danger occurs when the wounded healer has not resolved, or cannot control, his own injury. The helping professional's career can follow either of two paths. The more difficult, but ultimately more satisfying, road leads to a painful confrontation with his own problems and weaknesses, and ultimately to self-knowledge. Ideally, he overcomes the difficulties; at worst, he is forced to resign himself to insuperable handicaps. In either case, though, the end result is a clearer perception of his ambitions and needs and their relationship to the task at hand. He can approach others with honesty, compassion, and humility, knowing that he is motivated by genuine concern, and not by some ulterior motive.

The other path is easier but often disastrous. The psychotherapist comes, consciously or unconsciously, to see in his profession a means of *avoiding* the need to deal with his problems. He gains authority and power to compensate for his weakness and vulnerability. He learns slippery techniques that enable him to justify his actions in almost all circumstances, and perhaps even to shift blame onto somebody else. In his work with his patients, the entire therapeutic relationship is perverted and turned to the service of his hidden purpose. The therapist is there not to treat the patient but, by circuitous and well-concealed means, to treat or protect or comfort himself. The patient is not an object of empathy and altruism but an unsuspecting victim who is taken into the therapist's realm of personal needs and subjective impressions and assigned a role there that he does not recognize and would not want. And in the course of this strange, unacknowledged process, the patient's own problems may be neglected.

In choosing his profession, the therapist-to-be may even make his problems much worse, because he discovers a justification for divorcing himelf from the emotions that have caused him so much pain. He is to become a cold, accurate instrument instead of a sloppily warm and vulnerable human being. He may console himself with the heady deceit that he is martyring himself for the good of others: rather than live a happy and self-interested life, he says, he will forgo his own satisfaction in order to transform himself into someone who can do greater good. The flaw in this idea is that he is not being selfless at all but seeking, through the very medium of ostentatious self-denial, a perverse gratification of his personal needs. For such a therapist, the wound has become sealed off, prevented from causing pain but also left inaccessible to healing. Since his energy is directed toward defending the status quo, he is diverted from the arduous and humbling process of self-examination which might otherwise have made him whole, and is forced, continuously and forever, to work just to stay where he is. With this sealed-off problem now at the center of his personal and professional life, the further along he goes the more difficult and costly it becomes to try to correct the mistake. His situation is almost Faustian: he has sold his hopes of redemption in the future for power, comfort, and knowledge in the present.

THE PARALLELS IN THE WORLD OF RELIGION ARE conspicuous and instructive. The Church has often been regarded as a haven for the emotionally disturbed. Like studies on the mental state of psychotherapists, studies of the clergy are contradictory and emotionally charged. Overall, however, they suggest a high incidence of family problems and narcissistic disorders, and a host of other problems involving interpersonal relations and self-esteem. In the course of my research I spoke to several psychotherapists who had begun their careers as ministers, and who now specialize in treating the emotional problems of their erstwhile professional colleagues. Some of these problems are incidental to the occupation, or result from its peculiar pressures and strains, but others seem to be both causal and recurrent enough to rate as a mild but characteristic clerical pathology.

One type of clergyman, like one type of psychotherapist, is a repentant sinner who has recognized his or her weakness and can therefore align himself with other mortal men in the search for salvation. Another kind, the sealed-off sinner in his most extreme form, is the rigid and damning preacher who exhorts and chastises his flock from above, who has no sympathy for their weaknesses, and who may hurt his congregants by condemning their transgressions, instead of helping by leading them, through understanding, to righteousness. These preachers are so deeply beset by uncertainty and unresolved problems that they have organized their external life through sheer brute force and imposture, but they have left their internal life untouched. They cannot understand their congregants because they cannot understand themselves, and they cannot constructively help with many emotional problems because the solution they have adopted themselves is to cap such tensions tightly and hold them unseen.

Perhaps the most interesting and significant problem shared by many "healers," which has been described by a number of therapists, is that of the person, often a first-born or only child, who was rushed through childhood too quickly, without the warmth, the protection, and the love that children deserve, and who was obliged to become a little adult. Such people grow up believing that hard work and responsibility are the only things that give them value in others' eyes. They have a chronically low sense of self-worth and a stunted ability to receive genuine love or friendship from others; only their selfishly selfless labors make them feel satisfied with themselves. As a result, they may be driven into a veritable frenzy of wholesale helping, which is motivated not by altruism but by a desperate need to fill an inner vacancy—an effort that ultimately helps very little, because, like trying to fill a bucket with a hole in the bottom, it can never succeed until they have attended to the necessary repairs. As one man, a Jungian analyst and an Episcopalian minister who has treated many clergymen, describes the problem: "They give too much, without knowing how to take, and it has an effect on them as well as on their families. They build up even more of an inhibition against being able to appropriately take things for themselves, which is taboo. They can justify this attitude with all sorts of theological jargon that says 'It is more blessed to give than to receive,' and so on. They are into loving their God and loving their neighbor, but they forget that little, crucial, additional thing: 'as thyself.'

"These people are pathological givers, and so they become servers, pastoral counselors, and so on, and they can even be good at it, to a degree, but they become impoverished after a while. They have given so much that they finally run out of spiritual and nervous energy, and what remains is the underlying resentment. You find a great deal of resentment and sourness among the clergy. Just go and interview your garden-variety Catholic priest in the parish. Get to know him a little bit, and you will find a lot of anger and bitterness, even though he will maintain a façade of benevolence and contentment. He has given more than he had to give, and gotten very little back."

In choosing the ministry as a profession, these wounded

THE CHILDREN OF PSYCHOTHERAPISTS PORTRAY THEIR THERAPIST PARENTS AS EXCEPTIONALLY LONELY AND UNHAPPY, SOCIALLY OSTRACIZED AT SCHOOL, AND ABUSED AT HOME.

healers have embarked on an ultimately doomed quest, one that perverts the purpose of their work. One bishop summed up the issues quite neatly when he said that in screening candidates for the ministry, one of the questions he asks himself is, "Is this a whole person seeking to express his wholeness through the ministry? Or is this a person trying to *find* his wholeness in the ministry?"

William Dewart, a clinical psychologist who works primarily with clergymen, points out another interesting, common problem. One of the lures that drew these people to the Church was a position of authority that might help them to compensate for their feelings of inadequacy and emptiness and to escape from painful impositions by others. "Some go into the clergy believing that 'in the end, I answer only to God.' That is a very nice arrangement, they suppose, because God is a spiritual entity, after all, and His love is unconditional. They won't have to deal with a foreman or boss, no changes of administration. It's just you and God, who, after all, called you in the first place. At least that's what they believe when they begin. But before they know it, they find themselves running up against authority and issues of power everywhere, from the vestry of their own small parish all the way up to the bishop of the diocese. For example, in the Episcopal Church the canons provide for the bishop to make the final decision regarding the very question of one's calling to an ordained priesthood. So the poor individual unconsciously seeking the priesthood in hopes of circumventing issues of authority and power will certainly find himself walking straight into one of the more authoritative, political organizations in the world."

Among psychotherapists this is rarely a problem, except among those entering a psychoanalytic institute, who may feel that the institute's teachers and training analysts hold despotic power over their fate. Indeed, the psychotherapist in private practice is responsible to no outside authority. Information about what he does comes only from what he chooses to tell and from the perceptions of his patients, who tend to mistrust their own judgment. The therapist truly has the independence that the clergyman hoped for; he is the solitary ruler of his microcosmic domain. This unusual circumstance tends to exacerbate whatever problems he brought to his profession and to add novel difficulties.

In an important paper titled "The God Complex," published in 1913, Ernest Jones, a pioneer psychoanalyst now best remembered as Freud's biographer and chief English-language ambassador, described a set of character traits resulting from a pathological unconscious belief that one is God. People with this complex do not wander the streets proclaiming themselves the deity but have both a concealed, insidious faith in their own importance and entitlement, and an inability to conceive of others as comparably important, which color every aspect of their relations with the world.

> The type in question is characterized by a desire for aloofness, inaccessibility, and mysteriousness, often also by a modesty and self-effacement. They are happiest in their own home, in privacy and seclusion, and like to withdraw to a distance. They surround themselves and their opinions with a cloud of mystery, exert only an indirect influence on external affairs, never join in any common action, and are generally unsocial. They take great interest in psychology, particularly in the so-called objective methods of mind-study that are eclectic and which dispense with the necessity for intuition. Phantasies of power are common, especially the idea of possessing great wealth. They believe themselves to be omniscient, and tend to reject all new knowledge. . . . The subjects of language and religion greatly interest them. . . . Constant, but less characteristic, attributes are the desire for appreciation, the wish to protect the weak, the belief in their own immortality, the fondness for creative schemes, e.g., for social reform, and above all, a pronounced castration complex.

Oddly enough, this comes very close to being a description of many psychotherapists, or even a job description for psychotherapy. Some of the qualities are ones that psychotherapists go out of their way to cultivate as part of their professional persona, and the training process may encourage them. Indeed, Jones said that people with God complexes were more likely than others to go into psychology and related professions. He hastened to add that they were not drawn to psychoanalysis, his own specialty, for it required intuition and an ability to empathize with others. A great many analysts and analytically oriented therapists, however, plod through their jobs on the basis of dogma, with little empathy at all. Jones himself was notable for his lack of psychological intuition, and was a curious mixture of radicalism and conservatism. He left medicine and Wales, his native land, which threatened in separate ways to hold power over him, yet once he had embraced Freudian psychoanalysis he became its most inflexible defender. His belief in the powers of psychoanalysis, by his own admission, bordered on grandiosity:

> Perhaps, indeed, in centuries to be, the medical psychologist may, like the priest of ancient times, come to serve as a source of practical wisdom and a stabilising influence in this chaotic world, whom the community would consult before embarking on any important social or political enterprise. Mere megalomania, it may be said. Perhaps, but it is my living faith none the less, and only our descendants will be able to say if it was a misplaced one.

Freud himself had a strong element of grandiosity, insisting that he was not a man of science, an observer, an experimenter, or a thinker, but a conquistador. His bitter relations with Jung, Adler, Rank, and others who strayed from his patronage and guidance are in keeping with Jones's image of the man who can tolerate no god but himself.

In any psychotherapist, for that matter, an unusual degree of self-assurance is essential. After all, the therapist's patients are people whose attempts to conduct their own lives have failed, to some degree, and who are seeking help from another. However much therapists may wish to play the part of mere mediators rather than guides, the situation forces them into a position of superiority in which, by whatever direct or subtle means, they must assert their notion of what is good for their patients above what the patients may believe to be proper in the management of their own lives. Moreover, therapists need self-confidence and poise, combined with a great deal of humility, to withstand the emotional onslaught of the patients' unreasonable expectations and assumptions. Patients force therapists into a position of superiority through their idealization: the therapists must have wonderful marriages, perfect children, cultured and profound interests, clear and correct understanding of issues. Many patients want to be like their therapists, to adopt facets of their therapist's tastes and mannerisms, and some patients go on to become therapists or counselors themselves, because the profession has emerged in their minds as the most perfect of all occupations. Patients do not simply want advice from their therapists: as children, they expected magic from their parents, and often with their therapists—thanks to the transference—they entertain similarly unrealistic hopes that their fears will be soothed and their problems miraculously resolved.

The field of psychotherapy inevitably attracts people with God complexes, and it is custom-designed to exacerbate the condition when it exists. Psychiatrists sometimes expect, and are often expected by others, to address questions that lie well outside the range of their expertise. They are expected to do so simply because they study human beings and, by erroneous implication, are therefore supposed to understand all things human. Psychiatrists comment on the law, politics, art, literature, and ethical questions, which nothing in their training has qualified them to comprehend any better than any other intelligent and educated person. Above all, within the therapeutic situation itself therapists who do not have the personal strength and equilibrium to resist the temptations of power and to see the patients' adoration as the epiphenomenon of their actions that it is may subside into self-importance.

> Each profession carries its respective difficulties, and the danger of analysis is that of becoming infected by trans-

> ference projections, in particular by archetypal contents. When the patient assumes that his analyst is the fulfillment of his dreams, that he is not an ordinary doctor but a spiritual hero and a sort of saviour, of course the analyst will say, "What nonsense! This is just morbid. It is a hysterical exaggeration." Yet—it tickles him; it is just too nice. And moreover, he has the same archetypes in himself. So he begins to feel, "If there are saviours, well, perhaps it is just possible that I am one," and he will fall for it, at first hesitantly, and then it will become more and more plain to him that he really is a sort of extraordinary individual. Slowly he becomes fascinated and exclusive. He is terribly touchy, susceptible, and perhaps makes himself a nuisance in medical societies. He cannot talk with his colleagues any more because he is—I don't know what. He becomes very disagreeable or withdraws from human contacts, isolates himself, and then it becomes more and more clear to him that he is a very important chap really and of great spiritual significance, probably an equal of the Mahatmas in the Himalayas, and it is quite likely that he also belongs to the great brotherhood. And then he is lost to the profession. We have very unfortunate examples of this kind. I know quite a number of colleagues who have gone that way.

This description by Carl Jung is probably exaggerated, which is fortunate in one obvious sense, though unfortunate in another, inasmuch as therapists of the sort described are not necessarily lost to the profession but may continue to practice. They can justify their attitude to themselves and to others—but someone who wields power in the name of some perceived ultimate good is always potentially dangerous. The zealot can find a moral excuse for oppressing others that is unavailable to the mere bully or the charlatan.

If viewed clinically, the god complex can be related to narcissism, a personality disorder whose chief features are well established. Those with narcissistic personality disorders have grandiose self-images, often entertain unrealistic notions of their abilities, power, wealth, intelligence, and appearance, and feel entitled to things they haven't earned, simply by virtue of their inherent greatness. This exalted view of themselves, however, lacking the comfortable and certain support of reality, is very fragile. Narcissists constantly need admiration and praise from others and can be incongruously devastated by relatively unimportant failures, which threaten the fragile tissue of their belief. A paradoxical indifference to the wishes and feelings of others, combined with a simultaneous dependency upon their praise, is a particularly striking feature of narcissists. Many of them have a deep-seated sense that they are frauds—as in many ways they are.

Narcissists are much more concerned with the appearance of things than with the reality; thus their ambitions tend to have a driven quality but to be empty of genuine sustained interest or pleasure. They are ethically empty, though their fundamental amorality is often masked by an intense but superficial show of morality and social, political, or aesthetic concern. Since these cosmetic ethics do not touch them personally, however, narcissists may readily change their views or entertain conflicting ethical beliefs.

Their relations with others tend to be emotionally hollow and exploitative, since narcissists are ultimately interested only in themselves (failing, in a profound way, even to perceive other people as separate from themselves) and are thus unable to maintain equal give-and-take relationships. They are insensitive and lacking in empathy; their views of others are chiefly projections from within themselves, and therefore vacillate between idealization and debasement. Frequently they believe other people to be basically unscrupulous, unreliable, false, and opportunistic. Though they may make an extravagant show of generosity and concern for others, this behavior inevitably proves to be just that—a show, which serves to polish the fine image they strive to hold of themselves.

Various schools of psychoanalytic thought postulate different origins for narcissistic disorders, but all agree on the fundamental outlines. Narcissists were deprived in infancy and childhood of the affection and the deep emotional interactions with their parents that would have allowed the normal development of a distinct sense of the difference between self and other and a feeling of personal value. According to the psychoanalysts Heinz Kohut and Alice Miller particularly, pathology in the parents (who are often narcissistic themselves) kept them from treating the child as an independent person and responding to him on his own merits, and led them instead to use the child for their own gratification. As a result, the child's sense of self was stunted and his sense of value was structured around his ability to comprehend and fulfill his parents' wishes. As Miller comments,

> This ability is then extended and perfected. Later, these children not only become mothers (confidantes, comforters, advisers, supporters) of their own mothers, but also take over the responsibility for their siblings and eventually develop a special sensitivity to unconscious signals manifesting the needs of others. No wonder that they often choose the psychoanalytic profession later on. Who else, without this previous history, would muster sufficient interest to spend the whole day trying to discover what is happening in the other person's unconscious?

Thus the peculiar miseries of the narcissist's childhood have encouraged him to develop a sensitivity to others' needs and a knack for anticipating and dextrously catering to them. **These are extraordinarily useful in the practice of psychotherapy, as is a need to exercise these talents and to achieve the approval of others. The very same qualities, however, ultimately hinder the therapist's ability to help patients or to raise children who are free of emotional problems, because the empathy and altruism are basically false. Meanwhile, the profession he has entered presses him further than ever from the chance of cure.**

One of the best ways to avoid or counteract feelings of grandiosity is to cultivate genuine human loves and friendships. By dealing with people as equals, in symmetrical relationships in which the corners tend to get knocked off people's fantastic monuments to themselves, and in which they may grow comfortable with their shortcomings through others' acceptance of them, they can learn to be real, solid human beings who take true pride in genuine strengths and are able to recognize and deal with genuine weaknesses. Healthy, loving marriages, in particular, wean people from lonely grandiosity, and also mitigate the effects of their particular problems on their children.

Unfortunately, this is not the sort of marriage many psychotherapists seem to have or to seek out. When measured in superficial statistical terms, psychiatrists have a divorce rate insignificantly higher than the rate among other medical specialists, and considerably *lower* than the rate among the general professional population. Their marriages, however, according to one respected research team, often appear to be remarkably distant and formal, based on shared intellectual and recreational activities rather than on affectionate interaction. Moreover, considerable anecdotal evidence suggests that therapists, both men and women, tend to marry troubled and dependent partners who will not counteract their narcissistic disturbances but will supply the admiration they crave. It is said that they marry their patients—which is sometimes even literally true—and end up in relationships that are anything but equal. The psychiatrist Richard Robertiello, speaking from professional and personal experience, writes,

> [Therapists] tend to be drawn to partners who have rather serious emotional problems and who are looking for a wise understanding person who will help, support and perhaps "cure" them. . . . They are drawn by their own feeling of grandiosity and omnipotence. They think they will be able, by their love and caring and wisdom, to make this person happy, especially one who has frustrated several previous therapists in their efforts to accomplish this. Of course, the therapists feel very noble and generous and altruistic in this endeavor.
>
> But their satisfactions are hardly only altruistic. They start off having tremendous adulation and admiration from their "sick" mates. They begin in an unchallenged position of superiority and control. They are always "right" or "healthy" and their mate is always "wrong" or "sick." In addition to all of the narcissistic gratification this provides, it also gives a perfect assurance of acceptability and a near-guarantee against being abandoned.

Ultimately, this sort of relationship is not very profitable for either person involved. The therapist may eventually outgrow his spouse and come to resent the dependence that originally brought them together. "I used to complain that I saw outpatients all week long, and then had an inpatient on my hands every weekend," Robertiello says. But growth on the part of the spouse can pose a threat to the therapist. The couple may end up in a stale relationship, where even the gratification of adoration and dependence wears thin. Meanwhile, the whole household revolves around the initial narcissistic demands of the therapist, and the subordinate spouse may come to function more as a part of this pattern than as an autonomous entity. "My father was very shy and insecure," says one woman, a lawyer and the daughter of an analyst, "and he insisted that the family provide him with a lot of reassurance all the time. He stayed very close to home in every way—his office was in the house—and there was this ritual that my mother had to tell him how wonderful he was even though he wasn't, and how great the things he did were even when they weren't. That seems to be why he needed her."

Close friendships are the other curative, but psychotherapists, as it happens, tend to have very few friends. Therapists explain this away as a result of the tremendous demands of their professional lives—long hours, teaching, society meetings—but such rationalizations seem forced. Statistics show that psychiatrists have more free time than almost any other medical specialists and that compared with many lawyers and businessmen—people not noted for a paucity of friends—psychotherapists do not have demanding schedules. Moreover, having little time does not automatically mean that one cannot make friends.

The real reason for the lack of friendships often appears to be a much more unpleasant, unconscious one. Many therapists do not need friends, because they live vicariously through their patients, just as clergymen seek love and self-worth vicariously through devotion to a congregation. For people who are uncomfortable with others and with themselves, the therapeutic situation offers an unparalleled opportunity for asymmetrical intimacy. The rules of therapy demand that the patient tell the therapist everything, while the therapist is under no obligation to reveal anything at all and thus can minimize the risk of pain incurred in normal human relationships. Life in the office can be exciting. One therapist told me the story of an analyst who retired and looked forward to the joy of reading novels but was dreadfully bored after a few months, because fiction did not possess the immediacy and veracity of clinical cases. And therapists who are allowed entry into their patients' lives are repaid for this privilege by the patients' grateful adoration. "My father had an inability to relate with his family or other people," says an analyst and the son of an analyst, "and his way of being close was through his patients. It was a way for him to have an interaction, but there was always a wall, or a desk, or a couch to protect him."

The Swiss psychotherapist Adolf Guggenbühl-Craig describes the tragic consequences to the therapist of this kind of vicarious living.

> His own private life takes a back seat to the problems and difficulties of his patients. But a point may be reached where the patients might actually live for the analyst, so to speak, where they are expected to fill the gap left by the analyst's own loss of contact with warm, dynamic life. The analyst no longer has his own friends; his patients' friendships and enmities are as his own. The analyst's sex life may be stunted; his patients' sexual problems provide a substitute. . . . His own psychic development comes to a standstill. Even in his non-professional life he can talk of nothing but his patients and their problems.

> He is no longer able to love and hate, to invest himself in life, to struggle, to win and lose. His own affective life becomes a surrogate. Acting thus as a quack who draws his sustenance from the lives of his patients, the analyst may seem momentarily to flourish psychically. But in reality he loses his own vitality and creative originality. The advantage of such vicarious living, of course, is that the analyst is also spared any genuine suffering. In a sense this function too is exercised for him by others.

The particular danger for the patient, against which therapists must be vigilant but often are not, is that the therapy begins to settle in as part of the patient's life rather than remaining an active process through which he can reintegrate himself into living. The patient may begin to look forward to sessions excessively and to live his life for the unacknowledged purpose of interesting and pleasing the therapist. Problems may apparently be resolved and changes made because the patient feels that this is what the therapist wants; such changes have no profound or permanent effect, because they are performed more for dramatic value or the therapist's approval than from a sense of inner need. Patients do not want to leave the idealized therapist; nor, in the pathological relationship described above, is the therapist motivated to help the patient leave. In the worst case, the entire therapy is poisoned, because ultimately, unconsciously, the therapist cannot bear to cure the patient, for then he would lose him. He therefore perpetuates a curious relationship of a kind that he may have had with his parents and that he may inflict not only on his patients but also on his children.

I have heard such stories again and again. One of the first and most dramatic accounts came from a respected psychoanalyst who had always admired and sought to emulate his analyst father, had gone to the same medical school and analytic institute, and had set up his practice in the same city. He dated the beginning of his most significant personal growth from the time his father, during a period of illness, asked him to take over some of his cases.

"I agreed. I wasn't that busy. I was in analytic training and was getting some supervision analyzing, and I thought this would be more grist for the mill. Besides, I figured I could do it as well as anybody else, and I never thought about the possible consequences of this kind of involvement with him. But in the course of doing this two or three times, I began to realize that my father had a number of patients who were very dependent on him. He charged them low fees, for one thing. That should have been a clue. But then, more important, with a number of his patients I realized that he had no good idea of the difference between maintenance, support, and cure. With some of them he had developed a kind of *collusion*; they needed him, and he needed them."

What both alarmed and helped this man most of all was his realization that the same process was at work in the relationship between his father and himself. He idolized his father, and his father depended on this idolization, much as he did in his relationships with his patients. Though his father was willing to help him grow to a certain degree, and though the son benefited in many ways from his closeness to his father, at some point his independence worked against his father's interests—both the father's selfish interests and his inappropriate wishes for his son. "I saw the contrast in the relationships between my psychoanalyst and me and my father and me. My analyst was providing me with an opportunity to grow up, while my father, apparently, didn't want me to go through the same sort of pain he had experienced growing up." Gradually the son established his own independence: he divorced his wife, having married in part to please his father, moved to another state, and eventually abandoned full-time psychoanalysis in favor of a psychiatric practice whose orientation was altogether removed from that of his father's.

Several teaching analysts and psychotherapists agree that what poses as professional dedication is often at heart a morbid addiction. A training analyst in New York has discussed with men the unwillingness of analysts to leave their practice even when they reach retirement age. "They may say that they can't give up the income, or offer some other explanation, but what they really miss is feeling needed. Personally, I think that it is unethical and immoral for analysts to practice beyond a certain time in life. You can say a word for experience, but how much experience is experience? You can't really say that a seventy-year-old's experience is better than that of someone who is fifty-five. There comes a time when you are simply repeating the same experiences. Yet analysts will not retire. They *won't*. Myself, I don't take on new patients anymore. I do consultations or see an occasional ex-patient, and mostly do teaching or supervising. But someone who is now in his eighties, a New York analyst whom everyone knows, said to me the other day, "I have time," meaning that he wanted some referrals. I told a friend, and she said I should have replied, 'Not much.' What is someone like that doing for his patients? He can't see as well, he can't remember as well, he can't hear as well, but he's still in there, and nobody's going to tell him what to do, and since there are no rules or laws or need for operating-room privileges, nobody can stop him, and he'll just keep doing it. And, transferential feelings being what they are, the patient doesn't have enough sense to move on or move up. Sometimes patients actually stay because they feel sorry for the therapist. I've known cases like that."

For most patients the problems of the wounded healer are irrelevant. Most people who seek therapeutic help need the benefit of knowledge, experience, and objectivity, and the opportunity to devote a specific amount of time to the careful scrutiny of whatever is wrong with their lives. The narcissistic therapist's sealed-off wound and secret self-centered agenda may have no discernible effect on this simple program. But in cases that demand more from the therapist, or tread close to his own problems, or issue challenges that his therapeutic persona cannot easily handle, serious harm may be done.

BEATING DEPRESSION

Treatment of mood disorders is psychiatry's greatest success story. As the biological roots of the illness become better understood, the stigma is subsiding

It is as if the person Dr. Peter Kent used to be is now buried somewhere inside this man who cannot summon the energy to get out of bed, who lies for hours staring blankly, sighing, his thoughts traveling in bleak circles. Kent's colleagues at the hospital have been told by his secretary that the 41-year-old cardiologist is on "personal leave," nothing more. They have not been told about the psychiatric ward that resembles an exclusive college dormitory, about the faint institutional smell, Monet's vision of Giverny on the wall, the living room where patients play pool or sit smoking cigarettes. They do not know that Kent is, for the moment, spending his afternoons in group therapy and watching the "Oprah Winfrey Show."

Kent's secretary is protecting him from what people—his patients, other doctors, the public—might think. It is very hush-hush, his illness. Indeed, this magazine is protecting him, too. We have changed his name in order to write about him, creating a new identity for this altered, sluggish self, the ailing Dr. Kent who finds it painfully difficult to string words into a sentence, who yawns every few minutes and shifts his gaze away, up to the ceiling, over to the daffodils on the table. "It's like being in quicksand," he says. "There's a sense of doom, of sadness."

The need for secrecy is troubling. Kent has not embezzled money, cheated on his income tax or seduced 16-year-old girls. He is not a bad person; on the contrary, his gentleness and quiet concern must be reassuring to patients who are recovering from heart attacks or facing bypass surgery. He is guilty only of having fallen victim to an illness that, because it affects the mind and the personality, is still tinged with shame, as if to suffer from it were somehow an admission of poor character, or weak will.

Though it is more common than diabetes, serious depression—the kind that can lead to suicide or land one in a mental hospital—remains an issue that can unhorse presidential candidates or bind a family in embarrassed silence. There are signs, however, that this view is shifting, that science is at last making headway against fear. Those who have sampled depression's dark offerings are speaking out, describing both the depth and harrowing intensity of their ordeal. Some of their faces are familiar: An actress, a prominent attorney, a talk-show host, a businesswoman. Most recently, author William Styron, writing in *Vanity Fair,* has described his own plunge into despondency, "a veritable howling tempest in the brain," that nearly cost him his life. With each declaration the curtain is drawn back a little further, a kind of mental *glasnost* reminiscent of the thaw that followed Betty Ford's public discussion of her struggle with breast cancer.

There are wider reflections of the changing climate. Large corporations, once oblivious to the impact of psychological factors, are beginning to pay more attention to their employes' state of mind, realizing that mental well-being is essential for high productivity and lower medical costs. They have reason for concern: A recent study by the Rand Corporation found that depression can be as disabling as coronary-artery disease or arthritis, with depressed individuals spending more days in bed than those with chronic lung or gastrointestinal problems. And, perhaps sensing growing interest in the subject, the media, too, have become expansive when it comes to mental illness. Public television this winter launched a new series, "Moods & Music," spotlighting the link between creativity and mood disorders (see next page). Says Dr. Robert Hirschfeld, chief of the Mood, Anxiety, and Personality Disorders Research Branch of the National Institute of Mental Health (NIMH): "People are now recognizing depression as an illness and not a character flaw."

1 in 12 Americans

In part, this new-fledged openness

rests upon an expanding body of research that in the last three decades has given scientists a much greater understanding of mood disorders—illnesses that will afflict more than 20 million Americans at some point in their lifetime. The treatment of depression and manic depression is "psychiatry's No. 1 success story," says Dr. Frederick Goodwin, administrator of the U.S. Alcohol, Drug Abuse and Mental Health Administration and co-author of *Manic Depressive Illness,* to be published by Oxford University Press this spring.

A new generation of drugs allows a sophistication and flexibility in treatment that was not possible in the past. One such antidepressant, Anafranil, also used to treat obsessive-compulsive disorder, won final approval from the Food and Drug Administration last month. Other medications are in the pipeline. For the first time, studies are also beginning to reveal how and where psychoactive drugs exert their action on the brain. Further, scientists have taken the initial steps toward solving the difficult problem of which pharmacological treatments work most reliably for different manifestations of the illness. Experts know more, too, about the types of psychotherapy best suited to defeating the feelings of hopelessness and paralysis that infuse the depressive state (see "Tailoring Treatment . . .").

By far the most powerful lever for changing public attitudes comes from the growing body of work that establishes depression as a disease that is biologically based, at least in its most disabling forms. Both severe depression and manic depression involve dramatic physiological changes, and the evidence points to a hereditary vulnerability that is then triggered by environmental stress. Using high-tech scanners, chemical probes and genetic mapping techniques—the newest tools of a rapidly developing science—researchers are starting to fill in the unknowns of an immensely complicated equation, one capable of leaving the brain, as Lord Byron imagined it in *Childe Harold,* "In its own eddy boiling and o'erwrought, A whirling gulf of phantasy and flame."

Mood disorders take many forms, and researchers historically have been hard pressed to draw iron-clad distinctions among types, or even to differentiate reliably between "normal" dips in mood and the psychic transformation that constitutes depressive illness. Confusing the issue further is the colloquial use of the word *depression* to describe a range of unpleasant, but inevitable, consequences of living. One is "depressed" after a bad day at the office, or the breakup of a love relationship.

Clinical depression is at once more intense and longer lasting than the brooding funks that seize everyone from time to time. Of patients hospitalized for depression, 40 to 60 percent suffer from the disease in its classical form, once referred to as "melancholia." Submerged in recrimination and self-doubt, these patients lose their appetite, suffer an array of bodily aches, show little interest in sex and awaken in the early-morning hours. They may pace the floor in agitation, or their speech and movement may be drastically slowed, almost as if they had suddenly developed a peculiar and sudden form of brain damage. Yet this facade of lethargy is deceptive. In fact, says Dr. Philip Gold, chief of the NIMH Clinical Neuroendocrinology Branch, severe depression may be a state of hypervigilance and intense arousal: "Such patients are so overwhelmed and overstimulated," says Gold, "that they just kind of sit still."

Winter's discontent

Less common than melancholia is a pattern in which the symptoms are reversed. Patients eat more than usual and sleep for long hours, only reluctantly emerging into wakefulness. In recent years, more and more patients have also been reporting to clinics with still other forms of depression that researchers are only beginning to categorize. In seasonal affective disorder (SAD), despair sets in

MELANCHOLY'S CREATIVE SIDE

"As an experience, madness is terrific I can assure you, and not to be sniffed at," British novelist Virginia Woolf once wrote in a letter to a composer friend. Woolf, author of *To The Lighthouse* and *Orlando,* among other works, careened from feverish periods of writing to weeks immersed in bottomless gloom, according to the memoirs of her husband Leonard Woolf.

Neither the novelist's mood swings nor the conviction that her work was enhanced by them is unusual in creative individuals. Indeed, mood disorders seem to have a predilection for artistic victims, and the list of painters, composers and writers who suffered from depression—or, even more commonly, manic depression—is a long one. "Creativity involves making associations between unrelated ideas," says Kay Jamison, associate professor of psychiatry at Johns Hopkins University School of Medicine and executive producer of the PBS series "Moods & Music." "In a slightly manic phase, you can link things that before were just isolated ideas."

George Frideric Handel, who scholars believe may have been manic depressive, composed his "Messiah," a work that takes almost 4 hours to perform, in a mere three weeks—presumably riding on the frenetic high of his illness. Gustav Mahler, in a letter to a friend, described with uncanny precision a type of "rapid cycling" manic depression in which moods shift precipitously, sometimes within weeks or even days. "The fires of a supreme zest for living and the most gnawing desire for death alternate in my heart, sometimes in the course of a single hour," Mahler wrote.

Poets Anne Sexton and Robert Lowell, Vincent van Gogh and photographer Diane Arbus all fought the demons of mental disintegration, and all managed to turn the battle to their creative advantage. Far too often, however, artists also pay with their lives, choosing suicide as a balm for their psychic wounds.

The link between creativity and mood disorders is validated by research. Harvard University researchers Dr. Ruth Richards and Dennis Kinney gave creativity tests to 33 Danish patients diagnosed with manic depression or a milder form of the illness. The same tests were given to their relatives. The scientists found that both patients and relatives scored higher than normal subjects. Similarly, in a study of creative writers enrolled in the prestigious University of Iowa Writers' Workshop, psychiatrist Nancy Andreasen discovered that 80 percent of the writers had suffered at least one episode of depression or mania in their lifetime, compared with 30 percent in a control group of lawyers, hospital administrators and social workers. The writers also showed a significantly higher incidence of alcoholism than the other subjects. It is possible, suggests Andreasen, that the sensitivity, openness, adventuresome nature and independent character of creative individuals in some way makes them more vulnerable to mental illness, in particular mood disorders.

with the disappearance of the lingering daylight hours of summer and persists for as long as short days and the cold winter sun remain. As spring returns, however, patients with SAD feel their energy return. Their desolation lifts, and their lives return to normal. "Dysthymia," on the other hand, is a chronic, if milder, form of depression that can last for months or even years. Researchers estimate that nearly 9 million Americans are locked in dysthymia's dispiriting grip. "It's like a low-grade infection," says Virginia Commonwealth University clinical psychologist James McCullough. "Dysthymics never really feel good."

At the most extreme end of the spectrum, a depressed patient can cross the border into psychosis. "I heard a voice, a male voice; it was the voice of death," says a 31-year-old entertainer, hospitalized for severe depression after she told friends she was afraid she might hurt herself or someone else. "The voice said, 'Hey, kiddo, you know I'm waiting right on the horizon for you.' It was telling me how my body was going to die, trying to catch me off guard. 'Jump in front of that car,' it told me."

Mania shares this departure from reality. Possessed of limitless energy, thoughts racing, manic-depressive patients in the elated phase of the illness may stay up all night, insist they are in touch with creatures from outer space, become uncharacteristically promiscuous or run up thousands of dollars in credit-card bills. One woman, a West Coast business executive, packed her briefcase, put on her best tailored suit and flew to Washington, D.C. Her mission: To convince the Federal Bureau of Investigation that a dangerous conspiracy threatened national security. The FBI agents were perplexed. Should they heed the woman's conservative attire and articulate manner or their hunch that something about her tale was not quite right?

The demographics of depression have changed dramatically in the last half-century. Cornell University psychiatrist Gerald Klerman and Columbia University epidemiologist Myrna Weissman, reviewing studies tracking fluctuating patterns of illness in 10 countries, have found that in developed nations, including the U.S., rates of depression increased markedly for postwar baby-boomers—those born in the period between 1945 and 1955—with the incidence peaking between 1975 and 1980. This upward trend seems to have been only temporary, however. Klerman's newest data, still unpublished, suggest that as the baby-boom generation turns 40, "the turmoil is subsiding," the curve sloping downward again. Suicides also declined in the '80s for baby-boomers, Klerman says, and rates of depression for those born in succeeding decades show a similar downward trend.

A host of theories

What accounts for these shifts? Researchers can only speculate. Fiercer competition in the labor force during the 1960s and '70s, a greater gap between expectations and fulfillment than in previous generations, increased drug use and greater mobility all have been proposed as possible reasons for the increases in the 1970s. Some even suggest that a change in biological factors is at work, but conclusive evidence for any of these theories is not yet in hand. Nor can experts at present convincingly account for changes in the male-to-female ratio among depressed patients. Women with "unipolar" depression—that is, without manic swings—have traditionally outnumbered men 3 to 1. But Weissman has found indications that men are catching up, with women now diagnosed with the illness at rates only twice those of men.

I should have done things differently.

This is one of the thoughts that Peter Kent cannot stop thinking as he eats chicken teriyaki for lunch in the psychiatric ward's dining room, or walks down the long, gray-carpeted hallway. He has a mental image of himself talking on the telephone, listening to his fiancée tell him it is over. He can see himself calling a few weeks later, hearing the metallic whir of her answering machine, her voice saying (impossibly, astoundingly), "You have reached the residence of Mr. and Mrs. . . ."

There were other things—events that, though he did not know it at the time, were leading him toward this spinning descent. Problems in his medical practice. Arguments with a friend. Indeed, there is the matter of his illness seven years ago, an episode of mania that lasted for several weeks, causing him to believe that a stranger was, in fact, his father in disguise. Yet none of these things is, in itself, an explanation, a solution to the riddle of "Why here, why now?"

Tracing the origins of mood disorders, illnesses that affect not only behavior and physiology but our very sense of ourselves, is a formidable task. For mind and body are inextricably joined, and everything we imagine, dream, experience or fear is ultimately translated into the firing of nerve cells and the ebb and flow of chemicals in the brain. How do we sort out the events that began internally, in a strip of DNA or a malfunctioning neuron, from those that have their roots in external events: A broken love affair, the death of a friend, the loss of a job? It is with this conundrum that scientists who would understand mental illness struggle. The answers that emerge are always somewhat murky, always two-sided, always a compromise of nature and nurture—which, after all, work hand in hand.

Yet there are some certainties. Researchers now know, for example, that certain forms of mood disorder—specifically manic depression and severe, recurrent, unipolar depression—run in families. This fact is demonstrated by dozens of research projects, including a 1986 study that examined the family pedigrees of depressed adults adopted as children and found an increased incidence of mood disorders in biological, as opposed to adoptive, relatives. As Columbia University's Weissman puts it: "Depression is a family affair."

Both depression and mania are also accompanied by changes in brain chemistry, though these changes are not fully understood. In the early days of research, scientists thought in terms of relatively simple models of chemical imbalance: Depression, for example, was thought to stem from an insufficiency of norepinephrine, one of many substances mediating the transmission of nerve impulses in the brain. Now, few experts talk about "too much" or "too little" of a single chemical. Instead, they believe mood disorders are the result of a complex interplay among a variety of chemicals, including neurotransmitters and hormones.

Genetic legacy

How much of this is influenced by heredity? The consensus is that genetic factors are at work, and in the last few years, laboratories all over the world have set out to track down the gene, or multiple genes acting in concert, that predispose an individual to depression or manic depression. This search has proceeded in fits and starts. Discoveries are announced, only to be called into question when other scientists fail to duplicate the findings. Most recently, the highly publicized results of a 1987 study of manic depression in the Amish—results that seemed to locate the gene for the illness on the short arm of chromosome 11—fell through when a research team re-analyzed the Amish pedigree, adding new subjects.

The team, which included some of the original researchers, concluded in an article published in *Nature* last November that while the evidence for a genetic marker in the Amish is still strong, the chances are slim that it is on chromosome 11. Another study, this one of an Israeli family, linked the gene for manic depression to the X chromosome. But so far, attempts to replicate this association have also been unsuccessful. Nonetheless, few researchers doubt that genetic studies will eventually yield results.

TAILORING TREATMENT FOR DEPRESSION'S MANY FORMS

Drugs and psychotherapy are targeting specific symptoms

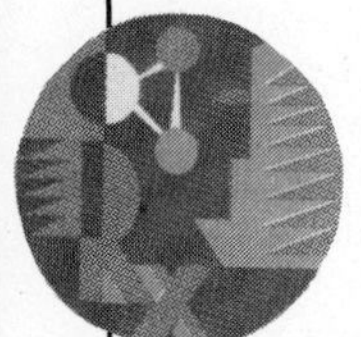

A hot bath or some friendly encouragement may be all it takes to banish a normal case of the blues. But the "black dog" of depression, as Winston Churchill once described it, does not respond to jollying, distraction, or well-meaning exhortation. A depressed person cannot merely "cheer up" or "snap out of it." Yet depressive illnesses are eminently treatable, and with expert assistance—including medication, psychotherapy and in some cases hospitalization—up to 80 percent of patients can get better.

Antidepressant drugs form a cornerstone of therapy for mood disorders because they work relatively quickly (most show their effects in two to three weeks) and often produce dramatic results in launching patients on their way back to health. Today, doctors have a wider range of drugs to choose from than in the past. More than 20 antidepressants are available by prescription, and new drugs, with fewer side effects and more-specific action, are being tested in the laboratory. Perhaps just as important, professionals are noticing a change in patients' attitudes toward mood-elevating drugs. Says Dr. Daniel X. Freedman, Judson Braun Professor of Psychiatry at the University of California at Los Angeles: "You see fewer patients who pit themselves against the medicine, as if their integrity or ability to exercise willpower were at issue."

Chemistry of mood. Antidepressants work by altering the levels of brain chemicals, and different drugs target different substances when they first enter the brain. Scientists are finding that these highly specific effects make some classes of drugs more helpful than others in treating various types of depression. The so-called tricyclic antidepressants, for example, appear more effective in combatting the disturbed sleep patterns, apathy and appetite loss of melancholic depression. Another group of drugs, the "monoamine oxidase inhibitors," seem to work well for patients suffering from "atypical depression," that is, eating and sleeping more than usual, rather than less.

Of particular interest to psychiatrists are two drugs that recently entered the market. Prozac and Anafranil both act principally to increase brain levels of serotonin, a neurotransmitter that scientists believe plays a role in some forms of depression. Anafranil just received approval by the Food and Drug Administration in January and is expected to be available in pharmacies this month. Prozac, approved in 1987, has fewer side effects than most antidepressants, is energizing rather than sedating and has proved much less toxic in overdoses—a boon since antidepressants are often used in suicide attempts. A third drug, Wellbutrin, has a unique chemical structure and also produces fewer side effects than most mood-elevating medications.

For some years, the gold standard in treatment for mania's frenetic highs has been lithium carbonate, a salt that was in use as a therapy for gout in the 1950s when an Australian researcher noticed its quieting effects. Lithium works well for about 70 percent of patients in the manic phase of "bipolar" disorder, and can act as an antidepressant as well. Now, however, two antiseizure drugs—carbamazepine and valproic acid—also provide relief for some manic patients when lithium doesn't, and they can be combined with lithium for greater effect. Says Dr. Victor Reus, professor of psychiatry at the University of California at San Francisco: "We are clearly much more sophisticated in the recognition and treatment of bipolar depression than we were even five years ago."

Yet as effective as they are, psychiatric drugs are far from perfect. All have side effects, most commonly annoyances such as dry mouth and constipation, but in rare cases there can be more serious consequences. Nor does medication work for everyone. Some people don't respond to drugs; others find side effects intolerable. Experts caution that once you find a drug that works, it's important to stay on it long enough. Dr. David Kupfer, of Western Psychiatric Institute in Pittsburgh, recommends taking an antidepressant for at least four months after the major symptoms of depression disappear. Studies show that this decreases the chance of falling ill again.

When drugs aren't right. Sometimes using any drug is too risky. Elderly patients often react unpredictably to medicine, for example, and sometimes the risk of suicide precludes waiting the weeks needed for a given drug to take effect. In these cases, psychiatrists may turn to electroconvulsive therapy (ECT), a technique still recovering from the dubious reputation it acquired in the 1960s. ECT has been refined in recent years, and generally works quickly. Like drugs, however, it can have side effects: Patients may suffer memory loss and confusion right after treatment, and there are reports of longer-term memory problems.

Other innovative treatment methods for specific forms of depression have sprung up in recent years. In light therapy, for example, patients sit for a few hours each day in front of very bright, full-spectrum lights, a tactic found effective for sufferers of seasonal affective disorder.

Though medication plays an important role in treating severe depression, few experts would argue that it is, by itself, sufficient. Indeed, some types of moderate or mild depression may respond to talking therapy alone. The consensus is, however, that in most serious cases drugs and psychotherapy complement each other and are best used jointly. A recent National Institute of Mental Health study demonstrated that two forms of short-term psychotherapy—cognitive therapy, which helps change negative patterns of thinking, and interpersonal therapy, which addresses problems in personal relationships—are effective even in treating severe depression. They work more slowly than a standard antidepressant, however. Other kinds of brief therapy, including those that draw their guiding principles from psychoanalysis, may also succeed, but they have not yet undergone as much rigorous study. Ultimately, Dr. T. Byram Karasu suggests in this month's *American Journal of Psychiatry,* research on talking therapies may reveal that each has specific strengths, allowing therapists to pick and choose, tailoring psychotherapy to an individual patient's needs.

Even when they do, however, heredity will not tell the whole story. Depression and manic depression appear to be triggered by stress. And in some milder forms of mood disorder, experience—rather than genetics—may play the starring role. Traumatic events clearly are capable of precipitating changes in mood and behavior. In particular, scientists consistently find that being the child of a depressed parent may double or even triple the risk of depression in later life. Parents who suffer from depressive illnesses, these studies indicate, are more likely to be withdrawn, critical, inconsistent and irritable in child-rearing. Their own pain, expressed in this way, may thus become a burden for their offspring. According to a new report published last month, some children in this difficult atmosphere develop intense, exaggerated feelings of guilt—states of mind that then pave the way for depression and other emotional problems.

Losses in childhood

Perhaps most devastating is the loss of a parent in childhood, either through death or abandonment. The evidence suggests, according to British psychoanalyst John Bowlby, that those who have lost a parent, especially the mother, are more likely to develop serious psychiatric problems and, more specifically, to become psychotically depressed and suicidal. Work by University of London researchers George Brown and Tirril Harris demonstrates that women who lose their mothers before the age of 17 are significantly more prone to depression as adults. The crucial factor, Brown and Harris say, is how the father, or parental surrogate, provides for the child: "Inadequate care . . . roughly doubled the risk of depression in adulthood."

Any true understanding of mood disorders must take into account this intricate interplay between psychology and biology. NIMH psychiatrist Dr. Robert Post and others have done just that in the theory of "kindling," an attempt to explain the fact that episodes of mania

RESOURCES AND INFORMATION ON DEPRESSION

Help is readily available for the millions who suffer

The warning signs of depression:

- Persistent sad, anxious or empty mood
- Feeling hopeless or worthless
- Loss of interest or pleasure in activities, including sex
- Sleep disturbances (early-morning waking or oversleeping)
- Decreased appetite, losing weight or eating more than usual
- Recurrent thoughts of death or suicide
- Difficulty concentrating, remembering, making decisions
- Irritability, excessive crying
- Physical symptoms such as headaches, digestive disorders, nausea or chronic pain

The warning signs of mania:

- Increased energy and decreased need for sleep
- Unrealistic or exaggerated beliefs in abilities
- Inappropriate elation
- Increased talking, moving and sexual activity
- Racing thoughts
- Impulsive behavior without regard to consequences

Where to go for help:

- See your family doctor to rule out other illnesses
- Medical-school psychiatry department
- Community mental-health center
- Local mental-health association

JEAN TUTTLE FOR USN&WR

The National Alliance for the Mentally Ill (NAMI)
P.O. Box NAMI-Depression
Arlington, Va. 22216

DEPRESSION/Awareness, Recognition, Treatment (D/ART)
National Institute of Mental Health
Rockville, Md. 20857

National Depressive and Manic Depressive Association
53 West Jackson Blvd.
Box USN
Chicago, Ill. 60604

National Mental Health Association
Information Center
1021 Prince Street
Alexandria, Va. 22314

The National Foundation for Depressive Illness
P.O. Box 2257
New York, N.Y. 10116
Include $5 and a self-addressed, stamped envelope for literature

American Psychiatric Association
1400 K Street, N.W.
Suite 501—Dept. USN
Washington, D.C. 20005
Include a self-addressed, stamped envelope for literature

National Association for Research on Schizophrenia and Depression
60 Cutter Mill Road, Suite 200
Great Neck, N.Y. 11021

Books

Depression and Its Treatment: Help for the Nation's #1 Mental Problem, by John H. Greist, M.D., and James W. Jefferson, M.D. (American Psychiatric Press, Washington, D.C., 1984; $7.95).

Overcoming Depression, by Demitri F. Papolos, M.D., and Janice Papolos (Harper & Row, New York, 1987; $9.95).

Control Your Depression, by Peter M. Lewinsohn et al. (Prentice Hall Press, New York, 1986; $9.95).

Feeling Good: The New Mood Therapy, by David D. Burns, M.D. (New American Library, New York, 1980; $4.95).

Do You Have a Depressive Illness? by Donald F. Klein, M.D., and Paul H. Wender, M.D. (New American Library, New York, 1988; $7.95).

Is Your Child Depressed? by Joel Herskowitz, M.D. (Pharos Books, New York, 1988; $14.95).

and depression appear initially in response to some external stress, but later seem to acquire a momentum of their own. Repeated low-level stresses, Post suggests, might build up until they trigger a manic swing in mood, much as experimenters can "kindle" seizures in the brain by delivering low-level electrical shocks to cells deep in its interior. Or conversely, the brain may become progressively "sensitized" to the effect of environmental stress. Eventually, bouts of illness may occur with no help from outside events.

Such analogies are approximations, hypothetical road maps for an as yet uncharted territory. Yet those who suffer in depression's depths or negotiate mania's precarious heights may count themselves fortunate. Emerging from their illness is not dependent upon perfect scientific knowledge, and tools for treatment are already in hand.

What will happen when he goes home?

Peter Kent's psychiatrist at the hospital asks him this. The nurses who monitor his mood, who cajole and counsel him, who keep track of how much he eats and whether he wakes up at night, ask him this as well. His chances of full recovery are good, but not assured. Perhaps 30 percent of severely depressed patients "get better on antidepressants but do not get completely well," says Dr. Jan Fawcett, chairman of psychiatry at Rush Presbyterian–St. Luke's Medical Center in Chicago.

Leaving the hospital, Kent will rest for a while, filling his time with volunteer work before returning to his medical practice. In part, how the cardiologist fares will be determined by other people. His colleagues. His friends. Can they accept a doctor who has become a patient? He has his doubts: "They would look at it negatively," he says. "It's best if they don't find out." Yet it is possible, though far from certain, that Kent is mistaken and that he will find good will where he expects ostracism or disdain. It is possible that the time for secrecy is nearly over, that what Styron has called "Darkness Visible" is, at last, an illness like any other.

---

by Erica E. Goode
with Nancy Linnon and Sarah Burke

THE TRUSTING HEART

Type As, take note: Ambition won't kill you; it's hostility that can be fatal.

Redford Williams, M.D.

Redford Williams, M.D., has specialized in various aspects of behavioral medicine and research for more than two decades. He is professor of psychiatry, associate professor of medicine, and director of the Behavioral Medicine Research Center at Duke University Medical Center in Durham, North Carolina.

We have always been encouraged to have trusting hearts. This is what the world's religions have taught for well over two thousands years, and, more personally, what our parents and teachers have tried to instill in us. Now there is another reason: Scientific evidence shows that trusting hearts live longer, healthier lives.

This breakthrough stems from the ongoing research on what has come to be known as Type A behavior. As a result of the pioneering work of two San Francisco cardiologists, Meyer Friedman and Ray Rosenman, nearly every American is now aware that Type As are people who are always in a hurry, keenly ambitious and competitive, and easily moved to hostility and anger by everyday annoyances. Nearly everyone also has come to believe that Type As are at much higher risk of suffering a heart attack or dying from coronary disease than their less impatient, less competitive, and less hostile Type B counterparts.

Just as the American public was about ready to add Type A behavior to the list of those risk factors—smoking, high cholesterol levels, high blood pressure, and too little physical exercise—needing attention in their self-improvement programs, reports began to appear suggesting that perhaps the Type A story was not as simple as it had first seemed. Many studies, for example, failed to find increased risk of heart attacks in Type As.

The confusion occasioned by these negative studies, which began to appear in the late '70s, is now starting to clear—the result of major research efforts at various centers around the United States aimed at clarifying and refining our understanding of the relationship between Type A behavior and coronary heart disease.

As an active participant in this "second generation" research, I believe the findings are now sufficiently clear that we can be confident in telling you the good news and the bad news about Type A behavior. The good news is this: Not all aspects of Type A behavior are equally toxic. It now seems clear that being in a hurry and being ambitious and competitive are not, taken alone, putting you at risk of having a heart attack or dying from coronary disease.

Now for the bad news: Hostility, anger, and their biological consequences are the toxic part of Type A behavior. Hostility and anger not only account for the increased risk of developing coronary heart disease among Type A persons, but may also increase the risk of suffering other life-threatening illnesses as well. The other aspects of Type A behavior—such as being in a hurry and being competitive—appear to be harmful only to the extent that they activate one's hostility and anger.

It follows, therefore, that the most important thing you can do to decrease your coronary risk if you are a Type A person is to learn to reduce your hostility and anger.

The driving force behind hostility is a cynical mistrust of others. Expecting that others will mistreat us, we are on the lookout for their bad behavior—and we can usually find it. This generates the frequent anger to which the hostile person is prone, and that anger, combined with a lack of empathy for others—a natural consequence of the poor opinion we hold of others in general—leads us to express our hostility overtly, in the form of aggressive acts toward others.

Probably the most characteristic attitude of the person with high levels of cynical mistrust is suspicion of the motives of people he or she doesn't even know. Imagine you are waiting for an elevator and the elevator stops two floors

From *New Age Journal,* May/June 1989, pp. 26-30, 101. Adapted from *The Trusting Heart,* by Redford Williams, M.D.

above for a bit longer than normal. You may begin to think, "How inconsiderate! You'd think if people wanted to carry on a conversation, they'd get off the elevator so the rest of us could get to where we're going!" You cannot see the people two floors above you, you cannot hear them, and you have no way of knowing what is really holding up the elevator. Yet, in the span of a few seconds, your cynical mistrust has led you to draw hostile conclusions about the unseen people in the elevator, their selfish motives, and their inconsiderate behavior.

When expressed toward loved ones, cynical mistrust can have especially undesirable effects. Even if you don't utter a word, the anger or disgust you feel is written on your face. The message you give to your husband, wife, or child is that he or she is incompetent, that you believe he or she did it on purpose, and that he or she is in danger of being rejected by you.

What's worse still, these kinds of communication have effects on the behavior of others, causing them to act in ways that meet our expectations, to fulfill our cynical prophecies.

And what about people whose cynicism is so high that anger is experienced too often? If the thoughts I described earlier are the "words" of hostility, then emotions—the intense feelings of irritation, rage, frustration, of wanting to lash out at the source of these feelings—are the "music" of hostility.

YOU CAN TELL when the thoughts indicative of cynical mistrust are generating anger in you not only by the appearance of the emotions just described, but also by the increasing physical symptoms of the fight-flight response. These symptoms, most of which stem from the effects of the outpouring of adrenalin (epinephrine), include a change in your voice to a higher pitch (adrenalin tightens your vocal chords), an increase in the rate and depth of your breathing, an awareness that your heart is racing and beating harder, a sensation of tightness in the muscles of your arms and legs, and a general feeling of being "charged up," ready for intense action.

If you frequently experience these feelings, it is likely that your anger quotient is too high, so high that you may belong to the group that is at increased risk of developing serious health problems in the future. Indeed, it is likely that the hormones—epinephrine, norepinephrine, and cortisol—poured out during these anger episodes produce long-term biological consequences, leading over time to disease.

It is also possible that less-than-efficient stifling of these hormonal effects by the calming branch of your nervous system could affect the biological pathway to disease. By leaving you at the continuing mercy of the unpleasant effects of adrenalin on your body, your weak calming branch could also be responsible in part for your feeling a need to do something "extra" to reduce these distressing feelings.

This need is the source of another toxic aspect of hostility: the aggressive behavior that results when the pressure from our cynical thoughts and anger becomes too much to bear without doing something, usually some kind of aggressive act directed toward the person who has gotten our cynical thoughts going.

Probably the most characteristic attitude of the person with high levels of cynical mistrust is suspicion of the motives of people he or she doesn't even know.

Over time, sadly, it becomes easier for the hostile heart to express anger toward family members or friends; most people manage to bridle their anger in the company of complete strangers. However, have you been known to express your irritation to someone you never saw before two minutes ago? This can take the form of addressing that person, ranging from the mild ("I believe you have too many items in your basket for this express checkout line") to the not-so-mild ("Hey, you can't go through this line with that many items!"). It can also take the form of turning around to the person behind you, pointing to the sign above the line, and grimacing.

The first clue that your behavior in a given situation is hostile can be gleaned from your answer to the question, "What is my purpose in doing this?" If at least part of your purpose is to punish the other person, to make him or her feel bad for what he or she has done, then you are guilty as charged—even if another part of your purpose is to achieve some reasonable goal of your own. If "righteous indignation" describes your state of mind as you say what you say or do what you do, it is highly likely that your intention is at least in part hostile.

It *is* possible to reduce our hostility, to become more trusting. I believe this not only because of my own experiences, but also because of some very important research conducted by Meyer Friedman. In this study, the Recurrent Coronary Prevention Project (RCPP), Friedman and his colleagues recruited one thousand male heart attack victims—all Type As—to participate in a study evaluating various preventive approaches following a heart attack. Two thirds of the men, about 650, were randomly assigned to a behavior-modification treatment program designed to reduce both the time-urgency and free-floating-hostility aspects of their Type A behavior; the other third, about 350 men, were assigned to a standard, state-of-the-art cardiac rehabilitation program.

After the treatment programs were completed, independent assessments showed that the men in the behavior modification group had decreased their Type A behavior (both time urgency and hostility) by a substantial degree. Those in the standard cardiac rehabilitation group had also decreased their Type A behavior, but to a much smaller extent. These results provided strong evidence that it is possible to reduce the time-urgency and hostility components of the Type A behavior pattern.

More important, there was a significant reduction in the rate of recurrent heart problems in the behavior modification group. Subsequent follow-up of the men in the RCPP has also found reduced mortality rates in the behavior modification group. So, it is possible to change some aspects of Type A behavior, and, at least in men who had a heart attack, this change appears associated with a better prognosis.

These findings, suggesting that behavior changes *following* a heart attack may reduce the risk of having a second attack, support the theory that reducing hostility should be beneficial in preventing a first heart attack. Indeed, it is in this area of primary prevention—avoiding the initial development of disease—that the greatest potential benefits are to be found.

TO HAVE A MORE TRUSTING heart is not easy. It requires you to work toward three separate but related goals:

• Reduce your cynical mistrust of the motives of others.

• Reduce the frequency and intensity with which you experience negative emotions of anger, irritation, frustration, rage, and the like.

• Rather than behaving aggressively toward others, learn to treat others with kindness and consideration. Develop your positive assertiveness skills for use in those unavoidable situations.

In other words, to have a more trusting heart, you will need to change your thoughts, your feelings, and your actions. Sound difficult? To help you, I've devised the following twelve-step program:

❤

Step One: *Monitor Your Cynical Thoughts*

To learn more about the frequency and kinds of situations that trigger your cynical thoughts, carry around with you a little pocket notebook—your hostility log. Whenever you realize you are thinking cynical thoughts, make an entry. Every entry should include the time and place, who did what to stimulate the cynical thoughts, the actual thoughts that went through your head, the emotions you felt, and any action you took.

Keeping the log will sharpen your ability to recognize your cynical thoughts, angry feelings, and aggressive behavior—and, eventually, help you stop them before they get started.

Review your hostility log at the end of each week, looking for common themes. You may be surprised at how often your hostility is aroused by trivial events. In fact, you are likely to realize that many, perhaps most, of the entries represent situations in which your own cynical mistrust was the major cause of the emotional reaction and the unpleasant behavior that resulted.

❤

Step Two: *Confession Is Good for the Soul*

Remember all those TV ads in which some famous person says, "Hello, I'm__________, and I'm a recovering alcoholic"? As Alcoholics Anonymous has learned through long experience, the open acknowledgement that we have a problem, want to do something about it, and actively seek the support of important people in our lives to do so can play a major role in our ultimate success. Therefore, let your spouse or a close friend know that you have recognized you have a hard time controlling your hostility, and that you hope he or she will be supportive of your efforts to change.

Your acknowledgement of your problem is an act of trust—and trusting thoughts and behavior can promote beneficial effects. If the other person is able to be supportive and help you in your efforts, you will in essence be rewarded for being more trusting.

When you notice the cynical thoughts starting to build, simply start to meditate right there, wherever you are.

❤

Step Three: *Stop Those Thoughts!*

How do you stop them? Simply tell them to stop. "Thought stopping" is a well-known behavior modification technique that has proven effective in helping patients who excessively ruminate on the same thought all day long.

Here is how it works:

As soon as you realize you are having cynical thoughts, yell as loudly as you can (in your mind), "STOP!" Those thoughts *will* actually stop, and, if you are lucky, the anger also will be cut short. If the thoughts start when you are alone, by all means go ahead and yell out loud, at the top of your lungs, "STOP!"

❤

Step Four: *Reason With Yourself*

You are a rational being, so go ahead and try to reason with yourself. When cynical thoughts begin as you stand in a bank line, start a silent speech to yourself that goes something like this:

"All right, you suspicious person, here you go again, laying all these nefarious intentions on that little old lady. Lighten up! You know darn well she didn't get out of bed this morning saying to herself, '(Insert your name) has to deposit his check down at the bank today. I'll just follow him down there, jump ahead of him in line, and really take forever. I won't even have a pen to fill out my deposit slip. I can't wait to see him burn when I get there ahead of him in line.' "

You *know* that that elderly woman didn't really arise this morning with the main goal in her life being to get your goat. The rational approach—even if it isn't the whole solution—is worth the help it can offer.

❤

Step Five: *Put Yourself in the Other Person's Shoes*

With your silent monologue in the bank line, you also were accomplishing something else: a feeling of empathy. When you put yourself in the elderly woman's shoes in a joking way, imagining that she planned her day around irritating you, you could not avoid seeing how ridiculous your suspicions about her motives actually were. You might also gain the same sense of perspective by trying to understand another person's behavior from his or her viewpoint; in most cases, you will find your anger slipping away. Empathy and cynical anger are incompatible.

❤

Step Six: *Learn to Laugh at Yourself*

You were doing something else in that silent monologue: You were laughing at yourself. You were making fun of your own suspicious nature, perhaps even smiling as you went through the patently silly scenario of this elderly woman planning her day around aggravating you. Humor is a fine strategy for deflecting your cynical mistrust and defusing your anger.

❤

Step Seven: *Learn to Relax*

If you can't arrest your cynical thoughts by "thought stopping," by reasoning with yourself, or even by laughing at yourself, then it may be time for you to call upon a powerful technique that has been used for centuries to gain control over one's thoughts: meditation.

But to become proficient enough in this relaxation technique to be able to call upon it at will, you'll need to practice it regularly—even at times when you aren't "stressed out."

To begin a meditation, sit quietly and upright in a comfortable chair. Let your chin rest comfortably on your chest, your arms in your lap. Close your eyes. Begin to pay attention to your breathing. Every time you inhale and every time you exhale, pay attention to the sensations of air flowing across the membranes in your nose and mouth, the feeling of your lungs filling and emptying.

After you have done this for a few breaths, begin to repeat silently to yourself a single word every time you breathe out. The word you choose doesn't have to mean anything in particular. It can be a nonsense word you make up, or simply the number *one*. Try a word that conjures up the emotion you are trying to evoke through this strategy: *peace, love, trust,* or *patience.* Try several different words to see what works best for you.

Initially, you will find that thoughts intrude and that soon you are off on a thought stream, no longer attending to your breathing and saying the word you chose. Don't worry; just return to paying attention to your breathing and saying the word with each exhalation. As time goes on, and with practice, intruding thoughts will become less of a problem.

After you have practiced meditation for about ten to fifteen minutes twice daily for one to two weeks, you will be ready for a shortened version that can help you stop the cynical thoughts out in the "real world." When you notice the cynical thoughts starting to build, simply start to meditate *right there,* wherever you are. You don't have to go into a lotus position, close your eyes, or do anything that is going to make you look foolish in public. Just fix your attention on some object nearby, attend to your breathing, and say your word silently every time you breathe out. Do this until the elevator comes, until you get to the head of the bank or supermarket line, or whenever the need arises.

This will draw your mind's eye away from the habitual pattern of your cynical thoughts. It will counter the anger you might be feeling, if your thoughts have already progressed to that stage. It will also calm your cardiovascular system, as well as other bodily systems involved in responding to stress.

❤

Step Eight: *Practice Trust*

I alluded earlier to the potential benefits of trusting other people, when I suggested that you solicit the help of a spouse or friend. It is a valuable strategy.

Begin by looking for opportunities in which, if you trust someone else and it doesn't work out, no real harm will have been done. For example, if you are a cynical sort, you probably don't trust the airline ticket agent to assign you a good seat—you simply tell him or her you want, say, seat 14C.

Use such a situation to practice trust. When you get up to the check-in counter at the airport, instead of demanding "14C!" try saying, "Oh, whatever seat you pick is fine with me." I'll bet that, more times than not, you'll end up in a better seat than the one you would have picked for yourself.

❤

Step Nine: *Learn to Listen*

When you break in on someone during a conversation, it sends the message that *your* ideas are more important than his or hers. Done often enough, this causes others to withdraw from you, since you are telling them by your behavior that you have no interest in their words or ideas.

To prevent this, learn to listen. If you have to, force yourself to keep your mouth shut until the other person is finished. If what you planned to say is important enough, you'll remember to say it later. Your attentive posture will send this message to the other person: I value you and your ideas. It's irresistible, and it certainly will help focus that person's attention on you when it's your turn to speak.

❤

Step Ten: *Learn to Be Assertive*

When you are truly being mistreated by another person, what should you do? Any normal human being will become angry when mistreated badly enough.

If the offending person is not someone with whom you will need to have further contact in the future, the best response is probably to put a check beside that person's name in your mental notebook and resolve to have as little to do with him or her as possible. It is hard enough to learn to be more trusting yourself, without having to contend with others who are unwilling or unable to make the same effort. Still, it will be good practice for you to treat such people as well as you can when it is impossible to avoid them.

But what if the offending person is someone you will not be able to avoid—a close family member, a coworker, or a person who, despite his or her hostility, has other redeeming features that make you want to keep his or her friendship? Here is where the neglected art of assertiveness comes to the rescue.

It is one thing to lash out aggressively at another in a way that gives that person the message that he or she is uniformly bad. It is quite another thing to inform the person, calmly and without rancor, what it is specifically about his or her behavior—notice I said *behavior,* not *personality* or *innate selfishness*—that is bothering you, and why. This approach has the advantage of providing the other person an attainable goal: Even if his or her personality is pretty well fixed, nearly everyone is capable of changing specific behaviors, especially if you ask in a nice way.

❤

Step Eleven: *Pretend Today Is Your Last*

If you are still finding it hard to put these suggested changes into effect, you might try this strategy: Pretend you have just learned you have a fatal illness and that you have only a few weeks, or even one day, to live.

Many times, when I interview heart patients and ask them about anger and how they handle it, I hear, "Oh, I used to get angry a lot, but since my heart attack I've realized that all these nitpicking things that used to rile me so aren't really worth the candle."

Why wait until you've had a heart attack to start doing something about your hostility?

❤

Step Twelve: *Practice Forgiveness*

One final strategy: Simply forgive those who have mistreated and/or angered you. Rather than continuing to resent them and to seek revenge, try to understand the emotions of those who have wronged you. You may find that the weight of anger lifts from your shoulders, easing your pain and also helping you to forget the wrong.

These are steps you can take yourself. Like anyone trying to learn new skills, you may find the going rough at times. Most medical schools, and many of our larger hospitals, have rehabilitation programs for heart patients (and wellness programs for healthy folks). If you feel that extra help would benefit you, seek out one of these programs. Many of them employ group sessions, which appear to be effective because they enable hostile persons to realize that they are not alone in their cynical beliefs, and to profit from the experience of others.

WHEN STRESS BECOMES DISTRESS

Your best friend just told you she's been going to a therapist. *A therapist?* you think. *Well, she's always been a little crazy, but not that kind of crazy. Why would she need to see a therapist?* You always thought that people going for therapy became dependent on their therapist—going week after week, year after year, getting help with every decision. And your mom always told you only sick people need therapy. "Not people like us," she said. "We can handle our own problems." But your best friend isn't sick, so how do you explain this?

The truth is, the majority of people in therapy in the United States are not disabled by emotional or mental difficulties but need help with the stresses they find in everyday living. Even the most mentally healthy among us has difficulty coping now and then. Your friend isn't sick or weak, she's just resourceful enough to reach out for help when she feels she isn't coping well and needs some support.

And there's no need to worry she'll become dependent on her psychotherapist. According to Richard Ketai, MD, director of Middlesex Memorial Hospital's Community Mental Health Clinic (CMHC), 90% of people who see a psychiatrist or psychotherapist do so only 10-12 times. Clinic Psychologist Bob Reynolds assures that patients do not learn to rely on their therapist for advice. The idea behind psychotherapy, he explains, is to help patients discover what they need to do for themselves.

Anyone, regardless of age, sex, race, religion, occupation or economic status, can develop an emotional or mental problem that requires professional help. In addition, according to the American Psychiatric Association, one in five Americans suffers from a clearly diagnosable mental disorder involving a degree of incapacity that interferes with employment, education or daily life.

Fortunately, we've come a long way since the days when people with any hint of mental illness were stoned, burned at the stake or warehoused in insane asylums. Over the past quarter century especially, researchers have made great strides in the diagnosis and treatment of mental illness. They are now fairly certain that many psychiatric disorders have physical causes, such as chemical imbalance in the brain.

Medications have proven to be very effective in controlling or eliminating the symptoms due to chemical imbalance. Very often, medication is prescribed in combination with psychotherapy, which is a kind of "talk therapy" that helps people to better understand themselves and their problems and to change their lives in beneficial ways.

Psychiatrists, who are medical doctors specializing in the diagnosis and treatment of mental and emotional illness, can prescribe medicines as well as provide psychotherapy. Psychologists and many social workers are also trained to use psychotherapy to help people cope with their mental illness or help healthier people cope with crises and other stressful aspects of everyday living.

Middlesex Memorial Hospital's Department of Psychiatry provides a full range of mental health services for Middlesex County area residents of all ages, including inpatient psychiatric care, outpatient mental health services, and both inpatient and outpatient substance abuse treatment.

When Hospitalization Is Needed

The Hospital's inpatient Psychiatric Unit is a short-term, intensive-treatment, 28-bed Unit. A person with an emotional or mental problem might be admitted to the Unit by a psychiatrist if he (or she) is unable to adequately control symptoms outside the Hospital, needs to be observed more closely for diagnosis or regulation of medication, presents a danger to himself, or has lost touch with reality. Patients come to Middlesex Memorial on a voluntary basis. "They may be reluctant," says

From *Healthline*, Spring 1990, pp. 2-5. *Healthline*, published by Middlesex Hospital, Department of Public Relations, Middletown, CT 06457.

Department of Psychiatry Chairman Gerald Burke, MD, "but they realize there is a problem and are willing to come for help."

Twenty-two beds are reserved for patients who are able to be up and dressed and participate in the Unit's therapeutic programs. Six beds make up the Psychiatric Observation Unit, which is for patients who are more acutely ill or psychotic (out of touch with reality), patients who are elderly or infirm and need a more hospital-like environment, or patients who might be a danger to themselves. The Psychiatric Unit does not accept patients who are assaultive, homicidal, or unwilling to stop abusing alcohol or drugs.

What are the benefits of hospitalization for someone with a psychiatric illness? In addition to giving the physician a chance to observe the patient more closely and better regulate medication, he or she can also order diagnostic tests and evaluations. Another benefit of hospitalization is that it removes the patient from the situation he is in. "We rarely look at a psychiatric disorder as an isolated kind of thing; it takes place within a family, within a job, within an environment. And very often, the stress is in the environment," explains Dr. Burke. "Hospitalization removes the patient from the environment and gives him a chance to sort things out."

He continues: "Family members and co-workers might be fed up, impatient or incapable of understanding. The staff in the Psychiatric Unit is more accepting of psychiatric illness, more understanding about its manifestations, and more willing to help the patient work out his problems."

The Psychiatric Unit has a very active therapy program, which keeps the patients meaningfully involved all day. Dr. Burke explains why: "You'll find, on units like this, that the more structure you have, the less chance there is of patients decompensating or acting in self-destructive ways. We minimize these problems by keeping our patients involved and interacting."

Patients in the Psychiatric Unit participate in various kinds of group activity designed to help in their recovery, including group psychotherapy, art therapy, assertiveness-training, communication skills and life skills. There is also an activity-planning group, in which patients and staff plan weekend activities; a transition group, to help patients make the transition from Hospital to home; and recreational therapy, which helps patients make better use of their leisure time. Recreation is also used to encourage socialization and to help patients handle aggression constructively, according to Dr. Burke. The Hospital has memberships at the Middlesex YMCA for patients, who go there with staff members several times a week.

The Unit also offers work therapy, in which patients may work a few hours a day in the Gift Shop or elsewhere in the Hospital. By working, patients begin to rebuild confidence in themselves and feel more comfortable about making the transition from Hospital to home.

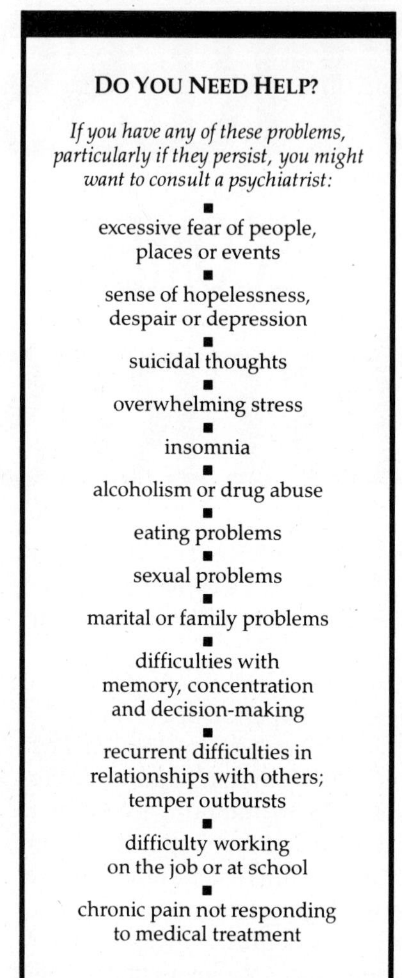

DO YOU NEED HELP?

If you have any of these problems, particularly if they persist, you might want to consult a psychiatrist:

- excessive fear of people, places or events
- sense of hopelessness, despair or depression
- suicidal thoughts
- overwhelming stress
- insomnia
- alcoholism or drug abuse
- eating problems
- sexual problems
- marital or family problems
- difficulties with memory, concentration and decision-making
- recurrent difficulties in relationships with others; temper outbursts
- difficulty working on the job or at school
- chronic pain not responding to medical treatment

Source: Connecticut Psychiatric Society

In addition to a staff of registered nurses and psychiatric technicians, MMH's Psychiatric Unit has two full-time social workers who do patient and family assessments, couples and family therapy, and discharge planning. It also has a three-person occupational therapy staff and a full-time, fully qualified recreational therapist. The medical staff — nine privately practicing psychiatrists with admitting privileges at MMH and four staff psychiatrists — are key players in treating patients in the Psychiatric Unit.

"Our staff works with the patient's private psychiatrist," says Dr. Burke. "Together, we plan treatment — figuring out what will work by assessing the patient's problems and the strengths he has to address those problems — and we review the plan on a weekly basis. The physician and staff work together to address the individual patient's issues."

The average length of stay for a patient in Middlesex Memorial's Psychiatric Unit is 15 days. Usually, after discharge, he will continue therapy on an outpatient basis with his therapist or psychiatrist or with a staff member of the Middlesex Substance Abuse Treatment Center.

In Times of Crisis

For most people, exposure to mental health services first comes in a crisis. Middlesex Memorial Hospital offers a Crisis Intervention Service in its Emergency Department to help people in acute crisis who do not know where else to turn. Assisted by funding from the State Department of Mental Health since January 1987, the Crisis Intervention Service is primarily intended to help indigent, chronically mentally ill people who are brought into the Emergency Room. But because of its location in the Hospital Emergency Room, the Crisis Intervention Service functions as a resource to many in need. Crisis Intervention Workers Joel Shaul and Leanne Hunter are available from 2 p.m. to midnight, every day, to help people resolve acute crises and assist them in getting any additional help they need.

"Many of the people who come to a hospital emergency room don't have medical problems, though they do have problems that need to be addressed," says Shaul, who has a master's degree in social work. "Being a crisis worker here is consistent with the way Middlesex Memorial treats people: People who come in here with non-medical problems are taken seriously; we try to help them all we can."

Often, says Shaul, "We help basically healthy people who are reacting to the stress of a really bad day." For instance, the crisis workers can provide assistance to family members of critically injured or dying patients who are brought into the Emergency Room. Shaul and Hunter are also called upon to deal with problems such as acute depression and suicide attempts, alcohol and drug abuse, rape, child and spouse abuse, and homelessness. One half to two thirds of the cases the crisis workers become involved with have substance abuse as a co-existing problem, according to Shaul.

When the crisis workers are called upon for assistance, their first role is to evaluate the person and aid the Emergency Room physician in determining what kind of help the patient needs. Some people require only an evaluation and brief follow-up; others are referred to private psychiatrists in the community, to MMH's Community Mental Health Clinic, or to services provided by the State Department of Mental Health. "Psychiatric services are diverse, complicated and confusing to the lay person," says Shaul. "So, we often act as brokers for the mental health system: We have contacts with nearly all the psychiatric providers in the community, and we have a good feeling for who can get help where."

Hunter and Shaul, who are staff members of the Community Mental Health Clinic, also see patients who call the Clinic in a crisis requesting an immediate appointment.

Crisis intervention differs from psychotherapy, according to Shaul, in that its goals are to stabilize the crisis and/or restore the person to his previous level of functioning, whereas the primary goal of psychotherapy is to help a person function better than ever before. "We assess the problem and evaluate how the patient is coping with it, offer some support and follow-up services, and the patient can usually take it on his own from there," explains Hunter. "That's what makes us different — we're not looking to address a long-term need for psychiatric services."

"People end up in an emergency room because they feel very bad suddenly. If their symptoms had grown over time, it is more likely they would have called a mental health clinic or a private psychiatrist and made an appointment for the next opening," Shaul says. "We're more likely to see a person who has a crisis in his life like an argument with his girlfriend and goes to the Portland Bridge to jump off. He never gave any thought to seeking conventional psychiatric services."

He adds: "We are virtually the only mental health professionals in the community available on a walk-in basis at night. We're here to help when people need us."

RIDDEN WITH GUILT

21 clues to unburdening an over-active conscience and building up healthy self-esteem

Joan Borysenko

Joan Borysenko is cofounder of the Mind/Body Clinic at Harvard University and author of Minding the Body, Mending the Mind *(Addison-Wesley, 1986).*

ALL OF US CAN REMEMBER feelings of shame. This incident happened when I was 14. Standing at a bus stop outside school, I felt the inexorable slithering of nylon against flesh. I stood paralyzed with fear. My undies were sliding down my legs and I was about to be revealed as different, unworthy, a loser, a jerk. Mercifully, I was saved by my knobby knees and long skirt, and I retreated into the school before I was discovered.

Shame feels like a sudden severing of our connection with the outside world. It leaves us feeling emotionally naked and revealed as being something other than what we thought we were. It breaks the bridges that bond us to one another and leaves us feeling vulnerable and alone. The feeling of belonging and connectedness with others is basic to a sense of self and shame temporarily destroys that sense. It is so powerful, it has been called the "master emotion" because childhood experiences of shame can determine how we experience other emotions for the rest of our lives.

THE RULE OF THE PACK

Shame is innate. We don't need to learn how to feel ashamed. In its grip we suddenly stop and hold our breath. Our eyes are downcast and we hang our head. There is paralysis of action rather than the attempt to fight or flee. Instead of blood flowing to muscles, it rushes to the skin and we blush, often revealing our vulnerability against our will. We are beaten and we know it. In thinking about why such a powerful physiological reflex occurs, it is interesting to speculate on shame's survival value.

Human beings are social creatures. We are pack animals by nature. If you've ever owned a dog, you know quite a bit about the instinctive behavior of a pack animal. When you yell at Fido for chewing the cord to the refrigerator, he looks submissive and ashamed. He lowers his head, crawls on his belly, beats his tail abjectly against the floor and begs for mercy with his big brown eyes. You are the "top dog" in his pack, and his inherent ability to feel shame when he oversteps his boundaries leads to ritual submissive behavior that calls off attack.

While an analogy between human beings and dogs is necessarily oversimplified, I do believe that shame has survival value in the human social hierarchy as well. I once saw a little boy of about three grabbing at brightly colored packages in the supermarket. His father responded with such an outburst that I was terrified. But in response to the tirade, the little boy hung his head in shame. The father looked at him for a minute, then continued down the aisle. It may be that some abusers find it more difficult to hurt a submissive victim.

Shame also has a higher-order social value. It is a core component of the painful remorse that accompanies healthy guilt. It signals our recognition that we have violated societal standards and is therefore critical to the development of conscience. According to personality theorist Erik Erikson, every three-year-old must come to terms with opposing desires. On the one hand, the child wants his own way. On the other hand, he wants to honor the societal mores he has begun to internalize.

If this stage of psychosocial development is properly completed, the child becomes "socialized to the pack" and understands that his own wants are secondary to a greater good. He has learned to experience healthy guilt. As we grow up, healthy guilt and its accompanying psychic pain motivate us to take responsibility for our misdeeds in a process of admitting our mistake, reflecting honestly on its cause, understanding how it could have been prevented and resolving not to let it happen again. This cycle renews and deepens self-respect. It is called forgiveness. Forgiveness permits us to see our mistakes as opportunities to learn, rather than as proof of how "bad" we are. It is an essential aspect of healthy guilt that enables us to reconnect with our true selves and others.

From *Health*, March 1990, pp. 78-80, 92. From *Guilt Is the Teacher, Love Is the Lesson*, by Joan Borysenko.

SHAME AS A FALSE IDENTITY

While the capacity to feel shame is a requirement for the development of healthy guilt, conscience, compassion and empathy, it can take on a life of its own. In *Shame: The Power of Caring* (Schenkman Books, Inc., 1985), Gershen Kaufman distinguishes between shame as a passing emotion and as an *identity,* where we feel alienated, deficient, despairing and helpless in general, rather than as a reaction to a specific event.

The latter kind of shame signals the loss of our true identity and value as a human being. We feel incapable of forgiving ourselves. Our real and imagined "crimes" fester within us and become incorporated into our beings. We see ourselves as flawed, inferior. Having a shame-based identity in turn gives rise to distorted thinking: "No one could love me as I am. I need something outside myself to be whole and okay."

This skewed thinking can lead to a whole range of addictive behaviors. Whether we choose to recover a temporary sense of power and connectedness through alcohol, drugs, sex, work, perfectionism, dependent or controlling relationships or even some forms of religious belief and practice, we are really seeking the same thing: self-respect and a connectedness with a larger frame of meaning.

The cure for shame and guilt-ridden behavior begins with psychological self-awareness and behavior change but goes beyond that to a reconnection with the spirit, the source of our being. Spiritual connection is the polar opposite of the isolated, unworthy feeling of unhealthy shame. This is why the so-called 12-step programs, offered by Alcoholics Anonymous and other groups that are not only psychologically sophisticated but also spiritually based, are such a potent force for healing shame and addiction.

RELIEVING THE BURDEN OF TOO MUCH SHAME

The first step toward recovering from a shame-based identity is identifying its attributes. Below are 21 such characteristics. Recognizing any of these within yourself is not an invitation to self-criticism. It is an opening for self-awareness.

1 *I really know how to worry.* The immediate escalation of any event into a world-class catastrophe is what psychologist Albert Ellis calls "awfulizing." With little or no objective evidence we come to conclusions of unprecedented gloom and doom. This kind of worry is the outer projection of our innermost fear—that of our own destruction. For without the knowledge of love, fear is all that remains and we can never feel safe.

2 *I'm overcommitted.* Overcommitment is based on the illusion that we can recapture our love, and that of others, by collecting achievements that prove our worth. Furthermore, overcommitment is an addiction that keeps us anesthetized to the anxious, empty feelings that inevitably surface if we are left alone without distractions. It also blocks the process of recovery.

3 *I'm a compulsive helper.* In reaching out to others, we naturally try to give them the love we so desperately need ourselves, but since we don't know how to love ourselves, our attempts to save others often backfire.

4 *I'm always apologizing.* Feeling that everyone else is the judge and jury of our souls, we apologize continually, often making ourselves obnoxious.

5 *I often wake up feeling anxious or am anxious for days or weeks.* We worry about all the things we might have done wrong or might soon do wrong. If we are overcommitted, we worry about how we can manage our obligations and who will be angry with us when we don't. Our anxiety often masks anger as well. After all, those people we are helping, saving or showing our achievements begin to look like our persecutors sometimes.

6 *I'm always blaming myself.* "It's all my fault" is the endless refrain. You think you are stupid, or lazy, or a jerk, or a loser, or you suffer from some other fatal flaw that is central to your constant self-criticism. This kind of pessimistic thinking is a hallmark of unhealthy guilt and reinforces the helplessness at the core of shame as an identity.

7 *I worry about what other people think of me.* Perhaps we finished a big project and feel pretty good about it. If the feedback is positive, we feel elated. But if there is any negative feedback, even though it will improve the project, all of our good feelings evaporate. We don't hear feedback as a dialogue about ideas, we hear it as an indictment of self. This is called attachment to praise and blame. When we have granted other people the power to determine our worth, it means we are helpless.

8 *I hate it when people are angry with me.* Our antennae are always sniffing the air for anger. The boss is preoccupied this week; we deduce that she is angry at us. When someone actually confronts us with anger, we feel so vulnerable that we will do almost anything to get off the hook.

9 *I'm not as good as people think I am.* Someday people are going to find out that we are frauds. Other people in our shoes are much more competent than we are. This impostor syndrome afflicts many competent people who define their worth in terms of what they can produce rather than who they are. In fact, the problem is that we don't really *know* who we are, so we feel empty and confused.

10 *I'm a doormat.* We are trying so hard to be good that we are often the one who takes on the extra project. In family situations "doormatting" creates the famous martyr complex, which is guaranteed to make us vastly unpopular in spite of our efforts. After all, few people care to play the role of the ungrateful, lazy, ne'er-do-well that the martyr needs for self-definition.

11 *I never have time for myself.* Even though we know that exercise, meditation and plain old rest make us feel better, something else is always more pressing. When we don't take time to restore ourselves, we reinforce the sense of isolation and helplessness that underlies unhealthy guilt. We're not really living. And we're not really happy.

12 *I worry that other people are better than I am.* In guilty thinking, success and failure are constant themes, breeding envy and competitiveness.

13 *"Must" and "should" are my favorite words.* Musts and shoulds are a great way to motivate yourself as a human *doing*, but they block the joy of human *being*.

14 *I can't stand criticism.* Even garden-variety questions are often perceived as critical assaults. Self-defense against reproach is what we think protects us from the rejection and abandonment that we fear so much. Tragically, our defense consists of dishing out the same rejection that we fear, so no one wins.

15 *I'm a perfectionist.* Statistically, it is a fact that no one can do his or her "best" 100 percent of the time. Half the time we do better than our average and half the time we do worse. It takes nerve to believe that we can or should outwit natural laws. But that's what perfectionists do.

16 *I worry about being selfish.* We are often angry at the very people we are bending over backwards to assist because helping them leaves so little time and energy for ourselves. Instead of acknowledging our anger as a signal that things are out of balance, we interpret it as a sign that we are selfish.

17 *I hate to ask for help.* Most guilty people find it's much easier to give than to receive. Yet giving and receiving are really the poles of the battery between which love flows. So refusing to receive is not an act of generosity at all, it's a subtle kind of selfishness.

18 *I can't take compliments.* We thrive on approval. But when it's freely given, we push it away, focusing instead on possible imperfections that might invalidate the compliment.

19 *I worry that I am being punished for my sins.* When something bad happens, the spiritual pessimist believes that "God is punishing me for my sins." It is the antithesis of spiritual optimism, which is based on knowing God is love and the faith that life's bad events are occasions for soul growth, not punishments for unworthiness.

20 *I worry about my body a lot.* Worrying about the body deflects attention from emotional self-awareness. It's one more way of numbing the pain of inner shame.

21 *I can't say no.* This little word fills the guilty with fear. Since we so desperately need approval, saying no is a risk. Someone might think we are bad or selfish. There's nothing in it for us but anxiety and rejection.

VICTIMS OF OURSELVES

Psychologist Nathaniel Branden calls self-esteem the reputation we have with ourselves. When we live our lives out of shame and believe that we are unworthy, that reputation is low—we have low self-esteem. Because the deep sense of inadequacy that accompanies shame is too much to bear, we develop defense mechanisms to protect ourselves from our tendency to be self-destructively judgmental. Since our own anger is often too frightening to acknowledge, for example, we tend to project it outside of ourselves and see other people as blaming, aggressive, unfair or controlling. In thinking of ourselves as the victims of others, we can disown the reality that we are actually victims of ourselves. The more we insist on not being aware, the more trapped we become.

Rooting out the characteristics of unhealthy guilt rests on the ability to accept the fact that we are each a composite, a mosaic of different thoughts, emotions and choices of behavior. That doesn't make us "bad," it just means that we have certain "growing edges." Rather than thinking in terms of good and bad, we should think in terms of conscious or unconscious—aware or unaware. The more aware we are, the farther along the road to recovery from guilt we will progress.

We can be kind and selfish, loving and occasionally judgmental, a nice person and very angry at the moment. No matter who we are, we will make mistakes. But if we can accept our humanity with open-mindedness and awareness, rather than censoring ourselves out of shame, we will be more capable of choosing behaviors that maximize our freedom and our happiness.

HEALTH'S CHARACTER

Hans J. Eysenck

Hans J. Eysenck, Ph.D., D.Sc., is one of the world's most cited psychologists. He is a professor at the Institute of Psychiatry of the University of London, where he started the discipline of clinical psychology in Great Britian. He is a pioneer in the use of behavior therapy as well as research in personality theory and measurements.

Imagine this: A simple, six-question test predicts whether you are likely to get cancer or heart disease or to stay healthy. These predictions would not be based on traditional medical risks such as smoking or obesity but on your personality.

If the test indicates that you have a disease-prone personality, there would be some short-term behavior therapies (no radiation treatments, no surgery, no drugs) that protect you against cancer or a heart attack or help you live longer if you are already sick.

It sounds too good to be true, but it just might be. Dramatic results from studies completed in Europe over the past several years point to a very strong connection between certain personalities and specific illnesses. If the research I am about to describe holds up under ongoing scrutiny, we will be entering a new era of health care and disease prevention.

Theories about disease-prone personalities usually draw loud protests from the medical community, but such ideas are hardly new. The notion that people with certain personality characteristics are likely to develop coronary heart disease dates back more than 2,000 years to Hippocrates. The idea that people of a different personality type are more likely to develop cancer has also been around for a long time. These ideas are based on centuries of observations made by keen-eyed physicians; they should not be rejected simply because they were made without modern methodological and statistical expertise.

The world's most-quoted psychologist contends that a Yugoslav's controversial experiments prove that certain personalities are prone to cancer, others to heart disease. But you can learn to be prone to health.

The type of personality often ascribed to the cancer-prone individual combines two major features. One is an inability to express emotions such as anger, fear and anxiety; the other is an inability to cope with stress and a tendency to develop feelings of hopelessness, helplessness and finally depression. In the late 1950s, a Scottish oncologist, David Kissen, and I tried to test some of these ideas. We administered psychological questionnaires to patients coming to Kissen's lung cancer clinic before they were diagnosed as having cancer. We wanted to find out how readily these people expressed their emotions. We then compared those with a diagnosis of lung cancer to those with a non-malignant diagnosis. People who found it easier to express their emotions seemed to be protected from cancer, while those who could not suffered from cancer much more than chance would have predicted.

These results have been replicated by other researchers studying lung cancer in men and breast cancer in women. In general, the more recent studies characterized the cancer-prone person as unassertive, over-patient, avoiding conflict and failing to express negative emotions. However, many of these studies were small and had some technical problems with methodology, and other studies found no association between cancer and personality traits (see "Fighting Cancerous Feelings," *Psychology Today*, May 1988).

Coronary heart disease has also been linked to certain personality types, most often to the so-called "Type A" personality or behavior pattern, which was summarized by its discoverers in the late 1950s as "excessive and competitive drive, and an enhanced sense of time urgency". Later research in the '70s and '80s has shown that Type A behavior is actually composed of several different components and that many of them do not in fact predict coronary heart disease. The only components that seem to stand up to the test are tendencies towards anger, hostility and aggression.

But many studies of heart disease and behavior focused on people who were already ill, and it is possible that the disease caused the personality pattern, rather than the other way around. And several studies of healthy people using the Type A behavior scales and interviewing methods found a very weak link to heart disease or no link at all (see "Type A On Trial," *Psychology Today*, February 1987).

So the whole question of personality and disease has been shrouded in uncertainty, due to the absence of large-scale studies in which personality traits are determined first and the people under investigation are then observed for many years to see who dies and of what disease.

Three such studies have recently been completed and published, all of them carried out by Ronald Grossarth-Maticek, a Yugoslav psychologist who carried out his original research in the 1960s in his home country and then went to West Germany to work in Heidelberg. He took large random samples of people, measured their personality traits, smoking and drinking habits, physical health and other characteristics. He then checked on them for periods of 10 or more years to learn whether aspects of personality could be linked to death from cancer or heart disease or to a long and healthy life. Several American and British psychologists, including myself, have collaborated with him in recent years.

Grossarth-Maticek measured personality in two ways. He used a series of short questionnaires to look at various aspects of the cancer-prone personality and the heart disease-prone personality, as he conceptualized them. The most important questions measured tendencies toward hopelessness and helplessness, rational and anti-emotional behavior and a lack of angry responses to traumatic life events (it is a testament to Grossarth-Maticek's astuteness that his ideas in the early 1960s agree almost perfectly with the most recent results of American and British research in this field).

An alternative method of ascertaining personality involved lengthy interviews in which the subjects were allocated to one of four types: Type 1, cancer-prone; Type 2, coronary heart disease-prone; Types 3 and 4, relatively healthy people who could deal with stress in a non-self-destructive fashion. Grossarth-Maticek has also developed a short questionnaire that distinguishes these four personality types (see "The Health Personality Test"). You can take it and score yourself to find out your health personality.

Based on these personality types, Grossarth-Maticek was able to predict death from cancer among these people with an accuracy of 50 percent, which is six times higher than a prediction from cigarette smoking. Of the Type 1 people who died, almost half died from cancer, while fewer than one-tenth died from heart disease. About one-third of the Type 2 people died of heart disease, but only about one-fifth died from cancer. Type 3 and Type 4 showed relatively few deaths.

In the Yugoslav study, the people were for the most part the oldest inhabitant in every second house in a small town; however, Grossarth-Maticek also included a number of people who were suggested as being in a state of high stress. It is unscientific to throw together two different populations in one study, and adding stressed individuals to the study has been criticized, since it might have artificially strengthened the connection between the death rates and the disease-prone personality groups. But a recent reanalysis has shown that the connection is actually stronger without the stressed people.

Until recently, no large studies have determined personality first, then followed people for years to see who dies of what disease. A few years ago, Grossarth-Maticek completed three such studies.

Later, in Heidelberg, Grossarth-Maticek studied a random group of men and women between 40 and 60 years of age (see "Mind-Body Connections"). The overall number of deaths in this study was much smaller than it was in the Yugoslav study because the people in Heidelberg were much younger on average. However, as before, Type 1 people tended to die of cancer and Type 2 people tended to die of heart disease.

In Heidelberg, Grossarth-Maticek also examined a second group, closely resembling the first in age, sex and smoking habits. However, this second group of people was nominated as people suffering from severe stress. If stress plays an important part in causing death from cancer and heart disease, far more people in this group should have died of these illnesses. This was indeed so: Approximately 40 percent more people in the stressed group died of these diseases. These data are for a 10-year follow-up, and there was little change when a 13-year follow-up was completed.

These dramatic results, indicating a powerful role for personality and behavior in cancer and heart disease, lead to an all-important question: Can we prevent these deaths by changing people's personalities?

Grossarth-Maticek and I tried to use behavior therapy to teach cancer- and heart disease-prone people to express their emotions more readily, to cope with stress, to wean them of their emotional dependencies and to make them more self-reliant. In other words, we taught them to behave more like the healthier personality types. We used relaxation, desentitization, modeling, suggestion and hypnosis and other standard behavioral techniques (see "Steps To A Healthier Self"). The results were astonishing.

100 people with cancer-prone personalities were divided into two groups: 50 who received no therapy and 50 who did receive it. Far more people died of cancer (and of other causes) in the no-therapy group than in the therapy group. After 13 years, 45 people who got therapy were still alive. Only 19 were alive in the no-therapy group.

We tried a similar experiment with 92 heart disease-prone people, divided into therapy and no-therapy groups. Here too there were marked differences 13 years later, with 37 people surviving with therapy and 17 surviving without it.

These results were encouraging, to say the least; however, the therapy in these studies consisted of about 30 hours of individual treatment, which is fairly lengthy and expensive. We decided to look for ways to reduce the treatment time and expense.

We tried using group therapy, in which groups of some 20 people met for about six hours in all, on two or three occasions. Here too we found a marked difference in the number of people who died of cancer and coronary heart disease, again favoring the therapy group. In a third study, we tried short-term therapy on an individual basis, again with favorable results.

There is also evidence that similar treatment can prolong life in people who

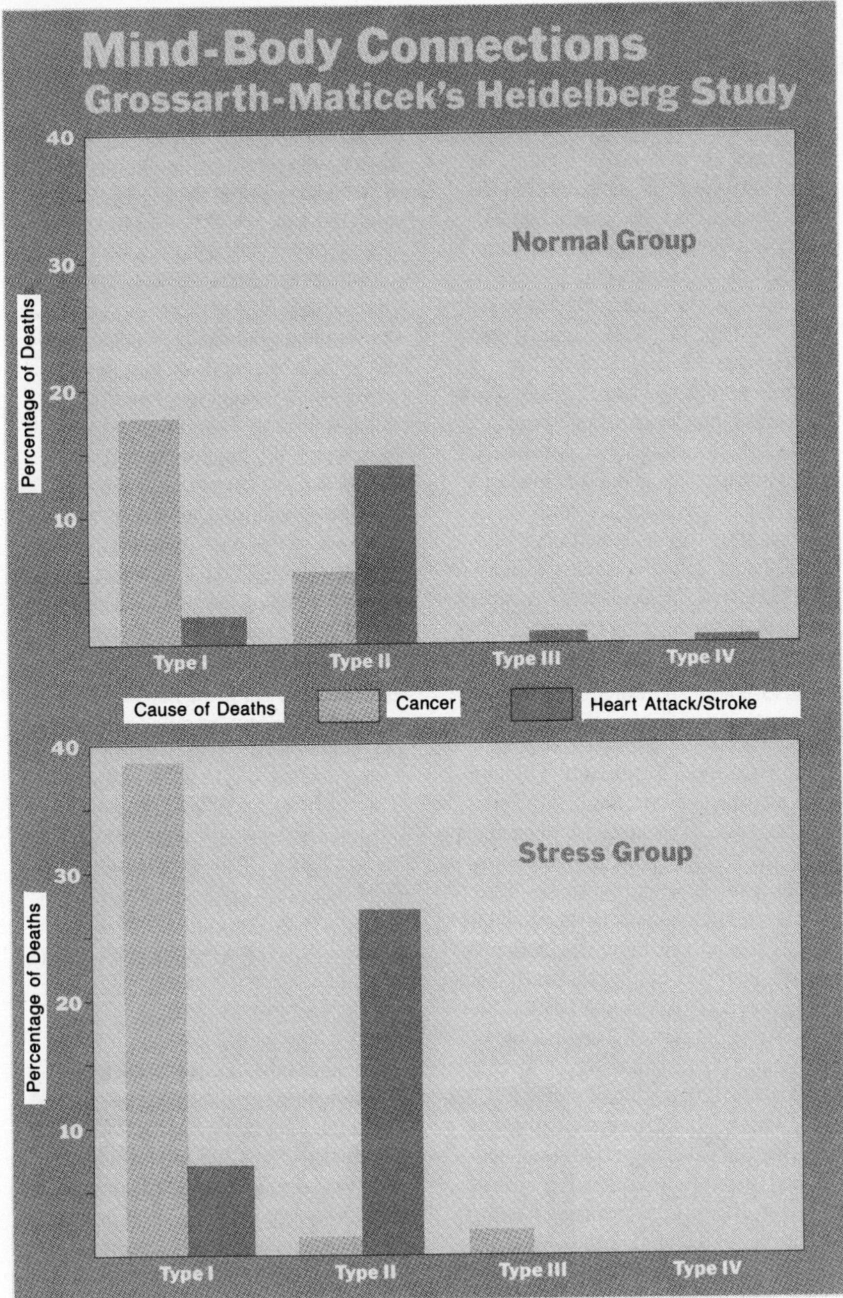

Top: More of the Type 1 (cancer-prone personality) people who died during a 10-year period in Heidelberg, West Germany, succumbed to cancer than died of heart disease. More of the Type 2 (heart disease-prone personality) people died of heart-related problems. These two diseases claimed only a small percentage of Types 3 and 4 (healthy personalities). Bottom: This mind-body pattern showed up to a much greater degree among people living under a lot of stress, indicating that stress can exacerbate these illnesses.

already have cancer. Grossarth-Maticek formed 24 pairs of cancer patients, each pair equal in age, sex, social background, type and extent of cancer and medical treatment. One person in each pair was allocated by chance to behavior therapy, one to a no-therapy group. Survival on the average was about five years for the therapy group and only three years for the other group.

In another study, we compared the effectiveness of behavior therapy as an adjunct to chemotherapy. Of 100 woman, all with terminal breast cancer, 50 elected to have chemotherapy and 50 rejected it. Half of each group also received behavior therapy. Survival rates were 11 months for those who received no type of therapy, 14 months for those who received only chemotherapy, 15 months for those who received only behavior therapy and 22 months for those who received both. The combined effect of both types of therapy is stronger than simply adding the individual effects of chemotherapy and behavior therapy.

The names and addresses of all participants in the preventive therapy studies were given to two independent research organizations, which were responsible for ascertaining death and cause of death. Thus there was reasonable control over the procedures.

Similar results, although using somewhat different methods and populations, have been obtained independently in the United States. In one study, psychiatrist David Spiegel and his colleagues at the Stanford University School of Medicine have reported on the effects of a psychotherapy group treatment for breast cancer patients. The average survival rate during the study was 35 months for the group in therapy, as opposed to just 19 months for the group that was not—a difference even greater than that reported by Grossarth-Maticek.

Psychologist Judith Rodin at Yale University Medical School has also found that a similar type of therapy can lower the cortisol levels of elderly women in a nursing home and prolong their lives. This is very important: Cortisol may be the link between personality and stress, on the one hand, and cancer on the other. Cortisol has often been linked with depression and feelings of hopelessness and helplessness; also, cortisol weakens the immune system, thus rendering it less capable of dealing with menaces such as cancer cells. This may be one way in which personality, stress and disease interact.

These results are impressive and suggest a revolution in medical practice. The type of therapy I've described would go a long way toward preventing early deaths from cancer and coronary heart disease. It would also significantly decrease the enormous health budget which has to pay for diagnosis and treatment, hospital care and operations, and so much else entailed by high rates of cancer and heart disease. Equally important, life prolonged through behavior therapy might not entail the very severe side effects of chemotherapy and other types of medical intervention.

I am not suggesting that we should completely reorganize modern medicine

Steps to a Healthier Self

KATARINA KOLB loved her married boyfriend, but he seemed to be much more concerned about his wife than he was about her. Katarina, a 38-year-old German woman, also felt rejected by her father but could not speak to him about it. And she had breast cancer.

Katarina—not her real name—felt depressed and hopeless. According to psychologists Ronald Grossarth-Maticek and Hans Eysenck, she had the classic personality traits of a person vulnerable to cancer. She repressed her anger and anxiety, and felt helpless to find ways to solve her problems.

To change this disease-prone behavior, Katarina took a course of treatment that Grossarth-Maticek and Eysenck call "autonomy training." During either individual or group sessions, therapists explain the difference between the healthy and disease-prone personalities and use relaxation methods, coping techniques and desensitization to help patients move toward the healthy personality style. Grossarth-Maticek and Eysenck use this approach with both cancer-prone and heart-disease-prone people. Individuals susceptible to heart disease learn to abandon the tendencies toward hostility and aggression that the researchers say put them at risk. The key change for cancer-prone people is to stop being overly passive.

Cancer-prone personality types often believe that they are incapable of meeting their needs on their own and depend on another person, job or institution to enhance their sense of self. Katarina, for example, could not get the support she longed for from her married boyfriend but felt she couldn't get along without him. Her feelings of helplessness and anxiety led to passive acceptance of the situation.

When the therapist asked Katarina to explain her behavior, she gained a sense of perspective on herself for the first time. "I've never really thought about this, but it's very destructive, really. Every time I get rejected I get depressed." At her therapist's suggestion, she began to write down ways to get rid of self-defeating behavior.

Her first step was to avoid confrontations with her father in which she knew she would end up feeling rejected. "I won't make demands on him, because when I do, I usually lose and I find that difficult to bear." The therapist helped her use mental imagery to picture several situations involving her father in which she had no expectations and did not need to make any demands.

Katarina reported success at her next session and said she was beginning to like and value herself. She was becoming less dependent on her father and boyfriend and wanted to find new, interesting activities to take her mind off her illness. "I will call up my girlfriend and ask her to go for a walk with me every day, and I will ask my old tennis partner whether he would like to come and have a game with me," she decided.

By the next session, Katarina had gone for several walks and had found three new tennis partners. She told her therapist that she wanted to be more relaxed; she wanted "a state in which inner inhibitions and fears are reduced, in which I believe in myself, trust myself and think I am doing the right thing." The therapist put her into a state of deep hypnosis and repeated some suggestions, created by Katarina herself: "I become more relaxed, happier and happier, and find myself in a wonderful landscape near the sea. I am at one with nature and free of all inhibitions. At the same time I can believe in myself and the success of all my wishes."

Eventually, Katarina sought ways to change her relationship with her boyfriend. He usually visited her once a day, promising to stay for a long visit but always left after only a short time. "Such behavior I will not tolerate any more!" she decided. Again, she used mental imagery, picturing unfulfilling moments in the relationship, and soon she had little desire to see her boyfriend again.

Mental imagery is also used to help other cancer patients combat their disease. Patients visualize white blood cells conquering a malignancy, and by doing so begin to feel some mastery over the illness, while also learning to release anger and resentment.

Autonomy training emphasizes avoiding behavior that leads to short-term solutions, such as escaping a personal rejection, but has long-term negative effects, such as an overall sense of helplessness. And Katarina had clearly reached a new level of autonomy. By ending her relationship with her boyfriend she chose long-term independence over the short-term goal of having some of her boyfriend's attention.

Grossarth-Maticek and Eysenck have found that the patients who succeed in changing their behavior in this way become more self-reliant, less demanding and less rigid than those who don't learn to make these changes. And for those who make the changes, Grossarth-Maticek and Eysenck's research shows that chances of getting cancer are greatly reduced. If they already have the disease, their lives should be prolonged by several years. While Katarina still had some self-doubts at the end of her therapy, she also had learned coping skills to deal with her problems. "I have experienced the negative consequences from putting one's self second," she said. "I shall always keep these consequences in my thoughts, act accordingly and feel good about myself."

—MIA ADESSA

on the basis of these results; obviously as in all such studies, there are faults and possible errors which make it imperative that an independent replication be carried out. No study is perfect, and science demands replication, particularly where life-and-death consequences are so strongly involved.

We obviously are only at the beginning of understanding the apparent interaction between body and mind, but as the Indian sage, Mahābhārata, said 4,000 years ago, "There are two classes of disease—bodily and mental. Each arises from the other, and neither exists without the other. Mental disorders arise from physical ones, and likewise physical disorders arise from mental ones." As the physicist has given up contrasting time and space and now deals with a space-time continuum, so we should stop talking about body and mind as separate entities and rather speak of a body-mind continuum. The study of this continuum will have vital consequences for our understanding of the human condition and may revolutionize our conception of disease, prevention and cure.

The Health Personality Test

THIS IS a short scale for rating yourself according to the four health personality types. This test is intended to illustrate the differences among the personality types. Indicate how closely the description in each question fits you by circling a number from **1** to **10** that best describes you or your situation. **1** means "Not at all" and **10** means "Very much."

1) Have you been repeatedly hopeless and helpless during the last 10 years of your life, either because of the withdrawal of persons who were very important to you and/or your failure to achieve particularly important aims in life? This hopelessness and depression was caused because these events made it impossible for you to satisfy your most important emotional needs, such as those for love, nearness, understanding and recognition. The cause might be the death of or separation from some particularly important person, causing disappointment and difficulties. How closely does this description fit your own case?

Not at all 1 2 3 4 5 6 7 8 9 10 Very much

2) Have you been repeatedly excited, annoyed and resigned in the last 10 years because people disturbed you and interfered with your plans? This excitement and annoyance was caused by your failure, in spite of constant effort to change the situation, allowing some person or persons to prevent the satisfaction of your all-important needs or the achievement of an all-important goal, such as happiness with a sexual partner or advancement at work. How closely does this description fit your own case?

Not at all 1 2 3 4 5 6 7 8 9 10 Very much

3) Considering the past 10 years, particularly your relations with people who were particularly important to you from an emotional point of view (either positively or negatively), which of the four reactions described below would be most descriptive of you and to what extent?

A) I seek and long for closeness and emotional contact with a person or persons who are at the moment too distant from me because of a death, a separation, lack of understanding on the part of my partner, or some shocking or too-demanding events. I would be willing to do anything to diminish this distance, but I do not succeed in reaching the wished-for intimacy. How closely does this description fit your own case?

Not at all 1 2 3 4 5 6 7 8 9 10 Very much

B) I seek distance or separation from one person or persons whose closeness to me (as a partner, in a work or other situation) I experience as crushing. In spite of my efforts I fail to achieve this distancing or separation, largely because of fear of the consequences, such as fear of financial difficulties. How closely does this description fit your own case?

Not at all 1 2 3 4 5 6 7 8 9 10 Very much

C) I alternate between great emotional closeness to a person who is important to me and great emotional distancing and separation. My actions only achieve a regular alteration of too-great closeness and too-great distance interspersed with moments in which distance and nearness are optimal. How closely does this description fit your own case?

Not at all 1 2 3 4 5 6 7 8 9 10 Very much

D) My relations with people who are important to me are neither crushingly close nor too-distant emotionally. Nearness and distance are for the most part optimal and regulated appropriately. I increase the distance from people who annoy me and decrease the distance to people with whom I interact positively. How closely does this description fit your own case?

Not at all 1 2 3 4 5 6 7 8 9 10 Very much

4) During the past 10 years, have you always been in a position to enjoy relaxation in various bodily activities, such as sports, work and sex, using these activities as a pleasant alternative to mental relaxation and activity? Yes/No
If the answer is No, were you prevented from doing so:
A) By the sudden or gradual change due to persons distancing themselves from you or by the loss of a position in a work situation?
B) Because of people or conditions disturbing or annoying you without your having the power to change them according to your desires, or to leave them?
C) Through people who alternated and made emotionally unacceptable demands on you while at other times distancing themselves from you.

5) In the past 10 years, have you repeatedly acted in such a way that emotionally negative (undesirable) consequences occurred? Were you unable to find ways of acting that led to more positive and desirable consequences, such as better interaction between you and emotionally important persons? How closely does this description fit your own case?

Not at all 1 2 3 4 5 6 7 8 9 10 Very much

6) Do you have frequent feelings of fear and anxiety (a general state of anxiety, a syndrome of anxiety, periods during which you suffer from anxiety, fears of being threatened or persecuted, fear of not being able to cope with life and its problems, fear of specific situations)? These fears should be relatively unrealistic, in the sense that you are in the position to avoid them if need be. How strong is this anxiety?

Not at all 1 2 3 4 5 6 7 8 9 10 Very much

HOW TO SCORE THE TEST. You get four scores on this test, not just one; each score corresponds to a health personality type. Type 1 is cancer-prone, Type 2 is heart-disease-prone, Type 3 is healthy with a tendency to act unconventionally and Type 4 is also healthy. You compare your four scores with one another, not to the scores of other people. The highest of your scores indicates your health personality.

Type 1 Add the ratings for question 1 and question 3A. If the answer to question 4 is "No" and the reason is A, add 10 more points. Add on the ratings for question 5 and question 6. Sum up the total.

Type 2 Add the ratings for question 2 and question 3B. If the answer to question 4 is "No" and the reason is B, add 10 more points. Add on the ratings for question 5 and question 6. Sum up the total.

Type 3 Add the rating on any part of question 3 to the rating on question 3C. If the answer to question 4 is "no" and the reason is C, add 10 more points. Add on the ratings for question 5 and question 6. Sum up the total.

Type 4 If your total score on questions 1, 2 and 3 was less than 15, give yourself 10 points. Add the rating on question 3D. If the answer to question 4 is "Yes," add 10 more points. If your rating on either question 5 or question 6 was less than 5 points, give yourself 10 points for that question. Sum up the total.

HEALTHY PLEASURES

ROBERT E. ORNSTEIN, PH.D., AND DAVID S. SOBEL, M.D.

Robert E. Ornstein, Ph.D., *teaches psychology at the University of California, San Francisco, Medical School.* **David S. Sobel, M.D.**, *is regional director of patient education and health promotion at the Kaiser Permanente Medical Care Program in northern California.*

A PROVOCATIVE NEW BOOK SAYS FEELING GOOD IS GOOD FOR YOU

Imagine the world without pleasure. Life would appear colorless and humorless. A baby's smile would go unappreciated. Food would be tasteless. The beauty of a Bach concerto would fall on deaf ears. Joy, delight, ecstasy, elation and happiness would disappear. The touch of a mother would not soothe; a lover could not arouse. Interest in sex and procreation would disappear. The next generation would wait unborn.

Fortunately, our life is not like that. There is a pleasure machine within our heads: Several brain centers respond to gratifying stimulation. Nerve pathways speed satisfying sensations to the brain, and packets of chemicals stand ready to transmit pleasure signals from one nerve cell to another.

This didn't happen by accident; human beings evolved to seek enjoyment to enhance survival. What better way to assure healthy, lifesaving behavior occurs than to make it pleasurable?

So evolution has connected health-promoting acts to pleasure. Enjoying food, sex, work and family is the innate guide to health. People recognize what is healthful by the joys of life, by their pleasurable feelings—a delicious nap, a full stomach, the gratification of sex. These sensations signal our brains that we are on the right track and should keep going. Good feelings and pleasures reward us twice: in immediate enjoyment and improved health.

Think about the healthiest, most robust people you know. What makes them vital? The most hardy people we know do not follow all the "correct" advice about health. Some assault the U.S. Senate Dietary Guidelines at nearly every meal. Many forgo regular medical checkups. They don't lead bland, "stress-free" lives. They simply expect good things of the world. They expect things to work out well; they expect their world to be orderly; they expect people to like and respect them. Most important, *they expect pleasure in much of what they do.*

The positive mood and expectation of pleasure in healthy people was so striking to us that we decided to find out how these people live. As a rule, they enjoy simple pleasures and stolen moments: watching the sun rise, building a model classic car, silly talk with their spouses, kids and pets. They highlight minor things that please them: a shotgun collection, playing the violin passionately (though terribly), cooking their favorite meals. These pursuits seem somehow to absorb some of the troubles of their active lives.

Most of the people we've talked to are passionate about their work, families and hobbies. Little troubles don't frazzle them. When his car was stolen,

From *American Health,* May 1989, pp. 53-58, 60, 62. From *Pleasures,* by Robert E. Ornstein and David S. Sobel.

Many people are not getting their minimum daily requirement of sensual pleasure

one said: "Can you drive me home? I wanted to talk more to you this afternoon."

Many robust people enjoy a good, hearty laugh—more often than not at themselves. Others bring an unbridled enthusiasm to everything they do and everyone they touch. They care more for people, animals, political causes or volunteer organizations than for micro-managing their blood chemistries or fiber intake. They see themselves as a part of life, not apart from it.

Don't get us wrong. We recognize well that exercising, not smoking, not drinking to excess, wearing seat belts, avoiding extreme sunburn, all contribute to a long, healthy life. Even so, the sum total of all these "good health habits" still doesn't add up to as much as we might believe, and it doesn't explain the essential vitality of some people. The healthiest people seem to be pleasure-loving, pleasure-seeking, pleasure-creating individuals.

There appears to be a physiology of hope, optimism and happiness that speaks to the heart, the immune system—in fact, the entire body. In one study, people who felt that many positive things would happen to them reported fewer physical signs of ill health and better physical well-being. Compared with optimists, pessimists also have measurable deficiencies in critical immune functions. And an optimistic way of viewing the world can promise better health and survival over the course of 20 to 30 years.

So Pollyanna was right: There are important reasons to believe in the best.

CIVILIZATION AND ITS DISPLEASURES

If pleasure is so health-enhancing, then why do we give ourselves such a bad time about feeling good? No one tries to prove to cats that they really should nap, purr and chase mice, or point out to puppies the joys of romping, sniffing or gnawing on a bone. Yet humans have a surprising and deeply rooted resistance to anything that smacks of simply offering a good time.

Our culture seems to have lost a vital perspective on what is *natural* for a human being to be, do and feel. Our health, as well as our quality of life, suffers greatly. Despite visible excesses by so-called pleasure-seekers, we haven't really learned to enjoy ourselves.

Or, more accurately, we've just forgotten.

If we think back to our pre-industrial ancestors, there were marked alternations between periods of intense effort and moments of complete idleness. The farmer might strain during planting and certainly during harvest, but there was little need to work in fallow times. One could live long parts of the year at one's own tempo—playing with the kids, watching geese fly, soaking up the morning sun, and taking (literally) a roll in the hay in the middle of the afternoon.

During the Industrial Revolution factory life became common. But our ancestors didn't happily relinquish control over their time. Historical records show that people hated taking up a tethered, regulated life. Their natural urges to seek pleasure had to be subjugated to the appetites of the industrial machine.

With the modern work ethic has come an almost involuntary dismissal of healthy sensuality and play. We have so learned to delay sensual gratification and curb our passions that many find it difficult to indulge themselves even when the time is right. The idea of napping, lovemaking, taking a walk, sitting idly watching the natural world, or just playing catch with a child somehow seems nonproductive. This view is needlessly shackling 20th-century society: Simple pleasures contribute to real productivity as well as health.

The work ethic is not the only cultural barrier to pleasure. Many religious leaders exhort us to view pleasure, particularly the sensual kind, as morally suspect and corrupting. Banishment from Paradise awaits those who indulge in the flesh, and a flaming hereafter is promised. The body is to be denied, passions reigned in, the mind disciplined.

Redeeming a natural and healthy sensuality requires us to buck strong historical forces. But our health, happiness and future depend upon understanding and reversing this deep-rooted cultural denial of sensual pleasures and leisure.

We need to restore some sensibility, too, to the pursuit of health. People increasingly view themselves as fragile and vulnerable, ready to develop cancer, heart disease or some other ailment at the slightest provocation. In the name of health people give up many of life's enjoyments.

The important point is that *worrying* too much about anything—including calories, salt, cancer and cholesterol—is bad for you. Living optimistically, with pleasure, zest and commitment, is good. Medical terrorism shouldn't attack life's pleasures.

It is time, now, to break the conspiracy against healthy pleasures. Feeling good pays off not only in immediate enjoyment but also in better health.

COMING TO OUR SENSES

Human beings evolved to find pleasure in sensory experiences: the sweetness of a peach, the swelling satisfactions of sex, the peaceful flow of a river, the view stretching from a mountaintop all the way to the horizon.

The human world has changed, though. Many sensual pleasures we're primed to receive are blunted in the modern world. City dwellers miss the glory of the sunrise and sunset as they hustle in their commutes. The synthetic foods in our markets bear little resemblance to the tasty real foods we were built to eat. Our ancestors heard the pleasant sounds of a stream and wind rustling in the trees, but for us it's the din of traffic.

Many people aren't getting their minimum daily requirement of sensual pleasures. Modern life has deprived us of too many of our sensory requirements. We need to regain a balance.

Some pleasures are close at hand.

TOUCHING THE HEART

We speak of something being "touching," implying a close link between physical contact and the emotional reactions of the heart. It's more than a metaphor: Our skin does speak to our hearts. And our hearts respond.

The result of touch depends on how someone is touched and how it feels to him or her. While tender hand-holding can slow the heart rate, pulse-taking by a nurse—if it provokes anxiety—can increase heart rate and prompt irregular beats.

For the most part, however, we find touching, especially light stroking of the arms, legs, back or chest, relaxing and pleasurable. From the pressure points of Oriental massage techniques to the kneading, stroking and gentle pummeling of Swedish massage, the various forms of skin stimulation have been credited with nearly every conceivable health benefit. Unfortunately, science has found little to support most of these claims.

Massage does seem to benefit patients with chronic anxiety, however. In one study, a group of patients with chronic muscle tension, body aches and pain got massage treatment. All had failed to respond fully to anti-anxiety medications, antidepressants and muscle relaxants, as well as standard relaxation training exercises. The researchers measured heart rate, muscle tension and skin resistance (a measure of stress) before and after deliberately stressing the subjects with blaring loud noises.

Then came the fun part. Each patient was treated to 10 sessions, each lasting 30 to 45 minutes, of deep massage. When the physiological measurements were repeated after the massages, each person improved in at least one of the measures: slower heart rate, lower muscle tension, decreased arousal. Most reported less tension, pain and need for medication.

The massage also apparently loosened their tongues. After the massage the patients seemed to speak much more freely and at greater length about their problems. Given our focus on psychotherapy or medication for mental problems, we might consider these touching alternatives.

Our society distances us from others; we don't give each other baths, hugs or massages much and today's parents don't carry their young long distances as their ancestors did. But touching helps us feel close to others. It may be as simple as scheduling a massage instead of a coffee break (companies that provide office rubdowns are springing up), or it may be the realization that it's been too long since you've caressed your child or lover.

Of course, our skin communicates much more than the pleasurable sensations of touch. We also have sensors for temperature, and when it comes to heat. . . .

SOME LIKE IT HOT

Most people like to get hot. We seek out sunny, warm climates, saunas, steam baths, hot tubs and solariums. Yet most research with respect to heat ignores our love of hot spots, focusing instead on the damaging effects of extreme heat.

One of the few areas in which heat's potential health benefits have been studied is the sauna. Exposure to high temperatures for brief periods produces major physiological changes: Stress hormones are released, the heart rate accelerates, respiration and sweating increase, and the skin flushes as the body struggles to maintain a normal body temperature.

Many people find saunas pleasurably relaxing; a brief sauna can decrease muscle and joint pain. One intriguing study in Czechoslovakia demonstrated that sitting in a sauna for 30 minutes increased blood levels of beta-endorphins, the internally produced chemicals that relieve pain and produce a sense of well-being and euphoria. So it may not be so far-fetched to speak of "sauna bathers' high."

Heat may also deplete our body stores of stress hormones. This makes us less likely to respond to stress later—a beneficial type of "burnout."

The healthy pleasures of saunas and hot baths may go well beyond physiological benefits. A dip in the heat is a great excuse for a protected, quiet rest period in an otherwise harried life.

LOOKING AT LIFE

We have an appetite for visual feasts. When given a choice between viewing a natural scene rich in foliage or an urban landscape devoid of vegetation or water, human beings nearly always favor the nature scene. This may come as no surprise, but there is now mounting evidence that such choices may be more than simple aesthetic preferences. Flooding our brains with rich, natural visual stimulation helps us recover from surgery, tolerate pain and manage stress.

When people view photographic slides of natural scenes, they report more positive feelings such as friendliness and elation, and fewer feelings of sadness and fear than those looking at manmade, urban scenes. Compared with cityscapes, natural scenes produce lower levels of arousal and more alpha brain waves, a brain state associated with wakeful relaxation.

We prefer certain types of landscapes, perhaps as a result of deep-rooted evolutionary experience. So try to include some elements from the natural environment in your home and at work. Plants, pets, windows with views of natural scenes, paintings or photographs of outdoor scenes, even an aquarium, can transform a lifeless manmade environment and reconnect you with nature.

MUSICAL MEDICINE

You are sitting in a darkened room. At moments you feel intense spine-tingling thrills that seem to begin at your neck and radiate up over your head and all the way down to the toes. You actually shiver with pleasure, get goose bumps; you may even weep. What could possibly be the source of such delicious sensations? Fabulous sex? A well-wrought movie? A glorious painting? The birth of a great idea?

Had you participated in this study at Stanford University, you would have been responding to music. Music is an ardent as well as healthy pleasure. One survey showed that some people find music more thrilling than anything else—including sex (which tied with "nostalgic moments" for sixth place on the all-time thrill scale).

Be it Bach, jazz, rock, gospel or pop, music is a mood mover. The right music at the right time brings us joy and serenity, soothes frazzled nerves, lifts us when we're down.

There seems to be a built-in response to certain tones: People uniformly describe high-pitched music as happy and playful, low-pitched music as sad and serious. On the other hand, tempo may be the most important factor for our hearts and our heads. Our hearts normally beat 70 to 80 times per minute. Most Western music is set (coincidentally?) to this tempo. Some studies have shown heart rate will synchronize with the beat.

Music therapy is useful in the treatment of many illnesses. It can ease pain, calm anxiety and lift the spirits of the terminally or chronically ill. It's now being used extensively for treating headaches, digestive problems, depression and other diseases with a strong emotional component.

THE EVOLUTION OF TASTE

Food is, fortunately, not one of the sensory pleasures that has disappeared from the world we've inherited. All animals feed, but only human beings savor food with such passion. We eat to nourish, to celebrate, to commemorate, but most of all, we eat for pleasure. Why else would we go to such trouble and expense in gathering, storing, preparing and finally, in one gustatory orgy, consuming our food?

We love variety and crave different taste sensations. This has led some experts to recommend that the road to weight loss is paved only with monotony. At least in the short run, facing a limitless smorgasbord of food is more likely to result in an orgy of calories than is choosing from a more limited menu. Yet there may be ways to indulge our craving for taste without overdoing it in the calorie department.

One researcher has increased dieters' satisfaction and the amount of weight they lose by boosting the *flavor,* but not the calories, in food. Here's where spices can be a boon for calorie counters (and others who want to enhance their taste sensations). Many tasty, low-calorie foods satisfy as much as high-calorie fare.

Eating slowly also allows time for satiety signals from the stomach to do their job. If you gulp down your food you may rush past the optimal level of satisfaction and into that postprandial stuffed feeling. Dieters who slowly sip a bowl of soup at the start of a meal feel satisfied earlier in the meal. For every additional calorie in the soup, dieters consume about two fewer calories in the main meal.

Remember, too, that you don't always have to eat when you crave food; even going for a walk instead may help to distract you.

GOOD SCENTS . . .

Smell is perhaps the most ignored and underappreciated of the human senses. Ever since our remote ancestors stood upright and headed for the trees, the two "distance senses"—sight and sound—have been our predominant means of gathering information about the threats and opportunities in our environment. Nevertheless, smell, because of its connection with the brain's emotion-generating areas, has a great, though often subconscious, influence on our moods and memories.

Egyptian papyrus fragments suggest that in the time of the Pharaohs the aroma of spices such as cinnamon was regarded as medicinal. In the traditional herbal medicines of ancient Greece, Rome, India and the Far East, too, perfumes were thought to have medicinal properties.

Fragrances inspire us. While savoring a pleasant fragrance we take slow, deep breaths and become relaxed. A strong aroma focuses our awareness, distracting us from less pleasant thoughts. Pleasant smells may also invoke positive memories or emotions with their associated beneficial physiological effects.

People with insomnia, anxiety, panic attacks, back pain, migraines and food cravings are now being treated with modern aromatherapy. For example, some patients with chronic pain are taught deep muscle relaxation while inhaling peach fragrance. Later, the patient simply takes a whiff of peach, and the relaxed state is quickly induced.

. . . AND GOOD SEX

Good sex puts a spring in your step, a sparkle in your eye, a glow in your skin. Some people claim sex helps them relax; others swear it helps them sleep better, eases menstrual cramps and other aches and pains, or even cures the common cold. We were surprised to find very little in the scientific literature when we researched the effect of a healthy sex life on happiness and well-being. But there is growing evidence that singer Marvin Gaye was right: There is such a thing as "sexual healing."

Testosterone is the hormone primarily responsible for the sex drive in both men and women. Female testosterone levels—and desire—are highest around the middle of a woman's menstrual cycle, when ovulation takes place and conception is most likely. Some women produce up to 10 times more testosterone than others, and these women tend to make love more often and enjoy it more.

Testosterone also has its tender side: It may help a man and woman bond together as a couple. In the long term, couples' testosterone levels tend to synchronize, and so does their desire for each other. This tends to make for a more contented, harmonious relationship.

Indeed, one of the most important benefits of sex may be psychological in nature. We're the only primates that engage in sex throughout the reproductive cycle, even at times when conception isn't likely. This sexual bond is basic to us as a species, and to our ability to raise more children.

Sexual fulfillment may help reduce the impact of certain stresses in a marriage. In a fascinating study, married couples monitored sexual intercourse and arguments on a daily basis. The result could be dubbed the "F Index": the frequency of fornication minus the frequency of fights. The higher the F index, the more likely they were to consider their marriages to be happy ones. For example, if a couple fights 10 times a month, but engages in sex 12 times a month, their F index is plus two, which points toward happiness.

Remember that sex fulfills many needs: being touched, being caressed, feeling close to others. Unfortunately, many erroneous beliefs—from upbringing, cultural traditions, media images—can interfere with sexual pleasures. Sex may be the first thing to go during times of physical and mental stress, from illness, pregnancy, parenting and aging. If your sexual relationship is a problem for you, give this essential pleasure the attention it needs to make it nourishing.

MAKING WORKOUTS PLAYFUL

"No pain, no gain" may at last be on its way to the graveyard of outdated health slogans. Human beings didn't evolve to run 26 miles at a time, but to walk. We didn't evolve to bench press 200 lb., but to carry 20 lb. to 30 lb. long distances.

So ease off. You don't have to kill yourself to save your life.

The exercise necessary to be healthy is much less than most people think, and doesn't have to involve burdensome regimens. It should be part of life. Gardening alone—hoeing, digging, pulling weeds and pushing a lawn mower—can boost heart rates by 20% to 25%. For a sedentary person that may be enough to improve health.

In a long-term study of nearly 17,000 Harvard alumni, those who burned as few as 500 calories a week in exercise had a 20% lower death rate. That modest workout could be achieved by a 15-minute walk each day, just over an hour of bicycling or a one-hour volleyball game per week! Granted, you might get even more benefit by burning 2,000 or more calories a week (death rates dropped another 10% to 20%). But the bulk of the benefit accrued to those who went from being complete couch potatoes to modest movers.

More important, gentle exercise makes you feel terrific. When you begin an exercise program you improve your mood and boost your confidence and sense of self-mastery.

Start by looking for opportunities to include more physical activity in the everyday things you do. You may not have time to "exercise," but you can build energetic activities into your life. Take the stairs instead of the elevator. Climb a hill. Walk through the park. Instead of driving to the store all the time, walk, and carry a bag of groceries home. Take seriously dancing, bowling, gardening, playing with children, or golf.

If you do enjoy the feeling of strenuous workouts, fine. But remember this is supposed to be *fun*.

LIFE-SAVING SIESTAS

Winston Churchill, a confirmed napper, wrote, "Nature had not intended man to work from eight in the morning until midnight without the refreshment of blessed oblivion, which, even if it lasts only 20 minutes, is sufficient to renew all vital forces." Most people imagine the natural sleep pattern is a single long period at night, but science is proving the value of napping.

When people in a laboratory are allowed to sleep without restriction, an interesting pattern develops. In addition to normal hours of night sleep, they begin to prefer a midday nap. Outside the laboratory, napping is quite common among college students and the aged, two groups often liberated from work-time demands.

The napless day we usually experience is probably an unnatural, fairly recent invention. Our early ancestors may have slept through the darkness of the night, hunted in the early morning, then escaped the midday heat by napping in a shady spot. Our biological rhythms appear programmed for a midday rest.

A catnap can refresh—relaxing the body, clearing the mind, and offering a break from the pace and stresses of daily life. You probably don't have to sleep to get the rejuvenation from an afternoon lie-down. A group of students were invited to either nap, rest quietly in a darkened room, or watch a video program on nature for one hour. After either napping *or* resting, they reported being more alert and clearheaded, and less anxious and fatigued.

ALL PLEASURES—GREAT AND ESPECIALLY SMALL

Which frames of mind and experiences really make human beings happy? Is it necessary to have intense moments of pleasure, or are little pleasures more important? Is happiness built up from many small occurrences or does it spring from a few fantastic events, such as one's first love, a long-awaited job promotion or a once-in-a-lifetime trip to Europe? The answers may surprise you.

In one study, a psychologist asked people to observe their moods over six weeks. Each person carried a beeper that recorded how he or she felt at any moment, and also rated happiness over the six-week period. Happiness, it was concluded, springs from *how much of the time* a person spends feeling good, not from momentary peaks of ecstasy. Simple pleasures—hours spent walking on a sunny day, gardening, running with the dog, or helping someone less fortunate—are more allied with happiness than strong feelings.

Don't bet your whole life on the big events—winning the lottery, becoming president of the company, or doubling your income. Instead, make sure you attend to the daily healthy pleasures of smells, tastes and sounds, rewarding relationships and meaningful work. The good feelings are likely to add up to a more optimistic view of your future and, perhaps, a longer, healthier life.

Glossary

This glossary of psychology terms is included to provide you with a convenient and ready reference as you encounter general terms in your study of psychology and personal growth and behavior that are unfamiliar or require a review. It is not intended to be comprehensive, but taken together with the many definitions included in the articles themselves, it should prove to be quite useful.

Abnormal Irregular, deviating from the norm or average. Abnormal implies the presence of a mental disorder that leads to behavior that society labels as deviant. There is a continuum between normal and abnormal. These are relative terms in that they imply a social judgment. *See* Normal.

Accommodation Process in cognitive development; involves altering or reorganizing the mental picture to make room for a new experience or idea.

Acetylcholine A neurotransmitter involved in memory.

Achievement Drive The need to attain self-esteem, success, or status. Society's expectations strongly influence the achievement motive.

ACTH (Adrenocorticotropic Hormone) The part of the brain called the hypothalamus activates the release of the hormone ACTH from the pituitary gland when a stressful condition exists. ACTH in turn activates the release of adrenal corticoids from the cortex of the adrenal gland.

Action Therapy A general classification of therapy (as opposed to insight therapy) in which the therapist focuses on symptoms rather than on underlying emotional states. Treatment aims at teaching new behavioral patterns rather than at self-understanding. *See* Insight Therapy.

Actor-Observer Attribution The tendency to attribute the behavior of other people to internal causes and the behavior of yourself to external causes.

Acupuncture The technique for curing certain diseases and anesthetizing by inserting needles at certain points of the body, developed in China and now being studied and applied in the West.

Adaptation The process of responding to changes in the environment by altering one's responses to keep one's behavior appropriate to environmental demands.

Addiction Physical dependence on a drug. When a drug causes biochemical changes that are uncomfortable when the drug is discontinued, when one must take ever larger doses to maintain the intensity of the drug's effects, and when desire to continue the drug is strong, one is said to be addicted.

Adjustment How we react to stress; some change that we make in response to the demands placed upon us.

Adrenal Glands Endocrine glands involved in stress and energy regulation.

Affective Disorder Affect means feeling or emotion. An affective disorder is mental illness marked by a disturbance of mood (e.g. manic depression.)

Afferent Neuron (Sensory) A neuron that carries messages from the sense organs toward the central nervous system.

Aggression Any act that causes pain or suffering to another. Some psychologists believe that aggressive behavior is instinctual to all species, including man, while others believe that it is learned through the processes of observation and imitation.

Alienation Indifference to or loss of personal relationships. An individual may feel estranged from family members, or, on a broader scale, from society.

All-or-None Law The principle that states that a neuron only fires when a stimulus is above a certain minimum strength (threshold), and when it fires, it does so at full strength.

Altered State of Consciousness (ASC) A mental state qualitatively different from a person's normal, alert, waking consciousness.

Altruism Behavior motivated by a desire to benefit another person. Altruistic behavior is aided by empathy and is usually motivated internally, not by observable threats or rewards.

Amphetamine A psychoactive drug that is a stimulant. Although used in treating mild depressions or, in children, hyperactivity, its medical uses are doubtful, and amphetamines are often abused. *See* Psychoactive Drug.

Anal Stage Psychosexual stage, during which, according to Freud, the child experiences the first restrictions on his impulses.

Animism The quality of believing life exists in inanimate objects. According to Piaget, animism is characteristic of children's thinking until about age two.

Antisocial Personality Disorder Personality disorder in which individuals who engage in antisocial behavior experience no guilt or anxiety about their actions; sometimes called sociopathy or psychopathy.

Anxiety An important term that has different meanings for different theories (psychoanalysis, behavior theory); a feeling state of apprehension, dread, or uneasiness. The state may be aroused by an objectively dangerous situation or by a situation that is not objectively dangerous. It may be mild or severe.

Anxiety Disorder Fairly long-lasting disruptions of the person's ability to deal with stress; often accompanied by feelings of fear and apprehension.

Applied Psychology The area of psychology that is most immediately concerned with helping to solve practical problems; includes clinical and counseling psychology, and industrial, environmental, and legal psychology.

Aptitude Tests Tests which are designed to predict what can be accomplished by a person in the future with the proper training.

Arousal A measure of responsiveness or activity; a state of excitement or wakefulness ranging from deepest coma to intense excitement.

Aspiration Level The level of achievement a person strives for. Studies suggest that people can use internal or external standards of performance.

Assertiveness Training Training which helps individuals stand up for their rights while not denying rights of other people.

Assimilation Process in cognitive development; occurs when something new is taken into the child's mental picture of the world.

Association Has separate meanings for different branches of psychology. Theory in cognitive psychology suggests that we organize information so that we can find our memories systematically, that one idea will bring another to mind. In psychoanalysis, the patient is asked to free associate (speak aloud all consecutive thoughts until random associations tend of themselves to form a meaningful whole). *See* Cognitive Psychology, Psychoanalysis.

Associationism A theory of learning suggesting that once two stimuli are presented together, one of them will remind a person of the other. Ideas are learned by association with sensory experiences and are not innate. Among the principles of associationism are contiguity (stimuli that occur close together are more likely to be associated than stimuli far apart), and repetition (the more frequently stimuli occur together, the more strongly they become associated.)

Association Neurons Neurons that connect with other neurons.

Attachment Process in which the individual shows behaviors that promote the proximity or contact with a specific object or person.

Attention The tendency to focus activity in a particular direction and to select certain stimuli for further analysis while ignoring or possibly storing for further analysis all other inputs.

Attitude An overall tendency to respond positively or negatively to particular people or objects in a way that is learned through experience and that is made up of feelings (affects,) thoughts (evaluations,) and actions (conation.)

Attribution The process of determining the causes of behavior in a given individual.

Autism A personality disorder in which ae child does not respond socially to people.

Autonomic Nervous System The part of the nervous system (The other part is the central nervous system.) that is for emergency functions and release of large amounts of energy (sympathetic division) and regulating functions such as digestion and sleep (parasympathetic division.) *See* Biofeedback.

Aversion Therapy A counterconditioning therapy in which unwanted responses are paired with unpleasant consequences.

Avoidance Conditioning Situation in which a subject learns to avoid an aversive stimulus by responding appropriately before it begins.

Barbiturates Sedative-hypnotic, psychoactive drugs widely used to induce sleep and to reduce tension. Overuse can lead to addiction. *See* Addiction.

Behavior Any observable activity of an organism, including mental processes.

Behaviorism A school of psychology stressing an objective approach to psychological questions, proposing that psychology be limited to observable behavior and that the subjectiveness of consciousness places it beyond the limits of scientific psychology.

Behavior Therapy The use of conditioning processes to treat mental disorders. Various techniques may be used, including positive reinforcement in which rewards (verbal or tangible) are given to the patient for appropriate behavior, modeling in which patients unlearn fears by watching models exhibit fearlessness, and systematic desensitization in which the patient is taught to relax and visualize anxiety-producing items at the same time. *See* Insight Therapy, Systematic Desensitization.

Biofeedback The voluntary control of physiological processes by receiving information about those processes as they occur, through instruments that pick up these changes and display them to the subject in the form of a signal. Blood pressure, skin temperature, etc. can be controlled.

Biological (Primary) Motives Motives which have a physiological basis; include hunger, thirst, body temperature regulation, avoidance of pain, and sex.

Biological Response System System of the body that is particularly important in behavioral responding; includes the senses, endocrines, muscles, and the nervous system.

Biological Therapy Treatment of behavior problems through biological techniques; major biological therapies include drug therapy, psychosurgery, and electroconvulsive therapy.

Bipolar Disorder Affective disorder which is characterized by extreme mood swings from sad depression to joyful mania; sometimes called manic-depression.

Body Language Communication through position and movement of the body.

Brain Mapping A procedure for identifying the function of various areas of the brain; the surgeon gives tiny electrical stimulation to a specific area and notes patient's reaction.

Brain Stimulation The introduction of chemical or electrical stimuli directly into the brain.

Brain Waves Electrical responses produced by brain activity that can be recorded directly from any portion of the brain or from the scalp with special electrodes. Brain waves are measured by an electroencephalograph (EEG). Alpha waves occur during relaxed wakefulness and beta waves during active behavior. Theta waves are associated with drowsiness and vivid visual imagery, delta waves with deep sleep.

Bystander Effect Phenomenon in which a single person is more likely to help in an emergency situation than a group of people.

Cannon-Bard Theory of Emotion Theory of emotion which states that the emotional feeling and the physiological arousal occur at the same time.

Catatonic Schizophrenia A type of schizophrenia which is characterized by periods of complete immobility and the apparent absence of will to move or speak.

Causal Attribution Process of determining whether a person's behavior is due to internal or external motives.

Cautious Shift Research suggests that the decisions of a group will be more conservative than that of the average individual member when dealing with areas for which there are widely held values favoring caution (e.g. physical danger or family responsibility). *See* Risky Shift.

Central Nervous System The part of the human nervous system which interprets and stores messages from the sense organs, decides what behavior to exhibit, and sends appropriate messages to the muscles and glands; includes the brain and spinal cord.

Central Tendency In statistics, measures of central tendency give a number that represents the entire group or sample.

Cerebellum The part of the brain responsible for muscle and movement control and coordination of eye-body movement.

Cerebral Cortex The part of the brain consisting of the outer layer of cerebral cells. The cortex can be divided into specific regions: sensory, motor, and associative.

Chaining Behavior theory suggests that behavior patterns are built up of component parts by stringing together a number of simpler responses.

Character Disorder (or Personality Disorder) A classification of psychological disorders (as distinguished from neurosis or psychosis). The disorder has become part of the individual's personality and does not cause him discomfort, making that disorder more difficult to treat psychotherapeutically.

Chromosome *See* Gene.

Chunking The tendency to code memories so that there are fewer bits to store.

Classical Conditioning See Pavlovian Conditioning.

Client-Centered Therapy A nondirective form of psychotherapy developed by Carl Rogers in which the counselor attempts to create an atmosphere in which the client can freely explore himself and his problems. The client-centered therapist reflects what the client says back to him, usually without interpreting it.

Clinical Psychology The branch of psychology concerned with testing, diagnosing, interviewing, conducting research and treating (often by psychotherapy) mental disorders and personality problems.

Cognitive Appraisal Intellectual evaluation of situations or stimuli. Experiments suggest that emotional arousal is produced not simply by a stimulus but by how one evaluates and interprets the arousal. The appropriate physical response follows this cognitive appraisal.

Cognitive Behavior Therapy A form of behavior therapy which identifies self-defeating attitudes and thoughts in a subject, and then helps the subject to replace these with positive, supportive thoughts.

Cognitive Dissonance People are very uncomfortable if they perceive that their beliefs, feelings, or acts are not consistent with one another, and they will try to reduce the discomfort of this dissonance.

Cognitive Psychology The study of how individuals gain knowledge of their environments. Cognitive psychologists believe that the organism actively participates in constructing the meaningful stimuli that it selectively organizes and to which it selectively responds.

Comparative Psychology The study of similarities and differences in the behavior of different species.

Compulsive Personality Personality disorder in which an individual is preoccupied with details and rules.

Concept Learning The acquisition of the ability to identify and use the qualities that objects or situations have in common. A class concept refers to any quality that breaks objects or situations into separate groupings.

Concrete-Operational Stage A stage in intellectual development according to Piaget. The child at approximately seven years begins to apply logic. His thinking is less egocentric, reversible, and the child develops conservation abilities and the ability to classify. *See* Conservation.

Conditioned Reinforcer Reinforcement that is effective because it has been associated with other reinforcers. Conditioned reinforcers are involved in higher order conditioning.

Conditioned Response (CR) The response or behavior that occurs when the conditioned stimulus is presented (after the CS has been associated with the US).

Conditioned Stimulus (CS) An originally neutral stimulus that is associated with an unconditioned stimulus and takes on its capability of eliciting a particular reaction.

Conditioned Taste Aversion (CTA) Learning an aversion to particular tastes by associating them with stomach distress; usually considered a unique form of classical conditioning because of the extremely long interstimulus intervals involved.

Conduction The ability of a neuron to carry a message (an electrical stimulus) along its length.

Conflict Situation which occurs when we experience incompatible demands or desires.

Conformity The tendency of an individual to act like others regardless of personal belief.

Conscience A person's sense of the moral rightness or wrongness of behavior.

Consciousness Awareness of experienced sensations, thoughts, and feelings at any given point in time.

Consensus In causal attribution, the extent to which other people react the same way the subject does in a particular situation.

Conservation Refers to the child's ability to understand laws of length, mass, and volume. Before the development of this ability, a child will not understand that a particular property of an object (e.g. the quantity of water in a glass) does not change even though other perceivable features change.

Consistency In causal attribution, the extent to which the subject always behaves in the same way in a particular situation.

Consolidation The biological neural process of making memories permanent; possibly short-term memory is electrically coded and long-term memory is chemically coded.

Continuum of Preparedness Seligman's proposal that animals are biologically prepared to learn certain responses more readily than others.

Control Group A group used for comparison with an experimental group. All conditions must be identical for each group with the exception of the one variable (independent) that is manipulated. *See* Experimental Group.

Convergence Binocular depth cue in which we detect distance by interpreting the kinesthetic sensations produced by the muscles of the eyeballs.

Convergent Thinking The kind of thinking that is used to solve problems having only one correct answer. *See* Divergent Thinking.

Conversion Disorder Somatoform disorder in which a person displays obvious disturbance in the nervous system, however, a medical examination reveals no physical basis for the problem; often includes paralysis, loss of sensation, or blindness.

Corpus Callosum Nerve fibers that connect the two halves of the brain in humans. If cut, the halves continue to function although some functions are affected.

Correlation A measurement in which two or more sets of variables are compared and the extent to which they are related is calculated.

Correlation Coefficient The measure, in number form, of how two variables vary together. They extend from -1 (perfect negative correlation) to $+1$ (perfect positive correlation).

Counterconditioning A behavior therapy in which an unwanted response is replaced by conditioning a new response that is incompatible with it.

Creativity The ability to discover or produce new solutions to problems, new inventions, or new works of art. Creativity is an ability independent of IQ and is open-ended in that solutions are not predefined in their scope or appropriateness. *See* Problem-Solving.

Critical Period A specific stage in an organism's development during which the acquisition of a particular type of behavior depends on exposure to a particular type of stimulation.

Cross-Sectional Study A research technique that focuses on a factor in a group of subjects as they are at one time, as in a study of fantasy play in subjects of three different age groups. *See* Longitudinal Study.

Culture-Bound The idea that a test's usefulness is limited to the culture in which it was written and utilized.

Curiosity Motive Motive which causes the individual to seek out a certain amount of novelty.

Cutaneous Sensitivity The skin senses: touch, pain, pressure and temperature. Skin receptors respond in different ways and with varying degrees of sensitivity.

Decay Theory of forgetting in which sensory impressions leave memory traces that fade away with time.

Defense Mechanism A way of reducing anxiety that does not directly cope with the threat. There are many types, denial, repression, etc., all of which are used in normal function. Only when use is habitual or they impede effective solutions are they considered pathological.

Delusion A false belief that persists despite evidence showing it to be irrational. Delusions are often symptoms of mental illness.

Dependent Variable Those conditions that an experimenter observes and measures. Called "dependent" because they depend on the experimental manipulations.

Depersonalization Disorder Dissociative disorder in which individuals escape from their own personalities by believing that they don't exist or that their environment is not real.

Depression A temporary emotional state that normal individuals experience or a persistent state that may be considered a psychological disorder. Characterized by sadness and low self-esteem. *See* Self-Esteem.

Descriptive Statistics Techniques that help summarize large amounts of data information.

Developmental Norms The average time at which developmental changes occur in the normal individual.

Developmental Psychology The study of changes in behavior and thinking as the organism grows from the prenatal stage to death.

Deviation, Standard and Average Average deviation is determined by measuring the deviation of each score in a distribution from the mean and calculating the average of the deviations. The standard deviation is used to determine how representative the mean of a distribution is. *See* Mean.

Diagnostic and Statistical Manual of Mental Disorders (DSM) DSM-III was published in 1980 by the American Psychiatric Association.

Diffusion of Responsibility As the number of witnesses to a help-requiring situation—and thus the degree of anonymity—increases, the amount of helping decreases and the amount of time before help is offered increases. *See* Anonymity.

Discrimination The ability to tell whether stimuli are different when presented together or that one situation is different from a past one.

Disorganized Schizophrenia A type of schizophrenia which is characterized by a severe personality disintegration; the individual often displays bizarre behavior.

Displacement The process by which an emotion originally attached to a particular person, object, or situation is transferred to something else.

Dissociative Disorders Disorders in which individuals forget who they are.

Distal Stimuli Physical events in the environment that affect perception. *See also* Proximal Stimuli.

Distinctiveness In causal attribution, the extent to which the subject reacts the same way in other situations.

Divergent Thinking The kind of thinking that characterizes creativity (as contrasted with convergent thinking) and involves the development of novel resolutions of a task or the generation of totally new ideas. *See* Convergent Thinking.

DNA *See* Gene.

Double Bind A situation in which a person is subjected to two conflicting, contradictory demands at the same time.

Down's Syndrome Form of mental retardation caused by having three number 21 chromosomes (trisomy 21).

Dreams The thoughts, images, and emotions that occur during sleep. Dreams occur periodically during the sleep cycle and are usually marked by rapid movements of the eyes (REM sleep). The content of dreams tends to reflect emotions (sexual feelings, according to Freud) and experiences of the previous day. Nightmares are qualitatively different from other dreams, often occuring during deep or Stage 4 sleep.

Drive A need or urge that motivates behavior. Some drives may be explained as responses to bodily needs, such as hunger or sex. Others derive from social pressures and complex forms of learning, for example, competition, curiosity, achievement. *See* Motivation.

Drive Reduction Theory Theory of motivation that states that the individual is pushed by inner forces toward reducing the drive and restoring homeostasis.

Drug Dependence A state of mental or physical dependence on a drug, or both. Psychoactive drugs are capable of creating psychological dependence (anxiety when the drug is unavailable,) although the relationship of some, such as marijuana and LSD, to physical dependence or addiction is still under study. *See* Psychoactive Drugs, Addiction.

Drug Tolerance A state produced by certain psychoactive drugs in which increasing amounts of the substance are required to produce the desired effect. Some drugs produce tolerance but not withdrawal symptoms, and these drugs are not regarded as physically addicting.

Effectance Motive The striving for effectiveness in dealing with the environment. The effectance motive differs from the need for achievement in that effectance depends on internal feelings of satisfaction while the need for achievement is geared more to meeting others' standards.

Efferent Neuron (Motor) A neuron that carries messages from the central nervous system to the muscles and glands.

Ego A construct to account for the organization in a person's life and for making the person's behavior correspond to physical and social realities. According to Freud, the ego is the "reality principle" that is responsible for holding the id or "pleasure principle" in check. *See* Id.

Egocentrism Seeing things from only one's own point of view; also, the quality of a child's thought that prevents him from understanding that different people perceive the world differently. Egocentrism is characteristic of a stage that all children go through.

Electroshock Therapy A form of therapy used to relieve severe depression. The patient receives electric current across the forehead, loses consciousness, and undergoes a short convulsion. When the patient regains consciousness, his mood is lifted.

Emotion A complex feeling-state that involves physiological arousal; a subjective feeling which might involve a cognitive appraisal of the situation and overt behavior in response to a stimulus.

Empathy The ability to appreciate how someone else feels by putting yourself in his position and experiencing his feelings. Empathy is acquired normally by children during intellectual growth.

Empiricism The view that behavior is learned through experience.

Encounter Groups Groups of individuals who meet to change their personal lives by confronting each other, discussing personal problems, and talking more honestly and openly than in everyday life.

Endocrine Glands Ductless glands that secrete chemicals called hormones into the blood stream.

Equilibration According to Piaget, the child constructs his understanding of the world through equilibration. Equilibration consists of the interaction of two complementary processes, assimilation (taking in input within the existing structures of the mind, e.g. putting it into mental categories that already exist) with accommodation (the changing of mental categories to fit new input that cannot be taken into existing categories) and is the process by which knowing occurs. One's developmental stage affects how one equilibrates.

Ethnocentrism The belief that one's own ethnic or racial group is superior to others.

Experiment Procedures executed under a controlled situation in order to test a hypothesis and discover relationships between independent and dependent variables.

Experimental Control The predetermined conditions, procedures, and checks built into the design of an experiment to ensure scientific control; as opposed to "control" in common usage, which implies manipulation.

Experimental Group In a scientific experiment, the group of subjects that is usually treated specially, as opposed to the control group, in order to isolate just the variable under investigation. *See* Control Group.

Experimental Psychology The branch of psychology concerned with the laboratory study of basic psychological laws and principles as demonstrated in the behavior of animals.

Experimenter Bias How the expectations of the person running an experiment can influence what comes out of the experiment. Experimenter bias can affect the way the experimenter sees the subjects' behavior, causing distortions of fact, and can also affect the way the experimenter reads data, also leading to distortions.

Extinction The elimination of behavior by, in classical conditioning, the withholding of the US, and in operant conditioning, the withholding of the reinforcement.

Extrasensory Perception (ESP) The range of perceptions that are "paranormal," (such as the ability to predict events, reproduce drawings sealed in envelopes, etc.).

Fixed-Action Pattern Movement that is characteristic of a species and does not have to be learned.

Fixed Interval (FI) Schedule Schedule of reinforcement in which the subject receives reinforcement for the first correct response given after a specified time interval.

Fixed Ratio (FR) Schedule Schedule of reinforcement in which the subject is reinforced after a certain number of responses.

Forgetting The process by which material that once was available is no longer available. Theory exists that forgetting occurs because memories interfere with one another, either retroactively (new memories block old) or proactively (old memories block new); that forgetting occurs when the cues necessary to recall the information are not supplied, or when memories are too unpleasant to remain in consciousness. *See* Repression.

Formal Operational Stage According to Piaget, the stage at which the child develops adult powers of reasoning, abstraction, and symbolizing. The child can grasp scientific, religious, and political concepts and deduce their consequences as well as reason hypothetically ("what if. . . .").

Frequency Theory of Hearing Theory of hearing that states that the frequency of vibrations at the basilar membrane determines the frequency of firing of neurons that carry impulses to the brain.

Frustration A feeling of discomfort or insecurity aroused by a blocking of gratification or by unresolved problems. Several theories hold that frustration arouses aggression. *See* Aggression.

Functionalism An early school of psychology stressing the ways behavior helps one adapt to the environment and the role that learning plays in this adaptive process.

Gene The unit of heredity that determines particular characteristics; a part of a molecule of DNA. DNA (dioxyribonucleic acid) is found mainly in the nucleus of living cells where it occurs in threadlike structures called chromosomes. Within the chromosomes each DNA molecule is organized into specific units that carry the genetic information necessary for the development of a particular trait. These units are the genes. A gene can reproduce itself exactly, and this is how traits are carried between generations. The genotype is the entire structure of genes that are inherited by an organism from its parents. The environment interacts with this genotype to determine how the genetic potential will develop.

General Adaptation Syndrome (GAS) The way the body responds to stress, as described by Hans Selye. In the first stage, an alarm reaction, a person responds by efforts at self-control and shows signs of nervous depression (defense mechanisms, fear, anger, etc.) followed by a release of ACTH. In stage 2, the subject shows increased resistance to the specific source of stress and less resistance to other sources. Defense mechanisms may become neurotic. With stage 3 come exhaustion, stupor, even death.

Generalization The process by which learning in one situation is transferred to another, similar situation. It is a key term in behavioral modification and classical conditioning. *See* Classical Conditioning.

Generalized Anxiety Disorder Disorder in which the individual lives in a state of constant severe tension; continuous fear and apprehension experienced by an individual.

Genetics The study of the transfer of the inheritance of characteristics from one generation to another.

Genotype The underlying genetic structure that an individual has inherited and will send on to descendants. The actual appearance of a trait (phenotype) is due to the interaction of the genotype and the environment.

Gestalt Psychology A movement in psychology begun in the 1920s, stressing the wholeness of a person's experience and proposing that perceiving is an active, dynamic process that takes into account the entire pattern ("gestalt") of the perceptual field. *See* Behaviorism, Associationism.

Glia Cells in the central nervous system that regulate the chemical environment of the nerve cells. RNA is stored in glial cells.

Grammar The set of rules for combining units of a language.

Group Therapy A form of psychotherapy aimed at treating mental disorders in which interaction among group members is the main therapeutic mode. Group therapy takes many forms but essentially requires a sense of community, support, increased personal responsibility, and a professionally trained leader.

Growth The normal quantitative changes that occur in the physical and psychological aspects of a healthy child with the passage of time.

Gustation The sense of taste. Theory suggests that the transmission of sense information from tongue to brain occurs through patterns of cell activity and not just the firing of single nerve fibers. Also, it is believed that specific spatial patterns or places on the tongue correspond to taste qualities.

Habit Formation The tendency to make a response to a stimulus less variable, especially if it produced successful adaptation.

Hallucination A sensory impression reported by a person when no external stimulus exists to justify the report. Hallucinations are serious symptoms and may be produced by psychoses. *See* Psychoses.

Hallucinogen A substance that produces hallucinations, such as LSD, mescaline, etc.

Hierarchy of Needs Maslow's list of motives in humans, arranged from the biological to the uniquely human.

Higher Order Conditioning Learning to make associations with stimuli that have been previously learned (CSs).

Hippocampus Part of the cortex of the brain governing memory storage, smell, and visceral functions.

Homeostasis A set of processes maintaining the constancy of the body's internal state, a series of dynamic compensations of the nervous system. Many processes such as appetite, body temperature, water balance, heart rate are controlled by homeostasis.

Hormones Chemical secretions of the endocrine glands that regulate various body processes (e.g. growth, sexual traits, reproductive processes, etc.)

Humanism Branch of psychology dealing with those qualities distinguishing humans from other animals.

Hypnosis A trancelike state marked by heightened suggestibility and a narrowing of attention which can be induced in a number of ways. Debate exists over whether hypnosis is a true altered state of consciousness and over to what extent strong motivating instructions can duplicate so-called hypnosis.

Hypothalamus A part of the brain that acts as a channel that carries information from the cortex and the thalamus to the spinal cord and ultimately to the motor nerves or to the autonomic nervous system, where it is transmitted to specific target organs. These target organs release into the bloodstream specific hormones that alter bodily functions. *See* Autonomic Nervous System.

Hypothesis A hypothesis can be called an educated guess, similar to a hunch. When a hunch is stated in a way that allows for further testing, it becomes a hypothesis.

Iconic Memory A visual memory. Experiments suggest that in order to be remembered and included in long-term memory, information must pass through a brief sensory stage. Theory further suggests that verbal information is subject to forgetting but that memorized sensory images are relatively permanent.

Id According to Freud, a component of the psyche present at birth that is the storehouse of psychosexual energy called *libido,* and also of primitive urges to fight, dominate, destroy.

Identification The taking on of attributes that one sees in another person. Children tend to identify with their parents or other important adults and thereby take on certain traits that are important to their development.

Illusion A mistaken perception of an actual stimulus.

Imitation The copying of another's behavior; learned through the process of observation. *See* Modeling.

Impression Formation The process of developing an evaluation of another person from your perceptions; first, or initial impressions are often very important.

Imprinting The rapid, permanent acquisition by an organism of a strong attachment to an object (usually the parent). Imprinting occurs shortly after birth.

Independent Variable The condition in an experiment which is controlled and manipulated by the experimenter; it is a stimulus that will cause a response.

Inferential Statistics Techniques that help researchers make generalizations about a finding based on a limited number of subjects.

Inhibition Restraint of an impulse, desire, activity, or drive. People are taught to inhibit full expression of many drives (for example, aggression or sexuality) and to apply checks either consciously or unconsciously. In Freudian terminology, an inhibition is an unconsciously motivated blocking of sexual energy. In Pavlovian conditioning, inhibition is the theoretical process that operates during extinction, acting to block a conditioned response. *See* Pavlovian Conditioning.

Insight A sudden perception of useful or proper relations among objects necessary to solve the problem.

Insight Therapy A general classification of therapy in which the therapist focuses on the patient's underlying feelings and motivations and devotes most effort to increasing the patient's self-awareness or insight into his behavior. The other major class of therapy is action therapy. *See* Action Therapy.

Instinct An inborn pattern of behavior, relatively independent of environmental influence. An instinct may need to be triggered by a particular stimulus in the environment, but then it proceeds in a fixed pattern. The combination of taxis (orienting movement in response to a particular stimulus) and fixed-action pattern (inherited coordination) is the basis for instinctual activity. *See* Fixed-Action Pattern.

Instrumental Learning *See* Operant Conditioning.

Intelligence A capacity for knowledge about the world. This is an enormous and controversial field of study, and there is not agreement on a precise definition. However, intelligence has come to refer to higher-level abstract processes and may be said to comprise the ability to deal effectively with abstract concepts, the ability to learn, and the ability to adapt and deal with new situations. Piaget defines intelligence as the construction of an understanding. Both biological inheritance and environmental factors contribute to general intelligence. Children proceed through a sequence of identifiable stages in the development of conceptual thinking (Piaget). The degree to which factors such as race, sex, and social class affect intelligence is not known.

Intelligence Quotient (IQ) A measurement of intelligence originally based on tests devised by Binet and now widely applied. Genetic inheritance and environment affect IQ, although their relative contributions are not known. IQ can be defined in different ways; classically it is defined as a relation between chronological and mental ages.

Interference Theory of forgetting in which information that was learned before (proactive interference) or after (retroactive interference) the material of interest causes the learner to be unable to remember the material.

Interstimulus Interval The time between the start of the conditioned stimulus and the start of the unconditioned stimulus in Pavlovian conditioning. *See* Pavlovian Conditioning.

Intra-Uterine Environment The environment in the uterus during pregnancy can affect the physical development of the organism and its behavior after birth. Factors such as the mother's nutrition, emotional and physical state significantly influence offspring. The mother's diseases, medications, hormones, stress level all effect the pre- and post-natal development of her young.

Intrinsic Motivation Motivation inside of the individual; we do something because we receive satisfaction from it.

Introspection Reporting one's internal, subjective mental contents for the purpose of further study and analysis. *See* Structuralism.

James-Lange Theory of Emotion Theory of emotion which states that the physiological arousal and behavior come before the subjective experience of an emotion.

Labeling-of-Arousal Experiments suggest that an individual experiencing physical arousal that he cannot explain will interpret his feelings in terms of the situation he is in and will use environmental and contextual cues.

Language A set of abstract symbols used to communicate meaning. Language includes vocalized sounds or semantic units (words, usually) and rules for combining the units (grammar). There is some inborn basis for language acquisition, and there are identifiable stages in its development that are universal.

Language Acquisition Linguists debate how children acquire language. Some believe in environmental shaping, a gradual system of reward and punishment. Others emphasize the unfolding of capacities inborn in the brain that are relatively independent of the environment and its rewards.

Latency Period According to Freud, the psychosexual stage of development during which sexual interest has been repressed and thus is low or "latent" (dormant).

Law of Effect Thorndike's proposal that when a response produces satisfaction, it will be repeated; reinforcement.

Leadership The quality of exerting more influence than other group members. Research suggests that certain characteristics are generally considered essential to leadership: consideration, sensitivity, ability to initiate and structure, and emphasis on production. However, environmental factors may thrust authority on a person without regard to personal characteristics.

Learned Helplessness Theory suggests that living in an environment of uncontrolled stress reduces the ability to cope with future stress that *is* controllable.

Learned Social Motives Motives in the human which are learned; include achievement, affiliation, and autonomy.

Learning The establishment of connections between stimulus and response, resulting from observation, special training, or previous activity. Learning is relatively permanent.

Lifespan Span of time from conception to death; in developmental psychology, a lifespan approach looks at development throughout an individual's life.

Linguistic Relativity Hypothesis Proposal by Whorf that the perception of reality differs according to the language of the observer.

Linguistics The study of language, its nature, structure, and components.

Locus of Control The perceived place from which come determining forces in one's life. A person who feels that he has some control over his fate and tends to feel more likely to succeed has an internal locus of control. A person with an external locus of control feels that it is outside himself and therefore that his attempts to control his fate are less assured.

Longitudinal Study A research method that involves following subjects over a considerable period of time (as compared with a cross-sectional approach); as in a study of fantasy play in children observed several times at intervals of two years. *See* Cross-Sectional Study.

Love Affectionate behavior between people, often in combination with interpersonal attraction. The mother-infant love relationship strongly influences the later capacity for developing satisfying love relationships.

Manic-Depressive Reaction A form of mental illness marked by alternations of extreme phases of elation (manic phase) and depression.

Maternalism Refers to the mother's reaction to her young. It is believed that the female is biologically determined to exhibit behavior more favorable to the care and feeding of the young than the male, although in humans maternalism is probably determined as much by cultural factors as by biological predisposition.

Maturation The genetically-controlled process of physical and physiological growth.

Mean The measure of central tendency, or mathematical average, computed by adding all scores in a set and dividing by the number of scores.

Meaning The concept or idea conveyed to the mind, by any method. In reference to memory, meaningful terms are easier to learn than less meaningful, unconnected, or nonsense terms. Meaningfulness is not the same as the word's meaning.

Median In a set of scores, the median is that middle score that divides the set into equal halves.

Memory Involves the encoding, storing of information in the brain, and its retrieval. Several theories exist to explain memory. One proposes that we have both a short-term (STM) and a long-term memory (LTM) and that information must pass briefly through the STM to be stored in the LTM. Also suggested is that verbal information is subject to forgetting, while memorized sensory images are relatively permanent. Others see memory as a function of association—information processed systematically and the meaningfulness of the items. Debate exists over whether memory retrieval is actually a process of reappearance or reconstruction.

Mental Disorder A mental condition that deviates from what society considers to be normal.

Minnesota Multiphasic Personality Inventory (MMPI) An objective personality test which was originally devised to identify personality disorders.

Mode In a set of scores, the measurement at which the largest number of subjects fall.

Modeling The imitation or copying of another's behavior. As an important process in personality development, modeling may be based on parents. In therapy, the therapist may serve as a model for the patient.

Morality The standards of right and wrong of a society and their adoption by members of that society. Some researchers believe that morality develops in successive stages, with each stage representing a specific level of moral thinking (Kohlberg). Others see morality as the result of experiences in which the child learns through punishment and reward from models such as parents and teachers.

Motivation All factors that cause and regulate behavior that is directed toward achieving goals and satisfying needs. Motivation is what moves an organism to action.

Motor Unit One spinal motoneuron (motor nerve cell) and the muscle fibers it activates. The contraction of a muscle involves the activity of many motoneurons and muscle fibers. Normally we are aware only of our muscles contracting and not of the process producing the contraction, although biofeedback can train people to control individual motor units. *See* Biofeedback.

Narcotic A drug that relieves pain. Heroin, morphine, and opium are narcotics. Narcotics are often addicting.

Naturalistic Observation Research method in which behavior of people or animals in the normal environment is accurately recorded.

Negative Reinforcement Any event that upon termination, strengthens the preceding behavior; taking from subject something bad will increase the probability that the preceding behavior will be repeated. Involves aversive stimulus.

Neuron A nerve cell. There are billions of neurons in the brain and spinal cord. Neurons interact at synapses or points of contact. Information passage between neurons is electrical and biochemical. It takes the activity of many neurons to produce a behavior.

Neurosis Any one of a wide range of psychological difficulties, accompanied by excessive anxiety (as contrasted with psychosis). Psychoanalytic theory states that neurosis is an expression of unresolved conflicts in the form of tension and impaired functioning. Most neurotics are in much closer contact with reality than most psychotics. Term has been largely eliminated from DSM-III.

Nonverbal Behaviors Gestures, facial expressions, and other body movements. They are important because they tend to convey emotion. Debate exists over whether they are inborn or learned.

Norm An empirically set pattern of belief or behavior. Social norm refers to widely accepted social or cultural behavior to which a person tends to or is expected to conform.

Normal Sane, or free from mental disorder. Normal behavior is the behavior typical of most people in a given group, and "normality" implies a social judgment.

Normal Curve When scores of a large number of random cases are plotted on a graph, they often fall into a bell-shaped curve; there are as many cases above the mean as below on the curve.

Object Permanence According to Piaget, the stage in cognitive development when a child begins to conceive of objects as having an existence even when out of sight or touch and to conceive of space as extending beyond his own perception.

Oedipus Complex The conflicts of a child in triangular relationship with his mother and father. According to Freud, a boy must resolve his unconscious sexual desire for his mother and the accompanying wish to kill his father and fear of his father's revenge in order that he proceed in his moral development. The analogous problem for girls is called the Electra complex.

Olfaction The sense of smell. No general agreement exists on how olfaction works though theories exist to explain it. One suggests that the size and shape of molecules of what is smelled is a crucial cue. The brain processes involved in smell are located in a different and evolutionally older part of the brain than the other senses.

Operant Conditioning The process of changing, maintaining, or eliminating voluntary behavior through the consequences of that behavior. Operant conditioning uses many of the techniques of Pavlovian conditioning but differs in that it deals with voluntary rather than reflex behaviors. The frequency with which a behavior is emitted can be increased if it is rewarded (reinforced) and decreased if it is not reinforced, or punished. Some psychologists believe that all behavior is learned through conditioning while others believe that intellectual and motivational processes play a crucial role. *See* Pavlovian Conditioning.

Operational Definitions If an event is not directly observable, then the variables must be defined by the operations by which they will be measured. These definitions are called operational definitions.

Organism Any living animal, human or subhuman.

Orienting Response A relatively automatic, "what's that?" response that puts the organism in a better position to attend to and deal with a new stimulus. When a stimulus attracts our attention, our body responds with movements of head and body toward the stimulus, changes in muscle tone, heart rate, blood flow, breathing, and changes in the brain's electrical activity.

Pavlovian Conditioning Also called classical conditioning, Pavlovian conditioning can be demonstrated as follows: In the first step, an *unconditioned stimulus* (UCS) such as food, loud sounds, or pain is paired with a neutral *conditioned stimulus* (CS) that causes no direct effect, such as a click, tone, or a dim light. The response elicited by the UCS is called the *unconditioned response* (UCR) and is a biological reflex of the nervous system (for example, eyeblinks or salivation). The combination of the neutral CS, the response-causing UCS, and the unlearned UCR is usually presented to the subject several times during conditioning. Eventually, the UCS is dropped from the sequence in the second step of the process, and the previously neutral CS comes to elicit a response. When conditioning is complete, presentation of the CS alone will result in a *conditioned response* (CR) similar but not always the same as the UCR.

Perception The field of psychology studying ways in which the experience of objects in the world is based upon stimulation of the sense organs. In psychology, the field of perception studies what determines sensory impressions, such as size, shape, distance, direction, etc. Physical events in the environment are called distal stimuli while the activity at the sense organ itself is called a proximal stimulus. The study of perceiving tries to determine how an organism knows what distal stimuli are like since proximal stimuli are its only source of information. Perception of objects remains more or less constant despite changes in distal stimuli and is therefore believed to depend on relationships within stimuli (size *and* distance, for example). Perceptual processes are able to adjust and adapt to changes in the perceptual field.

Performance The actual behavior of an individual that is observed. We often infer learning from observing performance.

Peripheral Nervous System The part of the human nervous system which receives messages from the sense organs and carries messages to the muscles and glands; everything outside of the brain and spinal cord.

Persuasion The process of changing a person's attitudes, beliefs, or actions. A person's susceptibility to persuasion depends on the persuader's credibility, subtlety and whether both sides of an argument are presented.

Phenotype The physical features or behavior patterns by which we recognize an organism. Phenotype is the result of interaction between genotype (total of inherited genes) and environment. *See* Genotype.

Phobia A neurosis consisting of an irrationally intense fear of specific persons, objects, or situations and a wish to avoid them. A phobic person feels intense and incapacitating anxiety. The person may be aware that his fear is irrational, but this knowledge does not help.

Pituitary Gland Is located at the base of the brain and controls secretion of several hormones: the antidiuretic hormone that maintains water balance, oxytocin which controls blood pressure and milk production and ACTH which is produced in response to stress, etc. *See* ACTH.

Placebo A substance which in and of itself has no real effect but which may produce an effect in a subject because the subject expects or believes that it will.

Positive Reinforcement Any event, that upon presentation, strengthens the preceding behavior; giving a subject something good will increase the probability that the preceding behavior will be repeated.

Prejudice An attitude in which one holds a negative belief about members of a group to which he does not belong. Prejudice is often directed at minority ethnic or racial groups and may be reduced by contact with these perceived "others."

Premack Principle Principle that states that of any two responses, the one that is more likely to occur can be used to reinforce the response that is less likely to occur.

Prenatal Development Development from conception to birth. It includes the physical development of the fetus as well as certain of its intellectual and emotional processes.

Preoperational Stage The development stage at which, according to Piaget, come the start of language, the ability to imitate actions, to symbolize, and to play make-believe games. Thinking is egocentric in that a child cannot understand that others perceive things differently.

Primary Reinforcement Reinforcement that is effective without having been associated with other reinforcers; sometimes called unconditioned reinforcement.

Probability (p) In inferential statistics, the likelihood that the difference between the experimental and control groups is due to the independent variable.

Problem Solving A self-directed activity in which an individual uses information to develop answers to problems, to generate new problems, and sometimes to transform the process by creating a unique, new system. Problem solving involves learning, insight and creativity.

Projective Test A type of test in which people respond to ambiguous, loosely structured stimuli. It is assumed that people will reveal themselves by putting themselves into the stimuli they see. The validity of these tests for diagnosis and personality assessment is still at issue.

Propaganda Information deliberately spread to aid a cause. Propaganda's main function is persuasion.

Prosocial Behavior Behavior which is directed toward helping others.

Proximal Stimulus Activity at the sense organ.

Psychoactive Drug A substance that affects mental activities, perceptions, consciousness, or mood. This group of drugs has its effects through strictly physical effects and through expectations.

Psychoanalysis There are two meanings to this word: it is a theory of personality development based on Freud and a method of treatment also based on Freud. Psychoanalytic therapy uses techniques of free association, dream analysis, and analysis of the patient's relationship (the "transference") to the analyst. Psychoanalytic theory maintains that the personality develops through a series of psychosexual stages and that the personality consists of specific components energized by the life and death instincts.

Psychogenic Pain Disorder Somatoform disorder in which the person complains of severe, long-lasting pain for which there is no organic cause.

Psycholinguistics The study of the process of language acquisition as part of psychological development and of language as an aspect of behavior. Thinking may obviously depend on language, but their precise relationship still puzzles psycholinguists, and several different views exist.

Psychological Dependence Situation when a person craves a drug even though it is not biologically necessary for his body.

Psychophysiological Disorders Real medical problems (such as ulcers, migraine headaches, and high blood pressure) which are caused or aggravated by psychological stress.

Psychosexual Stages According to Freud, an individual's personality develops through several stages. Each stage is associated with a particular bodily source of gratification (pleasure). First comes the oral stage when most pleasures come from the mouth. Then comes the anal stage when the infant derives pleasure from holding and releasing while learning bowel control. The phallic stage brings pleasure from the genitals, and a crisis (Oedipal) occurs in which the child gradually suppresses sexual desire for the opposite-sex parent, identifies with the same-sex parent and begins to be interested in the outside world. This latency period lasts until puberty, after which the genital stage begins and mature sexual relationships develop. There is no strict timetable, but according to Freudians, the stages do come in a definite order. Conflicts experienced and not adequately dealt with remain with the individual.

Psychosis The most severe of mental disorders, distinguished by a person being seriously out of touch with objective reality. Psychoses may result from physical factors (organic) or may have no known physical cause (functional). Psychoses take many forms of which the most common are schizophrenia and psychotic depressive reactions, but all are marked by personality disorganization and a severely reduced ability to perceive reality. Both biological and environmental factors are believed to influence the development of psychosis, although the precise effect of each is not presently known. *See* Neurosis.

Psychosomatic Disorders A variety of body reactions that are closely related to psychological events. Stress, for example, brings on many physical changes and can result in illness or even death if prolonged and severe. Psychosomatic disorders can affect any part of the body.

Psychotherapy Treatment involving interpersonal contacts between a trained therapist and a patient in which the therapist tries to produce beneficial changes in the patient's emotional state, attitudes, and behavior.

Punishment Any event that decreases the probability of the preceding behavior being repeated. You can give something bad (positive punishment) to decrease the preceding behavior.

Rational-Emotive Therapy A cognitive behavior modification technique in which a person is taught to identify irrational, self-defeating beliefs and then to overcome them.

Rationalization Defense mechanism in which individuals make up logical excuses to justify their behavior rather than exposing their true motives.

Reaction Formation Defense mechanism in which a person masks an unconsciously distressing or unacceptable trait by assuming an opposite attitude or behavior pattern.

Reactive Schizophrenia A type of schizophrenia in which the disorder appears as a reaction to some major trauma or terribly stressful encounter; sometimes called acute schizophrenia.

Reality Therapy A form of treatment of mental disorders pioneered by William Glasser in which the origins of the patient's problems are considered irrelevant and emphasis is on a close, judgmental bond between patient and therapist aimed to improve the patient's present and future life.

Reflex An automatic movement that occurs in direct response to a stimulus.

Rehearsal The repeating of an item to oneself and the means by which information is stored in the short-term memory (STM). Theory suggests that rehearsal is necessary for remembering and storage in the long-term memory (LTM).

Reinforcement The process of affecting the frequency with which a behavior is emitted. A reinforcer can reward and thus increase the behavior or punish and thus decrease its frequency. Reinforcers can also be primary, satisfying basic needs such as hunger or thirst, or secondary, satisfying learned and indirect values, such as money.

Reliability Consistency of measurement. A test is reliable if it repeatedly gives the same results. A person should get nearly the same score if the test is taken on two different occasions.

REM (Rapid-Eye Movement) Type of sleep in which the eyes are rapidly moving around; dreaming occurs in REM sleep.

Repression A defense mechanism in which a person forgets or pushes into the unconscious something that arouses anxiety. *See* Defense Mechanism, Anxiety.

Reticular Formation A system of nerve fibers leading from the spinal column to the cerebral cortex that functions to arouse, alert, and make an organism sensitive to changes in the environment. *See* Cerebral Cortex.

Retina The inside coating of the eye, containing two kinds of cells that react to light: the rods which are sensitive only to dim light and the cones which are sensitive to color and form in brighter light. There are three kinds of cones, each responsive to particular colors in the visible spectrum (range of colors).

Risky Shift Research suggests that decisions made by groups will involve considerably more risk than individuals in the group would be willing to take. This shift in group decision depends heavily on cultural values. *See* Cautious Shift.

Rod Part of the retina involved in seeing in dim light. *See* Retina.

RNA (Ribonucleic Acid) A chemical substance that occurs in chromosomes and that functions in genetic coding. During task-learning, RNA changes occur in the brain.

Role Playing Adopting the role of another person and experiencing the world in a way one is not accustomed to.

Role Taking The ability to imagine oneself in another's place or to understand the consequences of one's actions for another person.

Schachter-Singer Theory of Emotion Theory of emotion which states that we interpret our arousal according to our environment and label our emotions accordingly.

Schizoid Personality Personality disorder characterized by having great trouble developing social relationships.

Schizophrenia The most common and serious form of psychosis in which there exists an imbalance between emotional reactions and the thoughts associated with these feelings. It may be a disorder of the process of thinking. *See* Psychosis.

Scientific Method The process used by psychologists to determine principles of behavior that exist independently of individual experience and that are untouched by unconscious bias. It is based on a prearranged agreement that criteria, external to the individual and communicable to others, must be established for each set of observations referred to as fact.

Secondary Reinforcement Reinforcement that is only effective after it has been associated with a primary reinforcer.

Self-Actualization A term used by humanistic psychologists to describe what they see as a basic human motivation: the development of all aspects of an individual into productive harmony.

Self-Esteem A person's evaluation of himself. If a person "likes himself," feels he can control his actions, that his acts and work are worthy and competent, his self-esteem is high.

Self-Fulfilling Prophecy A preconceived expectation or belief about a situation that evokes behavior resulting in a situation consistent with the preconception.

Senses An organism's physical means of receiving and detecting physical changes in the environment. Sensing is analyzed in terms of reception of the physical stimulus by specialized nerve cells in the sense organs, transduction or converting the stimulus' energy into nerve impulses that the brain can interpret, and transmission of those nerve impulses from the sense organ to the part of the brain that can interpret the information they convey.

Sensitivity Training Aims at helping people to function more effectively in their jobs by increasing their awareness of their own and others' feelings and exchanging "feedback" about styles of interacting. Sensitivity groups are unlike therapy groups in that they are meant to enrich the participants' lives. Participants are not considered patients or ill. Also called T-groups.

Sensorimotor Stage According to Piaget, the stage of development beginning at birth during which perceptions are tied to objects which the child manipulates. Gradually the child learns that objects have permanence even if they are out of sight or touch.

Sensory Adaptation Tendency of the sense organs to adjust to continuous, unchanging stimulation by reducing their functioning; a stimulus that once caused sensation no longer does.

Sensory Deprivation The blocking out of all outside stimulation for a period of time. As studied experimentally, it can produce hallucinations, psychological disturbances, and temporary disorders of the nervous system of the subject.

Sex Role The attitudes, activities, and expectations considered specific to being male or female, determined by both biological and cultural factors.

Shaping A technique of behavior shaping in which behavior is acquired through the reinforcement of successive approximations of the desired behavior. *See* Successive Approximations.

Sleep A periodic state of consciousness marked by four brain-wave patterns. Dreams occur during relatively light Stage 1 sleep. Sleep is a basic need without which one may suffer physical or psychological distress. *See* Brain Waves, Dreams.

Sleeper Effect The delayed impact of persuasive information. People tend to forget the context in which they first heard the information, but they eventually remember the content of the message sufficiently to feel its impact.

Social Comparison Theory proposed by Festinger which states that we have a tendency to compare our behavior to others to ensure that we are conforming.

Social Facilitation Phenomenon in which the presence of others increases dominant behavior patterns in an individual; Zajonc's theory of social facilitation states that the presence of others enhances the emission of the dominant response of the individual.

Social Influence The process by which people form and change the attitudes, opinions, and behavior of others.

Socialization A process by which a child learns the various patterns of behavior expected and accepted by society. Parents are the chief agents of a child's socialization. Many factors have a bearing on the socialization process, such as the child's sex, religion, social class, and parental attitudes.

Social Learning Learning acquired through observation and imitation of others.

Social Psychology The study of individuals as affected by others and of the interaction of individuals in groups.

Sociobiology The study of the genetic basis of social behavior.

Sociophobias Excessive irrational fears and embarrassment when interacting with other people.

Somatic Nervous System The part of the peripheral nervous system that carries messages from the sense organs and relays information that directs the voluntary movements of the skeletal muscles.

Somatoform Disorders Disorders characterized by physical symptoms for which there are no obvious physical causes.

Somesthetic Senses Skin senses; includes pressure, pain, cold, and warmth.

Species-Typical Behavior Behavior patterns common to members of a species. Ethologists state that each species inherits some patterns of behavior (e.g. birdsongs).

Stanford-Binet Intelligence Scale Tests that measure intelligence from two years through adult level. The tests determine one's intelligence quotient by establishing one's chronological and mental ages. *See* Intelligence Quotient.

State-Dependent Learning Situation in which what is learned in one state can only be remembered when the person is in that state.

Statistically Significant In inferential statistics, a finding that the independent variable did influence greatly the outcome of the experimental and control group.

Stereotype The assignment of characteristics to a person mainly on the basis of the group, class, or category to which he belongs. The tendency to categorize and generalize is a basic human way of organizing information. Stereotyping, however, can reinforce misinformation and prejudice. *See* Prejudice.

Stimulus A unit of the environment which causes a response in an individual; more specifically, a physical or chemical agent acting on an appropriate sense receptor.

Stimulus Discrimination Limiting responses to relevant stimuli.

Stimulus Generalization Responses to stimuli similar to the stimulus that had caused the response.

Stress Pressure that puts unusual demands on an organism. Stress may be caused by physical conditions but eventually will involve both. Stimuli that cause stress are called stressors, and an organism's response is the stress reaction. A three-stage general adaptation syndrome is hypothesized involving both emotional and physical changes. *See* General Adaptation System.

Structuralism An early school of psychology that stressed the importance of conscious experience as the subject matter of psychology and maintained that experience should be analyzed into its component parts by use of introspection. *See* Introspection.

Sublimation Defense mechanism in which a person redirects his socially undesirable urges into socially acceptable behavior.

Subliminal Stimuli Stimuli that do not receive conscious attention because they are below sensory thresholds. They may influence behavior, but research is not conclusive on this matter.

Substance-Induced Organic Mental Disorders Organic mental disorders caused by exposure to harmful environmental substances.

Suggestibility The extent to which a person responds to persuasion. Hypnotic susceptibility refers to the degree of suggestibility observed after an attempt to induce hypnosis has been made. *See* Persuasion, Hypnosis.

Superego According to Freud, the superego corresponds roughly to conscience. The superego places restrictions on both ego and id and represents the internalized restrictions and ideals that the child learns from parents and culture. *See* Conscience, Ego, Id.

Sympathetic Nervous System The branch of the autonomic nervous system that is more active in emergencies; it causes a general arousal, increasing breathing, heart rate and blood pressure.

Synapse A "gap" where individual nerve cells (neurons) come together and across which chemical information is passed.

Syndrome A group of symptoms that occur together and mark a particular abnormal pattern.

Systematic Desensitization A technique used in behavior therapy to eliminate a phobia. The symptoms of the phobia are seen as conditioned responses of fear, and the procedure attempts to decondition the fearful response until the patient gradually is able to face the feared situation. *See* Phobia.

TAT (Thematic Apperception Test) Personality and motivation test which requires the subject to devise stories about pictures.

Taxis An orienting movement in response to particular stimuli in the environment. A frog, for example, always turns so its snout points directly at its prey before it flicks its tongue. *See* Orienting Response.

Theory A very general statement that is more useful in generating hypotheses than in generating research. *See* Hypotheses.

Therapeutic Community The organization of a hospital setting so that patients have to take responsibility for helping one another in an attempt to prevent patients from getting worse by being in the hospital.

Token Economy A system for organizing a treatment setting according to behavioristic principles. Patients are encouraged to take greater responsibility for their adjustment by receiving tokens for acceptable behavior and fines for unacceptable behavior. The theory of token economy grew out of operant conditioning techniques. *See* Operant Conditioning.

Traits Distinctive and stable attributes that can be found in all people.

Tranquilizers Psychoactive drugs which reduce anxiety. *See* Psychoactive Drugs.

Trial and Error Learning Trying various behaviors in a situation until the solution is hit upon; past experiences lead us to try different responses until we are successful.

Unconditioned Response (UR) An automatic reaction elicited by a stimulus.

Unconditioned Stimulus (US) Any stimulus that elicits an automatic or reflexive reaction in an individual; it does not have to be learned in the present situation.

Unconscious In Freudian terminology, a concept (not a place) of the mind. The unconscious encompasses certain inborn impulses that never rise into consciousness (awareness) as well as memories and wishes that have been repressed. The chief aim of psychoanalytic therapy is to free repressed material from the unconscious in order to make it susceptible to conscious thought and direction. Behaviorists describe the unconscious as an inability to verbalize. *See* Repression.

Undifferentiated Schizophrenia Type of schizophrenia which does not fit into any particular category, or fits into more than one category.

Validity The extent to which a test actually measures what it is designed to measure.

Variability In statistics, measures of variability communicate how spread out the scores are; the tendency to vary the response to a stimulus, particularly if the response fails to help in adaptation.

Variable Any property of a person, object, or event that can change or take on more than one mathematical value.

Weber's Law States that the difference threshold depends on the ratio of the intensity of one stimulus to another rather than an absolute difference.

Wechsler Adult Intelligence Scale (WAIS) An individually administered test designed to measure adults' intelligence, devised by David Wechsler. The WAIS consists of eleven subtests, of which six measure verbal and five measure performance aspects of intelligence. *See* Wechsler Intelligence Scale for Children.

Wechsler Intelligence Scale for Children (WISC) Similar to the Wechsler Adult Intelligence Scale, except that it is designed for people under fifteen. Wechsler tests can determine strong and weak areas of overall intelligence. *See* Wechsler Adult Intelligence Scale (WAIS).

Whorfian Hypothesis The linguistic relativity hypothesis of Benjamin Whorf; states that language influences thought.

Withdrawal Social or emotional detachment; the removal of oneself from a painful or frustrating situation.

Yerkes-Dodson Law Prediction that the optimum motivation level decreases as the difficulty level of a task increases.

Source for the Glossary:

The majority of terms in this glossary are reprinted from *The Study of Psychology*, Joseph Rubinstein. ©The Dushkin Publishing Group, Inc., Guilford, CT 06437.

The remaining terms were developed by the Annual Editions staff.

Index

Credits/ Acknowledgments

Cover design by Charles Vitelli

1. Becoming a Person
Facing overview—United Nations photo by John Isaac.

2. Determinants of Behavior
Facing overview—Courtesy of Marcuss Oslander. 76—United Nations photo by L. Barns.

3. Problems Influencing Personal Growth
Facing overview—United Nations photo by L. Barns.

4. Relating to Others
Facing overview—United Nations photo by Michael Tzovaras. 166—United Nations photo by Margot Granitsas.

5. Dynamics of Personal Adjustment
Facing overview—United Nations photo by F. B. Grunsweig.

6. Enhancing Human Adjustment
Facing overview—WHO photo by J. Mohr.

PHOTOCOPY THIS PAGE!!!*

ANNUAL EDITIONS ARTICLE REVIEW FORM

■ NAME: ______________________ DATE: ______________________

■ TITLE AND NUMBER OF ARTICLE: ______________________

■ BRIEFLY STATE THE MAIN IDEA OF THIS ARTICLE: ______________________

■ LIST THREE IMPORTANT FACTS THAT THE AUTHOR USES TO SUPPORT THE MAIN IDEA:

■ WHAT INFORMATION OR IDEAS DISCUSSED IN THIS ARTICLE ARE ALSO DISCUSSED IN YOUR TEXTBOOK OR OTHER READING YOU HAVE DONE? LIST THE TEXTBOOK CHAPTERS AND PAGE NUMBERS:

■ LIST ANY EXAMPLES OF BIAS OR FAULTY REASONING THAT YOU FOUND IN THE ARTICLE:

■ LIST ANY NEW TERMS/CONCEPTS THAT WERE DISCUSSED IN THE ARTICLE AND WRITE A SHORT DEFINITION:

*Your instructor may require you to use this Annual Editions Article Review Form in any number of ways: for articles that are assigned, for extra credit, as a tool to assist in developing assigned papers, or simply for your own reference. Even if it is not required, we encourage you to photocopy and use this page; you'll find that reflecting on the articles will greatly enhance the information from your text.

We Want Your Advice

Annual Editions revisions depend on two major opinion sources: one is our Advisory Board, listed in the front of this volume, which works with us in scanning the thousands of articles published in the public press each year; the other is you—the person actually using the book. Please help us and the users of the next edition by completing the prepaid article rating form on this page and returning it to us. Thank you.

ANNUAL EDITIONS: PERSONAL GROWTH AND BEHAVIOR 91/92

Article Rating Form

Here is an opportunity for you to have direct input into the next revision of this volume. We would like you to rate each of the 54 articles listed below, using the following scale:

1. **Excellent: should definitely be retained**
2. **Above average: should probably be retained**
3. **Below average: should probably be deleted**
4. **Poor: should definitely be deleted**

Your ratings will play a vital part in the next revision. So please mail this prepaid form to us just as soon as you complete it.
Thanks for your help!

Rating	Article	Rating	Article
	1. Abraham Maslow and the New Self		28. Not Past Their Prime
	2. Erikson, in His Own Old Age, Expands His View of Life		29. Meet the People Who Never Quit Learning
	3. What Dreams Are (Really) Made Of		30. Reaching the Child Within Us
	4. Personality: Major Traits Found Stable Through Life		31. The Plowboy Interview: Elisabeth Kübler-Ross on Living, Dying . . . and Beyond
	5. Embattled Giant of Psychology Speaks His Mind		32. A Theory of Success and Failure
			33. A Plan That Works
	6. Managing Stress and Living Longer		34. Art of Anger Difficult for Women to Master
	7. The Risks of Rewards		
	8. Major Personality Study Finds That Traits Are Mostly Inherited		35. The Language of Persuasion
			36. "They Have Ears, But Hear Not"
	9. New Connections		37. Beyond Selfishness
	10. A Pleasurable Chemistry		38. The Dance of Intimacy
	11. Making of a Mind		39. The Indispensable Woman
	12. Winter Blues		40. The American Man in Transition
	13. Food, Mood, and Behavior		41. Success at Failure: Understanding Self-defeating Behavior
	14. Guns and Dolls		
	15. The New York Times Special Section: The Gender Card		42. Getting Better—Together
			43. Fixing the 'Between'
	16. Proceeding With Caution		44. No Life to Live
	17. Second Thoughts About a Gene for Alcoholism		45. When Bystanders Just Stand By
			46. Psychologists Find Ways to Break Racism's Hold
	18. The Changing Meanings of Age		
	19. Don't Act Your Age		47. Psychotherapy's Value Becomes a Key Issue as More People Use It
	20. Dr. Spock Had It Right		
	21. Sad Legacy of Abuse: The Search for Remedies		48. Wounded Healers
			49. Beating Depression
	22. Children After Divorce		50. The Trusting Heart
	23. The Taming of the Tube		51. When Stress Becomes Distress
	24. Scared Serious		52. Ridden With Guilt
	25. A Much Riskier Passage		53. Health's Character
	26. Ambitious Bulimics: Thinness Mania		54. Healthy Pleasures
	27. Understanding and Preventing Teen Suicide: An Interview With Barry Garfinkel		

(Continued on next page)

ABOUT YOU

Name_________________________________ Date__________

Are you a teacher? ☐ Or student? ☐

Your School Name ______________________________

Department ______________________________

Address ______________________________

City____________________ State __________ Zip __________

School Telephone #______________________________

YOUR COMMENTS ARE IMPORTANT TO US!

Please fill in the following information:

For which course did you use this book? ______________________________

Did you use a text with this Annual Edition? ☐ yes ☐ no

The title of the text? ______________________________

What are your general reactions to the Annual Editions concept?

Have you read any particular articles recently that you think should be included in the next edition?

Are there any articles you feel should be replaced in the next edition? Why?

Are there other areas that you feel would utilize an Annual Edition?

May we contact you for editorial input?

May we quote you from above?

No Postage Necessary if Mailed in the United States

ANNUAL EDITIONS: PERSONAL GROWTH AND BEHAVIOR 91/92

BUSINESS REPLY MAIL

First Class Permit No. 84 Guilford, CT

Postage will be paid by addressee

DPG **The Dushkin Publishing Group, Inc.**
Sluice Dock
Guilford, Connecticut 06437